T0306363

THE ILLUSTRATED ENCYCLOPEDIA OF
TRUCKS

COLES & SONS
SCANIA
124
420
T606 AOK
SCANIA
SCANIA

THE ILLUSTRATED ENCYCLOPEDIA OF

TRUCKS

A GUIDE TO CLASSIC AND CONTEMPORARY TRUCKS AROUND THE WORLD, INCLUDING 700 PHOTOGRAPHS

PETER J. DAVIES

LORENZ BOOKS

This edition is published by Lorenz Books
an imprint of Anness Publishing Ltd
info@anness.com
www.lorenzbooks.com www.annesspublishing.com

A CIP catalogue record for this book is available from the British Library.

Publisher: Joanna Lorenz
Senior Editor: Felicity Forster
Designer: Michael Morey
Production Controller: Ben Worley

PUBLISHER'S NOTES

Where possible, weights are quoted in units appropriate to the manufacturer's country of origin. A UK "imperial" ton is 2240lbs or 1016kg. A US "short" ton is 2000lbs or 907kg. A metric tonne is 2204lbs or 1000kg. A glossary of truck terminology appears at the back of the book. Although the information in this book is believed to be accurate and true at the time of going to press, neither the authors nor the publisher can accept any legal responsibility or liability for any errors or omissions that may have been made nor for any inaccuracies.

ACKNOWLEDGEMENTS

The publisher would like to thank Peter J. Davies for supplying the photographs used in this book, and the following picture libraries:
(t=top; b=bottom; l=left; r=right; c=centre; u=upper; lo=lower)
AB Scania: pp23 (t), 216 (t, c); Ashok Leyland: p76 (br, lo, br); N. Baldwin: p97 (t); Bering Truck Corp: p82 (t); BMC Sanayi ve Ticaret AS: p85 (t, b); Daimler AG: pp16 (t), 23 (b), 108 (c), 183 (t), 184 (tl, b); E.T. Davies: p253 (c); F. Gambut: p93 (b); A. J. Ingram: pp 77 (bl), 79 (c, b), 87 (br), 96 (t), 97 (c), 103 (b), 109 (t, cb), 125 (b), 138 (t, c), 139 (b), 155 (t), 157 (b), 172 (c), 180 (t), 191 (b), 197 (b), 201 (b), 203 (b), 210 (t), 226 (t), 230 (t), 236 (t); M. Haeder p91 (bc); Iveco: p77 (cl); N. Jansen: p173 (cl); P. Love: pp92 (bl), 172 (b), 191 (uc), 227 (c), 248 (t); Mack Museum: p174 (tc); MOL n.v: p190 (b); National Motor Museum: pp14 (c), 15 (t); Nicolas: p192 (b); Oshkosh Truck Corp: pp52 (b), 53 (tr), 195 (c); R. Pearson: p52 (t); Peterbilt Motors Co: p201 (tr); M.D. Phippard: pp 62 (lor), 77 (tr), 87 (t); M. Platt: p63 (br); Reed Business Information: p100 (b); Roman SA: pp108 (t), 231 (b); Skoda-LiAZ: p225 (b); P. Sposito: pp63 (tl), 113 (b), 202 (c), 232 (b); A. Syme: p253 (t); R. J. Stanier p224 (bl); E. van Ingen-Schenau: p157 (u), p252 (b); R. Tew: p62 (bl); J. Thompson: p253 (b); Tony Stone Images: pp10–11, 2–7, 38–9, 56–7; Karl-Heinz Wenzel p186 (tl).

CONTENTS

INTRODUCTION

Trucks influence our daily lives far more than we think. Like them or loathe them, they play a vital role in maintaining the living standards to which modern society has become accustomed. From the 3-ton box van going about its high-street deliveries to the largest long-haul rigs on international journeys, every truck is carrying a commodity that will eventually benefit us in some way.

While most of us are sleeping, there are trucks of all kinds being loaded with fresh food, bread, newspapers and parcels to be driven through the night for next-day delivery. Nearly everything we eat, everything we wear and everything we use on a daily basis travels at some stage by truck.

It might be difficult to see the relevance of some loads to our lives – raw materials, coils of steel, logs, chemicals – but such commodities will eventually reach us in another form. Steel ends up in the form of cars, washing machines and beer cans; logs end up as paper or sawn timber; chemicals end up in toiletries, pharmaceuticals and household cleaners – all things that the average consumer takes for granted.

The need for trucks has grown steadily as manufacturing has become more centralized over the years. It might be argued that the availability of a fast, efficient road-haulage industry has itself encouraged such centralization. Once upon a time local communities tended to be self-sufficient. At the turn of the 19th century, road systems were almost non-existent. The growth in railways and canals during the 19th century had suppressed development in roads and road vehicles. It wasn't until the World War I era that governments both in Europe and North America began concerted road improvements.

In America the Federal Aid road plan got underway with each state setting up its own highway authority. From the passing of the 1921 Federal Highway Act, designated Federal Aid roads were jointly financed by the government and state highways departments. Funds were also raised by the introduction of fuel tax and road-user tax.

In the UK, existing roads were in urgent need of improvement since even the major arterial routes passed through tiny villages and market towns, which formed serious bottlenecks. The British Ministry of Transport was formed in 1919 to regulate the transport industry and road development, although such government bodies appeared to be more concerned with protecting the railways. Germany took the lead in Europe with a large-scale program of Autobahns

in the 1930s. It was after World War II that major road building plans were instigated in most European countries. Britain's first motorway was opened in 1959.

With the development of national highway networks, trucking came into its own. The rapid bulk movement of food supplies transformed the agricultural industry and brought the consumer a wider choice at lower cost. Manufacturing sprang up in semi-rural locations away from city congestion. The trucking industry developed in parallel with the highways and industry in general. Agriculture and the consumer soon became dependent upon the hundreds of thousands of trucks that carried the raw materials and manufactured goods over longer and longer distances.

The trucking industry plays an important role in most nations' economies, not least in providing employment for hundreds of thousands of people. The many related industries, including truck manufacturing, retailing, servicing, bodybuilding, parts manufacture and tyre services, are equally significant employers. Despite the enormous benefits that trucks have brought to our quality of life, the public at large regards them with disapproval. There is a popular notion that trucks are, at best, a necessary evil. Environmental groups devote much energy to discrediting the trucking industry, which has done little to defend itself.

At the other extreme there is a small but dedicated pro-truck element. Truck enthusiasts, though few in numbers, have done much to promote the positive aspects of trucking and to preserve trucking heritage. There are active bands of preservationists, especially in the UK, Europe, North America, Australia and New Zealand, who painstakingly restore old trucks and record history for future generations. Vintage truck shows enable the public to see trucks in a new light and to appreciate the engineering achievements of the past century or so. Trucks are, however, first and foremost, functional machines designed for an important job of work.

This book introduces the fascinating world of trucks – the enormous variety of makes and types, and the multitude of roles they perform to keep the wheels of industry turning.

159
FREIGHTLINER
159
FREIGHTLINER
Washington
18641PR
ORE.
P.U.C.
MKZ 775

THE WORLD OF TRUCKS

In one sense the world of trucks has changed enormously, as new technology and improvements in the infrastructure have enabled heavier, faster trucks to be developed. In another sense the basic function of a truck is the same as it ever was – to transport a load from one place to another as economically and as safely as possible. Trucking companies undertake to deliver the goods on time, regardless of the weather and the distance involved. For most of the time it is the driver who takes responsibility for the safe arrival of the load. While some truck drivers are engaged on regular hauls with one type of load, others, known as "roamers" or "trampers" in the UK, travel from one location to another and can be away for a week or more, hauling a variety of loads ranging from soap powder or coffee beans to steel or breakfast cereal. In this modern age, truckers can be likened to the resourceful pioneers of old.

■ OPPOSITE *The timeless lines of this Freightliner cabover typify the United States trucking scene.*

■ LEFT *A dual-steer bonneted Pacific concrete mixer operating in British Columbia. It is powered by a Cummins L10 diesel engine.*

History of the Truck

Seen against thousands of years of history, the truck is a relatively new invention – it has existed for little over a century. During that period it has developed from a crude powered cart into a highly efficient marvel of modern technology. No one invented the truck *per se*; it emerged from a succession of early experiments by inventors in pursuit of a means of propulsion. When steam power became a reality in the 18th century it was only a matter of time before the high pressure rotative engine was developed. Alternative energy sources such as gas, oil and electricity gradually appeared, paving the way for a practical, self-propelled vehicle. The earliest vehicles were passenger carriers, but practical designs for steam wagons were emerging in the last decade of the 19th century. The first gasoline-engined truck appeared in 1896, and that's where the story begins.

WHAT IS A TRUCK?

■ ABOVE *Smooth aero-dynamic lines characterize the modern-day urban delivery truck such as this Leyland DAF 60 series.*

■ RIGHT *Four-wheeled box vans are much the same throughout Europe. This late 1970s FBW milk truck is typical of Switzerland.*

A truck can be described as a self-propelled load carrier but, within that general definition, there are so many variations that it is virtually impossible to single out a "standard" truck. Each country has its own system of transport legislation, which distinguishes trucks from other types of vehicle. In the UK and Europe, for instance, any goods vehicle over 3500kg/ 3.1 tons gross vehicle weight qualifies as a truck. Large goods vehicles (LGVs) are those over 7500kg/6.7 tons gross vehicle weight. In the United States trucks are divided into classes, heavy-duty trucks coming within Class 8.

The nearest thing to a standard truck is a general-purpose "flat" or box van used to transport a wide variety of goods. In this day and age such vehicles have diminished in numbers as more and more trucks are tailored to specific types of loads. Purpose-built self-loading equipment has become commonplace on trucks, especially in the construction industry. Temperature-controlled truck bodies are indispensable for the transport of fresh foods such as meat, fish, fresh produce, fruit and dairy products. Bulk tankers come in a variety of forms for liquids, powders and gases. These are often tailored to specific commodities, which can range from liquid chocolate and liquid tar to granulated sugar or cement powder.

Because of the vast number of different tasks performed by trucks, they are often custom built for specific types of operation. In specifying a truck, account has to be taken of axle loadings and the loaded truck's centre of gravity. Often auxiliary drives are installed for special equipment such as hydraulic pumps and compressors. At the same time a close eye has to be kept on unladen weight to ensure that the truck can take the net payload specified by the customer.

In the past 30 years or so the word "truck" has become almost universal, but this wasn't always so. "Truck" is an American term. In the UK the term was "lorry" or "wagon" and these terms are still popular among old established hauliers. In French it translates to "camion", in Spanish "camión", in German "lastwagen",

■ BELOW *North America is noted for its spectacular trucks like this Peterbilt conventional doubles outfit delivering bulk cement.*

■ LEFT *The UK truck scene is dominated by articulated outfits grossing up to 44 tonnes. This Scottish Scania 4-series hauls a tri-axle curtainsider.*

■ ABOVE *In the 1980s Swiss trucks like this Volvo CH230 garbage vehicle, were restricted to a maximum width of 2.3m/7.5ft.*

in Swedish "lastbil" and in Dutch "bedrijfswagen". Even so, the word "truck" figures in most vocabularies today. Though a truck is designed to carry loads, there are numerous variations which have fixed equipment but still come under the general heading of "trucks". These include recovery trucks, fire trucks, mobile cranes, cement pumps, drilling rigs, hydraulic platforms, ballast tractors and mobile exhibition trucks.

Despite efforts, especially within Europe, to harmonize weight legislation, there are wide variations between countries. Similarly, in the United States, transport law varies from state to state. Most other countries also set their own weight and length limits. The main factors on which truck legislation is based are axle weights, gross vehicle weight and overall length. Often individual axle weight limits are set low, while high gross vehicle weights are allowed by adding more axles. Road wear from heavy trucks is generally calculated on a combination of axle weights and outer axle spread – theoretically, the longer the outer axle spread and the higher the number of axles, the less road damage. With such a diverse range of national and state legislation, trucking companies have to conform to the lowest weights they are likely to encounter when their journeys take them across international or state borders.

■ RIGHT *Like the United States, New Zealand has some impressive long-haul trucks. This Seddon Atkinson Strato cabover grosses 44 tonnes on eight axles.*

EARLY ORIGINS

■ LEFT *In the 17th century the means of transporting goods was by teams of pack horses.*

From earliest times man has sought ways to transport heavy objects from one point to another. Ancient civilizations devised ways of moving large rocks to build monuments. It was discovered that wooden logs could be used as rollers to ease their task. The wheel was a logical development of the roller. Earliest evidence of the wheel dates from 3500 BC in the Sumerian civilization of Mesopotamia. By 2000 BC there were crude ox-drawn carts. The ox and horse served man's transport needs until the last two centuries, when the horseless carriage turned from a fantasy into a reality. The modern truck has evolved over the past hundred years, although indirectly it owes its existence to many bizarre experiments, which can be traced back more than 400 years.

As early as 1472 an Italian inventor came up with a carriage propelled by windmills. In the late 17th century, a Frenchman thought he had found the answer in rewindable clock springs. Steam power emerged as a practical means of propulsion during the 18th century, although the earliest record of steam power appeared in the writings of Hero of Alexandria in 116 BC with his description of the Ball of Aeolus – was released through a jet pipe, providing forward thrust. It is doubtful if any of these ideas met with success, but the quest for self-propulsion continued. The 17th century saw experimental carriages from Englishmen Ramsay and Wildgoose.

■ ABOVE *Cugnot's steam artillery tractor of 1770 was acknowledged as the world's first self-propelled road vehicle.*

■ BELOW *Trevithick's steam carriage of 1803 looked decidedly top heavy. Even so, it completed a number of successful journeys within London.*

Experiments with heat engines had taken place in various European countries during the 16th and 17th centuries. In 1663 the Marquis of Worcester patented a simple atmospheric engine which was used to raise well water at Vauxhall in London. In 1673 Dutchman Christian Huyghens is on record as exploding gunpowder inside a cylinder to operate a piston, but he was unable to control the violence of the explosion or to achieve any kind of regular cycle. In 1698 the earliest design of a steam engine was being patented in England by Thomas Savery. Referred to as the Savery "Fire" engine, it worked not just by steam but by atmospheric pressure combined with a vacuum created by condensing the steam in the cylinder.

By 1712 Thomas Newcomen, a Dartmouth blacksmith, had developed an improved engine

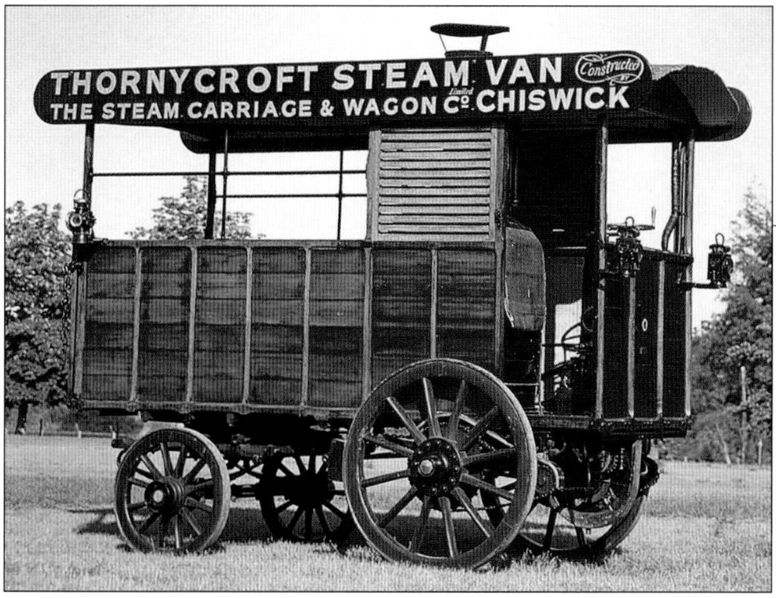

■ ABOVE *Britain's first commercial vehicle was this Thornycroft 1-ton steam van of 1896.*

based on Savery's design, and for the next 50 years or so his "atmospheric" engine was the most efficient means of powering machinery. In 1765 James Watt patented an atmospheric engine with a condenser, achieving greater efficiency and considerable fuel savings. Watt also filed a patent for a steam carriage in 1769, but it was not built. High pressure rotative steam engines for road vehicles were still to be developed.

In the same year that Watt was granted his steam carriage patent, Captain Nicolas Joseph Cugnot of the French Artillery completed the world's first steam-powered road vehicle. Cugnot was commissioned to build a second vehicle, his world famous Artillery Tractor, which was completed in 1770. Though crude and cumbersome, the vehicle was capable of hauling up to 5 tons at 5kph/3mph and had a range of about 1.5km/1 mile before running out of steam. Cugnot's design was inherently unstable, having a heavy boiler overhanging its single front wheel which was 1.3m/4.25ft in diameter and only steered through 15 degrees. Its instability was its undoing since it overturned while negotiating a corner, demolishing a wall. Cugnot was jailed for what was the first-ever motoring offence, and no further development took place.

About 15 years later William Murdock, a pupil of James Watt, designed a high-pressure engine and produced a working model, but Watt discouraged further development, dismissing high-pressure steam as impractical and dangerous. At the same time, steam development was beginning to take place in America with Welsh-born Oliver Evans of Philadelphia being granted a licence to operate steamers, although there are no records of any being built. However, Evans did build a 20-ton steam dredger which he mounted on a wheeled chassis in 1804 to travel under its own power the 2.5km/1.5 miles from his works to the Schuylkill River.

An important step forward was made in 1798 when Richard Trevithick built his first high-pressure steam carriage. He patented his design in 1802 and the following year produced a second carriage, which was to complete a number of trips carrying passengers from Leather Lane to Paddington in London.

Over the first four decades of the 19th century, new ideas were rife. There were numerous practical designs for steam road carriages, but they were all for passengers rather than goods.

For the next 50 years road vehicle development in the UK was stifled by draconian legislation laying the foundations of an anti-road culture which has survived to the present day. Other

■ BELOW *This 1901 5-ton steam lorry won the Mann Patent Steam Cart & Wagon Co. a silver*

countries, mainly Europe and America, moved ahead with new ideas.

Britain's attitude was summed up by the Locomotives on Highways Act of 1861, passed in 1865. Under it, all mechanically propelled road vehicles needed three attendants, one of whom had to walk 55m/60yd in front carrying a red flag. A speed limit of 3kph/2mph was imposed in towns, while 6.5kph/4mph was permitted on rural highways. The requirement for the red flag was dropped in 1878.

France, Germany, Italy and the United States continued to develop new, more efficient means of propulsion as well as inventing new systems for steering, suspension and drive transmission. In France during the late 19th century, Amédée Bollée, Georges Bouton and Leon Serpollet made important advances in high-pressure steam engines. In 1873 Bollée completed his advanced 12-seater carriage "L'Obéissant" which was one of the first with Ackerman steering. Another breakthrough was Serpollet's liquid-fuelled flash boiler announced in 1890.

In spite of legislation, there were brave attempts at building steam wagons in the UK during the 1870s. What must be the earliest British self-propelled load carrier was a massive vehicle built in 1870 by John Yule of Rutherglen. The 7.9m/26ft long by 4.9m/16ft wide wagon with driving wheels 2m/6.5ft in diameter was used to transport boilers to Glasgow docks, a distance of 3.2km/2 miles. In 1875 another one-off steam wagon weighing 4 tons was built by Brown & May of Devizes.

Progress was also being made on internal combustion engines. Jean-Joseph Etienne Lenoir built the first practical gas engine, albeit a rather inefficient affair relying on a single-stroke in which the charge in the cylinder was not compressed before ignition. The idea of compressing gas prior to firing had been thought of as early as 1838 by William Barnett, but 20 years elapsed before it was put to practical use. Early experiments with

■ ABOVE *In 1896 this Daimler Phoenix 1½-tonner with 4hp engine was the world's first gasoline-engined truck.*

■ BELOW LEFT *George Selden filed a patent for his road engine in 1879 and other manufacturers had to pay him royalties until 1911.*

■ BELOW RIGHT *All four-stroke engines operate on the Otto cycle. The third "ignition" stroke in the diesel cycle is the "combustion" stroke following fuel injection.*

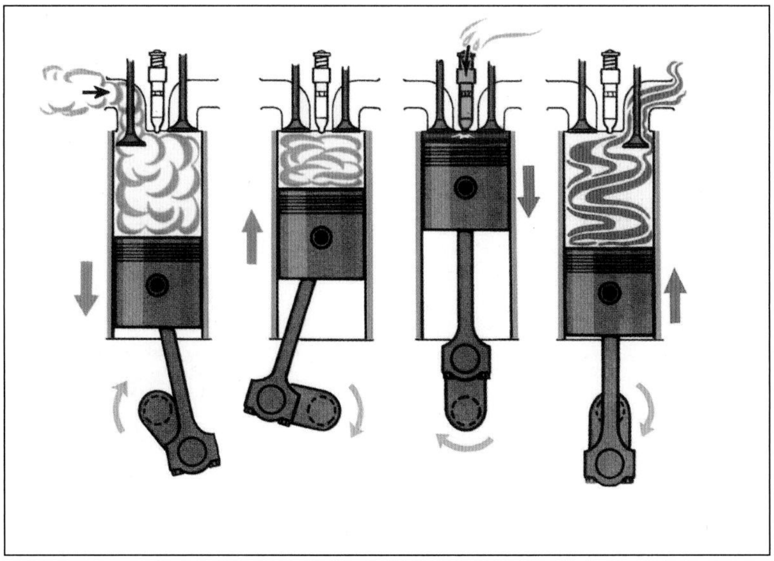

a four-stroke cycle (induction, compression, ignition, exhaust) were conducted by Alphonse Beau de Rochas in 1862 and patented by Dr Nikolas August Otto in 1876. All subsequent four-stroke engines have been based on the Otto cycle. The alternative two-stroke principle was patented by Sir Dugald Clerk in 1881.

There was rapid progress in engine design during the latter half of the 19th century. The discovery of oil in the late 1850s was an important step forward. By the early 1870s gasoline had become available and one of the earliest gasoline-engined vehicles was built by Siegfried Markus of Mecklenburg, Austria, in 1873. Significant development was also taking place in America during the 1870s, where George Brayton of Boston designed the first practical liquid-fuel engine. This was introduced into the UK in 1878 where further development was carried out by Priestman Bros. of Hull, who devised a method of blowing vaporized fuel into the cylinders, igniting it with a spark plug.

In 1879 George Baldwin Selden filed an idea for a "road engine" with the United States Patents Office. The patent was not approved until 1895. Following this, every manufacturer of gasoline-engined vehicles had to pay royalties to the holder of the Selden patent up until 1911. Ransom Eli Olds of Lancing, Michigan was helping to pioneer the United States motor industry in 1886 when, at the age of nineteen, he built his first steam car.

Britain was reawakening in the 1890s, thanks to a small number of entrepreneurs who recognized the importance of the motor industry. One was Sir David Salomons, who took the initiative to organize the first-ever horseless carriage exhibition. This was staged at Tunbridge Wells in 1895. Ironically, all five exhibits were European. Shortly after the exhibition, he organized the Self Propelled Traffic Association in collaboration with Frederick Richard Simms, who was a director of Daimler Motoren Gesellschaft. The association's objective was to persuade the British government to repeal the Locomotives on Highways Act, a goal finally achieved in 1896. The new Locomotives Act of that year lifted most of the restrictions but speed limits were still low, any truck over 2 tons being restricted to 8kph/5mph.

In Europe development of the gasoline engine had progressed dramatically during the late 1880s, the two leading figures being Germany's Gottlieb Daimler and Karl Benz. It was Daimler who introduced the first production gasoline-engined truck in 1896. The same year John Isaac Thornycroft built Britain's first practical self-propelled load carrier, the Thornycroft 1-ton Steam Van. The modern truck began to evolve from that point on.

THEY HELPED MAKE HISTORY ***(left to right, then down page)***

- ***Gottlieb Wilhelm Daimler (1834–1900) introduced the world's first truck.***
- ***Dr Rudolph Diesel (1858–1913) invented the diesel engine.***
- ***Edwin Richard Foden (1870–1950) developed Foden steamers and founded ERF.***
- ***Lawrence Gardner (1840–90) founded Gardner Engines.***
- ***Marius Berliet 1866–1949) founded Automobiles M. Berliet.***
- ***William Crapo Durant (1861–1947) founded General Motors Corporation.***
- ***Ransom Eli Olds (1867–1950) founded Oldsmobile and Reo Trucks.***
- ***John Michael Mack (1864–1924), with his brothers, founded Mack Trucks.***

THE TRUCK EVOLVES

In the space of 120 years trucks have evolved from crude self-propelled carts into highly advanced machines which the early pioneers would not have thought possible. Innovative engineering, legislation, competitive rivalry and customer demands all push technology on to new frontiers. Often refinements are forced by legislative changes concerning safety, pollution and road damage.

Quite apart from meeting legislative changes, trucks undergo periodic development to keep ahead of their competitors. Driver comfort and safety are important factors. At one time the driver sat on a hard wooden seat without even a windshield, let alone a cab roof to protect him. By World War I he had the luxury of a canvas hood, and by the 1920s semi-enclosed cabs brought a greater degree of comfort. Of course, the need for improved cabs was not just a comfort issue – as speeds and weights increased, safety considerations became more relevant.

■ ABOVE ***In the earliest trucks the driver had precious little protection from the elements. This Vabis dates from 1909.***

■ RIGHT ***By the 1930s fully enclosed cabs provided a degree of driver comfort, as on this Thornycroft Jupiter.***

■ BELOW ***Enclosed cabs came in 1930, but styling had progressed little by 1946 when this Maudslay Mogul was built.***

Recent developments have related to environmental issues. During the past two decades emission laws have put increasing demands on engineers to develop clean diesels. There have also been advances in 'intelligent' automatic transmissions. These aid fuel economy and component life by selecting the optimum gear ratio in all conditions.

Since 2001 developments in 'Telematics' tracking systems have enabled trucking companies to monitor vehicle and driver activity around the clock to further promote efficiency.

One development aimed at eliminating traffic collisions and improving efficiency is the idea of autonomous 'platooning' trucks in which convoys are controlled by the lead vehicle. Trials have been taking place on both sides of the Atlantic since 2015.

Despite ever tightening emission standards in both Europe (Euro 1, 1992 to Euro 6, 2017) and the United States Environmental Protection Agency standards, there are still calls from environmentalists to switch from diesel to fuels such as Liquified Natural Gas (LNG) or even electric propulsion.

■ ABOVE LEFT *Autonomous 'platooning' truck convoys are being trialled in Europe and in the United States.*

■ LEFT *The Tesla experimental electric semi-truck foresees future trends in long distance hauling.*

■ ABOVE *Mercedes-Benz Future Truck 2025 is a revolutionary concept featuring 'Highway Pilot' automated controls.*

MILESTONES FROM A CENTURY OF TRUCK EVOLUTION

1890s
1896 First gasoline-engined truck, from Daimler Motoren Gesellschaft.
1896 Thornycroft Steam Van introduced.
1898 Alexander Winton builds first gasoline-engined van in the United States.

1900s
1901 First mechanical road sweeper by John Collins, Connecticut.
1903 Dennis introduces worm-drive axle.
1909 Knox fifth wheel patented.
1909 First air suspension tried on commercial vehicles.

1910s
1912 All-wheel drive truck developed by FWD.
1917 Goodyear promotes pneumatic tyres on heavy trucks.
1919 Clessie Cummins begins diesel production.
1919 Dunlop and Goodyear pneumatic truck tyres introduced.

1920s
1920 Electric lighting taking over from paraffin and acetylene.
1922 Pagefield introduces first swap body system.
1924 First rigid six-wheelers.
1924 First direct-injection diesel engine announced by MAN.
1926 Hendrickson introduces walking beam suspension.
1926 Pneumatic tyres taking over from solids.
1928 First diesel-engined truck in UK (Mercedes-Benz).
1928 Hydraulic brakes available on trucks.
1928 Diesel engines under development in UK by Gardner, Leyland and AEC.
1929 Air brakes for trucks (invented by George Westinghouse for railway use, 1868).
1929 First British-built diesel truck, the Kerr Stuart.
1929 Enclosed cabs appear.

1930s
1930 Rear-view mirror compulsory fitment in UK.
1930 First rigid eight-wheeled steamer from Sentinel.
1931 Cummins diesel demonstrated in an Indiana truck.
1933 Kenworth first to offer Cummins diesel as standard.
1933 Kenworth offers sleeper cab.
1933 UK legislation leads to decline of steam trucks.
1934 First diesel and gasoline rigid eight-wheelers by AEC.
1936 Cabover trucks gain popularity in United States.
1937 Sterling introduces tilt cab.
1938 Kenworth launches torsion bar suspension.

1940s
1941 Producer gas trucks overcome fuel shortages.
1948 Cab improvements, more emphasis on styling.

1950s
1950 Kenworth experiment with gas turbine trucks.
1952 Reo and International Harvester introduce LPG-powered trucks.
1954 Volvo introduces turbocharged diesel engines.
1955 Glass fibre used in cab construction by Bristol.
1955 Firestone introduces tubeless truck tyres.
1956 Single-piece curved windscreens appearing.
1958 Dunlop Pneuride heavy-duty air suspension available.

1960s
1960 Synchromesh gearboxes on some heavy trucks.
1960 Rockwell taper leaf springs.
1962 First UK truck with tilt cab, the Foden S24.
1965 Fail-safe spring brakes in United States.
1966 First UK truck with spring brakes from ERF.
1968 Leyland gas turbine truck.

1970s
1973 Opec oil crisis leads to more economical engines.
1974 Chevrolet Titan gas turbine on operational trials.
1977 Roof top deflectors improve fuel economy.

1980s
1982 Length limits for tractors relaxed in United States. Long-nose conventionals gain popularity.
1985 Aerodynamic styling appearing on trucks in United States, influenced by Europe.
1986 Anti-lock braking systems for trucks.
1987 Detroit Diesel 60 series with electronic fuel control.

1990s
1998 Volvo with driver's airbag.
1998 Electronic disc brakes from Mercedes and Scania.
1999 Mercedes "driverless" trucks under development.

2000s
2001 Telematics mean drivers can be tracked round the clock.
2007 UK's last truck maker, ERF, closes.
2015 First driverless convoys tested in the United States and Europe.
2017 Tesla unveils electric 40-ton semi-truck with 500-mile range.
2018 Peterbilt displays autonomous '579' at Las Vegas Consumer Electronics Show.

THE DIESEL ENGINE

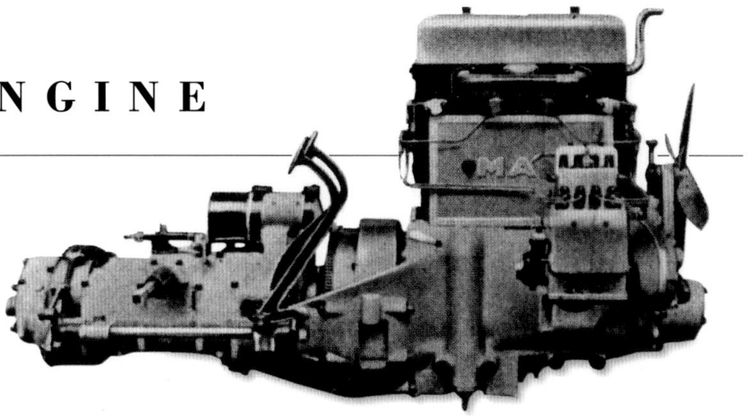

■ ABOVE *MAN's direct-injection 4-cylinder diesel engine of 1924 was the forerunner of the modern truck engine.*

The high-speed, automotive oil engine has been with us since the mid 1920s and, for the past half century, has been the staple power unit of heavy trucks all over the world. For most of that time it has gone under the name "diesel", although it has been argued that an automotive engine based strictly on Dr Rudolph Diesel's theory has never been built. Dr Diesel was born in Paris of German parents in 1858 and, after studying at the Universities of Augsburg and Munich, he developed his theory of an "economical thermal motor" which he patented in 1892.

■ LEFT *The unusual opposed-piston 3-cylinder Rootes TS3 two-stroke diesel introduced on Commer trucks in 1954.*

The essence of his idea was that when air is highly compressed it reaches a temperature hot enough to spontaneously ignite fuel brought into contact with it. His original design was fuelled by coal dust instead of oil, but a much modified engine developed at MAN of Augsburg in 1897 used fuel oil. Prior to Diesel's successful engine a number of other engineers had experimented with "crude oil" engines, which would run on high flash-point oil as opposed to gasoline.

Among them were George Brayton of Boston in 1874, Priestman Bros. of Hull in 1885 and Ackroyd Stuart, who took out patents for oil engines between 1886 and 1890. These included a compression-ignition engine with jerk pump injection, but with a lower compression ratio than Dr Diesel's. This required pre-heating when starting from cold. It was in December 1924 at the Berlin Exhibition that the first practical direct-injection engine appeared. This was the MAN 5 litre/305cu in 4-cylinder unit, which is regarded as the forerunner of the modern diesel. It developed 45bhp and was governed to a maximum of 1050rpm.

By the early 1930s new diesels were being developed by many leading truck manufacturers and specialist engine builders. Though the Cummins Engine Co. was by then well established, heavy-duty gasoline engines were to remain popular in the United States through to the 1960s. The economy benefits of the diesel became increasingly important with the oil crisis of the early '70s. Cummins, Caterpillar and Detroit Diesel are all major proprietary manufacturers in the United States,

■ BELOW *The Gardner 6LXB 180 was renowned for durability. Most British heavies used it, including Atkinson, Bristol, ERF, Foden, Guy and Scammell.*

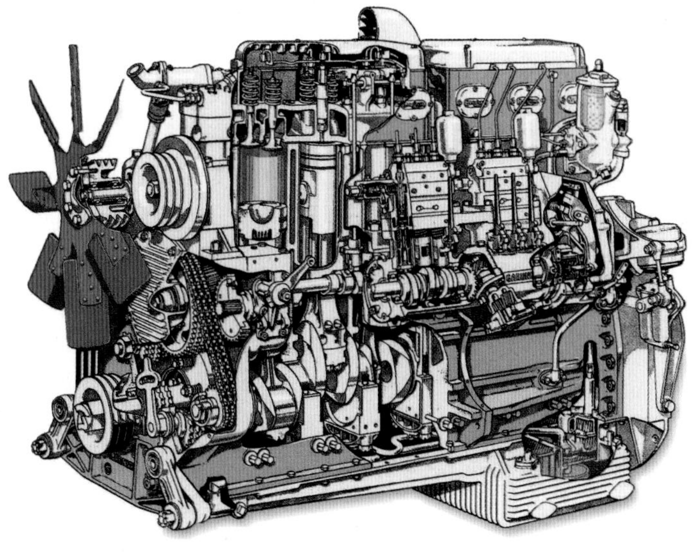

■ ABOVE ***The 400bhp Detroit Diesel 8V-92TA Silver Series two-stroke thrived on high-speed long-haul operations.***

while in the UK and Europe the most significant makers have included MAN, Mercedes-Benz, Deutz, Saurer, Volvo-Penta, Gardner, Perkins, Meadows and Rolls Royce.

Some manufacturers favoured the two-stroke diesel, which can develop a high power output from a smaller cubic capacity and is therefore lighter and more compact than four-stroke engines of equivalent power ratings. Noted two-stroke diesels were those of Detroit Diesel, Krupp, Foden and Rootes, the latter being of an unusual 3-cylinder opposed-piston type. Common drawbacks of two-stroke diesels are their tendency to generate high temperatures and to lack torque in the lower speed range. Four-stroke engines present less cooling problems and have a flatter torque curve, giving greater "lugging" power at low speed.

■ ABOVE ***The Cummins 11 litre/671cu in M series 6-cylinder diesel featured CELECT Plus electronic engine management.***

As demands for bigger, more powerful engines grew, some manufacturers, notably Detroit Diesel, Cummins, Mercedes-Benz, Deutz, Tatra, Perkins and Scania, turned to V engines with between 4 and 12 cylinders. These have the advantage of more compact dimensions than in-line units. Gardner, on the other hand, favoured the traditional in-line approach with their 150bhp 8LW, designed during World War II, and later their 8LXB 240 which was a highly successful design of the 1970s era. In recent years tough new emission laws have brought big advances in diesel engine technology with increasing use of electronic engine management, controlling fuel injection and timing with great precision. Not only has this reduced air pollution, it has also improved fuel economy by up to 25 per cent. Progress towards even leaner and cleaner diesel engines continues and, despite pressure from environmentalists to switch to gas or electric propulsion, diesels continue to be the preferred choice for heavy trucks.

■ BELOW ***Announced in 1987, the Detroit Diesel 60-series 6-cylinder four-stroke was the first to feature electronic fuel injection.***

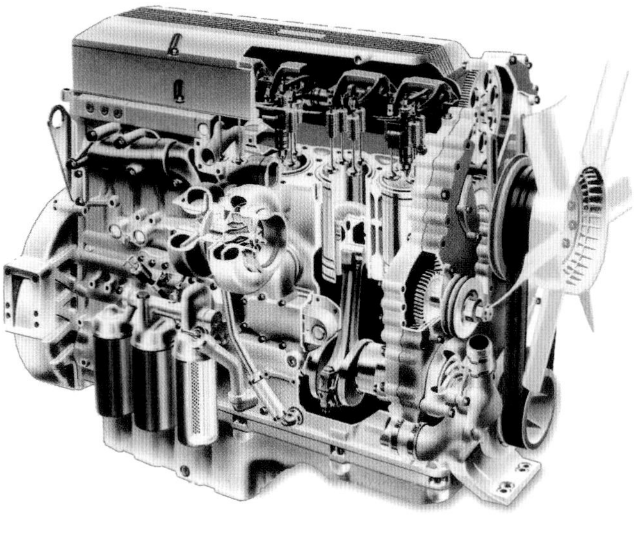

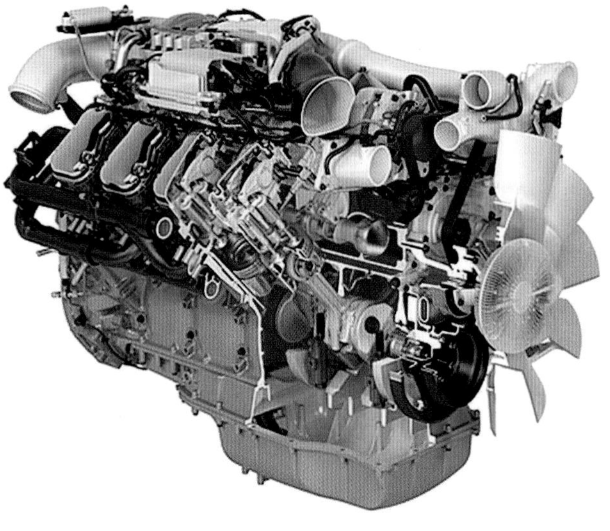

■ RIGHT ***The Scania 730hp, 16.4 litre R730 V8 diesel introduced in 2013 typifies the trend in truck engines for the 21st century.***

TRUCK ANATOMY

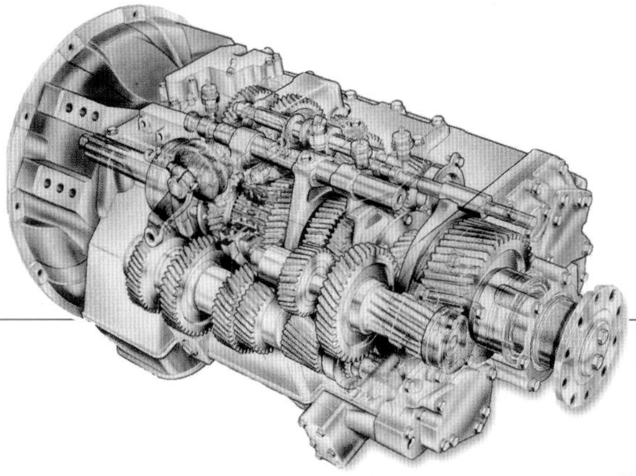

While huge advances in technology and component design have taken place, the fundamental anatomy of a truck has not changed for more than half a century. Most modern trucks still consist of a ladder-type chassis frame on to which the engine, transmission, suspension, axles, steering, braking system, electrics and cab are attached. Most chassis frames are constructed from high-tensile steel and can be of riveted, bolted or, in some cases, welded construction. Where weight is critical, frames are sometimes built from aluminium.

At one time most trucks had semi-elliptic multi-leaf springs front and rear, but big advances have been made in suspension over the past 30 years or so. Parabolic tapered leaf springs for improved ride and greater reliability became available in the 1960s. Most premium-quality trucks now feature air suspension. Hydraulic dampers are standard fitment for safe handling and even ride. Front axles, up to 8 tonnes capacity, are usually of I-section, forged from nickel steel for greater strength. Recirculating ball steering with integral hydraulic power assistance provides almost effortless control for the driver. Power steering pressure is delivered by an engine-driven pump.

The engine is the heart of the truck, and virtually all modern heavy trucks have turbocharged and intercooled in-line-six V8 or V10 direct-injection diesels. Typically these have net power outputs of between 300 and 600bhp. Most modern diesels are quiet-running with low exhaust emissions, achieved by sophisticated electronic fuel injection and timing control. Electric starting is most common, but some heavy diesels have compressed air starters.

Power is transmitted to the road through a clutch, gearbox and differential drive. To cope with high torque loadings most modern clutches are of the twin-plate type with air-assisted hydraulic actuation giving light pedal effort. Gearboxes can be constant mesh with sliding dog engagement or synchromesh and can have eight, nine, ten, thirteen or sixteen ratios. Most have a mainshaft and twin countershafts. As an alternative to manual gearboxes, semi and fully-automatic "intelligent" transmissions are available, relieving the driver of the responsibility of gear shifting.

Rear axles of between 10 and 13 tonnes capacity are generally of spiral bevel or hypoid gear type with single or double-reduction. Some axles have the secondary reduction gearing in the wheel hubs, reducing drive-shaft stress and enabling a smaller

■ ABOVE *A modern-day heavy truck synchromesh twin countershaft gearbox – the Eaton RTS 17316 16-speed range-change plus splitter.*

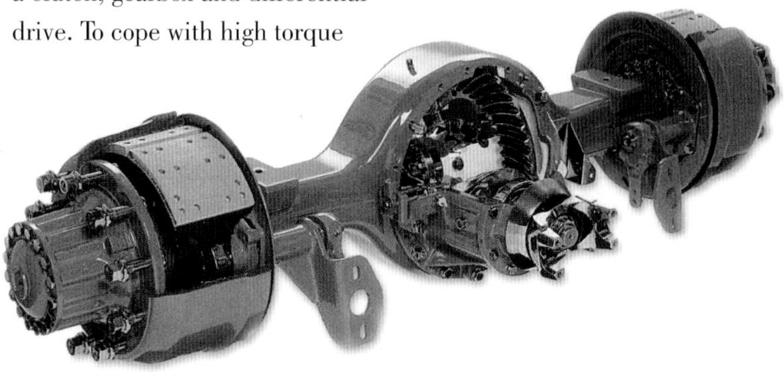

■ BELOW *A typical Meritor single-reduction hypoid heavy-duty rear axle as used by many leading truck manufacturers.*

■ LEFT *Since the 1960s most heavy trucks have featured tilt cabs. This is a 1981 Bedford TM4400 with Cummins E370 diesel.*

differential housing which gives improved ground clearance. The drive from the gearbox to the rear axle is transmitted by a propeller shaft with universal joints.

Braking is of paramount importance and modern systems are highly sophisticated. While internal expanding drum brakes are still the most common, increasing numbers of manufacturers are fitting disc brakes. Some fit front discs and rear drums, while some of the latest trucks have electronically controlled disc brakes front and rear. In nearly all cases brakes are actuated by compressed air through a complex system of valves. All trucks must have an independent secondary system by law.

Spring brake actuators keep the brakes applied on a stationary vehicle and they cannot be released until air pressure has been built up. Compressed air is supplied to chassis-mounted air tanks from an engine-driven compressor. Air systems have alcohol antifreeze equipment and are self-draining to expel moisture. To save wear and tear on the service brakes, many heavy trucks have engine brakes which utilize engine compression to retard the vehicle. In mountainous territories other auxiliary brakes such as electric transmission retarders are frequentlyfitted. Wheels and tyres have also benefited from technological advances over the years. Tubeless radials on single-piece wheel centres are standard on most modern trucks, and wheel centres are often of forged aluminium for lightness and smart appearance. For accurate concentricity, wheels are spigot-mounted.

■ ABOVE *Representing state-of-the-art trucks of the 1990s was the Scania 144L with a design gcw of 50 tonnes, a 14 litre/854cu in V8 diesel and disc brakes.*

■ BELOW *This sleeper cab on a Mercedes-Benz Actros is typical of current European sleeper cabs.*

The truck's electrical system serves vital functions, not only for starting and lighting, but for the many electronic devices that keep a modern truck operational. Most systems incorporate two high-capacity 12-volt batteries to give 24 volts. These are kept charged by an engine-driven alternator incorporating current voltage control.

The one feature that gives the truck its identity and means most to the driver is the cab. Over the past 20–30 years cabs have improved enormously inside and out. Modern styling not only adds prestige, but reduces wind drag to improve fuel economy. Interior appointments on long-haul cabs are now up to the best passenger-car standards, featuring velour or soft leather upholstery, carpeting, tinted glass, electric windows and many other refinements. Comprehensive instrumentation on wrap-around dash panels have become the norm, while interior noise has been reduced to car levels so that the modern trucker can listen to music or receive calls on his cab phone. Nearly all long-haul cabs now have well-appointed sleepers.

ROLE OF THE TRUCK

The average citizen spares little thought for trucks, save perhaps to complain at their presence on the highway. In doing so he is probably unaware that those very trucks might be delivering the goods that he expects to find at the supermarket the next day. Just about everything we own, from the bread we eat to the shoes on our feet, has to travel by truck. Likewise, the raw materials that go into manufacturing these products are also delivered by trucks. It is no exaggeration to say that modern society would quickly grind to a halt without an efficient, around-the-clock road-haulage industry.

Commodities that we take for granted have to be transported from factory to wholesaler and on to retailers. Beer, gasoline, milk, fresh vegetables, clothing, children's toys, newspapers, TV sets, soft drinks, sports gear and even motor cars all rely on trucks for delivery. Further back down the line, other

■ OPPOSITE TOP *Brewers rely extensively on their truck fleets to keep bars and clubs supplied with beer. This is a Swiss FBW.*

■ OPPOSITE MIDDLE *Food distribution is dependent on trucks. This famous New Zealand brand runs long-distance ERF B-trains.*

■ OPPOSITE BOTTOM *Keeping filling stations supplied is down to the large tanker fleets run by major oil companies.*

■ RIGHT *Car dealers are kept supplied by transporters carrying up to 10 cars at a time.*

trucks carry the grain, steel, plastic, fertilizer, cotton, chemicals, timber and countless other materials that go into the manufacture of such products. We rely equally heavily on other types of trucks too – those that collect our garbage, sweep our streets, clear the snow in winter, fight fires all year round and tow away broken-down vehicles.

A fundamental difference between road and rail is that road transport can survive without rail but rail freight is entirely dependent on road transport to provide collection and delivery at rail terminals. For complete flexibility and rapid turnaround, especially important when handling perishable cargoes, road transport is the only option. As long as we continue to expect the goods demanded by modern society, trucks will be needed to deliver them.

■ ABOVE LEFT *Supermarkets could not keep going without the thousands of trucks that deliver to them on a regular basis.*

■ ABOVE RIGHT *Hauling fresh milk over long distances requires large tankers.*

■ BELOW *Our daily bread supplies rely entirely on an efficient supply of flour from the millers. This is an Iveco EuroTech bulk flour tanker.*

Peterbilt
87803
Peterbilt
Peterbilt
8780

Truck Types

As the trucking industry developed, so did the need for various types of bodywork. The open truck was fine for most goods, and in inclement weather a tarpaulin could be used to cover the load. The box van or "tilt" van offered extra load security and complete weather protection. While liquids were originally carried in cans or churns on an open truck, bulk tankers were much more efficient. Loose loads such as coal, sand and gravel involved a lot of hard work with shovels until the dump body appeared. Eventually the variety of bodywork was almost endless. Box vans were adapted into insulated vans for meat and perishable goods. Later still, refrigeration equipment was available. Tankers were developed for powders and gases as well as a vast range of liquids. Over the years bodywork has carried on being adapted to suit customer requirements.

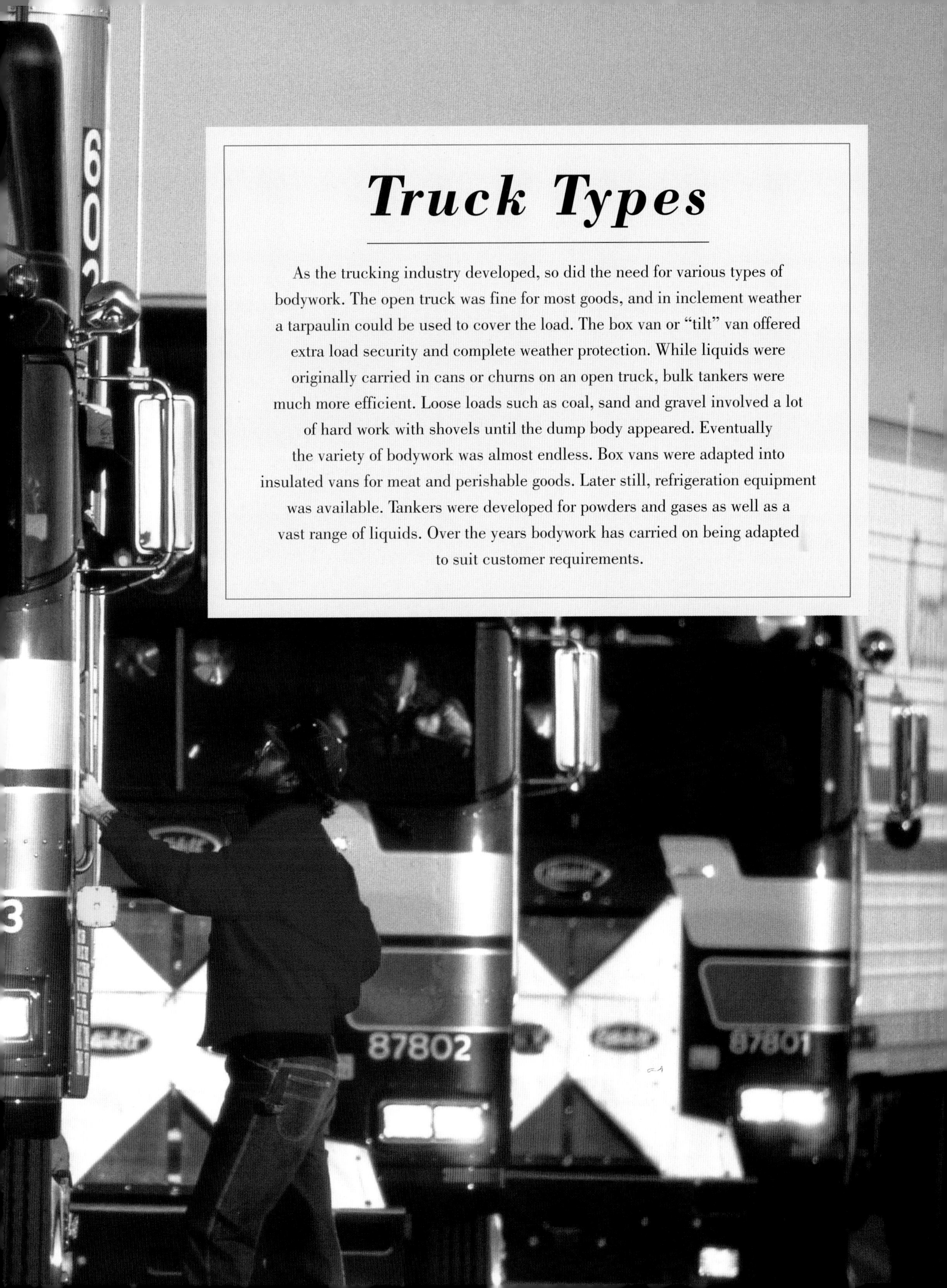

GENERAL-PURPOSE TRUCKS

Any truck not adapted for a particular product is a general-purpose truck. The most basic type is the flat-platform truck, usually fitted with a front loading board to prevent the load from moving forward under braking. In the UK they are known as "flats" or "platform trucks" while in Australia and New Zealand they are called "flat decks" or "trays". In the United States the popular term is "flatbed".

They have the advantage of lightness and ease of loading from the side, rear or above, but once loaded the cargo has to be restrained by ropes, chains or webbing straps, and loads needing weather protection have to be sheeted over. Sheeting and roping a large load demands special skill, and usually it is the driver's responsibility to ensure that the cargo is secure and does not pose a risk to other road users. Securing different types of products requires different techniques according to how stable they are and whether or not they can be damaged by the lashings themselves.

A sided body offers some load security. In most cases the sides are hinged so that they can be lowered to facilitate loading and

■ ABOVE *The open "flat deck" or "platform" truck is the basic general-purpose vehicle. This is a Mack MC working in New Zealand.*

■ LEFT *For heavy international transport throughout Europe, TIR tilts, such as this Swiss-registered White Road Commander, are the ideal option.*

■ BELOW *For all-round loading access, the platform truck is unrivalled, as clearly seen in this photograph of a Canadian Freightliner.*

■ CENTRE LEFT *Stake sides, as seen on this GMC, are popular as general-purpose trucks in many countries, including the United States.*

■ CENTRE RIGHT *The dropside truck has the advantage of greater load restraint. This early 1970s AEC is pictured at a large steel stockholder.*

■ BOTTOM RIGHT *For weather protection certain loads must be securely sheeted, as with this 21-ton load of bagged cement on a Leyland Constructor.*

unloading. One type of sided truck popular in many countries is the stake side which features fixed high sides made up of spaced-out horizontal boards. Such bodywork is well suited for agricultural use and for the carriage of loose, bulky items such as tyres.

A type of general-purpose bodywork common in Europe is the tilt, which is basically a dropside body with a tarpaulin cover supported by a strong framework. One advantage is that it can be sealed by Customs for cross-border international traffic while still offering the flexibility of an open platform truck for loading and unloading. It does, however, take considerable time and effort to strip down and reassemble.

Curtainsiders & Box Vans

By far the most common bodywork to come on the scene over the past 30 years is the curtainsider. This is, in effect, a van body with open sides and slide-back plastic curtains. These provide access for loading by forklift trucks. Once the body is loaded, the curtains are drawn along the full length and tensioned up – usually by special straps and buckles. As an extension to the curtainsider principle, there are now versions with sliding roofs for overhead loading. Another type, mainly for steel haulage, has a full-length sliding canopy that can concertina to either end of the load platform for overhead loading.

The other type of body seen in most countries is the box van. This usually has double doors or a roller shutter at the rear and often has a side door or shutter near the front end. It has the benefit of greater load security but the drawback of inferior loading access. Such bodies are sometimes fitted with sliding tracks or roller conveyors in the floor to facilitate the loading and unloading of goods in bins or on pallets. A relatively recent development has been the double-deck van body featuring an intermediate load platform. Van bodies are frequently fitted with hydraulic or electric tail lifts.

Another important version of the box-van body is the temperature-controlled van which

■ ABOVE *Maximum-capacity reefers such as this MAN five-axled artic from Aberdeen, haul meat to London's Smithfield market.*

■ LEFT *Temperature-controlled box vans are essential in dairy-products distribution. This cab-forward Peterbilt 320 operates in Canada.*

■ RIGHT *Curtainsiders provide full-length access for loading by forklift truck while offering load security for high-value cargo.*

■ BELOW RIGHT *Curtainsiders originated in the UK as Boalloy Tautliners. This International is New Zealand-based.*

■ BOTTOM *Box vans are popular in the United States, where this seven-axled International A-train is based.*

has insulated panelling and a built-in temperature control unit, usually used to chill the interior for the transport of fresh produce, meat, poultry and fish. These are frequently referred to as "fridge" bodies or "reefers" and generally have a refrigeration plant powered by its own small diesel engine which can be heard running even when the vehicle is stationary or unattended. All the bodywork described here can come in an almost endless variety of sizes, from compact units for 1 tonne or less to long semi-trailers for payloads of up to 30 tonnes.

TANKERS

Tankers come in two basic types – those for bulk liquids and those for bulk powders. The latter only became common during the 1950s, and during the past 40 years or so have become more and more sophisticated in design. The first bulk liquid tankers date from the early 1920s. Some early tankers for fuel oil were built in rectangular form, but as manufacturing techniques improved cylindrical and elliptical barrels became the norm. Because different commodities have different specific gravities, tanks tend to be tailored to particular products. Also, loading and unloading methods have to suit the behaviour of the product. For instance, some products foam profusely when poured while others can only be pumped when kept within a certain temperature range.

Some tanks consist of one single compartment while others can have up to five or six separate compartments for different grades or types of product. Most tanks for foodstuffs are manufactured from stainless steel for hygiene. Others may be glass-lined. Most are insulated and, where a higher than ambient temperature must be maintained, as with liquid chocolate, they can be fitted with

■ OPPOSITE TOP *An Iveco EuroTech articulated bulk powder tanker seen unloading near the Port of Rotterdam.*

■ OPPOSITE MIDDLE *Some tanks are housed in ISO frames which can be stacked with standard containers and loaded on to skeletal trailers.*

■ RIGHT *Highly polished modern tankers are among the best-looking trucks on the highway. This New Zealand Kenworth is a good example.*

■ ABOVE *Not all powder tankers tip. This ERF with Metalair-Feldbinder cement bulker is non-tipping and has pneumatic discharge.*

■ RIGHT *This Spanish Dodge foodstuffs tanker is passing through the dock area of Almeria.*

heating jackets. Depending on the product, tanks can be top filled or, where the product foams through agitation, they can be filled from below. The load may be discharged by gravity or pumped out, and tanks are usually lightly pressurized to assist discharge. When hazardous chemicals are carried, strict safety codes are applied and drivers undergo special training.

There are also flexible, portable rubber tanks which lie flat when empty so that other goods can be carried.

A whole range of powders are now transported in bulk tanks and these too require highly sophisticated unloading equipment. Commodities most commonly carried include cement, flour, gypsum, limestone, china clay, salt, pulverized coal, plastic granules, farm feeds and silica sand. Sometimes vehicles are equipped with a number of identical smaller tanks instead of one large one.

■ OPPOSITE BOTTOM *A large fuel distributor in Portland, Oregon, runs this impressive eight-axled A-train hauled by a Freightliner conventional.*

■ RIGHT *Doubles outfits are not legal in the UK. This smart chemical tanker is typical of British outfits which are limited to 16.5m length.*

DUMP TRUCKS

Dump trucks or "tippers" are mainly employed for the transport of construction materials such as earth, stone aggregates, sand and rock. However, dump trucks come in a wide variety of types, from four-wheelers for 2 or 3 tons payload to massive, heavy-duty articulated and drawbar outfits grossing 50 to 60 tons or more. Most dump trucks are equipped with hydraulic rams to raise the body. These can be front-mounted or underbody-mounted, the latter being the only option for three-way dump trucks, which can be tipped to either side as well as to the rear. Most hydraulic pumps are driven from a gearbox power take-off. As well as "open" dump trucks there are covered versions commonly used for grain and bulk feed. Even most open dump trucks carrying sand and aggregates are sheeted over nowadays, since stricter regulations regarding safety and pollution have come into force in many countries.

Dump-truck bodies, like those on tankers, generally tend to be purpose-built to cater for

■ TOP *The Peterbilt transfer dump is designed to tip its own load and then the trailer's load which is transferred into the truck body.*

■ ABOVE *Three-way dump trucks are common in Europe, especially in Germany, Italy and Switzerland. This is a Fiat with Romanazzi bodywork.*

■ LEFT *Seen at a quarry in the Spanish town of Carboneras is this 36-tonne Pegaso 2431K 8×4. It has forward-mounted underbody gear.*

■ ABOVE LEFT *Grossing 35 tonnes, this Mercedes-Benz 3538 end dump truck is seen working on a major road-building project near Iraklion Airport in Crete.*

■ ABOVE RIGHT *The MAN 35-332 8×8 dump truck has great performance on rough terrain. Here it is seen at work on a large drainage scheme at Magdeburg.*

certain types of loads. Those for heavy, dense materials like earth, clay and sand have lower sides and therefore less cubic capacity than those used on lighter materials such as coke, coal and grain. The latter are generally referred to as "high-sided bulk dump trucks" in the UK. Materials used in the construction of dump-truck bodies also vary. While light alloys are suited to lightweight, bulky goods, materials such as rock and granite ballast require harder wearing steel. Massive earthmovers, which operate off-highway, are designed to tip, but they are generally known as "quarry dumpers" as opposed to "tippers". Many bulk tankers are also equipped with tipping gear to aid discharge of the load.

■ RIGHT *With a design weight of 44 tonnes this 6-axled Foden outfit is the largest of its type allowed in the UK. It features Harsh triple-ram tipping gear.*

FURNITURE-REMOVAL VANS

The furniture-removal van, referred to as a "moving van" in some countries, is basically a large-capacity box van adapted for easy loading and unloading of furniture. In the UK it usually has a Luton head, which is an extension over the driver's cab. This takes its name from a type of high-volume van developed to carry hats, Luton once being the centre of the UK hat trade. Removal vans also have a dropped rear floor section behind the rear axle to save effort when loading and unloading. The rear door is usually in the form of a full-width tail board which is lowered to form a convenient ramp. Sometimes mechanical tail lifts are fitted instead.

Removal vans are operated by professional crews, specially trained in handling awkward and often valuable pieces of furniture, as well as being sensitive to customers' concerns about cherished possessions. Furniture moving can be strenuous work and very often access to properties is difficult in a large van. The cabs of many removal vans have extra seating to accommodate crew members. Journeys can vary from a few hundred metres/yards to

■ ABOVE *Pickfords, the oldest removal company in the world, ran this solid-tyred Leyland drawbar outfit in the 1920s.*

■ LEFT *A medium-weight Mitsubishi articulated removal van operated by the New Zealand division of Allied Pickfords.*

■ OPPOSITE BOTTOM *Longer distances covered in the United States demand larger removal vehicles like this Kenworth K100 of United Van Lines.*

■ ABOVE LEFT *This old-style bonneted Büssing with integral van body is typical of the furniture trucks once popular in Europe.*

■ ABOVE RIGHT *Volvo FL6 with Luton type van body is typical of the UK scene. This one is engaged in office removals.*

■ RIGHT *Lighter vans such as this GMC are useful for small consignments.*

hundreds of kilometres/miles. In the case of international removals, the furniture is sometimes transferred at the depot into an ISO container and a local crew takes over at the final destination.

As well as being used on household removals, furniture vans are used to deliver new furniture to shops and retail superstores. Similar vehicles are engaged in home deliveries of new furniture, and the skills needed for such deliveries are similar to those of the professional removal crews.

56
56

Specialized Trucks

There are limits to how far basic truck bodies can be adapted; certain loads need specialized bodywork. These can vary from self-loading cranes to completely purpose-built trucks like those for ready-mixed concrete or vehicle recovery. In the field of specialized trucks there are hundreds of variations to cope with specific operations. Municipal trucks are good examples – they have been designed to collect garbage, sweep and sprinkle streets, empty gulleys, service overhead cables and a host of other important tasks. Fire and rescue trucks come in a wide variety of types, as do recovery trucks. In the heavyweight sector, massive logging trucks and heavy-haulage trucks can transport hundreds of tons in one go. Military vehicles are another breed of specialized truck with sophisticated self-loading systems. The scope for special purpose-built trucks is almost endless.

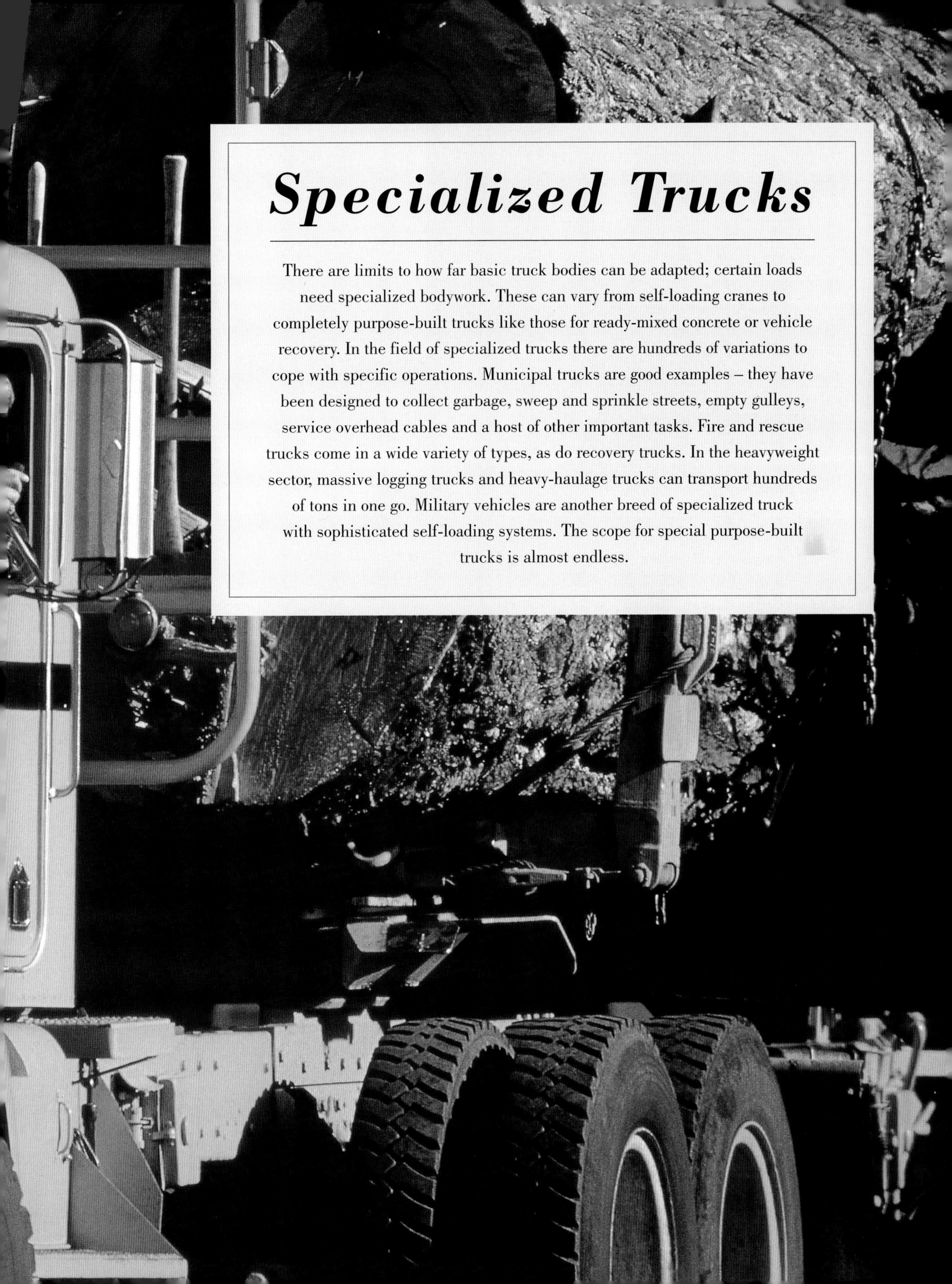

Concrete Mixers

Concrete mixers or "readymix" trucks have become an increasingly common sight over the years as the use of concrete has grown in the construction industry. Early designs by Jaeger & Co. and T. L. Smith Co. in the United States were built under licence in the UK by Ransomes & Rapier of Ipswich and Stothert & Pitt of Bath. Today a large proportion of concrete mixers are 6×4s with drums of 6 to 7cu m/7.8 to 9.1cu yd capacity, but often a customer might require larger or smaller quantities. To operate economically, concrete suppliers often run a variety of trucks with two, three, four or five axles to cater for various load capacities. A typical 8×4 truck can deliver 8 to 9cu m/10.5 to 11.8cu yd and some larger multi-axle mixers have drums of between 12 and 15cu m/15.7 and 19.6cu yd capacity.

Most concrete mixers have a separate engine to rotate the drum at various speeds. Some

■ TOP *1993 MAN 32-292 four-axled mixer truck with 9cu m/11.8cu yd drum in the Hasselhorst district of Berlin.*

■ ABOVE *This Terberg F2850 10×4 12cu m/15.7cu yd machine is one of a large fleet based near Rotterdam in The Netherlands.*

■ LEFT *In New Zealand the International ACCO is a popular basis for transit mixers. This is a 1997 ACCO-G with a lowered version of the Iveco Group cab.*

■ RIGHT *A construction site near Burnaby, Canada, is the setting for this Freightliner 40-ton dual-steer cabover of Kask Brothers.*

■ BELOW LEFT *A Foden 3000 series 8×4 concrete mixer.*

■ BELOW RIGHT *A nicely liveried DAF 85 series 8×4 of the John Fyfe Group.*

■ BOTTOM LEFT *Spanish Dodge 6×4 mixer grosses over 30 tonnes and carries around 7cu m/9.2cu yd.*

■ BOTTOM RIGHT *Canada is one of the best places to see giant mixers such as this dual-steer Mack in Vancouver.*

have a P.T.O. or hydraulic drive. The trucks are loaded at batching plants, which today have computerized controls to ensure correctly measured quantities of ballast, cement and water. Drum rotation is reversed during discharge. The trucks have special chutes that distribute the concrete on site. With the abrasive nature of the materials used, drums can suffer rapid wear. Regular cleaning is necessary to maintain efficient operation. Drivers take special care when cornering, owing to the vehicle's high centre of gravity.

Self-loading Trucks

■ ABOVE *A 1994 Iveco Ford Eurotrakker with Atlas 100.1 self-loading grab with a Kingshoffer 50 litre/3050cu in bucket.*

Self-loading trucks come in a very wide variety of shapes and sizes, from the basic 2/3-tonne four-wheeler with truck-mounted hydraulic crane to 50-tonne multi-axle rigids and heavy-haulage tractors. Such vehicles are most widely used in the construction industry, where heavy loads often need to be handled on remote sites. Self-loading cranes are a virtual necessity on trucks delivering bricks, building blocks and similar materials. Another common type of self-loading vehicle is the skip truck or "bin lifter", which has a hydraulically operated gantry for delivery and collection of garbage bins. An extension of this idea is the roll-on-and-off garbage container which is hooked to a hydraulic arm and dragged up on to the truck. Many dump trucks engaged on road repairs have their own truck-mounted loading shovels.

One self-loading truck popular in the UK during the 1960s and '70s was the Brimec, which could slide its loading platform rearwards and then tip to form a ramp on to which vehicles or plant machinery could be driven or winched. Similar vehicles are currently in wide use for car recovery. A Japanese system that appeared in the '60s involved raising the whole front end of the truck on big hydraulic rams until the rear of the body platform descended to ground level.

In recent years many trucks engaged on container traffic have been fitted with their own hydraulic swing lift equipment capable of lifting heavy ISO containers from alongside the truck. Yet another device that has become popular recently is the portable forklift truck, which can be carried on the rear of the trailer or truck, to be demounted at the delivery point.

■ LEFT *This 1995 Foden 4380 can lift up to 60 tonnes in one go with its Bonfiglioli P.67000TL self-loading crane.*

■ OPPOSITE BOTTOM *1995 ERF EC Olympic 6×2 for machinery transport has a rear-mounted Cormach 30000SE crane with a 30-ton capacity.*

■ LEFT *Side-lifter equipment, popular in New Zealand, can lift ISO containers weighing around 30 tonnes.*

■ RIGHT *Mitsubishi truck's novel system using hydraulic jacks that raise the whole front up until the body forms a ramp.*

■ LEFT *Brick and block deliveries are made easier by truck-mounted cranes, such as this Hiab mounted on a 1988 Seddon Atkinson 3-11.*

■ RIGHT *A common form of self-loader is the skip truck or "bin lifter". This one is mounted on a 1987 DAF 2100.*

GARBAGE TRUCKS

Garbage trucks were once little more than covered dump trucks with hatches through which dustbins or trash cans could be emptied. Over the past three or four decades they have become more and more sophisticated, beginning with the introduction of hydraulic compression equipment. In recent years increasing volumes of domestic refuse and garbage have led to bigger and bigger garbage trucks. Three and four-axled trucks at up to 32 tonnes gvw are now commonplace in most parts of Europe and the United States.

At one time garbage trucks were built on low-loading chassis with small wheels to make it easier for crews to manually empty the bins. Crew cabs have become standard in the UK, while in the United States crews generally ride on a platform at the rear of the truck. While many garbage trucks were once built on standard off-the-peg chassis, most are now on specially designed chassis providing low-entry crew cabs with large glazed areas. Automatic transmissions are the norm, making the driver's job much easier. At the same time many authorities have standardized wheeled bins of increased capacity, which can be pushed into place on mechanical hoists to relieve the crews of lifting. This not only improves hygiene, but speeds up operations for greater efficiency.

■ ABOVE *A GMC 6×4 garbage truck of the early 1980s engaged on household garbage collection.*

■ LEFT *Garbage trucks have become larger in recent years. This 1996 Seddon Atkinson Pacer 325 grosses 32 tonnes.*

■ ABOVE *This White GMC garbage truck in Canada has a tight turning circle for accessing service roads in housing estates.*

■ BELOW *The latest Mercedes-Benz has large glazed areas and a walk-in cab. Special "wheelie" bins ease the operator's workload.*

FIRE TRUCKS

There is always an air of excitement when the sirens sound and traffic pulls to one side to give the speeding fire truck right of way as it hurries to an emergency. Fire trucks have captured the imagination of children and adults alike. The design and complexity of fire engines have advanced dramatically since open appliances with warning bells roared through the streets with the brass-helmeted crew clinging bravely on to their handrails. Wooden escape ladders were superseded by alloy and, later still, by hydraulic platforms.

Gasoline engines remained popular for many years after most trucks had turned to diesel, as gasoline engines offer faster acceleration. In recent years, though, most UK and European appliances have favoured diesel power. Manual transmissions have also given way to automatic.

In the United States articulated fire appliances have been popular for many years, classic examples being from American LaFrance and Seagrave. Another noted manufacturer is Hahn. In Europe, Magirus is recognized as one of the pioneers of fire-appliance design, while Merryweather, Dennis, HCB Angus and Carmichael led the industry in the UK. Today, many UK brigades have turned to European makers.

■ ABOVE LEFT *A heavy-duty Mack CF pump escape operating in Auckland, New Zealand.*

■ ABOVE *Hydraulic hoists, as shown on this Dodge, have replaced the traditional turntable ladder.*

■ BELOW *Articulated fire trucks are seen mainly in the United States. This Seagrave dates from 1960.*

RECOVERY TRUCKS

Since the humble manually operated equipment of the 1920s, recovery trucks have evolved into highly sophisticated machines capable of removing a broken-down truck weighing anything up to 50 tonnes. Recovery specialists take pride in their trucks, which require considerable expertise to operate. Technology made great advances during World War II, and during the 1950s ex-army vehicles were to be seen in civilian guise at most garages. Much of the recovery equipment in common use originated from the United States, including the Holmes Twin Boom principle which first appeared in the '30s. Large transport fleets often purchased their own recovery trucks to be self-sufficient.

While most recovery vehicles once used a crane jib to lift the stricken vehicle, a revolutionary new underlift design appeared,

■ ABOVE *Dutch recovery trucks like this four-axled Scania 144G have enormous reserves of power and strength. It is powered by a 530bhp, 14 litre/854cu in V8 diesel engine.*

■ LEFT *This British-registered Magnum 6×4 is kept ready for heavy truck recovery on the M1 motorway and in mainland Europe.*

■ LEFT *Veteran International Harvester 6×4 heavy tractor forms the basis of this well-equipped New Zealand recovery truck.*

■ OPPOSITE *When a truck comes to grief, the heavy lifting gear is brought in. Air bags are being used to right this rolled artic on a British motorway.*

■ RIGHT *This ex-British Army Foden 6×6 features Swedish Ekalift AK6500 EA12 top hamper recovery gear with an 11-ton lift capacity.*

■ ABOVE *This ERF EC10 has 50/30 T3DWX Century underlift gear with a 15-ton extending top boom.*

originating from Sweden. It featured a powerful hydraulic boom which could be extended under the truck to support the front axle. This system is far superior to the high mounted jib, and in recent years it has become state-of-the-art. It is not unusual now to see purpose-built four-axle recovery vehicles with engines up to 500bhp and 12-tonnes underlift capability. At the other end of the scale there is still a call for lightweight self-loading recovery trucks for private cars, popular with motoring organizations and small garages.

LOGGING TRUCKS

Logging trucks are among the largest and most powerful of vehicles. Some of the best examples are found in Canada, New Zealand and Scandinavia. There are two classes of logging truck – those which can operate on the public highway and those which are restricted to internal journeys on private forestry roads. The on-highway trucks must conform to length and weight limits, while no such restrictions apply on private roads.

Certain manufacturers specialize in extra-heavy-duty logging trucks, among them the Pacific Truck & Trailer Co. and the Hayes Manufacturing Co., both of Vancouver. Autocar, Kenworth, Mack and Western Star are also renowned for their rugged tractors tailored to the logging industry. In Sweden, both Scania and Volvo produce high-powered, bonneted logging trucks, as does Sisu in Finland.

Some of the heaviest outfits feature a torque converter, engine brake, water-cooled service brakes and electric transmission retarder. Special trailers with bolsters are used to carry logs, and the larger outfits regularly haul three or more trailers, each carrying around 50 tons. Depending on the type of logs, the timber is either taken direct to pulp mills for paper making, to sawmills to be cut into standard sizes, or to the docks for export.

■ ABOVE ***A 38-tonne MAN six-axled artic loaded with pulpwood from the Welsh forests heads over the Plynlimon Pass en route to a paper mill.***

■ BELOW ***Typical of Canada's on-highway logging trucks is this Kenworth W900 seen at work in British Columbia.***

■ ABOVE *Grossing 150 tons, this nine-axled Mack outfit is restricted to the private forestry roads in the Kaingaroa forests on New Zealand's North Island.*

■ RIGHT *This early 1980s 24m/79ft seven-axled drawbar outfit can gross 52 tonnes under Swedish regulations.*

■ BELOW *A Bedford TM2600 6×4 prepares to load logs at a forestry site in the Scottish border region during the late 1970s.*

■ BELOW *Murupara, New Zealand, is the setting for this view of two on-highway logging trucks. In the lead is a 6×4 Pacific.*

Heavy-haulage Trucks

They're big, they're powerful, they're spectacular – heavy-haulage outfits are, by far and away, the most impressive of trucks. Gross train weights for such outfits can be anything from 500 to 1000 tonnes and sometimes as many as three or four tractors are coupled together to provide the tractive effort. Such colossal tractors can individually weigh up to 40 tonnes and are powered by turbocharged and aftercooled diesels producing over 600hp. They tend to be custom-built to individual operator's specifications by such companies as Faun and Titan in Germany, MOL in Belgium and Nicolas in France. Another specialist manufacturer is MAN-ÖAF of Vienna.

Among the traditional makers once famous for such super haulers were Scammell in England, Pacific in Canada, Kenworth in the United States, Willème in France and Trabosa in Spain. Depending on the type of load, special girder-frame trailers supported on front and rear bogies, each with up to 12 rows of wheels may be used. Alternatively, multiples of modular bogies might be used, linked together.

Often the movement of such massive loads is planned months in advance and involves specialist teams, including structural engineers to test the strength of bridges and to advise on any obstructions such as overhead cables. Normal traffic is usually stopped to keep the route clear and such loads are escorted by police outriders. So spectacular are some of the larger heavy-haulage outfits that enthusiasts will travel great distances to see them.

■ ABOVE *Hookers, the well-known New Zealand heavy-haulage specialists, are the owners of this British-built Scammell Contractor photographed on North Island in 1993.*

■ BELOW *Grossing around 530 tonnes, this outfit is carrying a GEC steam turbine with two German-built Fauns providing the traction.*

■ TOP *This transformer is being hauled by a 240-ton Scammell Contractor, typical of the British scene up until the 1980s.*

■ ABOVE LEFT *Waiting on the outskirts of Vienna is this Austrian MAN-ÖAF 48.792 8×8 with jeep dolly and Goldhofer trailer.*

■ ABOVE RIGHT *This impressive Mack-hauled outfit is seen loading up at Oslo Docks in Norway during the early 1980s.*

MILITARY TRUCKS

Mobility is crucial to military operations and, ever since the birth of the truck, the armed forces of the world have capitalized on the rapid movement of troops, supplies and equipment being made possible by motorized transport. Military and civilian vehicle development has progressed steadily since World War I and in many instances civilian trucks have benefited from the spin-off of advances in military designs. Military-vehicle production soared during World War II with the United States being the largest producer. Between 1939 and 1945 it supplied well over three million military vehicles for the Allied Forces.

Broadly speaking, military vehicles are divided into three classes – low, medium and high-mobility. Low-mobility 4×2, 6×4 and 8×4 types are usually based on standard civilian types. Medium-mobility 4×4, 6×6 and 8×8s are specially designed for on-off highway use with a good rough terrain capability, while high-mobility vehicles are designed for tactical support in combat areas and are often tracked types. Interchangeability of components is an

■ ABOVE *This Foden 8×6 medium-mobility DROPS vehicle features Demountable Rack Offloading and Pick-up Systems.*

■ LEFT *For over 20 years the Bedford MK 4-ton 4×4 was the workhorse of the British Army as well as many foreign armies.*

■ BELOW *1992 Oshkosh M1074 10×10 five-axled PLS (Palletized Loading System) truck, powered by a Detroit Diesel 8V-92TA.*

■ ABOVE LEFT *The legendary Diamond T 980 earned its battle honours during World War II hauling 45-ton tank transporters.*

■ ABOVE RIGHT *An Oshkosh M983 HEMTT tractor with a Detroit Diesel 8V-92TA two-stroke engine hauling a launch platform for patriot missiles.*

important consideration within each class to facilitate rapid repairs and maintenance. As a rule, military vehicles have lower weight ratings than their civilian counterparts – for instance, a 10-ton civilian truck would be rated at about 6 to 7 tons in military form. Often one basic chassis can be put to a number of roles, such as a general-service cargo truck, fuel and water tanker, troop carrier, field ambulance, radio truck or workshop.

There are hundreds of military vehicle types, from the humble Jeep up to the massive tank transporter, each with an important role to play. In recent years sophisticated designs for mechanical loading and unloading have been developed, like DROPS (Demountable Rack Offloading and Pick-up Systems) equipment which was adopted by the British Army in the late 1980s. This is mounted on Foden and Leyland/Scammell 8×6 chassis.

The United States Army has a similar system called the PLS (Palletized Loading System) based on an Oshkosh M1074 10×10 and M1076 three-axled trailer with a combined load capacity of 33 tons. The PLS has a degree of commonality with the 10-ton HEMTT (Heavy Expanded Mobility Tactical Truck) which is in wide use in a number of roles, including cargo truck with self-loading crane, fuel tanker, fifth-wheel tractor for Multiple Launch Rocket System and recovery truck. The Czech Republic manufacturer Tatra has a broadly similar range of logistic support trucks based on their latest T816 8×8.

Since the collapse of UK truck manufacturing the British Armed Forces now rely on foreign-built military vehicles including Oshkosh tank transporters and German MAN trucks built by Rheinmetall-MAN including the HX60 4x4 and HX77 8x8.

■ BELOW LEFT *A British Army DROPS truck based on the Scammell 8×6, showing self-loading equipment.*

■ BELOW RIGHT *While the UK once built its own military vehicles it now relies on foreign manufacturers. This shows a typical Oshkosh tank transporter.*

Mobile Cranes

Though not designed to carry a load, mobile cranes qualify for mention as heavy-duty road vehicles. Indeed, many early examples were mounted on truck chassis. Over the years they have become more highly specialized and virtually all current mobile cranes are purpose-built, Germany being the leading manufacturing country. Among the most impressive examples of mobile cranes are the eight-axled Mannesmann Demag-Gottwald TC3600, with a 650-tonne lifting capability, and the AC1600 18x8, nine-axled telescopic crane for a 500-tonne lift.

Liebherr also offer some massive examples, like the 800-tonne capacity 16x8 LTM1800.

Other German specialists are Faun with six-axled models up to 120 tonnes and Krupp with their KMK8400 16x8 for 400 tonnes and their colossal KMK11000 for 1000 tonnes. The latter travels in two sections on a total of 19 axles, the combined weight of the crane and the ancillary vehicle for the telescopic jib being 210 tonnes.

Of course, not every situation calls for such massive equipment, and there are numerous

■ LEFT *This 1987 Krupp 220 GMT eight-axled machine is capable of lifting 220 tonnes. It weighs 96 tonnes and has a 99m/325ft reach.*

■ BELOW *This eleven-axled monster, a Demag HC920, is one of the largest cranes operated by Hewden Stewart in the UK.*

■ ABOVE *A 1989 16×8 eight-axled Krupp KMK8400 operated by Grayston White & Sparrow, with a 400-tonne lifting capacity.*

smaller mobile cranes with lifting capacities ranging from 10 tonnes to 100 tonnes. One notable Spanish manufacturer is Luna Cranes of Huesca, which manufactures an eight-axled giant, the GT-300, for lifting up to 300 tonnes. Luna also build lighter cranes for between 20 and 75 tonnes. Historically, Fodens Ltd and Coles Cranes were significant builders of mobile cranes in the UK. Fodens were in the mobile-crane business as far back as the 1930s in conjunction with Smiths of Rodley, Leeds. A tie-up with Demag in Germany during the 1960s saw Foden mobile cranes powered by air-cooled Deutz diesel engines.

■ RIGHT *This 1980 Gottwald AMK200-103 weighs over 100 tonnes and lifts 200 tonnes up to 96m/315ft. The cab is adapted from MAN.*

■ RIGHT *This impressive machine is a 1981 Gottwald AK68-1 with a maximum lifting capacity of 850 tonnes. Fully extended, it has a reach of 178m/584ft and weighs 110 tonnes.*

National Differences in Truck Design

Despite the globalization of the modern truck industry, there are still wide variations in trucks of different nations. In much the same way as living creatures adapt to their surroundings, trucks evolve to suit the conditions in various parts of the world. What is right for hot, equatorial regions simply would not suit the freezing conditions of the arctic. Likewise, what suits the long, deserted highways of parts of Australia and America would not be right for the Alpine passes of Switzerland and Italy. Coupled with the climatic and geographical differences, there are wide variations in local legislation, itself being influenced by local conditions. Then there is the influence of local culture, which is reflected in the way trucks are styled and liveried. Such diversity adds great interest for the foreign visitor who cares to observe the transport scene.

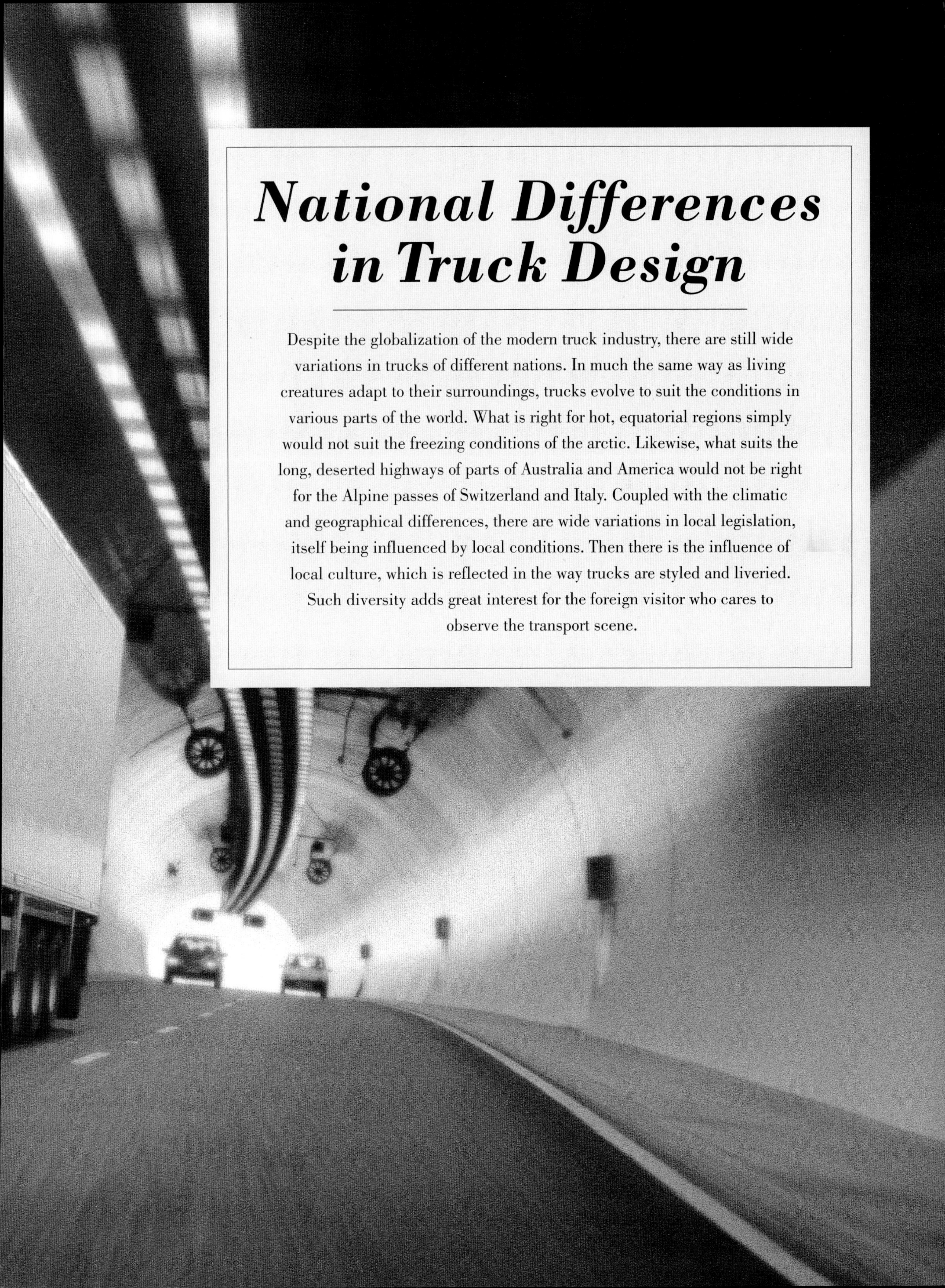

EUROPE

Despite some progress towards harmonization, the trucking scene in Europe still reflects the different priorities of individual nations. The growth of international traffic has gone some way to shaping a pan-European truck that can operate profitably without infringing local laws. The nearest thing to this is a 40-tonne gcw six-axled artic.

While the diversity of European trucks has diminished through federalization under European Community rule, full harmonization is still a long way off. Countries with high weight limits, such as The Netherlands, Sweden, Italy and Spain, are reluctant to agree to a lower weight limit, and Sweden in particular would not want to accept a shorter length limit. Such a move would render existing trucks and trailers illegal.

In Britain, traffic law favours forward-control or "cabover" trucks. Until the 1960s most British heavy trucks were rigids, the largest long-distance trucks being eight-wheelers with drawbar trailers grossing up to 32 tons. Artics gained popularity from 1964 when the law was changed to allow them to run at 32 tons instead of 24 tons. By European standards, British trucks tended to be under-powered, but the advent of new motorways from 1959 led to more powerful machines. This period also saw the beginning of roll-on/roll-off ferries between Britain and Europe.

Germany is the dominant force in European truck manufacture, while Sweden is also a major player. Germany's weight and length laws are similar to those in the UK, but Sweden

■ ABOVE *Belgium uses vehicles of Swedish, German and Dutch origin. This Scania was seen in Antwerp.*

■ RIGHT *The French stay loyal to home-produced trucks. This Renault Range T belongs to a leading French haulier.*

■ BELOW LEFT *Trucks from the old Eastern Bloc are a common sight in Western Europe, like this Polish Magnum.*

■ BELOW RIGHT *For a long time the Italian scene was dominated by eight-axled drawbar outfits like this OM.*

■ RIGHT *In the Netherlands transport legislation is more liberal and outfits like this can measure up to 25.25m and weigh up to 60 tonnes.*

■ BELOW RIGHT *Longer semi trailers (LSTs) up to 15.65m have been trialled in the UK since 2012 in a bid to improve efficiency.*

permits the use of drawbar combinations up to 24m/79ft, weighing 52 tonnes. The Netherlands has a thriving trucking industry and houses Europe's largest port at Rotterdam. The Dutch scene is dominated by heavy six, seven and eight-axled outfits grossing up to 60 tonnes.

Switzerland has lower weight limits, especially away from its borders, and since the 1970s has favoured the use of high-powered, rigid four-axled trucks. Until recently, many Swiss trucks were restricted to 2.3m/7.5ft width. France has had high axle and gross weight limits for many years, and this is reflected in the absence of French multi-axle outfits.

Spain also has high axle weights but there the preference, until recent years, has been for four-axled rigids on long-distance traffic. These are usually high-powered 8×2 vehicles with self-tracking fourth axles, grossing up to 36 tonnes. They were a development of the twin-steer six-wheeler which was originally adopted for its safety benefits on mountain roads.

Italian heavy trucks had something in common with those in Spain in that many are twin-steer six-wheelers with fourth axle conversions. However, most such Italian eight-wheelers operated with four-axled drawbar trailers grossing 44 tonnes. Traditionally, most Italian trucks featured right-hand drive for added safety when negotiating narrow mountain roads. Europe has aimed to harmonise truck weights and dimensions but there are still wide differences between individual countries. LSTs (Longer semi trailers) at 15.65m have been trialled in the UK despite environmentalists' opposition, while Holland already allows LHVs (Longer Heavier Vehicles) up to 25.25m in length.

■ BELOW LEFT *Liberal length limits allow Swedish trucks to run at 24m/79ft.*

■ BELOW RIGHT *German companies support their own truck industry. Drawbar outfits are very popular, such as this MAN.*

UNITED STATES & CANADA

With the stepping up of the Interstate highway network during the 1950s and '60s road transport overtook rail freight in America. In the late '30s the railways dominated freight movement but over 35 years that has been reversed. Road improvements enabled larger and more efficient trucks to be introduced. Many states allowed "doubles" outfits with two 12.2m/40ft trailers on a total of nine axles. These could gross over 60 tons and had high-power engines to maintain the 32kph/20mph minimum speed limit. Gasoline engines remained popular in America long after most countries had switched to diesel. The fuel crisis of the early '70s led to the decline of big, thirsty gasoline engines. At one time there was a 16.8m/55ft length limit in many states but current length limits apply only to trailers, allowing long-nosed "conventionals" with spacious sleepers. "Bridge Formulas" stipulate axle weights and minimum distances between sets of axles to minimize stresses on bridges. Michigan is noted for its liberal weight laws where rigs with 11 axles can gross over 74 tons. These have earned the nickname "centipedes".

■ ABOVE ***Canadian and United States trucks have much in common. Freightliner cabovers, such as this Canadian example, are a common sight in both countries.***

■ BELOW LEFT ***A classic eighteen-wheeler conventional photographed on Interstate 5 near the United States-Canadian border.***

■ BELOW RIGHT ***For years, visitors to Michigan were confronted by spectacular Centipede outfits grossing up to 74 tonnes, like this Brockway.***

While the majority of big Class 8 trucks are typical five-axled eighteen-wheelers, there are other types popular in certain states. One of these is the dromedary outfit, which consists of an artic with a very long tractor with its own van body. Such tractors can have three or four axles. Trucks engaged on long hauls must conform to the regulations in each state they enter or cross. Such are the variations in laws that the truck industry is geared to custom building. Unlike those in the UK and Europe, American manufacturers do not list standard specifications, but offer a wide choice of available options. This is generally referred to as a "modular build" approach.

East Coast rigs are generally workmanlike outfits, Mack and Volvo being popular makes, while the West Coast is dominated by glamorous long-nosed conventionals from Kenworth, Peterbilt and Western Star. The vast distances and extreme climatic variations encountered

■ RIGHT *Kenworth W900 Studio Sleeper conventional is the archetypal West Coast tractor, an icon of the United States trucking scene.*

■ BELOW RIGHT *The stretch-reach drawbar rigs, common in Washington State, are designed to meet local bridging formulas.*

by long-haul truckers in the States put extra demands on both driver and truck. To cope with this, most long-haul rigs have well-appointed sleepers that are like motor homes compared to the cramped sleeper cabs seen in Europe.

The American trucker has long been regarded as the modern-day cowboy – a resourceful free spirit upholding the legends of the great pioneers. This glamorous association, particularly true on the West Coast, has reached far beyond the shores of the United States – many truck drivers in the UK and Europe emulate the "steel cowboy" image with customized trucks and stetsons. The influence is particularly strong in The Netherlands, where truckers take enormous pride in their rigs. Australia and New Zealand have also developed their own trucking culture along American lines.

Canada's trucking industry parallels that of the United States to some extent, in that operators are faced with similar legislative differences between one province and another. Over the years trucking has overtaken rail freight. Trucks benefit from greater flexibility especially in accessing remote regions. Operators running to the Northwest Territories face extremely cold conditions and the climate varies greatly over such a huge country. High-powered doubles outfits are a common sight in most parts of Canada, some provinces allowing gross weights of up to 70 tons. Canadian doubles are usually of the B train type, consisting of two semis linked by a fifth wheel, while in the United States A trains, basically artics hitched to drawbar trailers, are more common.

In the past two decades there has been a marked increase in the use of dual-steer straight trucks hauling drawbar trailers, especially in British Columbia and the northwest of the United States. Canada is also noted for its four and five-axled concrete mixers. Most impressive of all are the massive logging trucks, particularly evident in British Columbia.

■ BELOW *Dromedary outfits, such as this Peterbilt 362E, consist of a load-carrying tractor hitched to a normal semi-trailer.*

OTHER COUNTRIES

■ ABOVE *This proud Moroccan driver is posing with his locally built Volvo N88. Note the large air filter on the far side.*

■ RIGHT *A Russian MAZ with TIR tilt trailer engaged on long-distance haulage in Eastern Europe.*

■ RIGHT *Zimbabwe is the only place one might have seen rarities like this Panda 6x4 tractor.*

■ BELOW *Israel saw a growth in multi-axle 60-tonners like this DAF 95 cement bulker in the 1990s.*

Road transport has become a vital part of the economy in most countries of the world. Eastern Europe had a truck-manufacturing industry from the beginning of the 20th century while the Russian Federation, formerly the USSR, entered the scene in the mid 1920s. Russia has some of the coldest regions on earth, and their trucks must be geared to cope with temperatures that few European makes could withstand. The emphasis is on ruggedness rather than driver comfort. As a consequence, most sales are within Russia and its neighbouring Eastern European countries.

Japan was also a relative latecomer to the truck industry, but by the '70s it had become a major player. Among Japan's most important export markets are Australia and New Zealand. Japanese trucks are now seen as state-of-the-art machines that can hold their own against any European and American competition.

Africa has a very varied transport industry. Within such a vast continent the conditions and priorities can be completely different according to the territory. In Morocco, Algeria and the Sahara regions many of the trucks are locally assembled Volvos featuring large heavy-duty air filters suited to the arid conditions. Bonneted trucks, including the Renault C range, are a common sight. In Central Africa road conditions demand particularly rugged trucks with "no frills", easy-to-repair specifications. Southern Africa has the most sophisticated transport system within the continent and, while there is little indigenous manufacturing, trucks are tailored to local needs by assembly plants set up by a number of European, American and Japanese companies. Heavy-duty long-haul trucks often consist of

■ ABOVE LEFT *India has its own breed of truck, represented by this ruggedly built Ashok-Leyland tanker.*

■ ABOVE RIGHT *Basic, easy-to-repair trucks like these old Bedford TJs abound in Nigeria and Central Africa.*

30.4m/100ft long 55-tonne gross doubles outfits known locally as "interlinks".

Trucks in the Middle East are a mixture of European and American types, and legislation on weight and length tends to vary from country to country. Heavy trucks are generally of very rugged build and some regions now permit multi-axle outfits of 60 tons gross. These are particularly prevalent in Israel. Doubles outfits are allowed on certain roads in Saudi Arabia. Trucks have to be specifically equipped to work in high temperatures and dusty conditions, so heavy-duty cooling systems and air filters are called for. Mercedes trucks have a strong presence in the region, with a well-established assembly plant located in Iran. Turkey has its own manufacturing industry building trucks under the BMC and Chrysler marques.

Pakistan and Afghanistan are noted for their highly colourful trucks, with elaborate bodywork featuring intricate decoration. Indian trucks are also individualistic in style. Most are locally built by Tata, which began as licence-built Mercedes, and Ashok Leyland which are now a mixture of old Leyland and Iveco-Ford Cargo designs. They are built along simple, rugged lines for ease of repair. This approach is prevalent in other parts of the world such as Southeast Asia, Indonesia and parts of Latin America. Cuba has a particularly interesting trucking scene, with many ageing trucks of American, Russian and Japanese origin, some of which date from the 1960s.

The most advanced trucking nations in the Southern Hemisphere are Australia and New Zealand where a wider variety of makes can be seen than almost anywhere else in the world. New Zealand heavies run at 44 tons, either in truck and drawbar trailer form or as doubles outfits, often on eight axles. They are noted for their smart liveries and impressive appearance. When it comes to impressive trucks though, there is nothing to compete with the spectacular Road Trains in Australia. These massive outfits, usually hauled by powerful American tractors, can consist of up to four trailers hauling payloads in excess of 100 tons. Many run on eighty or more tyres and have engines of between 600 and 750bhp. Most Road Trains are to be seen in the Northern Territory along the Stuart Highway which links Alice Springs to Darwin some 1500km/932 miles to the north. Such outfits are restricted to certain routes and are excluded from built-up areas.

■ BELOW *The largest on-highway trucks are found in Australia. This is a typical road train hauled by a Mack Super-Liner with 400bhp V8 engine.*

27
27
5922 TJ

A–Z of Trucks

The truck-building industry has been established for over a century. During that time many hundreds of manufacturers have come and gone: some have prospered to become world leaders while some have fallen by the wayside. Throughout history the industry has seen countless takeovers and mergers, and in recent years the trend has been towards globalization, with the bulk of manufacture in the hands of a few multi-national companies. This A–Z does not set out to include every single make, many of which are so obscure as to be of little relevance. Instead it lists all the leading truck manufacturers, focusing on famous makes, while taking a brief look at some lesser-known makes and short-lived specialist types, included for their historic interest. Takeovers and mergers are continually in progress, and in the future it is doubtless that more makes will be consigned to history.

■ OPPOSITE *A Western Star dual-steer four-axled concrete mixer loads up at a batching plant near Whistler in British Columbia.*

■ LEFT *A 1949 Gardner-engined Scammell Rigid 8 22-ton box van, once a common sight on Britain's trunk routes.*

SOUTHALL, LONDON, ENGLAND

AEC

■ BELOW *AEC's first volume-produced truck was this gasoline-engined solid-tyred Y type of 1916.*

The earliest truck from AEC was the 3 to 4-ton Y-type of 1916. The Associated Equipment Company was formed in Walthamstow, East London, in 1912 to build buses for the London General Omnibus Company. The factory was the former works of the Vanguard Omnibus Company which was merged into the LGOC in 1908. It was one of the first factories to use a moving assembly line. An estimated 10,000 Y-types were produced for the War Department and a civilian version went into production after World War I. Early AECs were powered by gasoline engines from Daimler or Tylor but from about 1920 the company built its own engines.

Development continued throughout the 1920s, the range consisting of the 201 and 204 (for 2½ tons), the 418 and 428 (4 tons), the 506, -07 and -08 (5/6 tons) and the 701, which was an experimental articulated vehicle. From 1928, pneumatics were becoming an option.

AEC joined forces with Daimler in 1926 but that association, under which the vehicles were sold as ADC, was to last only two years.

In 1926–27 AEC's truck sales were beginning to improve and a major investment was made in a new factory at Southall in London. Following the appointment of a new design engineer, John Rackham, the model line-up was transformed. From 1930 onwards, the trucks were given model names. The Mercury and Monarch for 3½ to 4-ton payloads were powered by a 4-cylinder engine, while the Majestic 6-tonner and Mammoth 7 to 8-tonner took a 6-cylinder unit. A new 6-cylinder diesel engine was also introduced.

New improved models were added to the AEC range during the 1930s, including the Matador 4×2 four-wheeler, the Mammoth Major 12-ton payload six-wheeler, and its larger counterpart, the 15-ton Mammoth Major 8. This was the first production rigid eight-wheeler. Its successors included the Mk.II (1935), Mk.III (1948), Mk.V (1958) and the Ergomatic (1964).

■ ABOVE *Large numbers of Matador 4×4s were supplied to the armed forces. Many went on to serve in civilian timber haulage.*

■ LEFT *AEC was the first to offer a rigid eight-wheeled diesel truck. This 1936 Mammoth Major Mk.II grossed 22 tons.*

■ LEFT *The Mandator Mk.V was AEC's last model type before the Leyland takeover. This one has an Oswald Tillotson cab.*

In 1948 AEC began a program of expansion, taking over the Maudslay Motor Co. and Crossley Motors, forming a new holding company, Associated Commercial Vehicles (ACV). Maudslay vehicles were phased out during 1950, replaced by AECs. The AEC range was expanded with the introduction of the lighter Mercury model in 1953, powered by the AV410 6-cylinder diesel. This was later developed into the AV470. Developments of the Mercury included the twin-steer Mustang of 1956 and the six-wheel Marshal introduced in 1960.

Heavy-duty Mk.IIIs were the Mandator (4×2), Mammoth Major 6 (6×2/6×4) and Mammoth Major 8 (8×2/8×4). There was a tractor-unit version of the Mandator. Bonneted versions of most models were offered, mainly for export. Until the mid 1950s AEC Mk.IIIs still featured exposed radiators but they were modernized from about 1956 with a concealed radiator and a wide "dummy" grille.

In 1958 the Mk.III range was replaced by the Mk.V (there was no Mk.IV except on bus models) which was a completely new design. The Mk.V had a very stylish cab built mainly by Park Royal Vehicles. AEC built only chassis with front panels so that customers could specify their own choice of cab.

During the 1950s AEC went from strength to strength, developing export business throughout the world. Plants were established in South Africa, Spain, Portugal, Belgium and South America, while AEC engines were supplied to Willème in France, Vanaja in Finland, OMT in Italy and Verheul in The Netherlands. In the late '50s AEC embarked on the production of dump trucks at the old Maudslay factory. AEC's empire continued to grow with the takeover of the old established Thornycroft company in 1961.

In 1962 AEC's expansion was brought to an end when the company was taken over by its rival, Leyland Motors Ltd. One by one, AEC's overseas interests were dissolved and, since Leyland Group products were competing with one another, some rationalization of model types was inevitable.

Very soon a new range was launched featuring a common style of Leyland Group cab, the Ergomatic. While it lacked the tasteful lines of the AEC's handsome Mk.V, it had the benefit of being a tilt cab, thus providing improved servicing access. The Mercury was also updated to take the Ergomatic cab and the AV470 was replaced by the more powerful 8.2 litre/500cu in AV505. The main power unit for the leading heavy models, the Mandator tractor and the maximum-weight Mammoth Major eight-wheeler, became the AV691 of 11.3 litres/689cu in capacity. The largest tractor units were the Mammoth Major Six and the twin-steer Mammoth Minor. For these and later Ergomatic models, the higher powered AV760 became a popular fitment.

An unsuccessful project to develop a new, high-powered V8 diesel engine to suit the heavy trucks of the 1970s tarnished AEC's image. A number of the engines went into production but they proved unreliable in service. The problem was blamed on lack of funding by Leyland. In reality Leyland itself was being starved of investment since it was led, under pressure from the UK government, into an ill-planned merger with British Motor Holdings in 1968. BMH car plants were subsequently being propped up by the truck business which, in turn, suffered big losses. AEC was one victim of this unhappy episode and, by the mid '70s, the writing was on the wall for the Southall company. The factory closed down in 1979.

■ LEFT *After 1964, most AECs had the Leyland Group "Ergomatic" cab as seen on this 1970 Mammoth Major eight-wheeler.*

GLASGOW, SCOTLAND

ALBION

Founded in 1899, the Albion Motor Car Company produced its first commercial vehicle – a half-ton van – in 1902. Its founders, Norman O. Fulton and T. Blackwood Murray, were formerly employed by the Glasgow based Mo-Car Syndicate which later became the Arrol Johnston Company, who themselves built trucks between 1904 and 1913. Albion's early vehicles were lightweight machines but in 1910 they launched their A10 truck for 3 to 4-ton payloads. This had a 4-cylinder gasoline engine and chain drive. The A10 met War Office requirements and a total of 6000 were built for service in World War I.

During the 1920s Albion's truck range expanded to include forward-control models, and shaft drive took over from chain drive. The distinctive rising-sun trademark appeared on their

■ RIGHT *One of Albion's most famous trucks was this chain-drive A10 3-tonner produced between 1910 and 1926.*

■ LEFT *The LK51 forward-control 4-tonner was a short-lived model built between 1931 and 1933. It had a 4-cylinder gasoline engine.*

■ BELOW *Albion entered the heavy-weight market with the CX range in 1938. This is a 1948 diesel-engined CX7N tanker.*

■ RIGHT *One of Albion's most successful post-war trucks was the Chieftain FT37. This dropside truck dates from 1958.*

radiators around 1928. Albion referred to their forward-control trucks as "overtypes", a term normally associated with steam lorries.

With the introduction of pneumatic tyres in the late 1920s, Albions began to take on a more modern appearance although their cab designs were still very basic. The heaviest truck model of the period was a 5-tonner, built along very rugged lines. During the early '30s a 6-ton payload four-wheeler and an 8-ton payload six-wheeler became available and some models were offered with diesel power using Gardner and Dorman engines. Albion developed their own diesels by the end of 1933. 1935 saw the introduction of one of Albion's most successful four-wheelers – the KL127.

That same year, the company took over Halley Motors Ltd of Yoker, Glasgow, who were building a similar product range. The Halley factory provided Albion with the additional capacity they needed to expand their range. In 1936 a short-lived maximum-capacity eight-wheeler – the T561 – was introduced, but few were built. Very soon a completely new heavy-duty truck range – the CX – appeared. This embodied two, three and four-axled trucks with payload ratings from 7 to 15 tons.

Albion were important suppliers of military trucks during World War II, their range including 3-ton 4x4s, 10-ton 6x4s and heavy-duty tank transporters. The immediate post-war range was the CX, more or less carried over from before the war, plus a choice of four-wheelers which were now given type names – the Clansman (5-tonner), Chieftain (5/6-tonner) and Clydesdale (7/8-tonner). An updated range of heavy trucks, designated the HD range, was launched in 1951, but almost immediately afterwards Leyland Motors announced the takeover of Albion.

Most of Albion's heavy trucks were then phased out as they competed with Leyland's own products, and the much reduced Albion offering consisted of medium-weight four and six-wheelers. Leyland's influence began to show in the late 1950s when an all-new pressed-steel cab – the LAD – became standard. The same pattern of cab appeared on Leylands. Albion briefly returned to the eight-wheeler market in 1958 with their Leyland-powered Caledonian, which was outwardly similar to Leyland's Octopus.

Following the formation of the British Leyland Motor Corporation in 1968, under which BMC trucks became part of the Leyland group, a new factory built by BMC at Bathgate was to become BLMC's medium truck plant. By 1972 production of Albions at their Scotstoun plant had been phased out, along with the Albion name. However, a Leyland range called the Blue Line continued to be built at Bathgate until 1981. These embodied Albion components and retained the Chieftain, Clydesdale and Reiver names.

■ ABOVE LEFT *The underfloor-engined Claymore of the mid 1950s was popular as a furniture van and as a brewery distribution truck.*

■ LEFT *The Reiver and Super Reiver were Albion's heaviest models during the 1960s. This example features the LAD Vista-Vue cab.*

MILAN, ITALY

ALFA ROMEO

■ RIGHT *A 1959 Alfa Romeo Mille 14-tonne gvw truck powered by a 6-cylinder diesel engine.*

The Alfa Romeo name is more usually associated with fast cars than with trucks. However, the company, whose origins go back to 1906, was a significant truck producer between 1930 and 1967. After launching a light truck at the 1930 Milan Show, Alfa (derived from Societa Anonima Lombarda Fabbrica Automobili) Romeo went on to build heavier trucks based on Büssing designs. These were generally of normal-control layout but the heaviest, including a three-axled model for 10-tonne payloads, had forward-control cabs. From 1945 onwards the range was predominantly forward-control. They were noted for their ample power output, their 900 model for 8-tonne payloads having a 9.5 litre/579cu in diesel developing 130bhp. In 1948 an unsuccessful design for independent front suspension using torsion bars was made. A stylish new model, the Mille, was introduced in 1957 for use as a 14-tonne gross four-wheeler, 32-tonne articulated outfit or 36-tonne drawbar combination. A 10-tonne six-wheeler with steering rear axle was also available. The Mille and its 900 forerunner were also built under licence by the Brazilian company FNM of Rio de Janeiro.

LITTLETON, COLORADO, USA

AMERICAN COLEMAN

From the beginning, Coleman Motors Corporation specialized in all-wheel drive trucks. Coleman, later known as American Coleman, began production in 1925. The first trucks were 4×4 and 6×6 types. They found favour with the highway authorities, the army, fire departments and airports. Off-highway trucks for the logging and oil industry also appeared. Crane carriers were supplied to the army during World War II, production of bonneted trucks restarting from 1945. The factory closed temporarily from 1949 to 1951 as the result of a strike. In 1968 American Coleman built a most unusual truck consisting of a four-wheel steer tractor which could be coupled to a semi-trailer to form a rigid, the tractor axles effectively acting as a dual-steer front bogie. They dubbed it the "Space Star" and it was powered by an 8V-71N Detroit Diesel. It never proceeded beyond prototype stage. The company continues to build 4×4 specialized trucks for airport, highway maintenance, dockyard shunting and fire-fighting, as well as carrying out four-wheel drive conversions to other vehicles.

MOSCOW, RUSSIA

AMO

AMO (Automobilnoe Moskovskoe Obshchestvo) began production in November 1924, exactly seven years after the end of the Great October Revolution, and marked the start of Russia's own motor-vehicle industry. The first truck, the AMO-F15, was based on a Fiat 1½-tonner. Predicting a massive demand for trucks in the USSR, the Moscow factory was extended in 1931 and another model, the AMO-2 for 2½-ton payload, entered production. This was replaced by an improved version, the AMO-3, in 1932. The factory was renamed Zavod Imieni Stalina in 1933 and the products were accordingly relaunched as ZIS. ZIS trucks were to continue in production until 1956 when the factory was once again renamed as the Zavod Imieni Likhacheva (ZIL).

■ ABOVE *The 1924 AMO F15 was basically a Fiat 1½-tonner built under licence. It was the first Russian truck, and forerunner of the ZIS.*

EAST KILBRIDE, SCOTLAND

ARGYLE

Argyle trucks were produced in small numbers between 1970 and 1973. The company was formed by Argyle Diesel Electronics Ltd but competition from larger manufacturers rendered the enterprise non-viable. Only one type of any significance was built, the Christina 16-ton gross four-wheeler powered by a Perkins 6.354 diesel engine with an Eaton Yale & Towne 5-speed gearbox and Eaton 2-speed rear axle. The cab was a standard off-the-peg pressed-steel unit from Motor Panels of Coventry and resembled those used on Seddon and Guy trucks. There were plans for a tractor unit and a rigid six-wheeler but the company ceased trading before they entered production. However, Argyle did produce one Cummins-engined heavy tractor called the Trilby for the British Steel Corporation. This one-off was designed to haul a 120-ton load.

■ ABOVE *The Argyle Christina was a short-lived make. It was assembled from proprietary components, including a Perkins 6.354 diesel, Eaton 2-speed axle and Motor Panels cab.*

NEWCASTLE-UPON-TYNE, ENGLAND

ARMSTRONG SAURER

■ BELOW *Early 1930s Armstrong Saurer trucks were built in the UK but based on Swiss engineering.*

During the 1920s a number of imported Saurer trucks had entered the UK and, in 1930, the Saurer company was seeking to set up a British manufacturing base. It was the Newcastle engineering company of Sir W. G. Armstrong-Whitworth that acquired the manufacturing rights and production commenced in 1931. The trucks were called Armstrong Saurers but were primarily of Saurer design. While bonneted trucks were typical of the Swiss market, British operators demanded forward-control or "cabover" types, so these were added specially for the UK.

The range included the Defiant four-wheeler with 4-cylinder diesel

and the 6-cylinder Dauntless four-wheeler. A six-wheeler went under the name Dominant. Gasoline engines were offered initially but were soon dropped. Saurer was renowned for its well-engineered diesel engines. Armstrong Saurer launched their Samson eight-wheeler in 1934. This was a very advanced machine with overdrive gearbox and eight-wheel air brakes. Despite encouraging sales during the mid '30s, production ended in 1937.

■ LEFT *The 22-ton gross Samson was a British development and was one of the first rigid eight-wheelers on the market in 1934.*

PRESTON, ENGLAND

ATKINSON

In 1907 Edward Atkinson and his brother Harry, together with a partner George Hunt, set up an engineering business, Atkinson & Co. at Frenchwood Avenue, Preston. The company soon moved to bigger premises at Kendal Street, undertaking motor and steam wagon repairs. It took on a repair agency for Alley & MacLellan, the founders of the famous Sentinel Steam Waggon, built at that time in Polmadie, Glasgow. By 1916 Edward Atkinson had decided to build a wagon of his own design, having relinquished the Alley & MacLellan agency when Sentinel moved to Shrewsbury in 1915.

While Atkinson produced a successful steam wagon, the post-war slump of the 1920s saw the company in financial difficulties. A brief but unsuccessful merger with Walker Bros. of Wigan, under which the products were called Atkinson-Walker wagons, ended in 1930. With no prospect of recovery, the company fell into the hands of the receivers who eventually sold it to St Helens-based speculators J. Jenkins, H. Johnson and J. Lytheer in 1931. At first the rescued company carried on with steam wagon repairs as well as carrying out third-axle conversions, but some experimental trucks were built in 1931 – one being a bonneted four-wheeler with Dorman diesel engine. Following the death of Edward Atkinson in 1932, a London businessman, W. G. Allen of Nightingale's Garage, bought the business and it was renamed Atkinson Lorries (1933) Ltd.

Soon it was decided to build diesel-engined trucks to compete with the likes of Foden and ERF. In 1935 Atkinson moved to bigger premises in Marsh Lane, Preston. Early Atkinsons featured Gardner diesels, Kirkstall axles and vacuum hydraulic brakes. In the six years up to the beginning of World War II only 50 trucks were built but they included four, six and eight-wheelers as well as twin steer six-wheelers. Atkinson was one of the few UK manufacturers to be allowed to continue civilian truck production during World War II, under

■ **TOP** ***An early Atkinson L1266. This 1937 six-wheeler was powered by a Gardner 6LW.***

■ **ABOVE LEFT** ***Atkinson briefly used a Krupp steel cab. This rare example operated in the UK.***

■ **LEFT** ***Atkinsons changed little during their first 20 years. This 1951 L1586 was basically a 1930s design.***

■ RIGHT *Atkinson retained the traditional exposed radiator to the last. This is a 1972 Defender with Mk.2 fibreglass cab.*

■ LEFT *One of Atkinson's largest trucks was the mighty Rolls Royce-powered Omega of the late 1950s.*

■ BELOW *The Viewline, seen here on a 6×4 heavy-haulage tractor, was offered between 1966 and 1972.*

the direction of the government. Shortages of Gardner engines led to the use of AEC diesels during the war.

Post-war demand was such that Atkinson moved again, into a new factory at Winery Lane, Walton le Dale in 1947. It was, by then, one of the UK's leading truck builders and it soon built up a healthy export trade. Throughout the 1950s and '60s Atkinson went on to produce a huge variety of road-going and specialized trucks. Its mainstream products were forward-control load carriers and it diversified into heavy-duty dump trucks and special oil-field tractors such as the massive bonneted Omega of 1957, which was powered by a 333bhp supercharged Rolls Royce C6.SFL coupled to a Self Changing Gears 8-speed semi-automatic gearbox and capable of hauling 90 tons over desert terrain.

The haulage range consisted of four, six and eight-wheelers powered almost exclusively by Gardner diesels. From 1958 all models could be ordered with a new Mk.1 fibreglass cab with a panoramic two-piece wrap-around windscreen. During the late 1960s the company offered an increasing choice of tractor units, including twin-steer and rear-steer six-wheeled versions. Engine choice was widening to include Rolls Royce and Cummins diesels. From 1963–64 a weight saving specification was offered in the form of Weightmaster models with a trimmed-down specification and lower-powered engines for the lightest possible unladen weight.

As Atkinson's world markets expanded, assembly plants were established in Australia, South Africa and New Zealand where vehicles were tailored to local operators' requirements. In 1968 it tried to increase its share of the European market by fitting Krupp steel tilt cabs when Krupp of Essen in Germany phased out truck production. Atkinson Vehicles (Europe) was set up in Antwerp, Belgium, but the venture was short-lived.

In the late 1960s models were given type names and the taller Mk.2 fibreglass cab was introduced. The main tractor units were the 4×2 Borderer and 6×2 rear-steer Leader. The most popular rigid was the Defender eight-wheeler, although some six-wheeled Searchers and four-wheeled Raiders were also built.

Atkinson Vehicles Ltd was taken over by Seddon in 1970, when Seddon-Atkinson was formed. The last Atkinsons were built in 1975. Seddon-Atkinson's independence was short-lived, however, as it was taken over by International Harvester in 1974.

The last hint of Atkinson's identity was when their "Circle A" badge continued to appear on Seddon-Atkinsons, which were produced at Oldham until 2004. Production, mainly of municipal vehicles, was then moved to Spain but ceased completely in 2006.

LONGBRIDGE, ENGLAND

AUSTIN

■ LEFT ***The Austin K2 box van of the late 1940s was nicknamed the "Birmingham Bedford".***

■ BELOW LEFT ***One of the first volume-built UK trucks with a tilt cab was the 1964 Austin FJ.***

■ BOTTOM LEFT ***The 1950 Loadstar was a modernized version of the earlier K4, dubbed the "K4 Series II".***

The Austin Motor Co. Ltd was established in 1908 but did not begin building trucks, other than light commercials, until 1913. Their first truck was a 2 to 3-tonner of unusual design, having a 29hp 4-cylinder gasoline engine mounted ahead of the radiator, a layout featured in Renaults and Macks of the era. Drive to the rear wheels was via a 4-speed gearbox and twin propshafts – one to each rear wheel. The semi-forward-control driving position and raked steering wheel meant that the steering column was fully exposed ahead of the dash panel.

Approximately 2000 of the early Austin trucks were built but the company left the truck market and did not return until 1939, when it launched a completely new range. That range was modelled to a degree on Bedford's, covering the 1½ to 4/5-ton payload bracket. They bore such similarities that they were often referred to as the Birmingham Bedford. Austin dubbed them the "K" models. Large numbers were built for military use during World War II.

After the war the K range continued with little change, but a stylish new model named the Loadstar entered the scene in 1950. Austin also began to offer a Perkins diesel-engine option. A significant event took place in 1951 with the formation of the British Motor Corporation by the merger of Austin and the Nuffield organization who produced Morris Commercial trucks. By the mid 1950s Austins and Morris Commercials were being commonized. A new range of forward-control models featured a bought-in steel cab manufactured by the Willenhall Motor Radiator Co. BMC's own diesel engines became available on the new models, the largest being a 5.1 litre/311cu in 6-cylinder unit for the 701 7-tonner launched in 1955. A 5.7 litre/347cu in version was introduced later.

Austin's (or by now BMC's) next design was the unusual "angle-planned" FG range which featured a new concept in cabs with entrance doors on the back corners. This was claimed to be a safety feature although it did allow the occupant to step out into the path of other traffic. By this time Austin and Morris trucks ("Commercial" had been dropped) were virtually identical under the BMC umbrella.

In 1961 a completely new BMC truck plant was opened at Bathgate in Scotland. A new model, the FJ, appeared in 1964 and was one of the first British trucks to feature a tilt cab. After the formation of the British Leyland Motor Corporation in 1968, created by the merger of British Motor Holdings and the Leyland Motor Corporation, Austins and their Morris counterparts were all badged as BMC, and from 1970 all carried the Leyland name and were marketed as the Redline range.

OGDEN, UTAH, USA

AUTOCAR

Louis S. Clarke, in partnership with his brother John, founded the Pittsburgh Motor Vehicle Co. in 1897 to build cars and light commercials. Fearing that the company name sounded too provincial, Clarke decided to change it to the Autocar Company in 1899. It was in 1908 that a small cabover truck, the XVIII ("18" in Roman numerals), was introduced. This rudimentary vehicle was very sturdily built and featured shaft drive. Just one year later a longer version, the XXI.U (21.U) appeared, the "U" signifying "under-cab" engine. That model remained in production until 1926. In 1919 it was joined by a larger, more powerful truck for 5-ton payloads, the Model 26.

In the late 1920s a new range of bonneted conventionals was launched, the largest being a six-wheeler with 6-cylinder gasoline engine. Payloads were up to 7½ tons. Throughout the 1930s Autocar built a wide range of medium and heavy trucks for loads of 3 to 12 tons, plus a heavy-duty 4×4, the DC10044. While most were bonneted there were cabovers too, such as the stylish UD model of 1937 which remained in production for over a decade. From 1938 certain Autocar types were also built by Kromhout in The Netherlands.

In 1953, following a downturn in the United States truck market, Autocar was taken over by White Trucks. Production was transferred to a new factory at Exton, Pennsylvania. From that point on Autocar concentrated on heavy-duty trucks tailored to customers' requirements and their name became synonymous with high-powered trucks for logging, mining and heavy haulage.

In 1974 Autocar production was transferred from Exton to a new plant in Ogden, Utah. New models with a stronger White influence appeared, such as the Construcktor 2 which featured a White Road Boss cab. In 1980 the White Motor Corporation went into receivership and Volvo of Sweden stepped in to purchase the company, which then became the Volvo White Truck Corporation. Autocar trucks continued to be marketed by the new organization and, as well as their heavy-duty machines, a new highway truck, the AT64F, was launched.

A joint venture with GMC Trucks was announced in 1988 when GM was pulling out of heavy trucks. The organization was called Volvo White Truck Corp. A new White GMC Autocar was launched, aimed at the construction industry. After 1995 'White GMC' was dropped and the trucks became Autocar. In 1997 Volvo purchased GM's remaining interest in Volvo GM and set up Volvo Trucks North America. Five models ranging from 4x4s to 8x4s, powered by Volvo, were offered until VTNA launched its VHD range in 2000. In 2001 Volvo licensed the Autocar brand to Grand Vehicle Works Holdings LLC of Indiana who continue to build the Xpeditor municipal chassis now powered by Cummins.

■ TOP ***1994 Autocar five-axled mixer has all-Volvo running units.***

■ ABOVE LEFT ***Concrete mixer based on Autocar 8×4 at work in Auckland, New Zealand.***

■ LEFT ***Autocar specializes in municipal vehicles like this low-cab, gas-powered Xpeditor 6x4 rigid.***

BRUSSELS, BELGIUM

AUTOMIESSE

■ LEFT ***A late 1950s Automiesse with licence-built Gardner diesel, seen in Antwerp, Belgium.***

■ BELOW LEFT ***Among the last Automiesse tractors was this sleeper-cabbed Büssing-engined machine operating in Brussels during the 1960s.***

Miesse SA was an old established heavy vehicle manufacturer which, prior to 1939, traded as Jules Miesse et Cie. The original company dated back to the turn of the century and built steam cars and trucks. Heavy trucks up to 5-tonnes payload with gasoline engines were introduced in the mid 1920s and car production ceased in 1926. Some of their heavy trucks were powered by their own 8-cylinder gasoline engine while others, in the early '30s, had Junkers two-stroke opposed piston diesels. From 1932 Miesse were given a licence to build British-designed Gardner diesels and these became standard fitment in most of their extensive truck range. One interesting vehicle introduced in 1939 was a rigid eight-wheeler with steering fourth axle and a payload capacity of 16 tons. One notable feature of this was a roof-mounted radiator. In 1939 the company was renamed Automiesse and the trucks were badged as such during the last few years of production.

After World War II Automiesse concentrated on heavy-duty trucks using Gardner engines, including the 8LW. To meet the higher power demands of their heavy 38-tonne tractors, Detroit Diesel and Büssing engines were specified. Production was dwindling in the late 1960s and the company closed in 1972.

OTHER MAKES

■ ADC (ASSOCIATED DAIMLER COMPANY)

SOUTHALL, LONDON, ENGLAND

Between 1926 and 1928 the Daimler Company, owned by BSA, and the Associated Equipment Company (AEC) formed a joint marketing agreement. Daimler had already been supplying engines to AEC for some years. The first ADCs were existing AEC designs but in 1928 a new lightweight ADC model, the 423/424, appeared. AEC-based goods vehicles such as the 418 3-tonner, the 507 5-tonner and the Ramillies 6-tonner, were all built as Associated Daimlers for a brief period but from 1928 ADC was disbanded, AEC and Daimler becoming separate companies again.

■ ASHOK LEYLAND

ENNORE, MADRAS, INDIA

Beginning in 1948 as Ashok Motors to assemble Austin cars, the company went on to assemble Leyland trucks in 1950. In 1954 Leyland Motors took a stake in Ashok and the company became Ashok Leyland. Most Ashok Leylands had locally built cabs. In 1987 Leyland's holding was bought by the Hinduja Group and Iveco Fiat SpA, and production of the old Ford Cargo began alongside the Leyland-based trucks. In 2007 Hinduja bought out Iveco and announced a joint venture with Nissan. The current Ashok Leyland range includes tractor units up to 49 tonnes and rigid trucks up to 37 tonnes gvw (gross vehicle weight) 10×4s.

■ LEFT ***This late 1920s ADC fuel tanker was based on an AEC design.***

■ ABOVE RIGHT ***The 1999 Ashok Leyland Comet 1611.***

■ RIGHT ***Ashok Leyland Cargo 1614 based on a Ford Cargo.***

OTHER MAKES

■ ASTRA

PIACENZA, ITALY

Astra was founded by Mario Betuzzi in 1948. After a few years in business reconditioning war-surplus trucks, Astra turned to assembling heavy dump trucks in 1954. In the 1960s it began building its own dump trucks powered by engines from Detroit Diesel, Mercedes and Fiat. By the late '70s it had cornered 50 per cent of the Italian market for such vehicles. Since 1985 Astra has been part of the Iveco Group and still produces heavy construction vehicles on two, three and four axles.

■ LEFT ***Part of the Iveco Group, Astra specialize in heavy-duty chassis for the construction industry.***

■ AVAILABLE

CHICAGO, ILLINOIS, USA

Available trucks were in production for 47 years, the company having been founded in 1910. The first truck was a chain-drive machine powered by an underslung 2-cylinder gasoline engine for ¾ ton. Larger trucks for 2-ton payloads were added and within five years or so Available was offering a choice of four types, the heaviest of which took a 5-ton payload. A Continental 4-cylinder engine was used. In 1920 a bonneted 7-tonner was announced, powered by a 50hp Waukesha engine, but demand was insufficient to continue production for more than a short period.

Throughout the 1930s and '40s Available offered a range of 4×2s and 6×4s in "normal" and "forward" control with a choice of engines. Models ranged from 4-tonners up to maximum-weight tractor-trailer combinations. Most of Available's modest production, which totalled around 2500 trucks, were sold to local customers. In 1957 the company was taken over by the Crane Carrier Corporation of Tulsa, Oklahoma.

■ LEFT ***An Available 10-ton payload six-wheeler from 1947.***

■ ABOVE RIGHT ***DAF engineering went into the development of the AVM heavy-duty trucks built in Zimbabwe.***

■ AVM

HARARE, ZIMBABWE

Since 1972 AVM heavy trucks, based on DAF designs but fitted with locally built cabs, have been assembled by Dahmer & Co. The company is 80 per cent owned by the British-based Lonrho Group. The vehicles, mainly 6×4s, are heavily built to withstand the demanding local operating conditions. Gross weights go up to 55 tonnes. DAF diesels and ZF gearboxes are used. The heaviest outfits have two trailers, built by Zambesi Coachworks in Harare.

■ AWD

DUNSTABLE, ENGLAND

AWD trucks were built at the former Bedford GM plant following General Motors' decision to withdraw from the UK truck market in 1986. David J. B. Brown, the founder of Artix Ltd, an articulated dump-truck company subsequently sold to Caterpillar, took over the business in 1987 and continued to build selected Bedford models under the AWD name. The Bedford name was retained by GM for its van range. Numerous special all-wheel drive prototypes were built, aimed at the military and export markets. Existing Bedford trucks were used as the basis for David J. B. Brown's patent Multidrive articulated 8×6 and 10×6 machines. Limited sales resulted in the closure of AWD in 1992 when the business was sold once again to Marshall SPV of Cambridge, who were granted permission to reinstate the Bedford name.

■ ABOVE RIGHT ***AWD used the Bedford TM cab for its prototype heavy tank transporter.***

■ RIGHT ***The AWD MTL33 was a Cummins-engined 8×6 with a driven trailer bogie.***

BOREHAMWOOD, ENGLAND

BARON

■ LEFT *The Baron 7-tonner was a simple, ruggedly built export truck for local assembly in developing countries.*

In 1957 Peter Boulas anticipated a demand for a rugged, no-frills truck that would withstand the harsh operating conditions of third-world countries. Historically, British manufacturers had dominated such markets with the likes of the Bedford TJ which was basic, reliable and easy to repair. Boulas feared that foreign influence was threatening British industry and designed the Baron 6 and 7-tonners, officially announced in 1964, after carrying out a seven-year market survey in the developing countries of Africa and the Far East. They were powered by a Perkins 6.354 diesel with 4-speed gearbox and Eaton 2-speed axle. Prototypes were built featuring pressed-steel front cowls by Airflow Streamlines who supplied similar designs to Commer and Dodge. Barons were to be exported in CKD (Completely Knocked Down) form for assembly in the third world. Just two versions were released – the 6-ton Master BN6 and the 7-ton Senior BN7. Baron withdrew from the market in 1970 through lack of demand.

MADRID, SPAIN

BARREIROS

■ LEFT *A Barreiros 82/35 twin-steer rigid eight-wheeler of the late 1960s with self-steering rear lift axle.*

■ BELOW LEFT *Twin-steer six-wheelers like this Barreiros 26/26 had safety benefits on twisting mountain roads.*

The manufacture of Barreiros trucks began in 1958 but the company's founder, Eduardo Barreiros Rodriguez, had begun an engineering business at Orense in north-west Spain some 18 years earlier. He specialized in converting gasoline engines to diesel and in 1951 transferred his business to Madrid where he began manufacturing diesel engines and, later, complete trucks. The first Barreiros truck was a 6-tonner called the Victor. Further medium-weight models bearing the names Halcyon, Condor, Azor and Super Azor appeared during the 1960s.

From 1963 the Chrysler Corporation bought into the company and by 1967 owned a majority holding. The name was changed to Chrysler Espana SA but the Barreiros nameplate was still used on the trucks until 1978. From then on the range was marketed under the Dodge brand. During the 1960s and '70s the range broadened to include maximum-weight tractor units and six and eight-wheelers.

In 1978 the French group Peugeot-Citroën acquired Chrysler's European truck interests when the American giant ran into financial difficulties. Just three years later Renault Véhicules Industriels took control of the Dodge truck operations both in the UK and Spain and the last vehicles to have the distinctive Barreiros cab were badged as Renaults. Renault updated some models with their Premier cab.

TIPTON, ENGLAND

BEAN

■ LEFT ***A 1928 Bean 30cwt truck powered by Bean's own 4-cylinder gasoline engine.***

While Bean was not a significant truck builder, it qualifies for brief mention. After setting up as A. Harper, Sons & Bean Ltd in 1923, the company produced a few light vans. It changed its name to Bean Cars Ltd in 1924 with plans to become a major volume producer with financial backing from the Sheffield steel-making company, Hadfields. Their products consisted of 1½ and 2½-ton payload trucks, the latter appearing in 1929 as the Empire model. A forward-control development of the Empire model for a 4-ton payload was announced in 1930 but, in the difficult trading conditions of the economic depression, the company was forced to close in 1931.

DALMUIR, SCOTLAND

BEARDMORE

Beardmore trucks might be seen as one of the lost causes of the UK industry. The name Beardmore became famous on taxicabs which were built in Paisley, Glasgow from 1919 to 1933. In 1933 production was transferred to Hendon in north London where taxi production continued until 1969. After the business left Paisley, William Beardmore Ltd – another branch of the Beardmore Engineering concern set up at nearby Dalmuir to build heavy trucks. They drew up plans for maximum-weight four, six and eight-wheelers for payloads of 8 tons, 13 tons and 15 tons respectively. A handful of four-wheeled 8-tonners were actually built but the company folded in 1937 before its final plans could be realized. William Beardmore Ltd had earlier been involved in the production of Beardmore-Multiwheeler road tractors.

■ ABOVE ***A 1924 Beardmore 1½-ton truck with integral van body.***

■ BELOW ***Beardmore-Multiwheeler tractors were based on the French Chenard-Walcker and were built at Beardmore's London factory. This is a 10-ton Cobra.***

LUTON & DUNSTABLE, ENGLAND

BEDFORD

■ LEFT *Bedford's 6-cylinder WLG 2-tonner of 1931 became a market leader in the UK.*

■ LEFT *The A type 5-tonner was built between 1953 and 1957 and had the option of a Perkins P6 diesel engine.*

The old established Vauxhall car company was taken over by General Motors in 1925. Around the same time GM had begun assembling Chevrolet trucks, first at Hendon in north London and then at Luton, in order to get a foothold in the UK market and, even more importantly, to gain access to the vast export markets of the British Commonwealth. Luton-built Chevrolet 30cwt U types with their powerful 6-cylinder gasoline engines sold well, and GM marketed them with a strong "British-built" message, choosing to brand the 1930 model as the Chevrolet Bedford. In 1931 a new 2-ton gasoline model, the W type, was launched as a "pure" Bedford and it featured many developments, including a heavy-duty rear axle with fully floating hubs and dual rear wheels. The new Bedford 2-tonners won a substantial share of the light truck market. An improved 30cwt model cloned from the last Chevrolet U type was introduced in 1932 as the Bedford WS. From that point the American identity disappeared completely and Bedfords were presented as a purely British product.

During the 1930s the range expanded to include the WT semi-forward-control model for 3-ton payloads, although the company openly described it as the truck for a 50 per cent overload, making it in effect a 4½-tonner. Plans for a completely new range – the K (1½ tons), M (2 to 3 tons) and O (4 to 5 tons) – were afoot in the late '30s but the launch coincided with the start of World War II. Full production was delayed until 1946. Meanwhile Bedford became a major supplier of military trucks and tanks. Around 250,000 were built for the war effort, including a hastily designed 4×4 called the QL.

In the post-war years the K, M and O models went into full production and they were joined in 1950 by the S type 7-tonner, called the Big Bedford. All were hugely successful and gave Bedford a big share of the home market as well as healthy worldwide export sales. From 1953 the K, M and O models were replaced by the A models which were mechanically similar but had a stylish new cab with strong American influence in its styling. Perkins diesel engines became a factory-fitted option to the standard gasoline engine.

Bedford's wartime experience with building 4×4s was put to use in developing their new 3-ton military R type, which was launched in 1952 and became the standard 3-ton truck for the Ministry of Defence. It also sold well in civilian form and to overseas military

■ BELOW LEFT *The OSS was a joint development between Bedford and Scammell Lorries and used Scammell's automatic coupling.*

■ LEFT *Announced in 1950, the S type 7-tonner had a 110bhp 6-cylinder gasoline engine with an optional Perkins R6 diesel from 1953 and, later, a Leyland O.350.*

customers. By 1954 Bedford production had outgrown Luton and was transferred to a new factory in Dunstable. The next significant launch was the legendary TJ model which won Bedford massive export business in the developing countries of the third world. The TJ continued to be built, often for local assembly abroad, right through to the 1990s.

In 1960 Bedford announced a new forward-control range, the TK, which replaced the S type. Heavier versions appeared during the 1960s and in 1966 the company entered the heavy-duty scene with the completely new KM featuring a 7.63 litre/466cu in diesel engine of their own design. Nineteen seventy-two saw another bold move when a 32-ton tractor powered by General Motors' own two-stroke 6V-71 Detroit Diesel was announced. Just two years later a complete range of heavy-duty trucks, the tilt-cab TM range, appeared. This did not enjoy the same success as earlier Bedfords and this, combined with the economic recession of the late 1970s, saw Bedford's business decline.

From 1983 General Motors' car and truck divisions were separated and Bedford became the UK Division of the GM Overseas Commercial Vehicle Corporation. Into a declining market Bedford launched a tilt-cab medium truck, the TL, but it was an underfunded development of the old TK and Bedford continued to lose orders to competition. Bids by GM to strengthen their UK truck manufacturing operations by the acquisition of the Leyland Group failed as a result of UK government intervention and, partially as a result of this, the American giant decided to withdraw from the UK truck business in 1986. The Bedford plant was sold to David J. B. Brown who resumed production of selected models under the AWD name. AWD only survived for five years and the remains of the once giant Bedford operation were sold to Marshall Special Purpose Vehicles of Cambridge. A handful of Bedfords have been built in the 1990s.

■ BELOW *The TK range was in production from 1960 to 1984.*

■ BOTTOM *The TM heavy-duty tilt-cab range appeared in 1974. This EWV8 32-tonner had a Detroit Diesel 6V-71.*

FRONT ROYAL, VIRGINIA, USA

Bering

■ LEFT ***Bering's cabover HD80ST tractor is based on the Korean Hyundai and has a Cummins or Caterpillar diesel.***

Bering was a short-lived manufacturer set up in the United States in 1997.
The Bering Truck Corp and its subsidiary, Bering Distribution LLC, manufactured, imported and distributed Class 3 to 8 trucks. The product range comprised 13 models using Cummins and Caterpillar engines combined with chassis that were sourced from the Korean company Hyundai. The company's range was divided into Light Duty (LD), Medium Duty (MD) and Heavy Duty (HD) groups. The 2-axled HD33M grossed 33,000lbs/15 tonnes, putting it in Class 7, while other HD models, the HD60ST, HD80ST and HD80TT tractor units and the HD67MX, HD65DP and HD83DP rigids fell within Class 8. The rigids were specifically aimed at the construction industry, the heaviest being the 38-tonne gross HD83DP, a cab-forward 8x4.

Production ended in 2001 after the company's agreement with Hyundai was terminated.

LYON, FRANCE

Berliet

■ LEFT ***Berliet's chain-drive 3-tonne CAT forward-control truck of 1913.***

■ BELOW LEFT ***The revolutionary Stradair 5-tonner of 1967 featured air suspension.***

■ BOTTOM LEFT ***The mid 1950s TLM was noted for its extravagant styling. This 35-tonne artic has those classic lines.***

The history of the company that was to become one of France's largest and most famous truck manufacturers dates back to the very beginning of motoring history. As long ago as 1894 Marius Berliet began experimenting with his own design of gasoline engine which he installed in a primitive car. In 1902, with financial backing from a rich Lyon merchant called Giraud, he produced a dual-purpose twin-cylindered vehicle with chain drive which could be transformed from a car into a truck by exchanging bodywork in a matter of minutes. This led to the introduction in 1906 of Berliet's first true commercial chassis, a chain-drive 2-tonne cab-over-engine machine powered by a 4-cylinder gasoline engine. Within a couple of years Berliet were offering models with 1½ to 4 tonnes payload capacity.

By the onset of World War I Berliet had added a forward-control 6-tonner to the range and a normal-control chain-drive 4/5-tonner designated the CBA. This was a particularly successful machine and 25,000 were built for the armed services. In the depressed market following the war, when sales were stifled by a glut of war-surplus trucks, matters were made even worse by the French government imposing a tax on profits gained during the war. Berliet ran into financial difficulties, going into receivership in 1921. By taking on reconditioning work and disposing of some assets, the company was able to survive to introduce a new and successful range of light commercials in 1924. Within two or three years Berliet was adding new models including heavier trucks up to 7½ tonnes payload. By now most models of 4 tonnes and below had pneumatic tyres and virtually all were of normal-control layout. Experimental diesel engines were being tried in 1930 and by 1931 they were

■ ABOVE LEFT *This 26-tonne GBH12 6×4 dump truck featured a 250bhp 6-cylinder diesel.*

■ ABOVE *The Berliet GAK drawbar outfit features the Relaxe cab which was very advanced when introduced in 1959.*

offered in what was an updated CBA chain-drive. The early engines were not as reliable as hoped but by 1933 an improved version was available and was offered in the new shaft-drive GD2. The CBA model was discontinued after 22 years in production. By the late 1930s diesel power was available in models from 3 tonnes and upwards, the heavy models being bonneted six-wheelers for 12 to 15-tonnes payload.

A few years after World War II Berliet's range took on a completely new look. The plain, sober styling of the late 1930s, appealing though it was, gave way to the sensational new GLR model with its protruding bonnet (hood) and curvaceous lines. Berliet built up an extensive export business in overseas countries. Trucks were exported as far afield as China. Berliet also began trying out some specialized heavy trucks including their biggest – the 1957 TOO 6×6 for oil exploration in the Sahara.

In 1967 Berliet was absorbed into Citroën. The first product of that joint operation was the highly unusual Stradair truck which embodied many innovative features. It had variable height air suspension, front-wheel drive options and a distinctive protruding bonnet (hood) with offset radiator which gave it a very striking appearance.

While bonneted heavy vehicles continued to be popular in France, Berliet also offered forward-control models which, from 1959, featured a stylish new cab dubbed the "Relaxe" cab. During the 1960s Berliet's range was quite complex with up to 120 different types on offer. They also had many overseas production facilities throughout the world, including Eastern Europe, China, North Africa, South America, Spain and Portugal. In spite of this, the French government felt that Berliet was vulnerable to foreign takeover and sought to merge the company with Saviem, which had been formed in 1955 by the merger of Renault, Latil and Somua. Eventually the merger did take place, in 1974 and, through Saviem, Renault took control of the Berliet empire.

In the meantime Berliet had come out with new models, the most notable being their TR260 with its Premier cab which was to become a familiar sight in many parts of the world. Another development in the 1970s was the Club of Four cab. This was a joint development by Saviem, Volvo, DAF and Magirus-Deutz. The cab, most familiar on Volvo's F7 and Renault's GR and GF ranges, was for a while fitted to Berliet-badged trucks.

However the Berliet name was shortly to disappear after Saviem was reorganized into RVI (Renault Véhicules Industriels) in 1978. Indeed, by 1980 Berliet's history had drawn to a close.

■ BELOW *Bharatbenz in India combines Mercedes and Fuso technology to build a new range of heavy-duty trucks like this '3128' dumper.*

CHENNAI, INDIA

BHARATBENZ

Daimler have long had a presence in India through their collaborative agreement with Tata back in 1954.

By the 1970s the Tata Engineering & Locomotive Co (TELCO) dominated the Indian market with trucks based on Mercedes designs. In the early part of the millennium Tata formed a joint venture with Korean Daewoo to market a new range based on their own designs.

Daimler India Commercial Vehicles (DICV) was formed in 2007 to build trucks badged Bharatbenz at a new plant in Chennai. Production got underway in 2012 and the trucks are already making inroads into the Indian market and are now in competition with Tata Daewoo.

LONGBRIDGE, ENGLAND, & BATHGATE, SCOTLAND

BMC

After the Austin Motor Company and Morris Commercial Cars Ltd were merged into the British Motor Corporation, formed in 1951, Austin and Morris trucks were progressively commonized and a new 7-ton payload model, the 701 was launched in 1955 as a BMC 7-tonner. The vehicle was powered by a BMC 5.1 litre/311cu in diesel engine.

Later the trucks reverted to being Austin or Morris but in 1968, after the formation of the British Leyland Motor Corporation, the trucks, by then produced at a new plant in Bathgate, Scotland, were badged BMC for a period of just two years. They were then integrated into the Leyland product range as Redline models and were all badged as Leyland.

■ LEFT *The 701 7-tonner made its debut in 1955 and was the first truck to carry the BMC badge.*

■ ABOVE *A BMC Mastiff artic powered by a Perkins V8 diesel engine.*

■ BELOW *The BMC VA was specially designed for parcel deliveries.*

■ BELOW *The BMC FG medium truck featured the "angle plan" safety cab.*

■ BOTTOM *A 1970 BMC Laird six-wheel, low-loading brewery truck.*

IZMIR, TURKEY

BMC

In 1964 the British Motor Corporation licenced a Turkish assembly plant, BMC Sanayi ve Ticaret A.S., at Izmir to build BMC trucks powered by licence-built Leyland diesels. Production began in 1966. In 1983 BMC signed an agreement with Volvo and, two years later, with Cummins. Following this they launched their 'Fatih' range of four models from 17 to 27 tons gross weight. The Fatih cab was based on the old Bathgate G cab fitted to the Leyland Redline models.

In 1994 BMC launched the 'Professional' range covering the same weights but featuring a stylish cab by Pininfarina. These were powered by Cummins B series 5.9 litre/366 cu.in. diesels. From 1998 to 2003 BMC Professionals were sold in the UK as the ERF EP6. BMC then set up a UK office to sell the trucks direct but their plans were cut short when their parent organisation, the Cukurova Group, racked up massive debts and their assets, including BMC, were seized by the Turkish Savings Deposit Insurance Fund. As a result the BMC went out of production but they have recently recommenced building military vehicles.

■ ABOVE RIGHT ***The 1999 BMC Fatih garbage truck used a modified version of the old Leyland G cab.***

■ RIGHT ***Ultra-modern styling by Pininfarina is a feature of the BMC Professional range.***

BRISTOL, ENGLAND

BRISTOL

■ LEFT *The Bristol HG6L was developed as an eight-wheeler for use by the British Road Services organization.*

■ BELOW *When British Road Services demanded articulated vehicles, Bristol introduced the HA6G with Gardner diesel.*

Production of Bristol trucks was twice interrupted by long spells of inactivity. The origins of the manufacturer can be traced back to 1874 and the formation of the Bristol Tramways Company which, in turn, became the Bristol Tramways & Carriage Company in 1887. This should not be confused with the Bristol Wagon & Carriage Works Ltd, which built steam wagons between 1904 and 1908.

Bristol was mainly concerned with the manufacture of gasoline-engined buses, but some were fitted with truck bodies during the period 1908 to 1914. After a small number of trucks were built for the War Department in 1915, production was suspended until 1919 but a few trucks were built during the 1920s.

The company was purchased by the Thomas Tilling Group in 1931 after which production was turned over fully to buses for Tilling's own operations. The Tilling Group was nationalized by the British government in 1948 so Bristol was then under state control. With the formation of British Road Services (BRS) as part of the new nationalized transport system, the controlling body, the British Transport Commission, decided to utilize the Bristol manufacturing plant to design and build a standardized maximum-weight goods vehicle. The trucks were built in two forms. The first was a 22-ton (later 24-ton) gvw rigid eight-wheeler (HG6L), the second a 24-ton gcw articulated tractor-trailer combination (HA6G, HA6L and HA6LL).

Leyland's 0.600 diesel was standard for the HG6L while the HA6G, HA6L and HA6LL were built with a Gardner 6LX or a Leyland 0.600 or 0.680. The first models, HG6Ls, appeared in 1952 and Bristol truck production continued until 1964 when new UK weight legislation rendered them obsolete. A plan to build a 30-ton gcw Bristol tractor unit, the HD, was shelved. From then on BRS, by then partly denationalized, only bought off-the-shelf trucks. Bristol themselves continued to build buses, with Leyland taking a substantial shareholding in the company during the late 1960s.

CORTLAND, NEW YORK, USA

BROCKWAY

■ LEFT *This multi-axle Brockway 761 series based in Michigan features a Mack R series cab.*

The Brockway Motor Truck Co. built its first truck in 1912 but the company's origins as the Brockway Carriage Co. dated back to the 1870s. The 1912 machine was an open-cabbed, chain-driven buggy-style vehicle with large-diameter cart wheels and was powered by a 3-cylinder two-stroke engine with air cooling. Four-cylinder Continental engines became standard fitment on subsequent trucks and Brockway was a significant supplier of military vehicles during World War I.

After the war they introduced models for 1½ and 3-ton payloads, with a more conventional layout and worm drive. A 5-tonner was added in 1921. Brockway soon grew to become one of the largest truck manufacturers in the United States. Four-cylinder Wisconsin engines were fitted in the late '20s and from 1928 that company's 6-cylinder engines were also used. The same year Brockway took over the Indiana Truck Corporation but in 1932, during the difficult trading conditions of the depression, they re-sold Indiana to the White Motor Corporation.

In 1934 Brockway launched what was one of the largest trucks on the market – the V1200, capable of hauling loads of 27 tons and powered by a massive American La France V12 gasoline engine delivering 240bhp. Sales were limited as axle weight restrictions in many States discouraged such machines. It was withdrawn from the range in 1937. During the late '30s the Brockway range listed 16 different models from 1½-ton trucks up to artics for 10-ton payloads, powered by Continental 6-cylinder gasoline engines.

From 1942 Brockway were engaged in defence work but the post-World War II era saw the introduction of the impressive 260 bonneted highway tractors for gross combination weights up to 32 tons. These were powered by 6-cylinder Continental gasoline engines and had Fuller gearboxes and Timken rear axles. This range was still Brockway's core product when the company was taken over by Mack Trucks. Under Mack ownership Brockway were to remain autonomous, although their first venture into forward-control tractors saw them adopting the Mack F Series cab. The first range announced under Mack ownership was the all-new Huskie, which featured a three dimensional Huskie emblem on the bonnet, echoing the famous bulldog motif of its parent.

From 1963 diesel engines from Cummins, Caterpillar and Detroit Diesel became alternatives to the standard Continental gasoline units, which were phased out completely in the late '60s. In 1968 Brockway dubbed their 5-speed gearbox and 2-speed axle package "Huskidrive". An 8-speed gearbox and 2-speed axle were also offered. One of Brockway's last models was the low profile, cab-forward Huskiteer in two and three-axled rigid form. In April 1977 Mack decided to close the plant down.

■ BELOW *A Brockway N527TL artic with Cummins NHC250 from the mid 1970s.*

BRUSSELS, BELGIUM

BROSSEL

■ BELOW *A late 1950s Brossel 32-tonne gcw tractor engaged on brewery transport in Belgium.*

Ets Brossel Frères (later Brossel Frères Borg et Pipe SA) built medium-weight bonneted trucks. In the post-war years the company produced derivatives of the FN 4×4 and the Ardennes artillery tractor. In the 1960s Brossel was absorbed into the Leyland Motor Corporation and some Leyland models were marketed in Belgium and France as Brossel before the company was wound up in the mid '60s. The last new range launched in January 1961 was called the Europ. This featured an adaptation of Leyland's fibreglass Vista-Vue cab and Power Plus diesel engine similar to the Leyland Beaver.

CHARLOTTE, NORTH CAROLINA, USA

BROWN

■ BELOW *Initially, all Brown tractor units were built for exclusive use by Horton Motor Lines.*

Brown was one of a number of low-volume manufacturers set up as an offshoot of a transport operator. In this case it was J. L. Brown, chief engineer of Horton Motor Lines, who designed and gave his name to the marque. Horton's had been operating a mixed fleet of Mack, Autocar, White and Corbitt tractor units, and J. L. Brown aimed to combine the best features of existing trucks into his own design. The first, designated the 21-R, appeared in 1939, powered by a Continental gasoline engine. Production continued until 1953 – an improved model, the 513, appearing in 1946. Cummins diesels were available from 1949. In all, approximately 1000 Browns were built.

BRASOV, ROMANIA

BUCEGI

■ LEFT *The 1962 Bucegi 5-tonne and Carpati 2 to 3-tonne were powered by a V8 gasoline engine.*

Bucegi trucks for 5-tonne payloads were built at the AB (Autocamioane Brasov) works from 1962 to replace the original SR 101 models. A lighter model for 2 to 3-tonne payloads was marketed as the Carpati. Power unit was a V8 gasoline engine. Both wore an SR badge on their bonnets (hoods) which stood for "Steagul Rosu" ("Red Flag"), the works where they were built. Production ended during the 1970s when Autocamioane Brasov switched to building trucks based on MAN designs. Since 1990 the company has traded as Roman SA and currently markets a wide range of trucks under the DAC brand (see "DAC", "Roman" and "SR").

BRAUNSCHWEIG, GERMANY

BÜSSING

■ BELOW *The driver of this 1903 Büssing 3-tonne truck had no protection from the elements.*

The motor-truck industry was still in its infancy when Heinrich Büssing set up his company at Braunschweig in 1903. That was the year he built his first truck – a 2-tonne payload machine powered by a 2-cylinder gasoline engine and featuring worm drive. That successful design was later built under licence by other companies in Germany, Austria, Hungary and by Straker Squire in England. Before World War I Büssing had already progressed to building heavy-duty trucks for loads of between 5 and 11 tonnes, powered by 6-cylinder engines. In 1923 Büssing introduced what was the first rigid three-axled truck and bus chassis in Germany and, during the '20s, cornered the market for such machines.

A number of other manufacturers were taken over by Büssing in the late 1920s. The first acquisition was Mannesmann-Mulag Motoren und Lastwagen AG of Aachen. Then the Elbing plant of Automobilfabrik Komnick AG was bought, followed a year or so later by Nacionale Automobil AG (NAG). After the last takeover Büssings was called Büssing-Nag until 1950. Büssing began building trucks with diesel engines around 1930 and pioneered the horizontal underfloor diesel in 1936.

During World War II Büssing once again supplied military vehicles,

■ RIGHT *A 1953 Büssing 12000 with 200bhp underfloor diesel engine. The truck grosses 24 tonnes or 32 tonnes with trailer.*

including 6×4 armoured cars and an 8×8 with all-wheel steering. After the war, civilian production resumed with a 5-tonne and later a 7-tonne truck chassis. In 1950 the company name became Büssing Nutskraftwagen GmbH and production was concentrated on underfloor-engined trucks which were to become the firm's speciality. Most tractor units and all normal-control trucks had vertical engines, but in the mid 1960s there was a version of their Commodore maximum-weight tractor unit, the 16–210, which had a horizontal diesel mounted under the cab ahead of the front axle, the gearbox being mounted halfway along the truck's chassis.

Büssing took over the Borgward plant at Osterholz-Scharmbeck in 1962 and built their military 4×4 4-tonner under the Büssing name until 1968. The factory was then sold to Faun-Werke GmbH. In 1969 links were formed with another major German truck manufacturer, MAN, and two years later the MAN takeover of Büssing was announced. The unique underfloor-engined truck range continued in production under the MAN-Büssing name through to the late 1980s.

■ ABOVE *The imposing Büssing 8000 bonneted tractor was a true classic of the early 1960s.*

■ LEFT *A Büssing BS22L with U12DA 280bhp underfloor engine for 38 tonnes gtw.*

■ BELOW *A 15-tonne gross Büssing with 7.5 litre/457cu in underfloor diesel engine engaged on furniture transport in Switzerland.*

OTHER MAKES

■ BELAZ

ZHODINO, BELORUSSIA

In November 1958, in the former road-building machinery works of Dormash at Zhodino, a heavy-duty 25-tonne tipping truck was assembled from components made at MAZ (Minsk Auto Zavod). That vehicle was designated a MAZ-525. The following year production began of 25-tonne dump trucks under the BELAZ (Belorussian Auto Zavod) name. In 1961 the first experimental 27-tonne BELAZ-540 dump truck was produced, followed in 1963 by the BELAZ-548 for 40-tonne payloads.

Full-scale production of the 540 27-tonner began in September 1965 and the 25-tonne version was discontinued. The 540 was a half-cab with 375bhp diesel engine. There was also a 540-A with 360bhp V-12 diesel and 3-speed hydro-mechanical transmission. In 1975 two 75-tonne and one 120-tonne BELAZ dump trucks were made. Two years later prototypes of a 110-tonne dump truck, the BELAZ-7519, were built and the 75-tonne dumper went into production.

■ ABOVE ***This early 1970s KrAZ 256, grossing 26 tonnes, was marketed as a Belaz 256B in the UK.***

Throughout the 1980s and '90s the product range has expanded with the introduction of airport tow tractors capable of hauling aircraft weighing up to 200 tonnes. An experimental 180-tonne dump truck, the 7521, was built in 1979. An even bigger machine, aimed at the mining industry, was a 280-tonne dump truck put into operation in 1990 at a Russian open-cast mine. The current BELAZ range features ten series of dump trucks ranging from 30 tonnes to the 75601, introduced in 2010 with a 360-tonne load capacity.

■ BELSIZE

MANCHESTER, ENGLAND

Belsize Motors Ltd was not in the truck market for very long and is better remembered for its fire engines. The company existed from 1901 to 1925 but did not begin truck building until 1911 when a shaft-drive 3-tonner was introduced. This was also used as a basis for charabanc bodywork. A 1½-ton truck appeared in 1914. Production tailed off after World War I and Belsize concentrated on vans and taxis.

■ ABOVE ***The 1911 Belsize 3-tonner had a 4-cylinder gasoline engine and shaft drive.***

■ BERNA

OLTEN, SWITZERLAND

Berna was an old established manufacturer that built its first truck, the K model, in 1905. It featured chain drive and a 2-cylinder gasoline engine located under the driver. At that time the company was called J. Wyss Schweicherische Automobilfabrik Berna. Not many of these early trucks were built. The same is true for a larger version which was also tried for a short period. The first successful heavy truck was a remarkably advanced machine launched in 1906. The G1 was a 5-tonner with a 6.3 litre/384cu in 4-cylinder gasoline engine, 4-speed gearbox and shaft drive to a double-reduction rear axle.

In 1906 the company was renamed Motorwerke Berna AG. In spite of their high standard of engineering, Berna trucks failed to sell in sufficient quantities to be viable and the company was faced with financial crisis within the first three years of its existence. Berna was rescued from closure in 1908 by a British firm, Hudson Consolidated, and was renamed once again as Berna Commercial Motors Ltd. A new range of goods vehicles for payloads of 1½ to 6 tonnes was introduced. After five years in British hands it returned to Swiss ownership as Motorwagenfabrik Berna AG. From 1914 to 1918 Bernas were also built under licence in the UK by Henry Watson & Sons Ltd of Newcastle-upon-Tyne.

In 1915 Berna launched the highly successful C2 with 4-cylinder gasoline engine. It was supplied in large numbers to the Swiss, British and French armies and was renowned for its ruggedness. Many thousands were built up until 1928, adapted to civilian operations. A new heavy truck, the G type, appeared after World War I and, to meet demand from Germany, Austria and other areas, licensed assembly plants were set up in Vienna and Budapest. By the late 1930s Berna sales were rivalling those of Switzerland's leading truck manufacturer, Saurer. In 1928 Berna began building Deutz diesel engines under licence.

The following year Adolph Saurer AG took a controlling interest in Berna and, although the Olten products continued to be marketed as Berna, an increasing Saurer influence was evident in their design. Saurer diesel engines ousted the licence-built Deutz units. The distinctive bonneted U range, based on the C type Saurer, appeared in 1936. During World War II a large number of Berna trucks were built for the Swiss army. They were virtually identical to the corresponding Saurer models.

After the war Berna added forward-control versions to the U range with a traditional but nevertheless pleasing

■ ABOVE ***Berna trucks were virtually identical to Saurer. This Swiss outfit is a 4VF with drawbar trailer.***

OTHER MAKES

appearance. For the remainder of Berna's existence their products were largely identical to those of Saurer. In the 1960s some Italian OM trucks were badged as Bernas following a marketing tie-up between Saurer and the Fiat group. Saurer themselves vanished in the early 1980s – after merging with FBW to form Nutzfahrzenggesellschaft Arbon & Wetzikon (NAW), the joint operation was absorbed into Daimler-Benz in 1982.

■ BERNARD

ARCUCIL, FRANCE

Camions Bernard was neither the oldest nor the largest of French truck manufacturers but in their 43-year history they did produce some very impressive road-going trucks. The company began as SA des Bennes Basculantes E. Bernard, who built hydraulic tipping gear. In 1923 Bernard produced a complete vehicle for a 2-tonne payload. Pneumatic tyres came as standard and the power unit was a side-valve, 4-cylinder gasoline engine of

■ ABOVE ***The Bernard TD15035 was powered by a licence-built Gardner 6-cylinder diesel.***

2.6 litres/158cu in. Three years later they introduced a high-speed, low-frame coach chassis powered by an American-built 6-cylinder engine.

The company name became Camions Bernard in 1929 and began building its own 3.6 and 5.2 litre/219 and 317cu in engines. A new range of bonneted heavy trucks was launched, developed from the earlier coach chassis. In 1932 an 8-cylinder $6\frac{1}{2}$-tonner with 5-speed gearbox was launched. This had automatic chassis lubrication as standard. Shortly afterwards Bernard turned to diesel power, having acquired a manufacturing licence from the British company Gardner. Four and 6-cylinder engines were built plus a 3-cylinder unit for lighter models. In 1935 a 15-tonne bonneted heavy six-wheeler with the 6-cylinder diesel and a remote mounted gearbox was launched.

Pre-war designs were continued after 1945, but production was concentrated entirely on trucks. New models in the early '50s featured full air brakes, 12.1 litre/738cu in diesels, disc transmission handbrakes and power steering. During the late '50s Bernard introduced higher-powered engines up to 200bhp and 10-speed transmissions. The early '60s range included 4×2 trucks and tractor units and long-wheelbase six-wheel rigids. The bonneted Bernard was perceived as old fashioned and sales declined. In 1963 Bernard launched forward-control versions of their trucks with a futuristic cab designed by Philippe Carbonneaux. Though modern it lacked the solid elegance of the old Bernard. In any case it came too late – in 1963 Mack Trucks took over the company and renamed it Automobiles Bernard. The trucks began to appear with Mack engines and transmissions. The alliance did not last and in 1966 Bernard closed down.

■ BORGWARD

BREMEN, GERMANY

Borgward were not a major player in the truck market. In their early existence from 1924 to 1938 they built light vehicles. In 1928 they took over Hansa Lloyd and used the brand names Goliath and Hansa Lloyd. From 1938 the company was re-established as Carl F. W. Borgward Automobile und Motorenwerke and trucks from $1\frac{1}{2}$ to 5 tonnes were introduced. All were available with diesel engines. Military vehicles, including half tracks, were built during World War II and after the war Borgward reintroduced a civilian 3-tonner. In 1949 the company became Carl F. W. Borgward GmbH. A 4-tonner, including a tractor-unit version, was listed. Improved models appeared in 1954 and forward-control versions in 1958. Financial problems forced the closure of the company in 1962.

■ ABOVE ***A late 1950s Borgward B544 powered by a 6-cylinder, 5 litre/305cu in diesel engine.***

■ BRUCE-SN

EDINBURGH, SCOTLAND

Unorthodox designs of truck sometimes emerge aimed at a specific type of operator. Brewery fleets have come up with various designs of ultra-low loading trucks for distribution work. The Bruce-SN was one example. Built in 1984 to Scottish & Newcastle Brewery's design, it was of front-wheel drive layout, the load carrying section being virtually a large box. The truck took its name from the late Alan Bruce, S & N's transport manager, who masterminded the design. Using a modified Bedford TL cab, the Bruce-SN was powered by a Cummins B-series diesel mounted with flywheel and gearbox facing forward, a transfer box taking the power to a Kirkstall steer-drive front axle. The truck featured single rear wheels. A similar experimental design was based on the Leyland Freighter. Neither type was to enter quantity production.

■ ABOVE ***This experimental front-wheel drive Bruce SN was developed specifically for brewery distribution.***

DETROIT, MICHIGAN, USA

CHEVROLET

■ LEFT *Chevrolet's production concentrated on light commercials during the 1920s and '30s.*

■ BELOW LEFT *A Chevrolet 2-ton payload truck of the early 1930s.*

■ BOTTOM LEFT *By the late 1930s Chevrolet had adopted a more stylish cab for their 2-tonner, designated the VD.*

■ BOTTOM RIGHT *The 1964 M80 tandem with dump body had a choice of V8 gasoline or V6 diesel engine.*

Chevrolet's early history is more concerned with cars, the first commercials – lightweight ½-tonners – appearing in 1918. The company was founded in 1911 by Louis Joseph Chevrolet, a Swiss racing driver, and William Crapo Durant, who had just lost control of the GM empire he had started in 1908. Through a number of shrewd business moves Durant regained control of GM, which absorbed Chevrolet in 1918. GM was already well established in the truck market. Chevrolet trucks, as distinct from car-based commercials, first appeared in 1926 and in 1929 the company introduced its famous "cast iron wonder" 6-cylinder of 3.2 litre/ 194cu in. The engine gained an enviable reputation for durability and smooth power.

From 1925 Chevrolet had begun fitting fully enclosed cabs as opposed to just offering chassis cowls. In 1930 they purchased the body works of the Martin-Parry Corporation of Indianapolis which enabled them to offer complete trucks with a variety of bodywork. Production was still largely concentrated on light trucks and pickups and Chevrolet boasted impressive truck sales volumes which had exceeded half a million by 1930.

Late 1930s models included the 1½-ton R model with its spoked wheels and splash-lubricated 4-cylinder engine. This was marketed in the UK. An important development was the LQ of 1929 which took the new 3.2 litre/ 194cu in overhead valve six. It was this that formed the basis for the British Bedford launched in 1931. At that time GM's heavy trucks were all badged as GMC and it wasn't until the late '30s that Chevrolet began to produce heavier models up to 2-tons payload, and true heavy-duty trucks were not to appear in the Chevrolet line-up until 1960.

The 60 and 70 series bonneted range came in 1961 and these marked a move into heavier trucks and artics. The forward-control T series tilt-cab range set Chevrolet firmly on the truck scene and from then on they progressed to maximum-weight line-haul trucks generally similar to their GMC stable mates. Detroit Diesel two-stroke engines and Fuller Roadranger transmissions were typical of the drivelines but during the 1960s big V6 and V8 gasoline engines were still available.

In the late 1960s Chevrolet developed a futuristic gas-turbine truck which was attractively styled and dubbed the "Titan 3". It boasted automatic

■ RIGHT *The Chevrolet Bison, with a choice of 6V-92TT Detroit Diesel or Cummins 14 litre/854cu in diesel engine, was introduced in 1976.*

transmission, power-operated tilt cab, electric windows, retractable headlights and built-in stereo radio and radio telephone. The truck did not go into production since it was basically a concept vehicle but it made quite an impact when it was exhibited at the New York World's Fair.

In 1970 the Titan name was reintroduced on a new cabover range for up to 34 tons gcw. Cummins diesels up to 320bhp were available. In 1976 the Chevrolet Bison conventionals, similar to GMC's General, were launched. One year later came the 90 Series Bruin for heavy-duty line-haul work. This too came with a choice of Detroit or Cummins diesels, and gasoline engines had by then been discontinued. Chevrolet continued to offer a full range of light and medium-weight trucks. Production of heavy-duty trucks was discontinued from 1980 and the company reverted to producing lightweight models.

■ BELOW LEFT *The 1970s Titan 90 was Chevrolet's heaviest cabover and offered a choice of Detroit Diesel or Cummins engine.*

■ BELOW RIGHT *This 1963 TM 80000 features a 180cm/72in BBC tilt cab.*

PARIS, FRANCE

CITROËN

■ LEFT *The medium-weight bonneted Citroëns of the 1960s era featured car-like styling.*

While Citroën's production was mainly concentrated on light vehicles from 1919 until the early 1930s, bonneted trucks in the 2 to 4-tonne payload class appeared in 1934. Frontal styling was clearly based on Citroën cars. A new truck range with modern styling appeared in 1954 as the 23 or 55 models for gvws of 3.5 to 9.3 tonnes. The lighter models had a 4-cylinder Perkins diesel option. A heavier 60 model was added for 9.8 tonnes gvw but, in tractor-unit form, could gross 13.75 tonnes or 17.4 tonnes with drawbar trailer. Semi-forward-control versions also appeared. The heavier models had a choice of Citroën 6-cylinder diesel or gasoline engines. Citroën's heavy trucks were phased out after the company acquired Automobiles M. Berliet in 1967. Some trucks were marketed as Citroën-Berliet until Citroën was merged into Automobiles Peugeot in 1974.

LUTON & DUNSTABLE, ENGLAND

COMMER

■ ABOVE *The updated Superpoise of the late 1940s had styling reminiscent of the Humber car.*

■ LEFT *The Commercar 3-ton truck of 1920.*

The Commer name came on to the market in 1926, but the history of the company began some 20 years earlier. A prototype truck was built in 1903, its design being centred around a revolutionary design of pre-selective gearbox invented by a talented engineer called Linley. The new enterprise was set up by Julian Halford who saw great possibilities for the new gearbox which eliminated sliding gears and thus the dreadful crashing sounds that drivers made with conventional gearboxes. The Commercial Car Company had been formed in 1905 at Lavender Hill in south London. The premises were unsuitable for large-scale truck production so, almost immediately, a site for a new factory was selected at Biscot Road, Luton, some 56km/35 miles away. The first Luton-built vehicles were completed in 1906.

While the initial prototype had been a 4-ton chain-drive forward-control machine of rudimentary design, the production trucks were bonneted types of similar load rating. In the ensuing five years the range expanded to include 1½, 2 and even a 7-ton model and Commercial Cars began exporting trucks to the United States, Canada, Australia, New Zealand and as far as Siberia. Their leading product was the chain-drive RC type although shaft-drive models were also tried. Some 3000 military trucks were supplied to the War Office during World War I.

■ BELOW *The Q type Commer Superpoise was announced in 1939 and production carried on after World War II.*

Tough post-war trading conditions saw Commercial Cars struggling to survive and in 1926 the Coventry-based car manufacturer Humber took over the company and the name was changed to Commer Cars. Just two years later both were absorbed into Rootes Ltd – a car distribution company set up by William and Reginald Rootes some years earlier. Under new ownership Commer designs were modernized and vehicles were built along more mass-produced lines. The Invader 2-tonner appeared, powered by a Humber Super Snipe engine. This

■ LEFT *The 1951 Commer QX featured a forward-entry cab and underfloor 6-cylinder gasoline engine.*

was followed by the G6 6/7-tonner with set-back front axle and a 100hp 6-cylinder gasoline engine. A 1½-tonner, the Raider, was also added to the range.

In 1935 the LN models entered the scene and with them came the first appearance of a radiator design which was later to grace the first Q model, Superpoise, launched in 1939. Karrier had joined the Rootes empire in 1934 and in subsequent years some commonization began to take place between Commer and Karrier models. In the post-war era a modernization program began with a restyled Superpoise introduced in 1948 with frontal styling borrowed from the Humber car. A completely new forward-control model, the QX, had many advanced features, including a forward-entry cab and an underfloor 6-cylinder gasoline engine. In 1954 Commer introduced their revolutionary Rootes TS3 (Tilling Stevens, 3 cylinder) two-stroke, opposed-piston diesel. Maidstone-based Tilling Stevens, who developed the engine, had joined the Rootes Group in 1949.

By 1953 Commer had outgrown the Biscot Road plant and moved to a new factory in Dunstable some 8km/5 miles west of Luton. Normal-control models were given a restyled cab which was also used on certain Dodge trucks.

■ ABOVE *The last model to carry the Commer name was the 1974 Commando.*

■ BELOW *This 1960 six-wheeler was powered by the unusual Rootes 3-cylinder opposed-piston TS3 engine.*

Commer introduced a factory-approved 10-ton six-wheeler with Unipower third axle. In 1962 a completely new forward-control cab was introduced on the C (TS3-engined) and V (Perkins-engined) ranges. Two years later, with the raising of UK weight limits, Commer launched their 16-ton gvw Maxiload. At about the same time, Dodge's parent company Chrysler bought a 46 per cent share in Rootes and by 1967 had gained full control of the group.

A process of integration between the Dodge, Commer and Karrier ranges began, all production being centred on Dunstable. Ultimately, the Commando range was launched in 1974 at which time the TS3 engine was phased out. By 1976 the Commer name had followed suit and all products were marketed as Dodge. Chrysler UK sold out to PSA Peugeot-Citroën in 1978. Later still, in 1981, Renault Véhicules Industriels took control of the company and the Commando models which had initially been Commer and featured new black plastic grilles became Renaults.

HENDERSON, NORTH CAROLINA, USA

CORBITT

■ LEFT *The 1948 Corbitt tractor was characterized by its exceptionally high driving position.*

One of America's pioneer automobile manufacturers, Corbitt was formed in 1899 and began truck manufacture in 1913. The early trucks were bonneted chain-drive 1-tonners with 4-cylinder Continental gasoline engines. By the '20s, as the Corbitt Motor Truck Co. (founded in 1916), they were one of America's largest truck producers with a range for 1 to 5-ton payloads. Heavier models up to 15 tons gvw were added during the 1930s. Medium-weight trucks of the '30s utilized the radiator grille and front-end sheet metal from the contemporary Auburn car. Military and civilian trucks were produced during World War II, including heavy-duty 6×4 tractor units. The post-war years saw an impressive range of bonneted and cabover heavy tractors. Volume truck production came to an end in 1952 when the founder, Richard Corbitt, retired. In 1957 there was an attempt to revive the Corbitt business with a build-to-order approach but this was short-lived.

MANCHESTER, ENGLAND

CROSSLEY

■ LEFT *A 25/30hp Crossley ambulance, a type supplied in large numbers to the allied forces in World War I.*

Although Crossley's origins date back to the 19th century when Sir William Crossley acquired world rights (excluding Germany) from Nicolas August Otto to develop his newly invented four-stroke gas engine of 1869, the company did not enter the truck market until 1932. Prior to that it specialized in engine manufacture and, from 1912, in military vehicles. In 1932 a range of forward-control diesel trucks for payloads of 3 to 7 tons was introduced. Three years later came their Atlas forward-control model, including a double-drive six-wheeler for 12 tons. Their brief presence in the civilian market was brought to an end at the outbreak of war in 1939. During World War II a 4×4 forward-control 3-ton truck, the Q type, was supplied in large numbers to the RAF. No further trucks were built and the company was absorbed, along with the Maudslay Motor Company, into Associated Commercial Vehicles in 1948. ACV marketed certain AEC vehicles under the Crossley name in some export markets through to the late 1950s.

BUDAPEST, HUNGARY

CSEPEL

■ LEFT *Csepel's forward-control range of the 1970s featured a French-designed Chausson cab.*

The Csepel Engineering Works near Budapest, Hungary, began truck production in 1950 with a bonneted 3-tonner based on a design from the Austrian company Steyr-Daimler-Puch. They also developed all-wheel-drive military trucks. At first Csepel also built their own diesel engines but later used Raba engines. In the 1970s the company was renamed Csepel Autogyar. Csepel trucks were exported to Asia and Africa under the Mogurt name. Following the collapse of communism Csepel lost the majority of its traditional markets and eventually faced bankruptcy. Now the company only produces components for trucks such as gearboxes as well as some complete bus chassis.

OTHER MAKES

■ LEFT *Caledon trucks built in Glasgow were originally inspired by World War I Commers.*

■ BELOW *Chenard-Walcker tractors had a unique coupling system to pull trailers.*

■ CALEDON

GLASGOW, SCOTLAND

The company that built Caledon trucks was originally Scotland's Commer (Commercial Cars) agent called Scottish Commercial Cars. In 1914 supplies of Commers dwindled as the War Department commandeered the company's production. In 1915 Scottish Commercial Cars marketed a bonneted chain-drive four-wheeler with a Dorman 4-cylinder gasoline engine which they named Caledon. The vehicle was fitted with a French-designed Dux gearbox built under licence.

Some heavier vehicles were built using Buda and Hercules engines. A Buda powered their largest truck, a 10-ton payload six-wheeler in 1924 which had a 6m/20ft long body. This was believed to be the first rigid six-wheel truck in the UK. Declining sales during the depression led Caledon into financial difficulties and the company was sold to Richard Garrett & Sons Ltd of Leiston, Suffolk. A couple of Garrett-Caledons were built but further production was abandoned.

■ CANADA

MONTREAL, CANADA

Between 1956 and 1958 the Canadian Car Co. Ltd, a member of A.V. Roe, Canada, and the Hawker Siddeley Group developed a heavy-duty tractor unit in both 4×2 and 6×4 form, in co-operation with Leyland Motors (Canada) Ltd. The trucks, for gcw ratings of 58,000lbs/26 tonnes up to 99,800lbs/45 tonnes, were powered by Leyland 0.680 6-cylinder diesel engines and had a choice of Spicer and Fuller transmissions. Eaton axles were used. Canadas were of bonneted layout using an International Harvester steel cab. The leading model was designated the 680WT. Canadas were manufactured at CCC's Diesel and Engineering Division of Can-Car at Longueuil near Montreal. Can-Car, Canada's leading producer of railway carriages, also built semi-trailers at their Fort William plant.

■ CHENARD-WALCKER

SEINE, FRANCE

Based at Gennevilliers, Seine, in France, Chenard-Walcker was set up in 1905 but only built light vehicles until turning to heavy-duty road tractors in 1919. These were bonneted short-wheelbase "tugs" for hauling independent trailers and featured the company's own unique design of trailer coupling. Load capacity of the early machine was around 5 tonnes but there was a later version for 10 tonnes. The tractors were marketed by subsidiary S.A. des Trains Chenard-Walcker-FAR. Licensed production by Minerva of Antwerp began in 1920 and, from 1930, they were also built under licence by Beardmore Multiwheeler in the UK. Those built in Antwerp were badged as Minerva. Heavy tractors for train weights of up to 25 tonnes were also offered. Some production of ordinary load-carrying 5 to 6-tonne trucks took place from the mid 1930s. The company was acquired by S.A. des Automobiles Peugeot in 1951.

■ CHINGKANGSHAN

NANJING, CHINA

The Chingkangshan bonneted 2½-tonne truck was first built in 1968 and is typical of Chinese vehicles that were produced in large numbers in several different factories. Chingkangshan trucks are built at the Chingkang Mountains Motor Vehicle factory in Kiansi province and are based on a Russian GAZ design, similar to the T'iao Jin and Yuejin 2½-tonne trucks from Nanjing which are built in large numbers for both military and civilian use.

■ LEFT *The Canada truck of the late 1950s was powered by a Leyland diesel.*

EINDHOVEN,
THE NETHERLANDS

DAF

■ LEFT ***DAF 30-ton rigid eight-wheelers became popular on the UK scene in the 1970s.***

Production of DAF trucks began in 1950 when the first forward-control 5-tonner was launched, powered by a Hercules 6-cylinder side-valve gasoline engine. A Perkins P6 diesel was optional. Prior to that, as DAF Aanhangenwagenfabrik NV, it had built trailers. The origins of the company date back to 1928 when its founder Hubertus van Doorne and his brother Wim began in general engineering. During the German occupation of The Netherlands experimental military vehicles were built. In the post-war period the brothers shrewdly foresaw a boom in demand for civilian trucks and, with support from the Dutch government, a new truck plant was built at Eindhoven in 1949. So successful were the early DAFs that the factory was enlarged just a few years later to six times its original size.

From 1953 DAF began using Leyland engines and from 1956 began building them under licence. The model range expanded rapidly as did export sales.

■ ABOVE ***The T1800 was DAF's first volume-produced heavy articulated truck.***

■ BELOW ***The 16DD bonneted range was powered by a licence-built Leyland 0.350 engine.***

■ BELOW ***In 2017 DAF relaunched its CF range with detailed improvements and subtle styling changes as seen on this UK articulated outfit.***

By 1958 they commanded a third of the Dutch domestic truck market. Soon DAF undertook its own development of Leyland's 0.350, 0.375, 0.600 and 0.680 diesels and was experimenting with turbocharged versions. Normal-control trucks were added to the range.

An important new model, the 2600, was launched in 1962 and this was to put DAF among the world leaders. It included maximum-weight rigids and artics for gross combination weights up to 40 tonnes, and featured a modern well-appointed cab for long-haul operations. DAF underwent further rapid expansion and a new cab and axle plant was opened at Ophasselt in Belgium.

In 1970 a new tilt-cab range was announced with increased power and gross weight ratings. DAF lost its independence in 1972 when the International Harvester Group bought a third of the company's shares. Some International components began to be introduced and for a brief period DAF offered a version of the American company's Paystar bonneted truck using DAF running units. DAF ran into further

■ RIGHT *The 2600 range became DAF's most important seller of the 1960s.*

■ BELOW *This DAF 2000 articulated bulk powder tanker dates from 1959.*

difficulties in 1975 following heavy investment in new facilities. Van Doorne's shareholding was reduced to 61 per cent in 1975 when the Dutch State Mines came to the rescue and purchased 25 per cent of DAF's shares.

A rigid 8x4, called the 2205, became available in the UK from 1975.

After International bought shares in DAF it took over Seddon Atkinson in the UK and bought a stake in the Spanish ENASA group which built Pegaso trucks. From 1978 International was forced, for economic reasons, to sell its European interests but the link between DAF, Seddon Atkinson and ENASA resulted in a joint Cabtec project developing a heavy truck cab used on all three makes. It went on DAF's new 95 series.

In 1987 when the British manufacturer Leyland ran into insolvency problems, DAF agreed a merger and subsequently the trucks were badged as Leyland DAF in the UK and DAF elsewhere. DAF concentrated on heavy vehicles while Leyland produced light and medium trucks, these being marketed as DAFs in the Netherlands. All was not well, however, and by 1993 Leyland DAF collapsed when DAF became bankrupt and was rescued by the Dutch and Belgian governments. The Leyland plant became Leyland Trucks Ltd but Leyland DAF dealers continued with both makes.

DAF launched its 75 and 85 series in 1993 followed by its flagship long-haul truck, the 95XF, in 1997. In 1996 DAF became a subsidiary of Paccar Inc which also bought Leyland Trucks in 1998. The Leyland name was dropped in 2000. The LF medium range appeared in 2001, featuring a Renault cab. At the same time the 75 and 85 series became the CF, featuring a face-lifted cab. The 95XF was updated in 2003 to become the XF95 with detailed improvements made to the cab. This had the DAF 12.6 litre XE diesel with 530bhp. For 2006 it underwent further improvements, becoming the XF105 with a new 560bhp, 12.9 litre diesel engine. This was developed into Paccar's MX-13 engine. Designed to meet European emission standards introduced in 2014, the engine's three output variants (410/460/510hp) power DAF's latest flagship truck, the Euro 6 XF, which began production in 2013.

GUILDFORD, ENGLAND

DENNIS

Dennis Brothers Ltd was formed in 1904 but John Dennis had began a cycle manufacturing business in 1895 and was joined by his brother Raymond in 1898. By 1901 they had begun producing cars, followed by their first commercial vehicle in 1903. A notable feature was its worm-drive rear axle, the first in Britain. As early as 1907 Dennis was offering a 5-ton payload truck with worm drive. From 1913 all production was to be concentrated on commercial vehicles, which included trucks, buses and fire appliances. The latter were to become synonymous with Dennis throughout its history. Engines were supplied by White & Poppe of Coventry, a company which Dennis took over in 1918 to become their engine plant until the early 1930s.

During World War I 7000 subsidy trucks were supplied to the War Department. Immediately after the war Dennis introduced a new 2½-tonner and in 1926 a truck range covering payloads of 4, 5 and 6 tons. These were powered by 5.7 litre/347cu in 4-cylinder gasoline engines. By then Dennis were building a very wide range of trucks, buses and municipal vehicles and had already achieved extensive export sales in many parts of the world. In 1933 the distinctive Ace 2½-tonner appeared, while a whole new truck range, including the Max 7½-tonner and the twin-steer Max Major for a 10½-ton load, was introduced in 1937. By now the heavier trucks had Dennis' own 4-cylinder diesel engine.

After World War II Dennis chose Pax (Latin for "peace") as the name for its popular 5-ton truck. New truck models were coming thick and fast in the late 1940s. These included the 1946 Horla 12-ton payload artic tractor, the 1946 Centaur four-wheeler and the Jubilant heavy-duty six-wheeler, which also appeared in 1946, powered by a 7.6 litre/463cu in 6-cylinder diesel. A very small number of rigid eight-wheeled Jubilants, no more than three, were also built in the early 1960s. As the 1950s drew on, Dennis concentrated more on buses and municipal vehicles but one interesting goods vehicle worthy of mention was the underfloor-engined Stork 3-tonner in 1952.

In 1957 the 14-ton gvw Hefty replaced the Max and by then Perkins engines were in wide use, as well as the occasional Gardner. In that same year the Centaur was replaced by the Condor. This and a lighter model, the Heron, had a modern style of forward-control cab.

■ ABOVE *The 1933 A model dropside truck took a payload of 2¼ tons.*

■ LEFT *The Dennis Horla tractor unit was based on the Pax and had a Dennis gasoline or Perkins P6 diesel engine.*

■ LEFT *1937 saw the launch of the Dennis Max for payloads of 7 to 8 tons.*

■ RIGHT *The Pax in both normal and forward-control was Dennis's best seller.*

■ BELOW LEFT *The 1974 Dominant had a fibreglass cab and Perkins 6.354 diesel.*

■ BELOW RIGHT *Dennis' last bid for a share of the market was with the Delta.*

One short-lived machine was the Paravan, a specially designed delivery van of 1958. It had an unusual angled up-and-over door on the left front corner and a Perkins P4 engine located behind the driver.

Dennis' position in the truck market was declining but in 1964 they made a bold effort to re-establish themselves with a Cummins V8-engined 32-ton tractor unit, the Maxim, plus a special low-loading Pax six-wheeler aimed at the brewery industry. By the late '60s Dennis' fortunes were at a low ebb, its once thriving truck and bus business having diminished, and it was relying almost entirely on municipal and fire vehicles, but the volume was insufficient. In 1972 the company was taken over by the Hestair Group, who also owned Yorkshire Vehicles and Eagle Engineering, both of whom specialized in municipal bodywork. A brief re-entry into the truck market came in the mid '70s with the Delta 16-tonner but home sales were few, the bulk of production being exported to the Middle East. With much of their business now given over to buses and municipal vehicles, Dennis were virtually out of the truck business, but they had one last assault on the 16-ton four-wheeler market in 1978 with a modernized Delta featuring a very square cab designed by the Ogle Design Group. This had the turbocharged Perkins T6.354 or a Gardner 6LXB but domestic sales amounted to a paltry 20 trucks per year. In 1983 Dennis pulled out of trucks except for municipal chassis. It was taken over by Trinity Holdings in 1989, becoming part of the Mayflower Group in 1998.

NORWICH, ENGLAND

DENNIS-MANN EGERTON

The Dennis-Mann Egerton was a semi-experimental one-off truck jointly designed by bodybuilder Mann Egerton of Norwich and the British Aluminium Co. of Greenford. It explored the benefits of super-lightweight-aluminium integral construction. With a gvw of 12 tons, the truck could carry an $8\frac{1}{2}$-ton payload. It featured an attractively designed cab built on an aluminium frame and skinned with embossed aluminium sheeting that did not require painting. A Dennis 5.5 litre/ 335cu in, 92bhp horizontal 6-cylinder diesel engine was used, similar to that fitted in the Dennis Pelican bus. The drive was taken to an Eaton 2-speed axle through a Dennis 5-speed gearbox. Other running units were those used in the Dennis Centaur truck. The truck was used on the British Aluminium Co.'s own transport fleet for about eight years and was later scrapped. A similar experimental Mann Egerton truck, rated at 14 tons gvw, was built in 1956 using Albion components.

■ ABOVE *The all-aluminium integral Dennis-Mann Egerton was one of the lightest trucks of its era.*

RATHCOOLE, REPUBLIC OF IRELAND

DENNISON

■ LEFT *The Dennison eight-wheeler used Rolls Royce diesel power.*

In 1977 Dennison Trailers of Rathcoole, Dublin, entered the truck manufacturing business with a small range of maximum-weight 4×2 tractors and 6×4 and 8×4 rigids. Its founder George Dennison had built up a successful semi-trailer business. That was sold to Crane Fruehauf and truck manufacture took over. The trucks had a choice of Rolls Royce or Gardner engines and a Motor Panels cab similar to that used on Fodens. Fuller gearboxes and Eaton rear axles were used. In 1979 Dennison began fitting Finnish Sisu cabs. Most of its sales were in Ireland but some 8×4 rigids and 4×2 tractors were sold in the UK. Stiff competition and low volumes forced Dennison to withdraw from the market in 1981. Dennison reverted to trailer manufacture.

CHICAGO, ILLINOIS, USA

DIAMOND T

■ LEFT *Diamond T trucks sold well, and some were built in semi-forward-control layout.*

■ BELOW LEFT *An early 1970s Diamond Reo C11464 6×4 conventional.*

C. A. Tilt began building cars in 1905 and when one of his customers requested a truck he obliged. That was in 1911 and the truck was a 1½-tonner with chain drive. Tilt's emblem of the Diamond T Motor Car Co. was his initial "T" set within a diamond which symbolized quality. The company built only trucks from 1911 onwards and as early as 1915 had built up a national reputation for its products which ranged from 2 to 5-ton payload. Diamond T Model B Liberty trucks were built in large numbers during World War I and development took place throughout the 1920s and '30s. In 1928 the trucks boasted 6-cylinder engines, spiral-bevel rear axles and all-wheel braking. By then heavier six-wheeled trucks were being offered for 12-ton payloads. In the mid '30s the trucks were given stylish new cabs and by 1937 the first cabover models were appearing. During World War II Diamond T built their legendary 6×6 trucks and 6×4 12-ton tank tractors which were widely used as heavy-haulage tractors after the war.

A new range was launched in 1947 and by 1951 lighter trucks had been dropped. From then on production was concentrated on heavy-duty trucks, both normal and forward-control. Also in 1951 a new design of forward-control tilt cab appeared. This was also used on certain Hendrickson and International trucks. Diamond T was taken over by the White Motor Co. in 1958 and the word "Car" in the company title was changed to "Truck". In 1961 production was transferred to the company's Reo factory, also in White ownership from 1957. From 1967 Diamond T and Reo products were merged and the trucks were renamed Diamond Reo, a sub-division of the White Motor Corp.

A range of heavy-duty conventionals and cabovers were built under the new name up until 1971 when White sold the division to Francis L. Coppaert of Birmingham, Alabama. Under new ownership and independent once again, Diamond Reo Trucks Inc., as it was now

■ RIGHT *This Diamond T 6×4 five-axled fuel tanker dates from the mid 1960s.*

called, developed some successful new models. These were the Royale cabovers with a choice of straight six, V8 or V12 engines, and the Apollo conventionals with a choice of Caterpillar, Cummins or Detroit Diesel power units. Their bonneted, heavy 6×4 tractor, the Raider, appeared in 1974. While sales were healthy in the early 1970s, Diamond Reo fell into financial problems in 1975 and the receivers were called in. The company was then purchased by one of the Diamond Reo parts distributors, Osterlund Inc. of Hansbury, Pennsylvania. From that point on one basic model, the bonneted Giant, was available in 4×2, 4×4, 6×4 and 6×6 form mainly for the construction industry.

CIUDAD SAHAGUN & MONTEREY, MEXICO

DINA

■ LEFT *The DINA 761 6×4 tractor was powered by Cummins NTC-335 diesel and grossed 35 tons.*

DINA Trucks was founded in 1953, taking its name from Diesel Nacional SA. The government-owned company began by building trucks based on bonneted Diamond T designs but later DINAs became based on 4×2 and 6×4 International Harvesters. In 1975 a new factory was opened at Monterey, mainly for smaller pickup trucks. In 1985 DINA came under the control of General Motors. Recently Grupo DINA launched its HTQ (High Technology and Quality) truck range which conforms to North American and European legislation.

DETROIT, MICHIGAN, & DELAWARE, OHIO, USA

DIVCO

■ LEFT *The Divco was the ultimate in purpose-built door-to-door delivery trucks.*

Although Divco specialized in door-to-door delivery vans they were such a memorable part of the American scene that no truck history would be complete without them. The distinctively styled vans were the invention of George Bacon, chief engineer of the Detroit Electric Vehicle Co. In 1922 he designed an electric delivery truck that could be driven from any one of four positions – front, rear and either running board. When it was discovered that electric traction was not as successful as gasoline power, Bacon set up the Detroit Industrial Vehicle Co. (Divco) to build a similar vehicle but with a Le Roi gasoline engine. The vans entered production in 1926. Numerous improved versions appeared up until the mid 1930s but the depression saw Divco being taken over by Continental Motors and renamed Continental-Divco Corp. In 1937 Continental Motors acquired the Twin Coach Co. of Kent, Ohio, and the vans were renamed Divco-Twin. It was at this stage that the famous snub-nosed pressed-steel van bodies appeared, a design that remained virtually unchanged until production finally ceased in 1986.

During its history Divco underwent many name changes. After Divco-Twin Truck Co. it became the Divco Corporation; the Divco Truck Division of Divco Wayne; and finally, in 1972, the Divco Truck Co., Correct Mfg. Co. The largest truck to bear the Divco name was a forward-control 6-ton refrigerated box van with separate cab and 5.4m/18ft long box-van body. The company's chassis cabs were also used for garbage trucks and a variety of other purposes.

KEW & DUNSTABLE, ENGLAND

DODGE

Dodge Bros. (Britain) Ltd was set up in Fulham, London, in 1922 as a subsidiary of its American parent. At first it was marketing American vehicles including light commercials up to 30cwt payload. In 1928 it moved to new premises at Park Royal, west London, by which time a wider range of trucks was being imported. Three years later Chrysler bought the Dodge operations. Chrysler had already absorbed the Maxwell Car Co., which had a UK distribution centre set up in 1914 at Kew in Surrey. Under Chrysler ownership the two operations were merged and Kew became the new home of Dodge Bros. (Britain) Ltd.

By 1932 a British Dodge 2-tonner was in production, powered by the American Dodge side-valve gasoline engine. Heavier models for 3, 4 and 5-ton payloads were added to the range in the '30s while the first all-British Dodge, with a Perkins diesel option, appeared in 1938. Some exports were already taking place to Australia and New Zealand where the trucks were badged Fargo. Wartime production was very limited as the factory switched to building aircraft, but from 1945 full production was resumed, the models being similar to the pre-war range. The largest truck was the 6-ton Major of semi-forward-control layout.

■ TOP ***A 1955 Dodge 7-ton dump truck with Perkins R6 diesel engine. It was nicknamed the "Parrot-Nose" Dodge.***

■ ABOVE ***The wartime Dodge Major 6-ton dump truck was powered by a Dodge gasoline engine with optional Perkins diesel.***

■ BELOW ***The Dodge 300 series had the forward-control Motor Panels LAD cab and a Perkins or Leyland diesel engine.***

The first new post-war range appeared in 1949 – the stylish 100 series with a modern Briggs steel cab which shared the same basic shell as the Thames ET6 and the Leyland Comet. It was sometimes referred to as the "Parrot-Nose" Dodge owing to its beak-like bonnet (hood). A 7-ton version with a Perkins R6 engine was added in 1953. In later years the 100 series formed the basis for the Premier truck range in India.

A completely new forward-control range, the 300 series was announced in 1957, taking Dodge into a heavier weight category. A 14-ton gvw model was available powered by an AEC AV470 diesel. Other power units for the 300 range included Perkins and Leyland. The range featured a Motor Panels steel cab dubbed the "LAD" (Leyland-Albion-Dodge), modified versions being used by both Leyland and Albion.

Meanwhile, in 1958 the bonneted range, now called the 200 series, received a more modern cab of streamlined appearance with a wider grille. An almost identical cab was introduced on Commer's Superpoise at the same time. In 1963 the 200 was

■ LEFT *The Spanish-built Dodge 38-tonne tractor was marketed in the UK as the R38 throughout the 1970s.*

revamped once again as the 400 series taking an American design of cab. Very few of these were actually sold in the UK, the model being aimed at the export market. An important new range entered the scene in 1964, the tilt cab 500 series. These marked the introduction of a Chrysler V8 diesel which was, in fact, a Cummins VALE built under licence. The heaviest model was now a 28-ton gcw tractor unit. The Chrysler V8 proved unpopular and Dodge later offered the Perkins V8-410 in response to demand. The successful 500 series enjoyed a 13-year production run.

Chrysler, Dodge's parent company, had owned a stake in the Rootes Group, owners of both Commer and Karrier, since 1964 and gained full control of the company by 1967. Dodge production was moved from Kew to the Commer-Karrier factory in Dunstable. The process of integrating Dodge, Commer and Karrier was completed by 1973 and from 1976 the Dodge name was applied to former Commer models, including the tilt-cab Commando that was launched in 1974.

In the early 1970s there was a strong demand for heavy tractor units but the 500 series had been developed to its limit at 28 tons. To cater for 32 tons and over, Dodge took the unusual decision to import the Spanish-built Dodge (formerly Barreiros) 38-tonne tractor and market it in the UK as the Dodge R38. Barreiros in Madrid had been bought out by Chrysler in 1967 and was renamed Chrysler Espana when the Barreiros name was replaced by Dodge. Dodge UK also imported the Barreiros-Dodge rigid eight-wheeler. Sales of the Spanish-built Dodges took off quite well but demand soon fell away and the model was dropped in 1982.

Chrysler were to suffer financial losses in their European operations in the late 1970s and decided to sell out to the French Peugeot-Citroën Group in 1978. Chrysler UK's business was renamed Talbot Motor Co. with the Dunstable truck operations being Karrier Motors. A few years later Peugeot sold Karrier Motors to Rènault Véhicules Industriels and eventually the Dodge name was phased out.

■ LEFT *The tilt-cab 500 series, launched in 1964 and powered by a Chrysler Cummins V8 diesel.*

■ BELOW *A 28-ton gvw eight-wheeled version of the 500 series was marketed during the early 1970s.*

DETROIT, MICHIGAN, USA

DODGE

John F. Dodge and his brother Horace formed a company in 1910 to manufacture automotive components and four years later began building cars. The cars formed the basis for light commercials. Following the death of the two Dodge brothers in 1920, their widows sold the company to a New York banking firm and the vice president and general manager, Frederick J. Haynes, linked up with Graham Brothers of Evansville, Indiana, who had supplied cabs and bodies for Dodge trucks, while their own Graham truck range used Dodge engines and drivelines. In 1927 Dodge Brothers absorbed Graham Brothers and the following year the bank sold the company to Chrysler. The heaviest truck at that time was a 2½-tonner and the products were called Dodge Brothers. A 4-tonner powered by a 6-cylinder gasoline engine was introduced in 1931. A heavier truck for up to 7½ tons with a straight-eight gasoline engine was available briefly from 1933–35, but Dodge's production was centred mainly on light to medium trucks. In 1936 the name was shortened from Dodge Brothers to Dodge. The heaviest truck model until the early 1950s was a 3-tonner. In 1951 a 4 to 5-tonner was introduced, but Dodge did not really enter the heavy truck market until 1960, their first tilt-cab L-line heavies appearing in 1964. Dodge's presence in the heavy truck market was relatively brief. After offering a range of maximum-weight tractor units with power ratings up to 335bhp from Cummins and Detroit Diesels, the company decided to pull out of heavy trucks in 1975 and concentrated once more on light commercials.

■ LEFT *The 1966 Dodge D800 conventional had a 6.7 litre/408cu in V8 gasoline engine.*

■ LEFT *The 1967 L700 223cm/88in wheelbase tilt-cab tractor was designed for urban distribution.*

■ BELOW LEFT *1953 marked the introduction of the Dodge 4-ton payload Job Rated truck.*

■ BELOW LEFT *The Dodge CNT900.*

■ BELOW RIGHT *The LN1000 had a choice of 121cm/48in, 185cm/73in or 200cm/79in BBC tilt cab.*

ADELAIDE, AUSTRALIA

DODGE

■ LEFT *The Australian-built Dodge Series 7 was available with gasoline or diesel engine.*

Dodge became established in Australia in 1939 but did not enter the truck market until 1958, when they introduced their own range of normal and forward-control trucks. They were a peculiar blend of American and British products, the normal-control models having a distinctly American looking cab while the forward-control versions featured the UK LAD cab. They were designated the 10 series and powered by V8 gasoline engines. In 1962, the Series 7 had a new cab with a strong American influence. This was to become the top seller with V8 gasoline engine and Rockwell 2-speed rear axle. Until then the trucks had also been marketed as Fargo and De-Soto.

A new truck plant was opened at Adelaide in 1974 and in 1975 more new Australian Dodge trucks were announced, including a version of the UK-designed Commando. In mid 1975 the range was further extended by marketing imported Mitsubishi Fuso heavy trucks which were badged Dodge. At the lighter end, the Mitsubishi Canter was also offered. Soon after Chrysler's withdrawal from the European truck business in 1978, Dodge of Australia were also to pull out of the market.

BOMBAY, INDIA

DODGE

Premier Automobiles Ltd (PAL) was established in 1944 and entered into an agreement with the Chrysler Group. The company went on to build a range of Dodge-based trucks in the 1 to 8-ton payload range. While some had locally built cabs, others featured the British Kew Dodge cab and some had American-style cabs. The trucks had a high local content and used licence-built Perkins engines or locally built gasoline engines. Some trucks were sold under the Fargo name. Both the Dodge and Fargo names were replaced by their own brand, Premier, from 1972. (See "Premier".)

KADIKOY, TURKEY

DODGE

Chrysler Sanayi AS began building Dodge trucks in 1964 based on American types but with locally built cabs. Heavier models were sold in chassis-only form. The trucks were also marketed under the De-Soto and Fargo names. Production of light, medium and heavy trucks continued until 2015.

SHIYAN, CHINA

DONGFENG

■ LEFT *Dongfeng EQ1310W of 2006 grosses 31 tonnes and is powered by a 296hp C300-20 diesel.*

Established in September 1969, Dongfeng Commercial Vehicles Ltd (DFCV) is part of the Dongfeng Motor Group (DMG) and ranks as China's second largest truck producer. In 2015 it joined forces with Volvo Trucks, the latter taking a 45 per cent stake. Dongfeng had previously had ties with Nissan dating back to 1969.

In the early '70s, production of Dongfeng began at China's Second Automobile Works (SAW) based in Shiyan, Hubei Province. The EQ140 was a gasoline engined bonneted 5-tonner. There was also a 6x2 designated EQ144. Another division is Dongfeng Luizhou Motor Co which builds trucks at Luizhou, including the Chenglong brand.

Currently Dongfeng's products include the KX long-haul trucks powered by Dongfeng-Cummins ISZ480, 13 litre/793 cu.in diesels; the KL with Dongfeng DDi11, 11 litre/670 cu.in diesels and KC 6x4 and 8x4 rigid trucks powered by the Cummins ISLe, 340hp. ZF gearboxes are specified. The trucks have cabs with up-to-the-minute styling.

OTHER MAKES

■ DAC

BRASOV, ROMANIA

DAC trucks were introduced in 1973, built at the Intreprinderea de Autocamione Brasov (Brasov Truck Manufacturing Works). Prior to that it was the S.R. (Steagul Rosu) Works, whose history dates back to 1921 when it was the ROMLOC Factory, which produced locomotives and rail wagons. The first DACs were based on the Bucegi which was powered by a V8 gasoline engine. As DACs they had a licence-built Saviem 6-cylinder diesel. DACs also build heavy dump trucks based on their own designs. In 1990 the company was privatized under the name of ROMAN S.A. Currently ROMAN trucks are badged DAC. The range includes two, three and four-axled trucks from 7 to 40 tonnes gvw and tractor units from 16 to 40 tonnes gcw, plus military and specialized trucks. Engines include Deutz, Navistar, Caterpillar and Renault diesels according to model. (See also "Bucegi", "Roman" and "SR".)

■ DAEWOO

CHOLLABUK-DO, KOREA

Daewoo trucks entered production at Kunshan in 1994. Annual production soon reached 2000. The trucks are modern well-equipped 4-, 6- and 8-wheelers and tractor units. Daewoo claims to be the first Korean manufacturer to have developed its own range as opposed to licence-built designs. Soon, overseas assembly plants were established. In 2004 Daewoo Commercial Vehicles was taken over by Tata Motors and renamed Tata Daewoo Commercial Vehicles. Its first heavy-duty range, the "Novus", was launched in 2005, followed by the "Prima" in 2008.

■ LEFT ***DAC tractor units have a wide choice of power units including Deutz, Navistar, Caterpillar and Renault diesels.***

■ DAIMLER

STUTTGART & BERLIN-MARIENFELDE, GERMANY

The name Daimler is linked to the origins of the motor vehicle. Having produced the world's first motor car in 1886, Gottlieb Wilhelm Daimler announced the world's first motor truck in 1896. That was based on the Riemenwagen car and was equipped with a rear-mounted V-twin gasoline engine, which drove the rear wheels through a system of belts and gears to ring gears on the wheels. Similar designs were built for loads of 1½ to 5 tonnes. Another model in 1897 had shaft drive and the engine was mounted underneath the driver at the front. By 1900 the final drive gearing was semi-enclosed to keep out dirt and to aid lubrication. By then a 4-cylinder engine had been introduced.

In 1901 Daimler Motoren-Gesellschaft took over a company previously set up by Daimler at Marienfelde called Motorfahrzeug und Motorenfabrik Berlin AG, and production of Daimler trucks was transferred there until 1914. Early experiments with diesel power were taking place during World War I and in 1923 a diesel-engined truck was exhibited at the Berlin exhibition. From 1924 Daimler began collaborating with Benz Werke and in 1926 the two companies merged to form Daimler-Benz, their products being sold as Mercedes-Benz from then on.

■ ABOVE ***Daimler's 1896 Phoenix was the world's first motor truck.***

■ LEFT ***Korean manufacturer Daewoo offer a comprehensive truck range.***

■ DART

WATERLOO, IOWA, & KANSAS CITY, MISSOURI, USA

From 1958 the Dart Truck Co. was part of Paccar Inc. of Bellevue, Washington, but its history dated back to 1903. The very first Dart was a ½-ton "high-wheeler" with underfloor engine and double chain drive. Between 1903 and 1907 Dart was based at Anderson, Indiana, as the Dart Manufacturing Co. but then the company opened a new factory at Waterloo, Iowa, where it was based until 1924. Early truck designs had 4-cylinder gasoline engines with chain drive but shaft drive was adopted in 1912. Bonneted 2 and 3-tonners were built up until the 1920s. For a brief period in 1924–25 it changed hands and became the Hawkeye-Dart Truck Co. In 1925 the name became Dart Truck Co. again and a factory was set

OTHER MAKES

■ ABOVE ***This bonneted De Dion Bouton with gasogene equipment dates from the late 1920s.***

up in Kansas City. During the 1930s a new range of $1\frac{1}{2}$ to 8-ton trucks appeared while heavy models for 10-ton payloads, plus an articulated version, were added in the late '30s.

At this stage Dart began building heavy off-highway trucks for the mining industry, a type in which it was to specialize later. Post-war models continued to include conventional medium and heavy tractor units but from the early 1950s Dart concentrated on heavy dump trucks. After the Paccar takeover they became KW-Dart until 1970, from which time the "KW" was dropped. Production of heavy dump trucks continued for a time, powered by Caterpillar, Detroit Diesel and Cummins engines. After a series of acquisitions by mining companies, Dart production ceased in the early 1990s.

■ DE DION BOUTON

SEINE, FRANCE

The company frequently referred to as De Dion began in 1884 as De Dion Bouton & Trepardoux. In their early years they built steam vehicles, including what is said to be the world's earliest articulated vehicle in 1894. Count Albert De Dion and Georges Bouton severed their relationship with Bouton's brother-in-law Trepardoux over Bouton's growing interest in gasoline engines. Gasoline-engined trucks appeared in 1906, the heaviest of which was a 5-tonner. In 1910 the distinctive circular radiator made its appearance. After World War I De Dion Bouton went through difficulties that lasted well into the 1930s. In 1930 a 5-ton truck was launched while a larger $6\frac{1}{2}$-tonner, the LY, followed in 1936. Sales were poor and production ceased in 1950.

■ DE-SOTO

DETROIT, MICHIGAN, USA, & ISTANBUL, TURKEY

Initially the De-Soto truck was the result of "badge engineering" on the part of the Chrysler Corporation who chose to use the De-Soto name on Dodge and Fargo trucks in certain export territories up until about 1960. For some years British Dodges were marketed as De-Soto in Australia and New Zealand.

In the 1960s Chrysler Sanayi AS of Kocaeli, Turkey, introduced their range of D series bonneted trucks which were marketed as Dodge and De-Soto and built at Kadikoy, Istanbul.

■ DELAHAYE

TOURS & PARIS, FRANCE

The very old established company of Emile Delahaye dated from 1898 and some early light trucks were built along similar lines to Daimler using rear-mounted 2-cylinder engines with belt drive. By 1904 chain drive had been introduced and a wide truck range was available by 1906. In the 1920s Delahaye were building $\frac{3}{4}$-tonne and 2-tonne bonneted trucks with 4-cylinder engines, shaft drive and pneumatic tyres, although heavier trucks retained solid tyres with chain drive.

Delahaye advanced into true heavy-duty trucks with diesel-engined 7-tonners in 1931. These had 6-speed gearboxes and 10 litre/610cu in 6-cylinder direct-injection engines built under licence from Fiat. By 1939 their 149 model had air brakes and a Gardner diesel engine. After World War II the company's main truck model was the modern, forward-control 163 type but sales were never to match those of the pre-war era. In 1954 Delahaye joined forces with Hotchkiss becoming Société Hotchkiss-Delahaye, but within two years the Delahaye truck operations came to an end.

■ DOUGLAS

CHELTENHAM, ENGLAND

Douglas currently specialises in heavy-duty airport terminal tractors but when the company was established in 1947 it built 4x4 forestry tractors based on the AEC Matador. Although many Matadors entered timber haulage there was a role for the Douglas Transporter with its higher-powered AEC 9.6 litre/590 cu.in. diesel with 125hp.

Other Douglas tractors included the Tugmaster, powered by a Perkins diesel. A 'dock spotter' tractor appeared in 1955. Douglas became part of Dennis Group PLC and continued to supply tractors like the Tugmaster NS8-220 for up to 35 tons. After joining Curtiss-Wright in 2011 Douglas continues to build airport tractors like the the TBL-600 with Cummins 760hp engine for towing the largest aircraft.

■ ABOVE ***Dodge trucks are badged De-Soto in certain countries. This example operated in Belgium during the 1960s.***

■ ABOVE ***A military-specification chain-drive Delahaye 3-tonne truck built in 1913.***

■ ABOVE ***The Douglas transporter had a high AEC content, including their 9.6 litre/ 588cu in diesel engine.***

SANDBACH, ENGLAND

ERF

■ LEFT *ERF's first truck was this CI4 6/7-tonner with Gardner 4LW engine, built in 1933.*

Edwin Richard Foden was the youngest son of Edwin Foden who founded the famous Foden steam-wagon company whose history dated back to 1856. By the early 1930s Fodens were struggling to sell steamers and ER, as he was called, was firmly convinced that the company should build diesels instead. His brother, William, had retired in 1924 and emigrated to Australia. A disagreement over policy led ER to resign and he and his son, Dennis, set up their own company called E R Foden just a short distance from Fodens' factory.

Production began in 1933 with a modern 6/7-ton payload forward-control four-wheeler powered by a Gardner 4LW engine. All the running units were bought in and, unlike Fodens, E R Foden were assemblers. The trucks sold well and very soon the E R Foden badge was altered to ERF. During the six years up to the outbreak of World War II the range expanded to include three and four-axled rigids and two-axled tractor units. They were also the first company to build a twin-steer six-wheeler. ERF was one of the few UK truck manufacturers to be allowed to continue production during the war and some wartime models were fitted with AEC engines when Gardners were in short supply. After the war, in 1948, a completely new range was introduced under the general designation of the V range, masterminded by chief engineer Ernest Sherratt who himself was an ex-Foden man. ERF went from strength to strength, developing an extensive export business.

■ BELOW LEFT *Introduced in 1948, this 22-ton eight-wheeler was part of ERF's V range with Jennings coachbuilt cab.*

Domestic vehicles had Jennings coachbuilt cabs, Jennings being an old established coachbuilder with whom ERF shared their premises at Sandbach. Later, in 1963, ERF absorbed the company as their in-house cab builder. For export, a steel cab was introduced in 1951, produced by the Willenhall Motor Radiator Co. This was also available on the home market but after a couple of years a completely new and strikingly modern cab with panoramic windscreen and oval radiator grille was introduced as the KV cab. A semi-forward-control version, nicknamed the "Sabrina", was added in 1958. The first appearance of the KV in November 1953 added to

■ LEFT *The KV models, first introduced in 1954, were noted for their ultra-modern styling and panoramic vision.*

■ RIGHT *The 34-ton gcw A series tractor units of 1972 had a choice of Cummins 6-cylinder or Gardner 8-cylinder diesels.*

ERF's prestige and the new models featured many improvements, especially in the braking system. ERF also became involved in building specialized export models for heavy-duty operation and options of Cummins and Rolls Royce diesels were offered during the late '50s. South Africa was a particularly strong export market for ERF.

The next major launch was the LV-cabbed range of 1962. It was with this range that ERF became the first UK manufacturer to offer fail-safe spring brakes. With an increasing demand for articulated vehicles in the UK, ERF began offering a complete matched artic during the '60s. Export demand continued to be healthy and an assembly plant was set up in South Africa in 1965 to build vehicles tailored to local requirements.

In the early 1970s Ernest Sherratt retired as director of engineering and his replacement, an ex-Chrysler man, brought in the A series which was based on a new design philosophy more akin to mass production ideas, especially in the design of frame and suspension. Engines included the Cummins NH220 and Gardner 8LXB 240. The A series formed the basis for a 38-ton European tractor with a steel Motor Panels tilt cab which ERF aimed specifically at the European market. Soon after, ERF's first true tilt-cab range, the B series, was announced. This featured the SP (Steel/Plastic) cab produced by a revolutionary new moulding technique.

Continuous improvements have been introduced to the ERF range since the mid 1970s resulting in the C series and later the E series, all using developments of the SP cab structure. The last major launch was in 1993 with the EC range. A top-of-the-range tractor unit appeared as the Olympic. In 1996 ERF, Britain's last independent truck builder, was bought by Western Star of Canada. Certain ERF-based models were then marketed as Western Star, like the Commander range that sold well in Australia and New Zealand. The mechanical content of the Commander series was predominantly American-sourced. ERF also marketed the Turkish-built BMC Professional as the ERF EP and assembled Isuzu trucks.

From August 1999 ERF production was transferred from Sandbach to Middlewich. In February 2000 Western Star sold the company to MAN in Germany. In 2002 ERF production was transferred from the UK to Europe, but ceased altogether in 2007.

■ ABOVE *The B series of 1974 featured a composite steel and plastic tilt cab as on this 1976 eight-wheeler.*

■ RIGHT *ERF, Britain's last truck manufacturer, closed down in 2007 and this ECT was the last ERF to enter service.*

CLEVELAND, OHIO, USA

EUCLID

■ LEFT *Euclid heavy dump trucks are powered by Detroit Diesel or Cummins engines.*

Euclid have always specialized in heavy off-road dump trucks, beginning with the 11-ton payload Trak Truck in 1934. The company was called the Euclid Crane & Hoist Company when it was founded in 1931. It was renamed the Euclid Road Machinery Co. in 1936 and a larger dump truck for 15-ton payloads was introduced. These early machines were the first purpose-built site dump trucks with scow-end bodies. Euclid added a range of specialized plant and vehicles including graders, loaders and crawler tractors. The load capacity of its dump trucks steadily increased. In 1953 the company was taken over by General Motors and remained under their control until 1968 when they were forced to sell it off under the Anti-Trust (Monopolies Commission) Regulations. By that time GM had set up Euclid (Great Britain) Ltd at Newhouse in Scotland where a wide range of Euclids were assembled. GM sold their Cleveland operations to the White Motor Corporation and the UK products were marketed under the Terex name. There were Euclid dump trucks for payloads from 22 to 170 tons. Daimler-Benz AG purchased the business in 1977 and in 1984 it passed to Clark Michigan. A year later Euclid was taken over by Volvo Construction Equipment. Sold again in 1992 to Hitachi, it traded as Euclid-Hitachi until the Euclid name was phased out in 2004.

■ LEFT *This articulated dump truck of the 1960s era is the nearest thing to a conventional truck in the Euclid range.*

OTHER MAKES

■ **EBRO**

BARCELONA, SPAIN

Ebro truck production began at Motor Iberica SA in 1956 with licence-built Ford Thames models. Just as the UK trucks took the name of a major English river, the Thames, so the Spanish-built Fords were called Ebro. Initially Ebros were similar to the Thames ET6 bonneted trucks while there was a semi-forward-control model loosely resembling the Thames Trader but having a locally designed cab. The D-series tilt-cab models formed the basis for a new range in 1968 for payloads up to 7 tonnes. Heavier models were added in 1976 as the P series for up to 27 tonnes gvw. In 1980 Motor Iberica was taken over by Nissan Motor Co who launched a new medium truck, the Atleon.

■ LEFT *In the late 1970s Ebro moved up the weight scale with their P range, using Perkins diesels.*

■ BELOW LEFT *In the 1960s semi-forward-control Ebros bore a vague resemblance to Thames Traders.*

OAKLAND, CALIFORNIA, USA

FAGEOL

Fageol Motors Co. was founded in 1916. An initial plan to build cars and tractors was dropped to concentrate on truck production. Bonneted trucks from $2\frac{1}{2}$ to 6 tons payload capacity were offered. These had 4-cylinder Waukesha gasoline engines and solid tyres. During the 1920s the heaviest model was discontinued and a new range was introduced for $1\frac{1}{2}$ to 5 tons as well as coaches. In 1925 coach manufacture, centred on another plant at Kent, Ohio, was absorbed into the American Car & Foundry Co., while truck production continued at Oakland. Trucks continued to undergo improvements, with the introduction of pneumatic tyres and electric lighting and starting. Heavier models for up to 10 tons with trailer appeared in 1930. Fageol ran into financial problems at this point and were reorganized as the Fageol Truck & Coach Company in 1932. Some impressive heavy-duty 6x4 tractor units were introduced during the 1930s but Fageol's trading position did not improve and the company was sold to Sterling in 1938. Sterling retained Fageol's distribution network but sold the manufacturing facilities on to T. A. Peterman who introduced the Peterbilt.

PRIBOJ, YUGOSLAVIA

FAP

Fabrika Automobila Priboj na Limu built medium-weight Austrian Saurer trucks under licence from 1951. Originally these were of normal-control layout but forward-control models were added to the range. Power units included Perkins and Leyland as well as locally built Famos diesels. From 1972 FAP's licence agreement with Saurer was replaced by an agreement with Daimler-Benz AG and subsequent vehicles, which include heavy-duty FAP-Famos 6x6 and 8x8 trucks, have featured Mercedes cabs.

■ RIGHT *The Yugoslavian-built FAP is based on a Mercedes design. This photograph shows the similarities of the two makes.*

GENNEVILLIERS, FRANCE

FAR

Tracteurs FAR began in 1919 by building Chenard-Walcker-designed road tractors. From 1937 they built the Scammell Mechanical Horse under licence as the Pony Mécanique. These continued in production until 1970.

■ RIGHT *This FAR Pony Mécanique of the French Railways SNCF was derived from Scammell's Mechanical Horse.*

KADIKOY, TURKEY

FARGO

The Fargo name badge was used to market Dodge trucks in certain territories from 1931. It is still used in Turkey.

■ RIGHT *The Fargo name badge is still used on trucks built at Chrysler's factory in Turkey.*

NÜREMBERG, GERMANY

FAUN

■ LEFT *This early 1960s Faun F66/47K was powered by an air-cooled Deutz diesel and grossed around 16 tons.*

Faun's history begins in 1918 with the merger of Fahrzeugfabrik Ansbach and Nürnberg Feuerloschgerate Automobillastwagen und Fahrzeugfabrik Karl Schmidt. The combined company was called Fahrzeugfabriken Ansbach und Nürnberg until the name was shortened to Faun-Werke AG in 1920, the trucks carrying the name Faun. Much of the production during the 1920s consisted of municipal vehicles, but a new range of trucks from 2 to 6-tonne payload appeared in the early '30s. There was also a heavy-duty 9-tonner powered by a Deutz diesel engine. 1934 marked the introduction of a six-wheeler and four years later a forward-control twin-steer four-axled rigid was introduced for a 15-tonne payload.

After World War II Faun offered a comprehensive range of trucks, both normal and forward-control. The normal-control models presented a very impressive appearance and covered the heaviest weight categories for articulated and drawbar operation. From 1969 Faun ceased production of normal on-highway trucks to concentrate on special vehicles, including crane chassis, airport crash tenders and heavy-haulage tractors which are still in production. Many feature 8×8 drive and high-powered diesels of between 700 and 800bhp. For a brief period during the mid 1970s a joint marketing agreement was established with Fodens Ltd in the UK to market dump trucks as Foden-Faun.

■ BELOW LEFT *This 1978 Faun HZ40.45/45 has a Daimler-Benz OM404 V12 diesel and was built for the Czech government.*

■ BOTTOM LEFT *A 1988 Faun 8×8 300-ton heavy-haulage tractor powered by a 19 litre/1158cu in 456bhp diesel with Allison automatic transmission.*

CHANGCHUN, JILLIN, CHINA

FAW

FAW (First Automobile Works) is a vast organization with links to many Far East and European manufacturers. The truck division is FAW Jiefang in Changchun, Jillin. When first established in 1953 it was heavily supported by Kruschev's Soviet Union. The Changchun factory was completed in 1956 and early trucks, based on the Russian Zis 150, began production in July 1956. The company grew into China's largest truck manufacturer and now has exports to over 70 countries and assembly plants in Pakistan, South Africa, Tanzania, Ukraine and Vietnam. Currently the trucks range from 1 to 50 tons payload, powered by Chinese engines from the Wuxi engine plant in Jiangsu Province. Power outputs are 260 to 460hp.

The J5P range of 2004 became the choice of leading long-haul fleets. In 2006 a new ultra-modern plant was completed in Changchun. The current J6P range of 2007 includes tractors up to 460hp plus 6x4 and 8x4 rigids. In 2017 sales topped 300,000. FAW is also developing self-driving trucks. Since 2014 the FAW Tiger 7.5-tonner has been marketed in the UK.

■ BELOW *FAW is a massive concern with extensive export business. This J6P tractor unit represents its 2018 range.*

WETZIKON, SWITZERLAND

FBW

■ LEFT *A forward-control 16-ton gross FBW four-wheeler with single-axle "pup" trailer.*

The founder of Franz Brozincevic et Cie Motorwagenfabrik Wetzikon AG was a Croatian engineer, Franz Brozincevic, who in 1909 designed a chain-drive truck for the Swiss Post Office powered by his own design of gasoline engine. Called the Franz, the truck was further developed into a range of shaft-drive machines for up to 5 tonnes payload. In 1914 the Franz operations were absorbed into Motorwagenfabrik Berna AG, Franz Brozincevic becoming Berna's general manager. After differences with Berna's management he resigned and established his own company, FBW, at the former premises of Schweizer Motorwagenfabrik. In 1922 FBW built their first 4-cylinder gasoline engine and introduced a double-reduction rear axle. Two years later a licence was granted to Henschel & Sohn to build FBW vehicles in Kassel, Germany.

During the 1920s FBW introduced a very advanced design for 5-tonne payloads. They were powerful trucks featuring small turning circles, pneumatic tyres and four-wheel braking, suiting them to mountain roads. FBW gained an excellent reputation for engineering. By the late '20s they had built their first heavy-duty chain-drive six-wheeler. FBW engines were fitted with a patented exhaust brake.

The first FBW diesel engine was announced in 1934, an 8.5 litre/518cu in 6-cylinder unit producing 100bhp. Wartime production concentrated on military vehicles for the Swiss army. The post-war years brought increased demand for heavy trucks in the construction industry. From the late 1940s a range of trucks was available, including forward-control models for 7-tonne payloads. A powerful new 11 litre/671cu in 6-cylinder horizontal engine with 145bhp was introduced in 1949. The range of trucks expanded during the '50s and '60s extending up to maximum legal weight. In 1968 lighter models were added to gain wider market coverage.

The 1970s saw impressive new models with turbocharged diesels in both vertical and horizontal forms. A very handsome tilt cab appeared on the forward-control models. In the late '70s there were 18 basic models in the FBW heavy-duty range. The 70N 4×2 and 80N 6×4 were bonneted types also marketed as the all-wheel drive 70X and 80X. Seven forward-control tilt-cab models included a 17-tonne gvw 4×2 (50V type), 21-tonne 6×2 (75V), 26-tonne 6×4 (80V) and, perhaps FBW's most impressive machine, the 28-tonne 85V 8×4 which appeared following increases in the Swiss weight limits during the '70s. In addition there were seven underfloor-engined models designated the U range in 4×2, 6×2 and 6×4 form. These were especially suited to municipal operations as well as general haulage. The lightest was the 13-tonne gvw 40U while the heaviest was the 6×4 80U at 26 tonnes gvw. To cover the lighter end of the range FBW marketed the Mitsubishi Canter 2-tonner and the heavier Fuso 6½-tonner as MMC-FBW.

In a declining market Switzerland's two truck makers, Saurer and FBW, joined forces in 1982 to form NAW (Nutzfahrzeuggesellschaft Arbon & Wetzikon) and were absorbed into Daimler-Benz.

■ LEFT *FBW built a wide variety of heavy-duty trucks, including bonneted tractors.*

■ RIGHT *Many FBWs were powered by the maker's own 5 and 6-cylinder underfloor diesel engines.*

TURIN, ITALY

FIAT

■ LEFT ***Fiat's 18BL was typical of their products from the World War I era.***

Though Fiat's origins as a car manufacturer date from 1899, the company did not build trucks until 1903. Beginning as F.I.A.T. (Fabbrica Italiana d'Automobili, Torino) the company became Fiat SpA from 1918. The original 4-tonne payload truck was a well thought-out design with cab-over-engine layout and a 4m/13ft load deck. It was powered by a 6.4 litre/390cu in 4-cylinder engine rated at 24hp. A shaft took the drive to a mid-mounted gearbox from which the drive to the rear wheels was by chains. A larger machine for a 5-tonne payload, powered by a 7.4 litre/451cu in 40hp engine came in 1906. The following year a normal-control layout was adopted.

In 1911 Fiat supplied motor trucks to the Italian forces engaged in the Italo-Turkish conflict in Libya. These were based on the Tipo 15 Bis and a more powerful version, the 15 Ter. They were believed to be the first motor vehicles used in war. Just before World War I the larger 18 series truck had entered production and this became one of the company's most important models during that era. There was also a larger 20B model and a type 30 heavy-duty tractor capable of towing up to 100 tonnes. Huge numbers of trucks were supplied to the Allied Forces during 1914–18.

In 1925 a new range of 2 to 2½-tonne trucks had pneumatic tyres. Light trucks based on these were built under licence by AMO in Moscow as well as by Mitsubishi in Japan, effectively founding those countries' truck industries. The same year, Fiat took over SPA Commercial Vehicles. Fiat concentrated on lighter trucks in the late '20s while heavier bonneted models up to 5 tonnes were built by SPA. In 1929 the Consortium Fiat Veicoli Industriale was formed, concentrating the marketing and production of Fiat, SPA and (from 1931) Ceirano vehicles at Fiat.

The first diesel engine appeared in 1930 and was installed in an 8-tonne Ceirano chassis. In 1931 the diesel-engined normal-control Fiat 632 4-tonner and 634N 6-tonner were introduced. The engines were 5.5 litre/335cu in 4-cylinder and 8.4 litre/512cu in 6-cylinder units. In 1938 Fiat acquired the share capital of OM (Officine Meccaniche) of Brescia but OM was allowed relative autonomy until finally absorbed into Fiat in 1970. Attractive, streamlined forward-control trucks for payloads of 3½ to 6½ tonnes were announced in 1939. These were the 625, 665 and 666 for gross train

■ ABOVE ***This Fiat 690N2 with Viberti fourth-axle conversion seen in Naples represents a typical Italian outfit of the 1970s era.***

■ LEFT ***A Fiat 6×2 with self-steering rear axle and a large-capacity integral van body.***

■ RIGHT *The 1939 Fiat 626N was powered by a 5.7 litre/348cu in diesel and could tow a 6-tonne trailer.*

■ BELOW RIGHT *This amusement-contractor's truck, a 626N, was still in service after more than 35 years.*

weights of 12 tonnes. The 666 was the heaviest, powered by a 9.4 litre/573cu in 6-cylinder diesel. They featured an easily removable engine which could be withdrawn from the front. A six-wheeler Fiat-SPA version, derived from the 666, in single and double-drive form, was developed as the A10,000 during World War II but finally went into production in 1945. It was designed for a 10-tonne payload.

Forward-control layout was now standard on Fiat heavies, as was right-hand drive which was considered safer when negotiating narrow mountain roads. In 1949 an improved range was launched, developed from the pre-war models. A completely new truck cab was introduced in 1952 and was to last right through to the late 1960s, gracing such models as the 642N and 643N four-wheelers, the 682T tractors, the 690N twin-steer six-wheelers, the 690T twin-steer tractor, the 693N six-wheeler and 683N and 683T rigids and tractors. Fiat France came into existence in 1966 with the acquisition of Unic and Turin-based Lancia Veicoli Speciali SpA was taken over in 1969.

A new generation of models appeared in 1970. Typical of these was the 4×2 619N rigid and 619T tractor unit, the 697N and T six-wheelers and the twin-steer 691N and T of 1971. Many of these twin-steer trucks were converted to 8×2 form by the addition of a fourth axle. All the new models were fitted with a new-style cab with wide grille and bumper-mounted headlights. Tilt-cab versions began appearing in the mid 1970s. In 1974 Fiat Veicoli Industriali SpA signed a joint agreement with the German manufacturing group Klockner Humboldt Deutz AG to form the Industrial Vehicle Corporation IVECO, which came into being on January 1st 1975. The Fiat name continued to appear on trucks until 1982 when the Iveco brand name was adopted for the group products.

■ BELOW *A maximum-weight five-axled articulated outfit used on international haulage by the large Polish company, Pekaes of Warsaw.*

SANDBACH, ENGLAND

FODEN

■ LEFT *The 1937 Foden DG4/7½ was powered by a Gardner 4LW diesel engine. DGs were built between 1936 and 1948.*

■ BELOW LEFT *Foden reluctantly gave up steamer production in 1934. This Speed Six was the last type built.*

The origins of the old established Foden company can be traced back to 1856 and the founding of an engineering business called Hancock & Foden which built agricultural machinery and steam engines. Its co-founder Edwin Foden went on to build steam traction engines and, in 1901, a successful steam lorry. Edwin's two sons William and Edwin Richard joined the company, and steam wagon production continued throughout the 1920s with such famous machines as the C type 5/6-tonner. By the late '20s steam wagon sales were losing out to internal combustion-engined trucks but Fodens Ltd (the company's title from 1902) still persevered with steamers. Edwin, the founder, had died in 1911 and his eldest son William had emigrated to Australia in 1924 leaving only Edwin Richard (ER) on the Board. ER foresaw the inevitable demise of steam and advocated a switch to diesel power, but he failed to convince other members of the Board. As a result ER left in 1932 and set up his own company, ERF, in partnership with his son Dennis.

ER's early experiments with diesels, beginning with a Gardner-engined 6-tonner in 1931, eventually formed the basis, albeit after he had departed, of a new range of Foden diesels that were phased in during 1934. Meanwhile steam-wagon production was discontinued, the last steamers being the highly advanced Speed Six and Speed Twelve under-types. The early '30s were difficult times for Fodens and the company came close to collapse. William Foden was persuaded to return to the company in 1935 and his presence raised the morale and fortunes of the firm. A new range of diesel trucks, the DG was launched in 1936, setting Fodens on a successful course to recovery. The Gardner-powered DGs were offered in 4×2, 6×2, twin-steer 6×2, 6×4, 8×2 and 8×4 form, plus tractor units for articulated use. Military versions of the 4×2 and 6×4 DGs were developed during World War II and DG production was resumed after the war.

Fodens' first new post-war model was the FG of 1948, featuring the stylish S.18 cab. Another development that had been underway during the 1940s was a two-stroke diesel engine. This was fitted in an eight-wheeled vehicle announced in 1948. The 4.09 litre/ 249cu in 6-cylinder two-stroke developed 126bhp at 2000rpm and

■ BOTTOM LEFT *This 1967 S21 represents Foden's leading type in the 1960s era.*

■ BOTTOM RIGHT *A 1971 S39 artic with 150 Gardner and 12-speed box.*

■ RIGHT *A 1979 30-ton gvw Foden eight-wheeled bulk cement tanker featuring the S83 cab.*

weighed only 500kg/1100lbs. A 4-cylinder version of 2.7 litre/164cu in capacity appeared in the FE.4/8 cab-ahead-of-engine four-wheeler in 1952. This truck, with its ultra-modern styling, was only built for three years. Meanwhile Fodens had entered the heavy-duty dump truck market, a field in which they were to become leading manufacturers.

Fodens' on-highway range continued to be updated throughout the 1950s and '60s. Twelve-speed range-change gearboxes became common fitment, especially on trucks with two-stroke engines. Gardner engines remained optional on all models. Fodens frequently introduced new cab designs, fibreglass becoming widely used from 1958 when their distinctive S.21 cab appeared. In 1962 came their S.24 cab, the first production tilt cab in the UK. Fodens was particularly successful in the field of rigid eight-wheelers. New UK weight limits introduced in 1964 led to a decline in eight-wheeler demand and most manufacturers were obliged to switch to building tractor units. One interesting machine offered by Fodens was the Twin-load – a dromedary-style load-carrying eight-wheeled tractor unit coupled to a single-axle semi. Unfortunately UK length limits made it impractical and only a handful of twin-loads were built.

Fodens Ltd was enjoying a substantial share of the truck market both at home and abroad during the 1960s but their fortunes took a down turn in the '70s. A substantial order for military vehicles helped them regain a footing in the mid '70s but more financial difficulties returned at the end of the decade. Meanwhile they had launched a heavy-duty range aimed at the European market but a combination of heavy investment and insufficient sales led the company into receivership in 1979.

Fodens Ltd was taken over by the Paccar Company in 1980 and renamed the Sandbach Engineering Company. Truck production restarted in a small way in 1981 with a much reduced workforce and a simplified range. Paccar, who also owned Peterbilt and Kenworth in the United States, introduced sweeping changes and a new breed of Foden emerged, benefiting from Paccar technology and production techniques. Most of the specialized vehicles were dropped and in-house component manufacture was discontinued. Production was concentrated on a rationalized range. Eight-wheelers, Fodens' traditional speciality, continued to be offered and a strong presence was maintained in that market.

The name Foden was reinstated into the company title, which became Foden Trucks in 1983. Military vehicles continued to form an important part of Foden's production. The civilian range was divided into the medium-weight 2000 series, the heavyweight 3000 series and the 4000 heavyweights. A wide variety of power units, including Caterpillar which in 1984 Paccar were the first to offer in the UK, and a wide choice of drive-lines and rear suspensions became available.

In 1996 Foden launched a top-of-the-range tractor unit, the high-roof 4000XL. In 1998 Foden moved away from fibreglass cabs with the new Alpha 3000, which featured a steel cab similar to that of the DAF 85 series, DAF having joined Paccar in 1996. The Sandbach factory was closed in 1999 and the company's production transferred to the Leyland plant near Preston. A face-lifted range, which was dubbed the "Next Generation", appeared in 2001 but dwindling demand led Paccar to end Foden production in 2006, bringing to a close 150 years of history.

■ RIGHT *Foden's last range was the "Next Generation" Alpha featuring an adaptation of DAF's CF steel cab.*

DAGENHAM, ENGLAND

FORD & FORD THAMES

■ BELOW *The Thames Trader was built from 1957–65. This is the Mk.II introduced in 1962.*

Ford's UK truck manufacturing operation went under the name Fordson from 1933–39, Fordson Thames from 1939–57 and Ford Thames from 1957–65. Prior to 1929, assembly of American Ford TT light trucks had taken place at the Trafford Park plant in Manchester which opened in 1911. In 1931 production was transferred to a new factory on the banks of the River Thames at Dagenham. The Thames name was adopted to give the trucks a distinct British identity. Fordson and Fordson Thames models are dealt with in their own sections.

The first significant Ford Thames model was the semi-forward-control Trader of 1957. It took Ford into a higher weight category, the heaviest model being a 7-tonner. This was also available as a tractor unit for 13.4 tons. There were six basic models for 1½, 2, 3, 4, 5 and 7-ton payloads. Those up to 3 tons had a choice of 4-cylinder gasoline or 4-cylinder diesel engine. Above that weight, 6-cylinder diesel and gasoline engines were also offered, while 6-cylinder engines were standard on the 7-tonners. An improved Trader Mk.II was introduced in 1962 for payloads up to 7½ tons and included a 17-ton gross tractor unit. At the same time a normal-control Trader featuring the German-style Koln cab became available. After the Thames name was dropped in 1965 this truck became the Ford K series.

■ LEFT *Ford's tilt-cab D series was launched in 1965 and became a market leader.*

■ BELOW LEFT *In 1975 Ford entered the heavy-duty market with their Transcontinental H series, built in Amsterdam.*

The dropping of the Thames name coincided with the introduction of the all-new tilt-cab D series in 1965. Henceforth UK-built trucks were marketed simply as Ford. The new D series was a highly successful range. Initially it covered the payload range from 2 to 8 tons while the heaviest D800 artic grossed 19 tons. A 16-ton gvw

■ LEFT *Ford built on the success of the D series with an even better range – the Cargo, launched in 1981.*

model, the D1000, was added in 1967. This was powered by a Cummins Vale V8 diesel. An artic version grossed 28 tons. The medium-weight D series took slant-six diesels developed from Ford's earlier 6D engines while the lighter models took a slant-four. For the first couple of years Ford also offered 4 and 6-cylinder Canadian-built gasoline engines mainly for the export market.

In addition to their 4×2 models Ford offered 6×2 and 6×4 versions for gross weights of 16 to 24 tons. A luxury Custom cab option was available on light and medium models while it was made standard on the heavy-duty models. Within a year of the launch of the D1000, Ford began offering their own V8 (actually the Perkins V8.510 built under licence) as an alternative to the Cummins Vale. Having achieved a leading position in the medium-truck market, Ford set their sights on entering the maximum-weight sector and designed a completely new range of heavies for up to 44 tons gcw, powered by Cummins 14 litre/854cu in diesels. However, though designed in the UK, the trucks were produced at Ford's Amsterdam plant in both left and right-hand drive. Dubbed the "Transcontinental", the big Ford featured an adaptation of Berliet's Premier cab. Assembly of the Transcontinental was transferred to the Sandbach Engineering Co. in 1981 when Paccar had spare capacity, but production finished altogether in 1982.

Ford's next major launch was that of the Ford Cargo range in 1981. This proved to be a market leader, putting Ford ahead of its traditional rival, Bedford. The new Cargo featured modern, up-to-the-minute styling and a high degree of driver comfort. With the demise of the Transcontinental, Ford introduced a range of heavyweight Cargo tractor units ranging from 28 to 38 tonnes gcw. The 38-tonners were powered by the Cummins L10 while those at 28 and 32 tonnes had Perkins, Cummins or air-cooled Deutz diesels.

In 1986 Ford sold its UK truck operations to the Italian Iveco group and subsequent vehicles were badged Iveco Ford. After making heavy losses, the Langley plant closed in October 1997, bringing UK Ford truck production to an end.

■ LEFT *The Transcontinental featured an adaptation of Berliet's Premier cab and Cummins 14 litre/854cu in diesel engine.*

■ BELOW *After production of the Transcontinental ended in 1982, Ford introduced heavier Cargo tractor units.*

DEARBORN, MICHIGAN, & LOUISVILLE, KENTUCKY, USA

FORD

While Ford built light commercials from their early days, they were generally car-derived. The TT launched in 1917 was a lengthened, heavier-duty version of the old Tin Lizzie for payloads of 1 ton. A succession of light trucks in the 1 to 2-ton payload class was built in the 1920s and '30s. In 1927 the famous Model T and TT – of which some 15 million were produced – ended. The more modern AA 1½-ton truck appeared in 1928. At first the AA had worm drive but in 1929 a spiral-bevel axle was made standard, as were offset steel disc wheels with dual rears on the heaviest model. The AA formed the prototype for the first Russian-built GAZ trucks (Gorkovoka Automobilova Zavod) in 1931.

The AA was joined by the BB in 1932, the first Ford commercial to feature the legendary V8 gasoline engine. Facelifted cabs offered in 1933/34 had raked radiator grilles resembling Ford cars. Semi-forward-control versions appeared later in the 1930s. Many thousands of military vehicles and armoured cars were produced for the war effort. It wasn't until the late '30s that Ford began to move up the weight range with their truck models. Restyled F6, F7 and F8 models for up to 3-ton payloads came in 1948, with a 6×4 version of the heaviest F8 model. Overhead-valve engines were introduced in 1952, replacing the old side-valve units which were phased out in 1954.

It was at this time that heavy-duty Fords began to appear for gross weights up to 24 tons. In 1957 the old fixed-cab forward-control models were replaced by the all-new tilt-cab C range and some diesel options became available. By 1960 big Ford commercials were in full production, the tandem drive T.950 Super Duty being the largest of these. The Super Duty V8 gasoline engine produced 270bhp. Other features included full air brakes, Fuller Roadranger transmission and power steering. The largest tilt-cab model, the C.800, was designed in articulated form and had the 205bhp HD V8. Fully automatic transmission was also available.

In 1962 the H series heavy-duty cabovers became available featuring a raised version of the C series tilt cab. This was Ford's first true line-haul

■ LEFT *Ford's legendary TT 1-tonner of the 1917–27 period was built at Trafford Park in the UK as well as in Dearborn.*

■ LEFT *The W series cabovers of 1970 were face-lifted with a new grille in 1975.*

■ BELOW LEFT *A seven-axled drawbar outfit in New Zealand being hauled by an LTL-9000 6×4 conventional.*

■ LEFT *An L-9000 concrete mixer based in Vancouver, British Columbia.*

■ BELOW LEFT *A 1960 C.750 milk tanker powered by a 302-HD V8 gasoline engine with the option of 5-speed synchromesh or Transmatic auto.*

truck. The H-1000 took Ford's Super Duty 8.5 litre/534cu in V8 gasoline engine developing 266bhp while the HD-1000 featured the Cummins in-line-six NH.220 at 220bhp. Drive-line choice included Fuller or Spicer gearbox, Eaton or Timken rear axles and Hendrickson rear suspension. In 1964 Caterpillar and Cummins V6 and V8 diesels were also offered.

In 1965 production of heavy trucks was transferred to a new plant at Louisville, Kentucky. The normal-control T range continued until 1972 but the new L line Louisville range was

launched to replace it in 1970. A new heavy-duty tilt-cab model, the W series, also made its debut in 1970. This was a completely new heavy tractor with a 132cm/52in BBC cab of very square appearance. An 208cm/82in BBC sleeper version was also offered. By then there was a choice of four different Cummins diesels covering 13 power ratings, two Detroit diesels covering five power ratings and Caterpillar diesels at 250 or 270bhp.

The Louisville or L line became one of Ford's best-known truck ranges and survived through to the 1990s. The W series was facelifted in 1975 with a grille resembling that of the Louisville. The old C series was also to survive into the early 1980s. In the late '70s the W series was replaced by the impressive new aluminium-cabbed CL-9000. A bonneted derivative of this model, the LTL-9000 for maximum-weight line-haul operation, was launched in 1981. While Ford's dominance of the light and medium market continued, it was losing sales in the highly competitive Class 8 heavy-duty sector. The superbly equipped Aeromax 120 conventional of 1991 was aimed to challenge the best that Kenworth and Freightliner could offer, but Ford's disappointing Class 8 sales led them to sell their heavy truck operations to the Freightliner Corporation in 1997. The products were subsequently renamed Sterling. Freightliner is a subsidiary of the Daimler AG.

GOLCUK AND ESKISEHIR, TURKEY

FORD

Truck production has been taking place at Ford's factory in Inonu, Eskisehir since 1983 but before then, going back to the early '60s, local assembly was being carried out on British based Thames Traders and, later, tilt-cab D-series and Transit vans.

Ford Otomotiv Sanayi AS is now a significant manufacturer jointly owned by The Ford Motor Co and former Ford dealers Turkish Koc Holdings whose history dates back to 1928.

Following the introduction of the Cargo in 1981 production was stepped up. In 1984 a large new factory was established at Inonu. In 1997 the company became Ford Otosan and Turkish engineers developed a completely new heavy-duty Cargo range launched in 2003.

In 2013 it unveiled the striking new face-lifted Cargo heavies, jointly developed with Ford Brazil. These include tractor units up to 56 tonnes gross and construction vehicles up to 39 tonnes gross. Power comes from Ford Otosan's own 6-cyl, Euro 6 'Ecotorq' diesels of 7.3 litre/438cu.in. and 12.7 litre/762 cu.in. with power outputs up to 460 bhp.

■ BELOW *Ford Otosan's current heavy-duty Cargos, like this 1846 tractor unit, are entirely engineered and built in Turkey.*

BARCELONA, SPAIN

FORD

Between 1920 and 1954 a range of Ford light trucks, based on American and British models, was built at Ford Motor Iberica, production being curtailed during the Civil War years from 1936–40. In 1956 a new range developed from British designs was launched under the Ebro name. The name was taken from the Ebro River, just as Thames was adopted for Ford's UK trucks.

COLOGNE, GERMANY

FORD

■ ABOVE ***German Ford FK4500 4½-tonners were powered by V6 two-stroke diesel engines of 120bhp.***

German-built Ford trucks appeared in 1935 with the BB 2-tonner. In 1936 a 3-tonner with the 3.6 litre/219cu in V8 gasoline engine was introduced. After World War II production of the 3-tonner continued and in the late 1940s it became known as the Ford Rhine. A 4-cylinder version was also available called the Ford Ruhr. From 1951 German Ford trucks were designated the FK series (standing for Ford-Köln). In 1956 a restyled range for payloads of 1.5 to 4.8 tonnes was announced, powered by V4 and V6 two-stroke diesel engines. The cab was also used on the normal-control Thames Trader and the later K series built in the UK. Truck production at Cologne ceased in 1971, the last models being based on the UK D series.

DAGENHAM, ENGLAND

FORDSON & FORDSON THAMES

British-built Ford trucks were re-named 'Fordson' in 1933, the first being the forward-control 'BBE' 2-tonner of 1934. Unlike its 'BB' predecessor, the BBE had longitudinal front springs instead of Ford's old transverse arrangement. The power unit was Ford's 3.6 litre/219 cu.in. V8 gasoline engine producing 85bhp. As well as 4x2s there were the 6x2 and 6x4 'Surrey' and 'Sussex' 6-tonners, converted by County Commercial Cars Ltd. A normal-control V8-engined 2-tonner, the 'Model 51', was announced in 1935. Another type produced from 1935 to 1937 was the unusual 'Tug' 3-ton light artic featuring a 3-wheeled tractor based on the 'Y' type 8hp car. There was also a 4-ton version with 10hp engine.

The forward-control range was enlarged in 1938 with a new 4/5-tonner. It was in 1939 that the trucks began to be marketed as 'Fordson Thames', Thames emphasising their British

■ ABOVE ***A Fordson Model 51 3-ton dump truck with 85bhp V8 gasoline engine and torque tube drive.***

■ LEFT ***The Fordson Thames 7V with V8 gasoline engine appeared in 1939 and production carried on until 1949.***

■ RIGHT *The Fordson Thames ET (English Truck) models of 1949 had a Briggs cab.*

■ BELOW RIGHT *Foton Auman has strong links with Daimler AG and is among China's leading truck manufacturers. This ETX model is seen near Beijing.*

identity. During WW2 Ford built large numbers of V8-powered military vehicles including 1.5-ton 4x2s, 1.5 and 3-ton 4x4s and 3-ton 6x4s. Civilian production resumed in 1945 with forward-control 7V trucks for 2- to 5-ton payloads. There were ten models including a tractor version for an 8-ton payload.

Unlike rivals Bedford, who only offered bonneted trucks, Ford only had the relatively cramped forward-control 7V. This led Ford to choose normal-control for its new Briggs cabbed 'ET6' and 'ET7' of 1949. The ET6 took the V8 gasoline engine while the ET7 had a Perkins P6 diesel. The new models covered a similar payload range to the 7Vs and still included the 'Surrey' and 'Sussex' 6x2 and 6x4 conversions by County. In 1953 Ford introduced its economical 3.6 litre/219 cu.in. 'Cost Cutter' 4-cylinder OHV gasoline engine. This formed the basis for Ford's first diesel, the 3.61 litre/220 cu.in. '4D' in 1954. With the arrival of the Thames Trader in 1957 'Fordson' Thames became 'Ford' Thames.

CHANGPING, BEIJING, CHINA

FOTON AUMAN

Founded in August 1966 the Beiqi Foton Motor Co builds trucks spanning 7.5 to 56 tons gross including tractors and 4x2, 6x2, 6x4 and 8x4 rigids, powered by diesels from the Foton-Cummins factory since 2006 or Weichai diesels built in Weifang, Shandong Province. Power outputs are up to 460hp.

Modern, stylish cabs are designed and built in-house to European standards. Heavy-duty trucks are the ETX and GTL, the latter being the premium range. Since 2009 Foton entered a 50/50 joint venture with Daimler AG to form the Foton Daimler Automotive Co. Foton have a European marketing operation in Moscow and a sales office in India. There are plans for assembly plants in India and Latin America.

DETROIT, MICHIGAN, USA

FREEMAN

Freeman trucks were of an unusual four-wheel drive design in which the front wheels were driven via a "live" axle positioned above a fixed axle, a system of bevel gearing eliminating the need for a differential. The trucks were in production from 1928–34 and there were three weight ratings. Power came from Buda 6-cylinder gasoline engines rated at 65, 75 and 100bhp. The heaviest model was capable of hauling two drawbar trailers, enabling a total payload of 20 tons to be carried. Initially trading as Freeman Motor Co., it later became the Freeman Quadrive Corporation.

■ ABOVE *The early 1930s Freeman 4×4 truck could haul two drawbar trailers and was powered by a Buda 6-cylinder gasoline engine.*

PORTLAND, OREGON, USA

FREIGHTLINER

■ BELOW *The Freightliner 6×4 conventional grosses up to 40 tons and features an aluminium cab to reduce tare weight.*

Freightliner is an example of an enterprising haulier building a truck to meet his own exacting standards and later successfully launching it on to the market. Leland James, president of Consolidated Freightways Inc. of Spokane, Washington, wanted something better than the existing truck manufacturers could offer in the late 1930s. In 1939 he set up a subsidiary under the name Freightways Manufacturing Corp. at Salt Lake City, Utah, to build a truck to suit CF's own needs. The aim was to build the lightest possible tractor unit through the use of light alloys. The product of Freightways' endeavours was the CF-100 diesel-engined cabover built in 1940. The Freightliner nameplate appeared in 1942.

CF were the only users of the early tractors, which were produced up to 1942 when war-time restrictions on materials forced a temporary shutdown. After the war, production was resumed at Consolidated Freightways' maintenance workshops in Portland, Oregon, and a new company, the Freightliner Corporation, was formed. The trucks were highly successful and by careful design and extensive use of aluminium, they could carry 1 ton more than most other trucks of similar size. In 1948 it was decided to market the Freightliner, and one of the first private carriers to purchase one was the Hyster Company. That truck, an 800 model, eventually clocked a total of four million miles and on retirement it was restored and presented to the Smithsonian Museum of History and Technology.

A sleeper cab was offered from 1949 and in 1951 Freightliner joined the White Motor Company of Cleveland, Ohio, in a joint marketing agreement whereby White became responsible for sales, service and distribution of Freightliners. The trucks were then badged White Freightliner. Many

■ BELOW LEFT *This dual-steer four-axled rigid can gross 60 tons with a trailer.*

■ BELOW RIGHT *An aluminium-cabbed 6×4 cabover with Cummins 14 litre/854cu in diesel.*

■ LEFT *An A train doubles outfit hauled by a Freightliner FLB-COE. Available power units include a 410bhp Cummins Celect diesel engine.*

■ RIGHT *Business Class Freightliners include the FL80 in various axle configuration.*

■ BELOW RIGHT *Freightliner's original cabover range was launched in 1942.*

■ BOTTOM RIGHT *This 2018 Freightliner Cascadia Evolution has sleek lines.*

refinements were introduced in the 1950s, with a newly designed cab appearing in 1953. That basic design continued with relatively little change for about three decades. A tilt version appeared in 1958 which could tilt to 90 degrees for complete maintenance access. The all-aluminium cab was designed as a strong riveted structure and featured a V-shaped windscreen with flat glass.

In 1974 Freightliner began offering a long-nosed conventional with a high degree of interchangeable parts with their cabovers. Once again these were among the lightest conventionals around. Freightliners use mainly Cummins diesels. By the late '70s the company had become one of America's major heavy-duty truck producers and had opened plants in Fremont, Chino, Indianapolis, and a Canadian plant in Vancouver. White trucks were forced to pull out of the joint marketing arrangement in 1977, and from that point on the trucks reverted to Freightliner. Daimler-Benz (now Daimler AG) had established a North American presence as long ago as 1964 and in 1981 it took over the Freightliner Corporation. As part of the world's largest producer of heavy trucks, Freightliner went from strength to strength and since 1991 has made significant in-roads into export markets. In 1992 Freightliner became the United States' number one Class 8 truck producer.

In 1995 the company entered the lighter Class 4, 5, 6 and 7 truck markets with the formation of their Custom Chassis Corporation. Freightliner also purchased American La France, the world's oldest manufacturer of fire appliances.

Some European influence showed in cab-over models with set-back front axles and aerodynamic styling. The Century class truck was unveiled in 1995, incorporating many technological advancements and improvements.
In 1997 Freightliner took over Ford's heavy truck operations and renamed them Sterling. Flagship of the current Freightliner range is the aerodynamically styled Cascadia Evolution, powered by a Detroit engine up to 505hp.

OTHER MAKES

■ FEDERAL

DETROIT, MICHIGAN, & MINNEAPOLIS, MINNESOTA, USA

After originally being set up as the Bailey Motor Truck Co. in 1910, the company name was changed that same year to the Federal Motor Truck Co. The first Federal was a bonneted chain-drive 1-tonner with a 4-cylinder Continental gasoline engine. Shaft drive was introduced in 1916, by which time a range of trucks from $1\frac{1}{2}$ to 3 tons was available. A 5-ton model appeared in 1917 followed by a 7-tonner in 1918. The lighter models had pneumatic tyres from 1921. By the mid '20s Federal was one of America's major truck producers. As early as 1929 a sleeper cab was being offered on the larger tractor units and pneumatic tyres and front-wheel brakes had become the norm. Bold cab styling was adopted in the late '30s and cabover trucks were added to the range from 1937. By 1939 Federal had produced over 100,000 trucks.

During World War II Federal built heavy-duty 6×6 wreckers with 180bhp Hercules gasoline engines plus a 20-ton 6×4 tractor powered by a Cummins two-stroke diesel of 130bhp. The distinctive Styliner range appeared in 1951, powered by Federal's own 145bhp Power Chief gasoline engine. In 1952 the company became the Federal Fawick Corporation but was taken over by Napco Industries in 1955, production being relocated at Minneapolis. For the last few years the company built specialized heavy vehicles in ever-diminishing numbers, and production ceased altogether in 1959.

■ LEFT ***A $1\frac{1}{2}$-ton payload Federal E6 type dating from 1931.***

■ LEFT ***This 6×4 Federal 2902 Styliner with dump body was built in 1954 and worked all its life in Australia.***

■ FLEXTRUC

ONTARIO, CANADA

Specialized 8×6 and 10×6 construction vehicles in articulating four-axle form are the main product of this company which took over the manufacturing rights of the Rubber Railway Company in 1979. The trucks are steered hydraulically by having a pivoted chassis. They have gross weights of 40 tons plus.

■ FOWLER

LEEDS, ENGLAND

Most of Fowler's products are outside the scope of this book since the company was mainly concerned with steam traction engines. Founded in 1880 as John Fowler & Co., they began building under-type steam lorries in 1924 using a vertical V-twin compound engine of 3hp. These never achieved the same success as vehicles from Sentinel or Foden. In 1931, when it was becoming clear that steam was losing out to the internal combustion engine, Fowler bid for a share of the diesel truck market by introducing their semi-forward-control Marathon 6 to 7-tonner. This had a 12.2 litre/745cu in direct-injection Fowler diesel developing 90bhp at 1400rpm. A three-axled version was also offered, plus a short-wheelbase dump-truck chassis called the Crusader. The trucks were heavy and expensive so sales were very limited. Gardner engines were tried in 1934 with little more success and Fowler production ceased in 1935.

■ LEFT ***Fowler were famous steam-engine builders who tried to market this Marathon 7-ton diesel truck in 1931.***

OTHER MAKES

■ LEFT ***Dutch manufacturer FTF used a British Motor Panels cab on its 6×4 tractor unit.***

■ BELOW ***The UK-built British Quad of 1918 was based on the FWD.***

■ FTF

WIJCHEN, THE NETHERLANDS

Floor's, a transport company, began building its own trailers in the 1950s. It assembled Mack trucks from 1952 and, following Mack's decision to set up a Dutch assembly plant in 1964, Floor's Handel en Industrie BV began building trucks under the FTF name in 1966. These incorporated many Mack components but later FTF used Detroit Diesel engines, Fuller and Allison transmissions and a Motor Panels cab. In latter years the range included 6x2, 6x4, 6x6, 8x4, 8x8 and 10x4 heavy trucks but from 1996 trucks were phased out and production reverted to trailers.

■ FWD

CLINTONVILLE, WISCONSIN, USA

Inventor Otto Zachaw came up with a patent constant-velocity joint in 1910 that led to the production of a steer-drive axle and in 1912, in partnership with his brother-in-law William Besserdich, founded the FWD (Four-Wheel Drive) Auto Company. A primitive 2-ton truck had been built as early as 1910 but it was during World War I that FWD trucks for 3 and 5-ton payloads began volume production. William Besserdich left to set up Oshkosh in 1917. FWD went on to build a wide range of trucks in conventional and cabover form. During World War II cabover versions of their SU bonneted truck were built for the armed forces – the familiar SU-COE models.

The 1950s saw a huge range of trucks for both on and off-highway use, including sleeper-cab 6×4 tractors for line-haul work. Specialized multi-wheel drive trucks like the Tractioneer appeared in the '50s and '60s, plus the unusual Teracruzer for desert use. From 1960 the company became the FWD Corporation, and in 1963 took over the Seagrave Corporation which specialized in fire-fighting equipment. Production of specialized trucks and fire appliances continued into the 1990s.

■ FWD

SLOUGH, ENGLAND

Considerable numbers of American FWD trucks were shipped to the UK during World War I, many finding their way into civilian ownership after the war. A British version, the British Quad was built under licence from 1918, using a Dorman engine. In 1927 FWD Motors launched a 6×6 powered by a 6-cylinder Dorman. Later, in 1929, FWD entered an agreement with AEC of Southall under which the trucks were fitted with AEC engines instead of Dormans. By then the British-built FWDs were so far removed from the original American-sourced trucks that the FWD name was dropped, and from 1931 the trucks were renamed Hardy.

■ BELOW ***A late 1960s FWD LB46-2641 Tractioneer with air load transfer.***

BIRMINGHAM, ENGLAND

GARNER

■ LEFT *A 2-ton Garner truck of the early 1930s.*

From 1915 Henry Garner of Moseley, Birmingham, assembled American Gramm-Bernstein trucks to meet wartime demand for civilian trucks in the UK. In 1925 Garner began building its own design of truck, a 2-tonner with Dorman engine. Production moved to a new factory at Tylesley in 1926 and in 1931 a new range of forward-control trucks up to 6-ton payload was introduced. For a brief period from 1934–36 Garner was taken over by steam-wagon builders Sentinel of Shrewsbury and the trucks were marketed as Sentinel-Garner. However, it was re-sold in 1936 to a consortium of ex-Dodge employees who set up a factory at Willesden in west London. A modernized truck range for 2 to 5-ton payloads was offered from 1937 up to World War II. After the war the company concentrated on building commercial bodywork.

LEISTON, ENGLAND

GARRETT

■ LEFT *A 6-ton Garrett undertype steam wagon of the late 1920s.*

One of the oldest names in the industry, Garrett's history dates back to 1856. They specialized in agricultural machinery and steam traction engines until 1904, when an experimental steam lorry was built. Garrett entered the steam-wagon market in earnest from 1909, first with overtypes and then, from 1927, with the more practical undertype layout. Garrett acquired the Scottish Caledon truck company in 1926 but a planned Garrett-Caledon gasoline truck did not enter full production, although two or three prototypes were completed. In 1928 a couple of oil-engined trucks were built, basically steamers fitted with McLaren diesel engines – these are reputed to be the first-ever UK diesel trucks. Just before the company folded in 1932, a 6-ton forward-control four-wheeler with a choice of Meadows gasoline engine or Blackstone diesel was announced, but there is no record of it entering production. From 1932–60 Garrett turned their attention to engineering.

GORKY, RUSSIA

GAZ

■ LEFT *The GAZ 53A 4-ton truck of 1969 had a V8 gasoline engine, but this example has a Perkins engine fitted.*

GAZ (Gorkovskij Automobilnyj Zavod) began in 1931 by assembling Ford AA trucks under licence. Products were based on American Fords until after World War II and were lightweight models with both civilian and military specifications. Post-war models consisted of the GAZ-51 general cargo truck for 5 tonnes, the 1½-tonne GAZ-63 4×4 and a dump truck designated the GAZ-93. A 2-tonne payload 4×4, the GAZ-66 was a cabover design powered by a 4.2 litre/256cu in V8 engine. From 1995 GAZ built light trucks for 1½-tonne payloads including the GAZ-3302 "Gazelle". The GAZ-66 was superceded by the GAZ-3308 2-tonner.

SEATTLE, WASHINGTON, USA

GERSIX

Gersix was the forerunner of today's Kenworth. The company was formed in 1917, having briefly been set up as Gerlinger in 1916. Louis and Edgar Gerlinger completed their first truck in 1917. This was powered by a 6-cylinder Continental gasoline engine leading to the choice of Ger-six as the make. The truck was a well-engineered, worm-drive bonneted machine. Until 1922 Gersix remained a low-volume producer, then two of the major shareholders, H. W. Kent and E. K. Worthington, reorganized the company, renaming it the Kenworth Motor Truck Co.

HIGH WYCOMBE, ENGLAND

GILFORD

■ LEFT *The early 1930s Gilford truck was partly inspired by Gilford's bus chassis.*

Gilford is probably remembered more for its buses than its trucks. The company began as E. B. Horne & Co. in north London in 1925 and became the Gilford Motor Co. Ltd in 1926. At first it imported Garford trucks from America but, because of import restrictions, it began building its own light commercials for 1½ to 2½-ton payloads powered by 4-cylinder Buda engines. During the 1930s it built trucks generally based on bus chassis. One model, the 1680T, was noted for its instantly recognizable Westinghouse Gruss air springs mounted on the front dumb irons. A normal-control version, the 168SD, was also available with goods bodywork. From 1927–33 Gilfords were built at High Wycombe, but production moved back to London in 1934. Poor sales forced the company into liquidation in 1935. For a brief period the factory was taken over by HSG (High Speed Gas) to build HSG-Gilford producer gas-powered trucks, but very few were built and HSG relocated to the Sentinel Waggon Works, Shrewsbury, in 1938, closing shortly afterwards.

EDERVEEN, THE NETHERLANDS

GINAF

■ ABOVE *Ginaf's speciality is extra-heavy-duty construction vehicles based on DAF engineering.*

In the 1950s Gebr Van Ginkel NV reconditioned old United States army trucks, converting them for civilian use, but in 1967 it began building its own 6×6 trucks – often based on Diamond T chassis. The company became Ginaf Automobielbedrijven BV from 1967 and went on to specialize in heavy-duty 4×4, 6×4, 6×6, 8×4, 8×6, 8×8, 10×4 and 10×8 trucks, aimed chiefly at the construction industry. Some early models had cabs produced by Van Dijk Coachbuilders but later models had DAF cabs as standard. Declared bankrupt in 2011, Ginaf was taken over by China Hi-Tech Group Corporation in 2012.

PONTIAC, MICHIGAN, USA

GMC

■ BELOW *A 1915 GMC SC type 1½-ton chain-drive truck with 4-cylinder gasoline engine.*

GMC trucks first appeared in 1912 following the earlier takeover of two pioneer truck manufacturers – Rapid and Reliance. Rapid trucks were the brainchild of brothers Max and Morris Grabowski, who built a rudimentary single-cylinder truck capable of 16kph/10mph back in 1900. The Rapid Motor Vehicle Co. of Detroit was officially incorporated in 1904 and in 1905 production was moved to Pontiac, Michigan. Max Grabowski fell out with his partners and left the company in 1907, setting up the Grabowski Power Wagon Co. but that enterprise was short-lived, going bankrupt in 1912. Shortly after taking over the Rapid Motor Vehicle Co., GM purchased the Reliance Motor Truck Co. of Owosso, Michigan, which had been formed in 1902. A new company, the General Motors Truck Co., was established following the acquisition of Reliance, to market both Rapid and Reliance trucks. In 1911 the two companies were merged and all production centred on Pontiac, the GMC nameplate being adopted the following year. Rapid trucks were generally of bonneted layout with 4-cylinder engines and chain drive to take payloads of up to 2 tons. Reliance trucks, on the other hand, were heavier-duty cabovers for 3½ to 5 tons payload, also primarily chain-drive. GMC trucks switched to shaft drive with worm axles in 1915.

■ ABOVE *This veteran 1906 Reliance 2-tonner was the forerunner of the GMC truck.*

■ ABOVE *The 1936 GMC T74 5-ton cabover had a 5.4 litre/330cu in gasoline "six".*

■ BELOW *The L5000 with 183cm/72in BBC tilt cab had a 182bhp V6 gasoline engine.*

After World War I production concentrated on the bonneted K series, covering payloads from 1 ton to 5 tons plus an artic version, the K101, which could take 15 tons. The heavier models had solid tyres. A Canadian production plant got underway in 1922. From 1925–29 GMC built the massive Big Brute K102.

During the late 1920s the K models were replaced with the more modern T-line trucks with pneumatic tyres and fully enclosed cabs. By 1931 GMC were offering four-wheelers, six-wheelers and artics for payloads of up to 15 tons. The company even built a range of semi-trailers. In 1933 engine improvements were introduced, the heavy trucks having new 10 litre/610cu in and 11.7 litre/713cu in gasoline engines with 7-bearing crankshafts. The same year saw the introduction of a full forward-control range. Sleeper cabs were now available too and all cabs were of very functional design. New streamlined cabs began appearing in 1935 on the T range. Medium trucks now had hydrovac servo brakes while the heaviest models had full air systems. Diesel power became available on some models in 1939, the engines being 3 or 4-cylinder two-stroke Detroit Diesels built by GM.

GMC's wartime production was an astonishing 560,000 military CCW 2½-ton 6×4 trucks plus 20,000 DUKW amphibious vehicles, making it the largest producer of the war period. From 1939 the company became the

GMC Truck & Coach Division of the General Motors Corporation. In the post-war era a comprehensive range from pickups to maximum-weight 6×4 tractors was offered. Memorable classics like the DW-970 conventional and the DF-860 cabover were available in the late 1950s, powered by the 6-71SE Detroit Diesel two-stroke rated at 210bhp. Noteworthy models of that same era were the 800/860 4×2 and W860 6×4 tractors with GM's own all-round air suspension, where compressed air was stored in a tubular front axle and in the rectangular section rear-radius arms.

The slab-fronted DFR 8000 cabover and DLR 8000 cab-forward models appeared in 1958 with aluminium 122cm/48in BBC tilt cab and air suspension. These originally had unusual I-section chassis rails. In 1963 they opted for conventional channel sidemembers and steel leaf suspension. While Detroit two-stroke diesels were common fitment, GM also offered their Torq-Flow four-stroke V8 diesels from 1964. Some medium-duty trucks were fitted with independent front suspension in the early '60s, but this was abandoned in 1963.

During the 1970s GM began commonizing more on the design of GMC and Chevrolet trucks. The Astro 95 cabover, launched in 1969, was the main line-haul tractor powered by the 71 series Detroit Diesel or with a Cummins option. The Chevrolet Titan was virtually identical. New additions to the range in the '70s were the Brigadier and General conventionals, the latter being the top-of-the-range Class 8 tractor. GM also offered Astro glider kits consisting of a new cab and chassis with front axle, aimed at owners who wanted to update an old truck, of any make, or to rebuild an accident-damaged truck. From 1980 the Astro 95 took on a new look with a full-width grille, but very little more came from GMC in the way of new heavy truck models after that. It entered a joint venture with Volvo of Sweden towards the end of 1986 resulting in the Volvo GM Heavy Truck Corporation, which eventually became Volvo Trucks North America.

■ ABOVE LEFT *A late 1950s bonneted GMC 620 tandem-axle truck.*

■ ABOVE RIGHT *This semi-forward-control articulated car transporter dates from the early 1950s.*

■ RIGHT *The 1979 GMC Brigadier tandem-axle tractor had a choice of Straight Six, V6 and V8 Detroit Diesel two-strokes or Cummins 14 litre/854cu in, with power ratings up to 350bhp.*

WOLVERHAMPTON, ENGLAND

GUY

■ LEFT *The 1920 Guy 2½-ton truck had shaft drive and solid tyres. It was powered by a 4-cylinder gasoline engine.*

The founder of Guy Motors, Sidney Slater Guy, was one of the pioneers of the UK truck industry. In 1913 he resigned from his position of works manager at the Sunbeam Motor Car Company and in 1914 formed Guy Motors at Fallings Park, Wolverhampton. The first truck was built that same year – a 1½-tonner which featured an overdrive 4-speed gearbox. In its early history Guy Motors was a significant producer of buses as well as trucks. In 1922 a heavy-duty articulated six-wheeler was introduced, plus a 3-ton electric truck. A number of military trucks were developed in the 1920s, including half tracks. Lighter trucks had pneumatic tyres from 1923. Already Guy were developing export sales in many parts of the world. Some heavy trucks were built in the early '30s, including the Warrior four-wheeler and Goliath six-wheeler powered by Gardner diesels.

■ LEFT *The 1954 Guy Otter 6-ton payload dump truck had a choice of Gardner 4-cylinder or Perkins 6-cylinder diesel.*

■ BELOW LEFT *In 1958 Guy Motors launched their Invincible Mk.II and Warrior range featuring bold styling and wrap-around windscreen.*

From 1933 the earliest examples of the famous Wolf 2-tonner, Vixen 3 to 4-tonner and Otter 6-tonner were appearing in both bonneted and forward-control form. There was also a low-loading six-wheel version of the Vixen called the Fox. Guy's famous Indian's head began appearing on the radiator caps in 1934. During World War II Guy designed and built the military 4×4 Quad Ant and a 4×4 rear-engined armoured car. During the war some civilian austerity models were offered, including the Vixant which was basically the Vixen with angular front-end sheet metal.

After the war the Wolf, Vixen and Otter resumed full production and in 1952 a new bought-in cab from Motor Panels began to appear. This was also fitted to the Otter tractor unit, specially developed in conjunction with British

■ RIGHT *A 1960 Otter 6-ton platform truck powered by a Gardner 4LK diesel engine.*

■ RIGHT *Guy's first heavy eight-wheeler was the 1954 Invincible, based on an AEC chassis.*

■ BELOW RIGHT *Guy's last truck model was the Big J4T launched after the company had been taken over by Jaguar Cars.*

Road Services, the nationalized UK transport organization.

In 1954 Guy extended up the weight range with new maximum-weight trucks of 4×2, 6×2, 6×4, 8×2 and 8×4 configurations. These were at first called Goliath, but were almost immediately relaunched as the Invincible range since the old Guy name "Goliath" had been claimed by a German van manufacturer. The Invincibles were based on AEC chassis engineering but were powered by Gardner or Meadows diesels. The heaviest Invincible grossed 24 tons gvw or 32 tons with trailer. The following year Guy launched the 14-ton gross Warrior with a stylish Motor Panels cab plus a more powerful version named the Formidable built mainly in tractor-unit form.

In 1958 Guy invested heavily in developing a completely new heavy-duty range, the Invincible Mk.II. This had a completely new chassis of very heavy proportions and a wide choice of engines from Gardner, Meadows, Leyland, AEC, Cummins and Rolls Royce. Perhaps its most memorable feature was its new ultra-modern cab with wrap-around windscreen and distinctive trans-Atlantic styling. A lightweight version, the Warrior, powered by an AEC AV470 engine, appeared the following year, developed from a prototype built by Guy's main dealer, TGB Motors, in 1958. However, Guy's finances were under some strain and the company was taken over by the Jaguar Car Company in 1961.

Jaguar breathed new life into Guy, which then traded as Guy Motors (Europe) Ltd. The range remained unchanged for three years or so until a new model, the Big J (signifying "Jaguar") was announced in 1964. This was a comprehensive range of four, six and eight-wheelers powered by a choice of engine but with the Cummins V6-170 and V6-200 as the leading fitment. The Big J featured a steel Motor Panels cab.

In 1964 the Jaguar company merged with the troubled British Motor Corporation to form British Motor Holdings. This in turn merged with the Leyland Motor Corporation in 1968 to form the equally troubled and top-heavy British Leyland Motor Corporation. Under Leyland ownership Guy was a small cog in the LMC machine and during the mid 1970s Guy was gradually phased out, disappearing completely by 1979.

OTHER MAKES

■ GENOTO

ISTANBUL, TURKEY

The General Motors-owned Genoto company, General Otomotiv Sanayi ve Ticaret A.S. of Istanbul, assembled Bedford TK trucks during the 1970s and '80s. The main model was the MSLR based on the KHL 13.5-tonne gvw chassis but with the addition of a 5-tonne capacity trailing third axle, bringing the gvw to 18.5 tonnes. Chassis engineering, including frame, suspension, brakes and steering, were all Bedford but Genotos were powered by a 130bhp 6-cylinder Mercedes-Benz OM352 diesel engine.

■ GOTFREDSON

WALKERVILLE, CANADA, & DETROIT, MICHIGAN, USA

Originally named the G & J (from the original company name of Gotfredson & Joyce Corporation) the Gotfredson was assembled from well-known proprietary units including Buda engines, Timken axles and Fuller transmissions. Production began in 1920 at Walkerville, Ontario, while an American plant in Detroit, Michigan, started production in 1923. The range included normal-control trucks for up to 7 tons payload. Gotfredson trucks sold well in Canada and many were exported to the UK. They were well-built trucks with handsome cast-aluminium radiators. From 1923 the company was called the Gotfredson Truck Corporation Ltd. Canadian production ceased in 1932 and the company was sold to the Ford Motor Company. The Detroit plant had run into financial problems in 1929 and had been rescued, reformed and slimmed down as the Robert Gotfredson Truck Co. As such it survived through to 1948. Products included heavy-duty trucks for up to 50 tons gtw powered mainly by Cummins diesels, Gotfredson having a Cummins sales and service franchise. Production figures were small, the trucks being custom-built.

■ GRÄF & STIFT

VIENNA, AUSTRIA

The Wiener Automobilfabrik vom Gräf & Stift was founded in 1895 and built its first truck, a 45hp 2½-tonner in 1909. It went on to build heavier machines for 3 and 5-tonne payloads, many being supplied to the Austrian Army. From 1926 production was concentrated on a 2½-tonne truck with pneumatic tyres. During the 1930s trucks up to 4½ tonnes payload were produced and the first diesel engines were offered.

After World War II the company became Gräf & Stift Automobilfabrik AG and

■ ABOVE *The 1970 Genoto was based on British Bedford engineering, but powered by a 6-cylinder Mercedes-Benz diesel engine.*

■ LEFT *The 1923 Gotfredson took its power from a Buda gasoline engine and featured pneumatic tyres and semi-enclosed cab.*

OTHER MAKES

■ RIGHT
A 1958 Graf & Stift LF-200/50 19-tonne gvw truck with sleeper cab.

■ BELOW RIGHT
GV flourished in the 1920s when heavy-duty electrics were in vogue.

production was concentrated on the 120 6-tonner powered by a 6-cylinder diesel of 125bhp. Forward-control models with a very attractive cab design appeared in 1957. These included maximum-weight trucks and tractor units powered by 6-cylinder Mercedes-Benz diesels, plus a twin-steer six-wheeler with a 200bhp two-stroke diesel. In 1970 the company merged with ÖAF, also of Vienna, becoming Österreichische Automobilfabrik Gräf & Stift AG, but henceforth all trucks were badged ÖAF.

■ GRUBE

WERDAU, GERMANY

The distinctive bonneted H3A truck was also built as the Sachsenring S4000. All these brands were part of the large IFA combine originally set up in 1948. Prior to 1952 the factory had built steam tractors for road haulage. These went under the Lowa name and were introduced in 1949. VEB Fahrzeugwerke Ernst Grube built Horch trucks including types H3A, H6 and the military G6 4×4. These were also marketed under the IFA (Industrieverband Fahrzeugbau Association) badge.

■ GV

LONG ISLAND, NEW YORK, USA, & BIRMINGHAM, ENGLAND

The General Vehicle Co. produced a wide range of battery electric trucks between 1906 and 1920. Payloads ranged from 1 to 5 tons. Production of GV trucks also took place in Birmingham, England, from 1916 and that operation continued until 1935. After 1921 lighter models were discontinued but heavy-duty models became popular with municipal users, breweries and railway companies. The largest machine was the articulated Giant for 10-ton payloads. GV in America briefly entered the gasoline-engined market from 1913–18, building German Mercedes 6-tonners under licence. They were first known as American Daimler but were renamed GV Mercedes.

GLASGOW, SCOTLAND

HALLEY

■ LEFT ***This Scottish-built Halley chain-drive 2½-ton truck was exported to a customer in Sydney, Australia.***

Established as Halley Industrial Motors Ltd in 1906, the company was formerly called the Glasgow Motor Lorry Co. Ltd, which was formed in 1901. Between then and 1906 it built steam wagons, the early ones being called Glasgow wagons. During the period up to World War I, Halley gasoline-engined trucks from 1½ to 6 tons appeared, the heaviest of which had Tylor engines. During the war Halley built some 400 3-ton subsidy lorries. By then Halley were building their own engines, including a 6-cylinder unit. In the post-war years the firm concentrated on a solid-tyred 3½-tonner but sales were poor in the depressed market. Nevertheless the range was expanded to include forward-control models.

After running into financial difficulties in 1926 they were rescued by the North British Locomotive Company. They re-formed towards the end of 1927 as Halley Motors Ltd. Much of Halley's sales around that period were of buses, municipal vehicles and fire engines. A rigid six-wheeler, the B53 model for 8-ton payload, was announced in 1929 and in the early '30s a range of trucks from 4 to 13 tons payload was offered. Diesel power was growing in popularity at that time and Halley offered a Perkins Leopard in their 4-tonner of 1934. However, Halley's fortunes did not improve and the company went into liquidation in 1935, their factory being purchased by Albion Motors Ltd.

DARTFORD, ENGLAND

HALLFORD

■ LEFT ***A Hallford chain-drive truck of the Bristol Tramways & Carriage Co.***

The very old established J & E Hall Dartford Ironworks originated in 1785 and the company's Hallford lorries appeared in 1907. The first 3-ton chain-drive was based on a Saurer design. By 1911 Hallford were producing their own engines and the truck range included models from 1½ to 5 tons. World War I production concentrated on 3-ton subsidy trucks powered by Dorman engines. After the war Hallford reverted to building their pre-war range, which still featured chain drive. From 1923 they offered a rigid six-wheeler for 10 tons payload, but in 1925 they withdrew from the market.

HANOVER, GERMANY

HANOMAG

■ LEFT ***A 1970 Hanomag-Henschel F-190 19-tonne gross four-wheeler with tilt body.***

Hanomag began building gasoline-engined trucks in 1925 but had built a number of steam lorries some 15 to 20 years earlier. Those early steamers dating from 1905–08 were Stoltz designs built under licence. Hanomag's first gasoline-engined truck was a ¾-tonne forward-control model. In 1933 an innovative design appeared in the form of an underfloor-engined forward-control 4-tonner with a horizontal 4-cylinder diesel. Hanomag went on to build heavier tractors for artic and drawbar use up to 15 and 20-tonne payloads, the heavier one having a 6-cylinder diesel. Hanomag's post-war range mainly consisted of light trucks up to 2½ tonnes payload. In 1967 a new range appeared, extending up to 5 tonnes payload. In the meantime, Hanomag had taken over the Tempo company which specialized in front-wheel drive vans. In 1968 Hanomag merged with heavy truck maker Henschel of Kassel to form Hanomag-Henschel. Only two years later Hanomag-Henschel was taken over by Daimler-Benz (now Daimler AG). Production of Hanomag-Henschel was phased out in 1973.

SLOUGH, ENGLAND

HARDY

The Hardy name replaced FWD in 1931 after the British FWD company signed an agreement with AEC Ltd to use AEC engines in their all-wheel drive trucks which previously used Dorman engines. AEC-engined Hardys also featured radiators and cabs closely resembling those of contemporary AECs. In the mid 1930s Hardy was absorbed completely into AEC and production was transferred to Southall in London. Hardy-AEC designs included the 8×8 roadtrain tractors exported to Australia during the mid '30s. The Hardy pedigree was also to be seen in AEC's famous Matador 4×4 medium artillery tractor of World War II. The Hardy name was not used after 1935.

WOLVERHAMPTON, ENGLAND

HAULAMATIC

■ LEFT ***The 1980 Haulamatic dump truck featured a Perkins V8 diesel engine and Allison automatic transmission.***

Haulamatic once marketed a Commer-based dump truck with beefed-up chassis and suspension before launching its own two- and three-axle models in 1969 with GM or Perkins V8 diesels and Allison automatic transmissions. In 1982 it was taken over by NEI Clarke Chapman. In 1990 it merged with Unipower, later acquired by Alvis. It then passed to the LH Group of Burton-on-Trent, becoming Heathfield Haulamatic, surviving until the late 90s.

VANCOUVER, CANADA

HAYES

■ LEFT ***Hayes specialized in massive heavy-duty logging tractors powered by a wide variety of engines.***

From 1934 trucks built by the Hayes Manufacturing Co. Ltd of Vancouver were referred to simply as Hayes but, prior to that, from their inception in 1928, they were called Hayes-Anderson. The company offered a wide range of trucks from 1½ tons upwards but came to specialize in logging trucks for the local lumber industry. Power units included Continental, Hercules and Leyland. They also built special low-loading dockside trucks.

In the late 1930s Hayes became Leyland distributors, supplementing their own range with Leylands. They also began using more Leyland components including axles and gearboxes. In the post-war years a range of on-highway trucks appeared and these continued to be updated and marketed throughout the 1950s and '60s. Engine choice now included Detroit Diesel, Cummins, Rolls Royce and Caterpillar. Three members of Hayes' management left in 1947 to form the Pacific Truck & Trailer Co. which was also to specialize in logging trucks. Meanwhile Hayes went on to build larger and more powerful logging trucks themselves throughout the 1960s and early '70s. The most impressive of these was the HDX1000, capable of hauling five trailers grossing up to 150 tons. The power unit for the HDX was a 430bhp Detroit Diesel V12. Mack Trucks took a two-thirds stake in Hayes from 1969 but in 1974 the company was sold to Paccar. Production ceased in 1975.

LYONS, ILLINOIS, USA

HENDRICKSON

■ RIGHT *1980 Hendrickson H3-38 6×4 tractor with Detroit Diesel.*

Swedish-born Magnus Hendrickson emigrated to the United States in 1887, settling in Chicago. A brilliant engineer, he built his first truck in 1900 and became chief engineer at the Lauth-Juergens truck company. Among his early innovations was a tilt cab, around 1911. Hendrickson left Lauth in 1913 and set up his own truck company, his first product being a chain-drive cabover. By 1920 he was offering three models from 2½ to 5 tons with shaft drive. A lighter 1½-ton model of 1922 had pneumatic tyres. From the outset Hendrickson built trucks for specialized operations, setting the pattern for their whole history. A significant development was the unique rocking-beam tandem-axle suspension unit that appeared on their first six-wheeler of 1926.

From 1933 Hendrickson formed close ties with the International Harvester Co. of Chicago, who gained exclusive rights to use the Hendrickson rear bogie. This arrangement lasted until 1948 when Hendrickson bogies were made available to other manufacturers. Meanwhile, some Hendrickson trucks featured International Harvester cabs. During the 1950s Hendrickson turned more and more to custom-built trucks and crane chassis, and a vast array of models was on offer, including aircraft refueller chassis, super-heavyweight trucks for 200 tons and more, fire appliances, dockspotters, as well as a range of on-highway trucks and tractor units. Production of these was centred on their Mobile Equipment division at Lyons, Illinois. In 1977 Hendrickson was acquired by the Boler Company and, while truck production did continue into the 1980s, the main products were suspension units and truck equipment of which Hendrickson continues to be one of the world's leading suppliers.

KASSEL, GERMANY

HENSCHEL

■ LEFT *A 1963 Henschel HS12KV powered by 132bhp 6-cylinder diesel.*

Prior to 1925 Henschel & Sohn GmbH built railway locomotives, but it was granted a licence in 1924 to build FBW trucks. The early FBW-based Henschel was a chain-drive 5-tonner but within a year a shaft-drive machine was available. In 1928 the company, now Henschel & Sohn AG, began building its own diesel engines and by 1930 the truck range included models from 2½ to 10 tonnes, the largest being a three-axled rigid. An articulated model was also available for payloads of up to 16 tonnes. Henschel then concentrated on a program of steam truck development based on the advanced Doble principle. Up to 18 heavy-duty steamers of modern appearance were built up until 1936. That year marked the appearance of a 300bhp 12-cylinder opposed-piston diesel engine. A range of military trucks was produced, but civilian production was resumed in the late 1950s. Bonneted trucks predominated but during the '50s a range of forward-control models became available, including some with underfloor engines. The company became Henschel-Werke GmbH in 1957, and in 1961 it formed a joint arrangement with Saviem under which Henschel was marketed in France as Saviem-Henschel. This arrangement only survived two years and was followed by an equally short-lived tie-up with the British Rootes Group, manufacturers of Commer trucks, to market their products as Commer-Henschel in Europe. That arrangement ceased in 1967 when Henschel was taken over by Rheinstahl, who already owned Hanomag and its subsidiary Vical & Sohn Tempo-Werke which built Tempo vans. Rheinstahl-Henschel AG was formed into Hanomag-Henschel Fahrzeugwerke GmbH in 1968 and the trucks carried Hanomag-Henschel name badges. Shortly after that, in 1970, the whole organization was absorbed into Daimler-Benz (now Daimler AG). The last trucks to bear the Henschel badge were built in 1969.

HEANOR, ENGLAND

HHT

Although HHT trucks were not available on the open market, they are worthy of mention as an example of a specialized product developed to suit a transport company's own needs. Heanor Haulage of Heanor, Derbyshire, specialized in the movement of heavy, abnormal loads. Having operated heavy tractors from Scammell, they used a Scammell Contractor frame as a basis for their own heavier and more powerful machine, which featured a four-axled 1+3 arrangement. The first HHT had a 388bhp Detroit Diesel 8V-92 two-stroke diesel, Lipe-Rollway clutch and 15-speed Fuller Roadranger transmission. Three Leyland 11-ton axles formed the rear bogie, one being a lift axle for unladen running. A Volvo F89 cab was used. Approximately five tractors were built in all, most of which were three-axle types.

■ ABOVE ***A three-axled HHT ballast tractor of 1978 built by Heanor Haulage.***

■ LEFT ***Heanor's first HHT was this Detroit Diesel-powered four-axled machine built in 1975.***

CALCUTTA, INDIA

Hindustan

Hindustan Motors Ltd was founded by the C.K. Birla Group in 1942 at Okha in the erstwhile state of Baroda, and was reregistered in 1950 with its head office in Calcutta. At first the company built a variety of British and American vehicles under licence but, from 1968, used the Hindustan nameplate on its trucks, which were based on the Bedford TJ. The normal-control J6, with detailed engineering changes to increase the gvw from 10.7 tons to 12 tons, used a cab based on the standard Bedford TJ, while a forward-control J6 featured a locally designed cab. Both were powered by Indian-built developments of the Bedford 5.4 litre/330cu in diesel and Bedford 4-speed gearbox. In 1982 the forward-control J6 was relaunched as the T.480 Mascot with 5-speed ENV gearbox as standard and larger fuel tank. By the early 1990s truck production had dwindled to nothing and Hindustan now build only cars and pickup trucks.

■ ABOVE ***Hindustan's forward-control 7-tonner of the late 1970s was based on the British Bedford's normal-control TJ, but uprated to 12 tons gvw.***

TOKYO, JAPAN

HINO

Hino's roots can be traced back to 1910 and the establishment of the Tokyo Gas Industry. This became the Tokyo Gas & Electric Industry Ltd in 1913 and from 1917 the subsidiary Motor Vehicle Division began building T.G.E. trucks. The first truck was the A type of 1918 followed by the B type 1½-tonner of 1921. Truck production continued through to the formation of Hino Heavy Industries in 1942 after which the Hino name badge was used. In 1946 the division was renamed the Hino Industry Co. Ltd and the first 15-tonne heavy articulated truck was introduced. The company was again renamed in 1948 as Hino Diesel Industry Co. Ltd to manufacture heavy-duty diesel trucks, and the range expanded to include dump trucks and 6×6 construction vehicles. Japan's first twin-steer

■ LEFT *A Hino TE dump truck for 6.5 tons payload powered by DS70 140bhp 6-cylinder diesel engine.*

■ LEFT *A 1966 Hino tilt-cab KC series for payloads up to 7½ tons. The KC was launched in 1961.*

■ BELOW *Hino's TC362E twin-steer 6×2 of the early 1970s had a gvw of 22 tons and carried around 15 tons payload.*

■ LEFT *A 1979 KL645 9.5-ton gvw four-wheeler with 165bhp 6-cylinder diesel operating in Norway.*

six-wheeler was launched by Hino in 1958. In 1959 the company became Hino Motors Ltd. At that time the leading truck types were the bonneted TA, TH and HD models. The TA and TH specifications were virtually identical at 12 tonnes gvw, the TA being a shorter-wheelbase version of the TH for dump-truck bodywork. The HD was shorter still for articulated use at gcws up to 22 tonnes. Visually their cabs echoed the American International KB8 styling. A six-wheel version, the KE100 for 13 tonnes gcw, was also available.

The 1960s saw a comprehensive truck range of both normal and forward-control layout, the latter having tilt cabs. Hino came under the control of the Toyota Motor Co. in 1966 and from then on it concentrated on medium and heavy-duty diesel trucks, the heaviest of which was their ZM 6×4 logging truck. In 1972 a new forward-control tractor unit, the HE model for 40 tonnes, was introduced. Hino assembly plants were established in numerous countries, including one in the Republic of Ireland, where J. Harris (Assemblers) Ltd built Hino's first 30½-tonne 8×4 model aimed at the Irish and UK market. This was a forward-control ZM type. Australia and New Zealand became particularly important markets for Hino. During the 1980s and '90s Hino's principal medium and heavy trucks have been the F series, the lightest being the 10-tonne gvw FC and the heaviest being the FS three-axled and FY four-axled rigids.

For a period during the 1980s Hino was second only to Daimler-Benz as the world's largest truck producer, but it has since been overtaken by expanding organizations like Paccar, Navistar and Volvo. In 1992 Hino introduced their advanced Super Dolphin PROFIA truck with motor-operated tilt cab. Since 2001 Hino has become a subsidiary of the Toyota Motor Corp and 2002 saw a marketing agreement reached with Scania. A brand new range of heavy trucks, the 700 series, appeared in 2006. These sold well in the UK but Hino sales diminished after Euro 6 emission standards took effect as Hino's diesels were not Euro 6 compliant.

■ LEFT *In the late 1970s this UK-registered HE335E grossed 32 tons and was powered by Hino's ED100 diesel engine of 235bhp.*

■ BELOW *Hino launched its 700-series trucks in 2006. This 8x4 model is seen in the UK.*

BARCELONA, SPAIN

HISPANO-SUIZA

■ LEFT *Exceptionally modern styling characterized the 66 7-tonner launched in 1944 by Hispano-Suiza.*

Hispano-Suiza's origins can be traced to 1898 and an unsuccessful project on the part of Emilio de la Cuadra to build a gasoline-electric truck, a project for which he enlisted the help of Carlos Vellino, a Swiss battery manufacturer. Vellino sent for his compatriot Marc Birkigt to help. Unfortunately Cuadra ran into financial difficulties and his enterprise was renamed J. Castro (one of the creditors) Fabrica Hispano Suiza d'Autómoviles, signifying the joint Spanish and Swiss enterprise in which Birkigt became a partner.

Up to 1908 Hispano-Suiza built cars, but a truck was then introduced. This was a 12/15hp 1-tonner. A chain-drive truck for 3 tonnes payload appeared in 1911 and larger trucks were built in military form. An even larger truck for 4 tonnes payload and powered by a 6.8 litre/415cu in 4-cylinder engine at 53hp appeared in 1915. Between 1916 and 1923 national pride saw truck production move to a new factory in Guadalajara and the products were called La Hispano. Hispano-Guadalajara ran into financial problems and was taken over by Hispano-Suiza, Barcelona, but the plant was closed down completely in 1931. During the Spanish Civil War truck production was very limited, and Hispano-Suiza's first important new model was the 66 announced in 1944. This beautifully styled 7-tonner had unique lines that were later to be inherited by Pegaso trucks. The 66G had a 110bhp side-valve 6-cylinder gasoline engine while the 66D had a 128bhp 6-cylinder diesel.

Just two years after the 66 appeared, the Spanish INI (Institute Nacional d'Industries) purchased Hispano-Suiza's truck operations as part of a nationalization plan and the Empresa Nacional de Autocamiones SA (ENASA) was formed to build trucks under the Pegaso name.

ZWICKAU, GERMANY

HORCH

■ LEFT *The Horch H3 was also built by Ernst Grube and marketed as the Sachsenring S4000 and IFA.*

Formed in 1912, Horch built trucks from 1913 mainly for military use. After World War I, as A. Horch & Co. Motorenwagenwerke AG at Zwickau, it continued to build trucks of between 1½ and 3 tonnes payload up to 1925. Production then turned to specialized vehicles and military trucks. From 1945 the name Sachsenring was applied to the products, which subsequently came under the IFA (Industrieverband Fahrzeugbau Association).

SEINE, FRANCE

HOTCHKISS

■ LEFT *The 1966 Hotchkiss Type 80 featured a tilt cab and a choice of 4-cylinder gasoline or diesel engine.*

The Hotchkiss Company was formed in 1914 but only cars were built until 1936 when a bonneted 2-tonne truck was introduced. It had a 4-cylinder, 2.3 litre/140cu in ohv gasoline engine. After World War II the truck evolved into the PL20 model which featured hydraulic brakes. Hotchkiss were not significant producers of trucks, their products being limited to the medium-weight class. In 1954 they merged with Automobiles Delahaye and in 1961 a short-lived arrangement began under which Hotchkiss marketed Leyland Albion and Scammell trucks in France. The PL range continued in production until 1967, with heavier trucks up to 4 tonnes payload being added from the early '60s. Hotchkiss' last completely new truck was the forward-control tilt-cab model launched in 1965 for payloads of 3.7 to 5.7 tonnes and with a choice of gasoline or diesel engines. Jeeps were also built under licence from Willys. Hotchkiss' truck production was merged into Citroën around 1970.

JINAN CITY, SHANDONG, CHINA

HOWO

■ RIGHT *Chinese giant CNHTC, the makers of Howo, have exported widely and this 8x4 is aimed at the UK.*

Howo is a brand of Sinotruck Group which is part of the CNHTC (China National Heavy-Duty Truck Co). The state owned organisation is China's third largest truck producer. The CNHTC originated in 1935 and entered truck production in the late 50s.

It was the first Chinese manufacturer to build a heavy truck, the Huanghe JN150 (see below). In 1983 it entered a joint venture with Steyr to build the 91 series. The CNHTC was re-organised in 1990, and in 2000 formed Sinotruck. Three years later it signed an agreement with Volvo Group and in 2013 formed links with MAN. Howo have a strong presence in Latin America and an assembly plant in Pakistan. There are plans to market some Howo trucks in Ireland and the UK.

SHANDONG PROVINCE, CHINA

HUANGHE

The Tsingtao Motor Vehicle Plant in Shandong Province, China, built an 8-ton payload truck designated the JN-150 from 1964. Prototypes had been built in 1959. The power unit was a 160bhp 6-cylinder diesel with a 5-speed gearbox. Since 1982 Huanghe trucks have been built at Jinan using "Roman" cabs.

SEOUL, KOREA

HYUNDAI

The Hyundai Motor Company was established in 1967 and entered the truck market in 1978. The trucks produced drew largely on British technology. Early Hyundai trucks were powered by Perkins diesels. Since the 1980s Hyundai have marketed a wide range from medium 4x2s up to heavy 8x4 models. Hyundai were also the basis for Bering trucks in the United States from 1997. In 2000 DaimlerChrysler entered a joint venture to build engines and in 2001 they planned to form the Daimler Hyundai Truck Co but this plan was abandoned in 2004.

HIGHLAND, ILLINOIS, USA

HUG

The Hug Company produced trucks, bodywork and trailers between 1922 and 1942, their products gaining a reputation for ruggedness and job fitness. This is not surprising since they understood the business from the customer's angle. Hug were a classic example of haulier turned manufacturer. The firm's founder G. J. Hug couldn't find a truck that would meet his needs on tough road-building work so he built his own prototype in 1921 – a solidly built 1-ton dump truck with a 34hp Buda gasoline engine and pneumatic tyres. During the 1920s and '30s Hug geared up to produce a wide range of trucks, many of which were fitted with dump-truck bodies. Heavy-duty bonneted 6×2 and 6×4 versions for payloads of up to 20 tons appeared in the '30s. The company also built cabover tractor units for maximum-weight line-haul operation. Typical were the 43LD and 43T powered by Cummins or Caterpillar 6-cylinder diesel or Buda gasoline engines. Fuller transmissions and Clark axles were used. At the lighter end of the range Hug offered models for payloads of 1½ to 2½ tons in both bonneted and cabover form. The company closed in June 1942.

■ LEFT *The D & R Transportation Co. of Lansing, Michigan, operated this seven-axled Hug 43LD A-train tanker with Cummins HA6 diesel in 1935.*

SALT LAKE CITY, UTAH, USA

IBEX

■ LEFT *The 1970 Ibex all-wheel drive tractor was powered by a Caterpillar 1676 8-cylinder diesel developing 340bhp.*

The Ibex Motor Truck Corporation specialized in heavy-duty, high-powered on/off-road trucks for construction, exploration and oilfield duty. They were mainly bonneted 4×4, 6×4 and 6×6 models powered by Cummins, Detroit Diesel and Caterpillar engines. Some cabover versions also appeared as well as specialized "dockspotter" tractors, and production began in 1963. In the 1980s production was concentrated on specialist airport service vehicles and terminal tractors.

ZWICKAU, WERDAU, & LUDWIGSFELDE, GERMANY

IFA

■ LEFT *The IFA W50 cabover 5-tonner was the workhorse of Eastern Europe for three decades.*

An association of manufacturers was formed in 1948 in East Germany to manage and co-ordinate state-owned truck production. The plants included Horch at Zwickau and Ernst Grube of Werdau where production of the H3, H6, G5 (6×6) and Sachsenring S4000 took place. From 1956 the VEB IFA (Industrieverband Fahrzeugbau Association) Werdau plant began production of the long-running W50 forward-control truck which was built in four-wheeler and articulated form, many thousands of which are still to be seen in the old Eastern Bloc regions. The last new model was the L60. In 1990 IFA Ludwigsfelde was taken over by Daimler-Benz (now DaimlerChrysler) and shortly afterwards production was switched to Mercedes light trucks and vans.

MARION, INDIANA, USA

INDIANA

■ LEFT *This model 95 box van for 2-ton payload dates from 1933.*

Indiana trucks were produced from 1911 through to the late 1930s. The bulk of production was in the light to medium-weight range. For the first nine years Indianas were built by Harwood-Barley Manufacturing Co., but in 1920 that became the Indiana Truck Corporation. Indiana used mainly proprietary engines and components. Engines in the earliest models were Rutenber gasoline units. Heavier models were added in the mid '30s. Five and 7-tonners were available using Waukesha and Hercules engines respectively. In 1928 the company was taken over by Brockway, but during the depression Brockway were forced to sell Indiana to the White Motor Co. From joining White in 1932 Indiana's production was moved to Cleveland, Ohio. Indiana claimed to be the earliest American manufacturer to offer a diesel truck, having co-operated with Cummins in 1931 to stage demonstration runs. The following year a 5-tonner with a 6-cylinder Cummins was offered. During the '30s production concentrated on the 2 to 7½-ton class, although a few heavier models were offered. Between 1936 and the company's demise in 1939, assembly of Indianas was undertaken in the UK by Indiana Sales of Wolverhampton.

MELBOURNE, AUSTRALIA

International Harvester

■ BELOW *The Australian-born ACCO range survives in the current ACCO-G series 2350 with choice of Cummins or International diesel power.*

Although International Harvester had a presence in Australia from 1912, production of Australian-designed trucks did not commence until the late 1950s. The first design was the military 4x4 2½-tonner for the Australian Army. The civilian AACO (Australian A-line Cabover) was developed from this in 1961. The squat, angular cab could not disguise its military origins but it proved a practical truck that would soon be seen all over Australia and New Zealand. Early models had a choice of International V.392 V8 gasoline engine or Perkins 6.354 diesel. Production was centred on Dandenong Works, Victoria. A large proving ground was built at Anglesea. A modernized tilt-cab range – the ACCO-A (Australian C-line Cabover) – was introduced in 1971. Normal-control trucks from 5 to 11.8 tonnes gvw and 24 tonnes gcw were also available, the cab on these being shared with Dodge. Twin-steer four-axled versions of the ACCO-A appeared in 1975 for a gcw up to 30 tonnes.

During the 1970s and '80s International's Australian operations underwent several changes of ownership. Following the formation of Seddon Atkinson in the UK in 1970, the Atkinson Australia subsidiary was sold off, becoming part of International Harvester Australia in 1973. Seddon Atkinson itself was absorbed into International Harvester's European operations in 1974, only to be sold to the Spanish group ENASA in 1983. ENASA had been part of International Harvester since 1978. By this time the ACCO-B range was in production with additional heavier-duty models up to 50 tonnes gcw.

International Trucks Australia Ltd (ITAL) became a separate operation from the parent company, International Harvester, when the latter curtailed its expansion plans and was re-formed as Navistar. ITAL built both Atkinson and International trucks for the Australian market, including Atkinsons fitted with the ACCO (or T-line) cab during the 1980s. In 1990 Iveco (Industrial Vehicle Corporation, formed in 1975), acquired ENASA, including its Seddon Atkinson subsidiary, followed in 1992 by ITAL. From the late '80s Iveco's influence had already shown itself in the E-series forward-control heavy-duty tractors that were based upon the Iveco TurboStar.

ITAL was taken over by Iveco in 1992 and the range in Australia became a mixture of Iveco and International lines, the long running ACCO cab surviving on the T-line. The ACCO was revamped in 1996 as the ACCO-G, using a lowered version of the Iveco EuroTech cab.

From 1995 ITAL offered an Australian-specification EuroTech and, in 1996, the bonneted 500E44 PowerStar, designed for the Australian market. ITAL now builds the latest PowerStar Mk.2 with a Strator style cab as well as the Iveco Stralis and ACCO range, the latter now featuring the Stralis style cab in lowered form. The PowerStar now has a choice of Iveco Cursor or Cummins power and train weights of up to 140 tonnes.

■ LEFT *Specially designed for the Australian market, the Iveco PowerStar Mk.2 '6400' model operates at up to 90 tonnes train weight in drawbar form.*

CHICAGO, ILLINOIS, USA

INTERNATIONAL HARVESTER

International Harvester's history dates from 1902, but the company's roots can be traced back to 1831 when Cyrus Hall McCormack invented the first mechanical reaper. By the turn of the century there were two large manufacturers of harvesters – McCormack and Deering – both in Chicago. In 1902 they merged with three other smaller manufacturers to form the International Harvester Co. Cyrus H. McCormack, the son of the original inventor, was president of the new organization. In 1907 IHC decided to expand into the production of light trucks aimed especially at farmers, and so was born their distinctive high-wheel Auto Buggy. Over the next few years more conventional trucks, including a 2-tonner, appeared and the International name badge was adopted in 1914.

By 1921 a range up to 5 tons payload capacity was available and a new production plant at Springfield, Ohio, was commissioned. A fully enclosed cab was introduced for trucks in 1927. The first diesel-engined models came in 1933. The C line heavy truck in rigid and articulated form featured new styling with a sloping, V-shaped aluminium radiator grille. There were 18 models in the range, including a 7-tonner. Six-wheelers for 10-ton payloads also appeared in the mid 1930s, featuring Hendrickson rear bogies. The D series replaced the C series in 1937, and further refinements were made to the styling. Cabover models were added to the range and a sleeper cab appeared in 1938.

In 1940 International's famous K line was introduced, and by then the company was one of America's largest truck producers. Wartime production included many thousands of military trucks, such as the semi-forward-control H-542, production of these also taking place at Marmon Herrington and Kenworth. The K re-entered production in 1946 as the KB, a truck to become a familiar sight in the UK and many other parts of the world. It formed the basis for the Russian ZIS and China's Jiefang trucks, which were virtually straight copies. The new

■ TOP ***International Harvester's early high-wheel Auto Buggy.***

■ ABOVE ***In 1921 International's Speed range included this 1-ton truck with shaft drive and pneumatic tyres.***

■ BELOW ***XL series cabovers, such as this Eagle 6×4 loaded with steel, could have Detroit Diesel or Cummins power up to 475bhp.***

■ RIGHT *A New Zealand specification heavy-duty bonneted 6×4 in the same class as the Fleetstar.*

■ BELOW *The KB8 conventional range was a great classic of the early post-World War II years.*

R series conventionals in the early 1950s featured a stylish all-steel cab built by the Chicago Manufacturing Co. and referred to by International as their Comfo-vision cab. It had a single-piece curved windscreen, sleeper option and distinctive grille with three horizontal bars on the lower portion. A lower version with high mounted headlights and a trapezoid grille went on the S series. The Fleetstar replaced the R series in the mid 1960s, this having a wide bonnet (hood) and grille. A version of this cab design became familiar on UK roads for a short period after International set up a manufacturing plant to build the medium-weight Loadstar models.

One attractively styled cab was the COF cabover. This tilt cab was originally a Diamond T design and had a long production run. A raised version of the same basic shell appeared on the heavy-duty VCO series. From the mid 1960s International used the "Star" suffix in most of their model types. The Loadstar was the medium and heavy range; the Fleetstar was the heavy-duty conventional range; the Paystar was the bonneted construction range; the Transtar, launched in 1971, was a maximum-weight line-haul range in bonneted and cabover form, while the Cargostar medium cabovers were developed from the COF range.

By the 1970s International was one of the largest truck manufacturers, with assembly plants and distributors throughout the world. In 1972 International were keen to expand into Europe, the UK assembly operations having petered out through lack of sales. The company entered talks with DAF of Eindhoven and acquired a 33 per cent holding in 1972. In 1974 International strengthened their European presence further by acquiring the newly formed Seddon Atkinson operations in Oldham, England. DAF had already undertaken a joint cab-development program with the Spanish group ENASA and in 1981 International bought a 35 per cent stake in that group too. However, after the series of European acquisitions, the International Harvester Group itself ran into difficulties and in 1984 was forced to pull out.

Notable products in that period included the 8100 city trucks, the 9200 tractor units for regional bulk haulage with power outputs of 280-470hp; the sleek line haul 9400 series with up to 550hp and the 9900 Eagle conventionals with 430-600hp. Current models include the 4000 series Durastar Class 5 and 6 city trucks, HV and HX construction vehicles and Class 8 RH regional haul and LT long haul tractors. Power comes from International's own engines or Cummins. Representing the ultimate in style for the image conscious trucker is International's stunning LoneStar, described as 'A Classic Reborn'. Despite its vintage looks it features the very best in cab comfort and boasts 605hp from its 15 litre/915 cu.in. Cummins X15.

■ LEFT *Aimed at the image-conscious long-haul trucker, the International LoneStar has striking retro styling.*

TOKYO, JAPAN

ISUZU

Isuzu's predecessor, the Tokyo Ishikawajima Shipbuilding & Engineering Co. Ltd, began building British-designed Wolseley A9 trucks under licence from 1922. These were built mainly for military use. The agreement with Wolseley terminated in 1927. Typical of the company's products in the early 1930s was the bonneted 2-tonne Sumida truck. In 1934 a research program into diesel engine production was put in place, and 1936 saw the development of a 5.3 litre/323cu in air-cooled diesel. The TX40 2-ton truck, with modernized cab strongly influenced by contemporary American styling, was in production in 1936. A new factory for heavy trucks was completed at Kawasaki in 1938, the Tokyo Jidosha Kogyo (Tokyo Automotive Industry) Co. Ltd having been formed in 1937, combining the motor divisions of the Ishikawajima Shipbuilding & Engineering Co. and the Tokyo Gas & Electric Co. The latter produced Japan's first truck in 1917 and also formed the basis for Hino Heavy Industries which went on to become a separate truck-building concern, being renamed Hino Motors Ltd in 1959 and which eventually merged with Toyota in 1966.

Diesel trucks were in full production by 1941. The company became Isuzu Motors Ltd in 1949 and the main truck model during the 1950s was the TX550 bonneted 6-tonner powered by a 6.1 litre/372cu in, 125bhp 6-cylinder diesel driving through a 5-speed overdrive gearbox. A military 6×6 development, the TW540, was also offered as well as a 5-tonne 4×2 with military pattern bonnet (hood) and wings powered by a choice of 5.6 litre/341cu in, 145bhp 6-cylinder gasoline or the 6.1 litre/372cu in diesel. In 1959 Isuzu's heaviest truck was the TD150 bonneted four-wheeler for 9-tonne payload. This was powered by a 10.18 litre/621cu in 6-cylinder diesel developing 180bhp and had air-assisted brakes.

During the 1960s, heavier and more powerful models were introduced. Typical of these was the bonneted 8-tonne gvw TD with a completely new pressed-steel cab with single-piece curved windscreen and four headlights. The power unit was the 10.18 litre/621cu in diesel uprated to 200bhp. The same engine powered a forward-control TD-E 8-tonner as well as 10-tonne payload 6×2 versions – the TP (bonneted) and TD-E (cabover). At the lighter end of the weight scale Isuzu offered the Elf forward-control

■ ABOVE ***The 1963 TD50-D 8-tonne hydraulic end dump truck has a 10.18 litre/621cu in DH100 6-cylinder diesel.***

■ BELOW LEFT ***A 1968 Isuzu TD50 for 15-tonne gvw.***

■ BELOW RIGHT ***The 1981 TWD25 all-wheel drive truck has 14-tonne gvw and a 150bhp 6BD1 diesel engine.***

■ RIGHT *The 1993 EXR300 A-train milk tanker has Isuzu's 6RA1-TRC 12 litre/732cu in turbo-intercooled diesel engine with 295bhp.*

2-tonners which were built at the Fujisawa car plant and embodied some Rootes Group engineering.

General Motors acquired a 35 per cent holding in Isuzu in 1971 and in 1973 a new range, the Forward, was introduced. The SBR and JBR at 9 tonnes and 12 tonnes gvw respectively were at the lower end, while the SLR grossed 16 tonnes. The SBG was a twin-steer six-wheeler at 21 tonnes gvw and the SPZ a 6×4 for 24 tonnes. There were two 38-tonne gcw tractor units too – the VPR 4×2 and the VPZ 6×4. Models from 21 tonnes gvw upwards were powered by the Isuzu E120 direct injection 12 litre/732cu in diesel. It was selected models from this range that GM chose to market as Bedfords in Australia and New Zealand, GM Holden carrying out the assembly.

Alongside the Forward range, Isuzu continued to offer their medium-weight TXD45/55 4×2 and TWD55 6×4 bonneted models, which by the 1980s were looking very old-fashioned. Heavier bonneted models were also available as the TDJ (16 tonnes gvw) and TDH (17.5 tonnes gvw) 4×2 and the 24-tonne gvw TMH and TMQ six-wheelers. An all-wheel drive range with a military-style cab, unchanged since the 1950s, the TSD 4×4 and TWD 6×6 also soldiered on into the '80s.

For 1980 Isuzu launched a facelifted forward-control range with the new 10PB1 14 litre/854cu in V10 diesel producing 292bhp. The range featured a new larger radiator and a set-back front axle. Throughout the 1980s and '90s Isuzu maintained a strong position in the truck market with healthy export sales. During the first two decades of the 21st century the principal models have been the C and E series heavy-duty trucks, the F series 2-, 3- & 4-axle models up to 30 tons and the N series light trucks. The top of the range E series trucks are marketed as the 'Giga' models. The new Isuzu Giga 'Second Generation' range was unveiled at the 2015 Tokyo Motor Show.

■ RIGHT *Early 1980s SPH rigid eight-wheeler and four-axled drawbar trailer operates up to 44 tonnes gtw in New Zealand.*

EUROPE

IVECO (INCLUDING IVECO FORD)

In the early 1970s Fiat of Turin recognized the need to increase its share of the world truck market if it was to survive in the face of competition from the market leaders like Daimler-Benz and Volvo. While Fiat had a virtual monopoly of its home market, commanding nearly 80 per cent of truck sales, it needed to expand if it was to remain profitable. It had already absorbed most of the major Italian manufacturers over the years, including OM and Lancia, while it also owned Unic, giving it a foothold in the French market. Fiat found a partner in Germany's Magirus-Deutz, the truck manufacturing division of KHD (Klockner Humboldt Deutz) of Ulm. The old established company was also looking for a partnership that would ensure its future independence and strengthen its position in the market, but in Germany there were no suitable companies. After a worldwide survey, Magirus-Deutz and Fiat agreed to set up a joint company to co-operate on truck development and manufacture. The earliest meetings took place in 1973 and IVECO (Industrial Vehicle Corporation) came into being on January 1st 1975. Part of the agreement was that Magirus-Deutz would be allowed to continue building the air-cooled diesels for which it was renowned. Group production facilities were to be reviewed to make best use of factories by concentrating like with like. Turin was to build heavy trucks, Ulm medium trucks and heavy construction vehicles, including the air-cooled-

■ LEFT *After the formation of Iveco in 1975 Fiat trucks began to display the new name badge on otherwise unaltered models.*

■ BELOW LEFT *Some, like this five-axled articulated cement bulker photographed near Pompeii, simply had the "I" logo on the grille.*

■ ABOVE *Iveco badges were added to UK Ford Cargos after 1986.*

■ LEFT *The 1997 Super Cargo has a design gross weight of 26 tonnes and 266bhp turbo-intercooled low-emission diesel.*

■ LEFT *Iveco became a make in its own right with the arrival of the TurboTech and TurboStar models of the 1980s.*

■ BELOW RIGHT *This UK-registered Iveco Cargo also carries a Ford badge. Outside the UK the model was badged Iveco EuroCargo.*

engined bonneted trucks. Brescia's OM factory was to build medium-weight vehicles and Trappes in France medium to heavy.

To satisfy all parties it was decided to locate Iveco's headquarters in a neutral country – The Netherlands. However, Iveco was still faced with problems integrating the various companies and factories into one corporate organization. While UNIC, along with the likes of OM and Lancia, had gracefully given up their individual identity and accepted their place under the Fiat dominated Iveco umbrella, Magirus-Deutz were no pushover. They fought to retain their individuality, while pride in their 110-year-old company made them reluctant to be swallowed up by a foreign group. As a result, after five years of uneasy co-habitation with Fiat, KHD pulled out of Iveco. The Magirus name remained with Iveco but Deutz regained its independence as an engine manufacturer and continued to supply engines to Iveco.

During these five years bold attempts had been made to give the Iveco Group products a corporate identity, but this had never gone beyond the addition of an italic "I" logo to their radiator grilles. From an early stage, however, heavy trucks from Fiat, OM, UNIC and Magirus-Deutz had all been given the Fiat tilt cab. Magirus was the only one to insist on including its famous "cathedral spire" trademark as well as the "I" logo. By the mid 1980s the Iveco brand name had replaced individual makes, and major restructuring was taking place to establish Iveco as a manufacturer in its own right. The truck that signified the true breakthrough for Iveco was the TurboStar of 1984. The important features of this highly successful truck were its cab and engine. While the cab bore a resemblance to its Fiat cousins, it was extensively redesigned with a 1.7m/5.5ft internal height and

■ RIGHT *Both Fiat eight-wheelers and their OM lookalikes were transformed into Ivecos after 1975.*

■ BELOW RIGHT *Iveco's Eurotech range of heavy duty tractor units was launched in 1992. In the UK they carried a small Ford badge too.*

■ LEFT *The Stralis represents Iveco's 2006 range in the 44-tonne artic sector.*

a sophisticated suspension system. There were two engines available – the 8210 13.8 litre/842cu in straight six turbo with 330bhp, or the 8280 17.2 litre/1049cu in V8 with 420, making it one of the most powerful trucks of the era and eminently suitable for long-distance inter-continental haulage.

The next major landmark in Iveco's development came in 1986 with the merger of Iveco and Ford's UK truck division. The result was Iveco Ford Trucks Ltd, with Iveco and Ford holding equal shares of 48 per cent each, the remaining 4 per cent being held by a merchant bank. Following the link-up, Ford badges were added to Iveco trucks for the UK market. Four years later came another milestone when Iveco added Pegaso (ENASA) to its ranks. This included Seddon Atkinson of Oldham, England which had become part of ENASA in 1983 when International Harvester sold off its European truck interests. Iveco made another important acquisition in 1992 in the form of International Trucks Australia Ltd.

A major model-replacement program came to fruition between 1991 and 1993. An attractive new design of forward-control Steel/Plastic cab, the Multi Purpose or MP cab, was introduced in various widths and heights to cover all models from 6 to 44 tonnes gvw. At the lighter end came the 1991 Eurocargo (badged Cargo in the UK) with rigids from 6 to 15 tonnes gcw and tractors up to 34 tonnes gcw. Then came the Super Cargo 17-tonne, two-axled and 26-tonne three-axled rigids. Four-axled Eurotrakker rigids built at Iveco's Spanish plant appeared in 1993. A lighter-weight version, the Trakker, was also available and built at the Seddon Atkinson factory in the UK. The old TurboTech with Fiat-style cab was replaced by the new EuroTech in 1992, featuring the new MP cab. The TurboStar premium long-haul tractor was replaced in 1993 by the high-cabbed EuroStar. Iveco was the dominant partner in the Iveco Ford merger, becoming the major shareholder in 1996 with 52 per cent. One year later UK truck production was phased out and the Langley plant was closed. A new Stralis was unveiled in 2002, with updated styling on the Eurocargo in 2003. The Eurotrakker was replaced by the Trakker in 2004. The Stralis Hi-Way won 'Truck of the Year' in 2013. Current models are powered by the Cursor 11 & 13 litre Euro 6 diesels.

■ LEFT *Former Magirus-Deutz trucks with air-cooled diesels were also rebranded Iveco in the late 1970s.*

■ BELOW *This Iveco Trakker 360 8x4 is seen at work in the UK.*

COLORADO SPRINGS, COLORADO, USA

JARRETT

James C. Jarrett Jnr of the J C Jarrett Motor and Finance Co. was in the business of selling trucks, but most of them were not up to the hilly conditions in the Colorado region. In 1921 he drew up a design for a more powerful truck with more suitable gearing. The specification included a Waukesha 6-cylinder gasoline engine, a 7-speed gearbox and a double-reduction rear axle. There were two load ratings of 2½ and 5 tons. The trucks were badged JCJ. No more than 300 were built during a 13-year production period, most going to local authorities.

KENOSHA, WISCONSIN, USA

JEFFERY QUAD

■ RIGHT ***The versatile Jeffery Quad 4×4 was built in large numbers during World War I.***

The four-wheel drive, four-wheel steer Jeffery Quad for loads of 1½ to 2 tons was developed primarily for military use in 1913. Prior to this the Thomas B. Jeffery Corporation had built a number of lightweight delivery trucks which were discontinued to allow volume production of the Quad. Production was also farmed out to other manufacturers to try to meet demand. The Quad was a very versatile machine with its 13.7m/45ft turning circle. Power came from a 36hp 4-cylinder Buda gasoline engine. Production continued until 1919 but from 1917 onwards the Jeffery Company was taken over by Nash Motor Co. of Pacine, Wisconsin, and the trucks were called Nash Quad.

JELCZ, K.OLAWY, WARSAW, POLAND

JELCZ

■ LEFT ***Some Jelcz trucks of the 1980s era still used diesel engines based on Leyland designs.***

Zaklady Samochodowe Jelcz SA formerly produced trucks under the Zubr name beginning in 1960, but from 1968 the Jelcz name badge was adopted. The Zubr A.80 8-tonne forward-control model featured a Wola diesel engine. The Jelcz 8-tonner appeared from 1968. From 1972 the range was updated using licence-built Wola-Leyland Power Plus diesels. The principal models were the 316 rigid six-wheeler and 317 tractor unit for 32 tonnes with the SW.680 diesel of 200bhp. A more powerful turbocharged version with 240bhp was also introduced. Jelcz used Steyr V8 diesels with 320bhp output for 6×4 tractors. Steyr axles were also used on some models.

As part of Grupa Zasada, Jelcz offered an extensive range of trucks featuring some 27 models from 16 to 42 tons including 4x2, 4x4, 6x2, 6x4 and 8x4 types. Engines included Mielec, Mercedes Benz, Iveco and Steyr. Since 2001 Jelcz has concentrated its production on military trucks for the Polish army.

WEST BROMWICH, ENGLAND

JENSEN

■ LEFT *Jensen's long lightweight chassis formed the ideal basis for large-volume furniture vans.*

Originally coachbuilders, the Jensen brothers decided to enter the truck business in 1938 with a lightweight integral design that could carry the maximum permitted payload but still be eligible to operate at 48kph/30mph. UK regulations passed in the 1930s restricted trucks over 2.5 tons unladen weight to 32kph/20mph. Jensen, by using a unique form of construction developed in conjunction with the Reynolds Tube Co., managed to build trucks to the maximum legal length of 8.4m/27.5ft with a load platform up to 7m/23ft and a payload capacity of 5 to 6 tons, while still not exceeding the 2.5-ton "tare" weight. A number of prototypes were built between 1939 and 1944 and production began in 1946. While the prototypes used Ford engines, production vehicles had Perkins P6 diesels and Moss 5-speed gearboxes. Later, an Austin 4-speed gearbox was used and a Moss rear axle was standard. When the UK length limit was increased to 9.1m/30ft in the mid 1950s, Jensen responded with their Freighter 6-ton models with a 7.7m/25.5ft body and an unladen weight of just 2-ton 19cwt as by this time the 32kph/20mph rule applied only to trucks over 3 tons. As well as the lightweight truck, Jensen produced a small articulated vehicle known as the Jen-Tug for urban deliveries. This was powered by a Ford gasoline engine, but later models had the 1.2 litre/73cu in 4-cylinder gasoline engine used in the Austin A40 car. Jensen's truck building activities ended in 1959.

■ BELOW *Jensen's chassis, cab and body were built as one integral structure to save weight.*

HEFEI, CHINA

JIANG-HUAI

During the period of Mao Tse-tung's Cultural Revolution of the late 1960s many provincial truck plants were established. The Jiang-Huai (or Chiang-Huai) HF.140 3-tonne forward-control entered production in 1969. It was powered by a 4.4 litre/268cu in, 120bhp 6-cylinder gasoline engine. Jiang-Huai also built a lighter model, the 2-tonne HF.130 and a heavy-duty 8-tonner designated the HF.150. Most are operated in Anhui province.

SHANGHAI, CHINA

JIAOTONG

The Shanghai Heavy Motor Vehicle Factory built trucks under the Jiaotong name, meaning "Communication". They are now called Datong. Gasoline and diesel engines of Shanghai manufacture are used and there are normal and forward-control models for 8 to 30 tonnes gcw. Truck production began in 1958. Applications include general cargo trucks, dump trucks, crane trucks, tractor units for semi-trailers and various municipal types such as fire appliances, street sprinklers and garbage trucks.

■ ABOVE ***This mid 1980s Datong (formerly Jiaotong) SH161 heavy-duty six-wheeled truck grosses 28 tonnes and carries a 15-tonne payload.***

CHANGCHUN, CHINA

JIEFANG

Jiefang is the original Chinese truck that later developed into the FAW. Sometimes called 'Jayfong', the name dates back to 1956 when the first CA-10 models were built, based on the Russian ZIS.150 which was itself a copy of the American International K series. The CA-10 was built in huge numbers, assembled in various plants throughout China. Other more modern Jiefang trucks from Dan Dong Automobile works in Lianoning Province have included the CA-141B cargo truck and a dump-truck version, the DD349. The No.1 Automobile Plant at Changchun also builds off-road dump trucks. Current trucks are badged FAW (First Automobile Works) and include new cab-over models in 4x2, 6x4 and 8x4 form (see 'FAW').

■ ABOVE ***The Jiefang CA102 dropside truck was powered by 95bhp gasoline engine and carried a 4-tonne payload.***

■ LEFT ***Typical of Chinese trucks is this FAW (Jiefang) drawbar outfit for up to 10 tonnes payload.***

BACKNANG, GERMANY

KAELBLE

■ LEFT *This 6×6 forward-control tractor was one of a wide range of Kaelble's custom-built heavy vehicles.*

Carl Kaelble Motoren- und Maschinenfabrik specialized in road tractors, crane carriers and, more recently, quarrying vehicles. The company history can be traced back to 1903, when it built its first high-speed gasoline engine. The first road tractor – the Suevia – appeared in 1925 and in 1933 a heavy six-wheel tractor was built for the German Railways. During the '30s larger tractors were produced with diesel engines up to 200bhp. After World War II Kaelble continued to build road tractors but entered the truck market too with a bonneted 7-tonne rigid with a 130bhp 6-cylinder diesel. From 1953 forward-control trucks for 6.5, 8 and 11 tonnes payload were introduced with in-line 6-cylinder diesels, plus a 13-tonner with a V8 diesel. During the late '50s Kaelble's K680 4×2 was a particularly impressive machine with its protruding bonnet (hood) and set-back front axle. This had the Kaelble GO130S indirect-injection 192bhp diesel and ZF AK6-75 gearbox. Payload ratings of 8.2, 10.2 and 11.4 tonnes were specified. Forward-control and tractor-unit versions were also available. Trucks were built through to the early 1970s when the company decided to concentrate entirely on specialized heavy vehicles, including a massive 500-tonne gtw 8×8 powered by a MAN V12 turbocharged diesel of 615bhp. During the late 1980s the company became CKG Kaelble-Gmeinder GmbH.

NABEREZHNYE CHELNY, RUSSIA

KAMAZ

In 1969 the Russians drew up plans for what was to be the world's largest truck plant at a site, determined by computer analysis, next to the Kama River east of Moscow. The plant, covering 103.6sq km/40 square miles and with a planned capacity of 150,000 trucks per annum, began production in February 1976. The models were all based on a new design of 6×4 heavy-duty tilt-cab truck powered by a 210bhp (later uprated to 220bhp), 10.85 litre/662cu in Kamaz 740 V8 naturally aspirated diesel engine. A turbocharged version, the 260bhp 7403, was also available. The rigid truck version for 22 tonnes gvw, or up to 36 tonnes with drawbar trailer, was designated the 53211 while the 54112 tractor unit grossed at 36 tonnes. Kamaz aimed to achieve export sales in many of the world's markets, including Western Europe, the UK, Australia and New Zealand. Their biggest markets have been East European countries. Another important export country has been Cuba. While production at times exceeded the 100,000 per annum mark during the 1980s and early '90s, at times it has been down to 10 per cent of its vast capacity. Currently the range includes 4-, 6- and 8-wheeled rigids, plus a choice of tractor units up to 75 tonnes gross weight. In 2012 the company produced its two millionth truck, and currently has a joint venture with Daimler AG.

■ ABOVE *The Kamaz five-axled artic of the mid 1980s grosses 36 tonnes and is powered by a V8 diesel engine.*

HUDDERSFIELD & LUTON, ENGLAND

KARRIER

■ LEFT *The 1956 Karrier Bantam 2-ton low-loader was a popular vehicle for drinks distribution.*

■ BELOW *A 1949 Karrier CK3 3/4 ton chassis forms the basis for this telephone maintenance truck.*

Karrier Motors Ltd of Huddersfield was formed in 1920 but, prior to that, back as far as 1907 was called Clayton & Co. Those early Karriers were noted for their excellent hill-climbing and manoeuvrability. They were A-types powered by Tylor gasoline engines. Bonneted models, called B-types, appeared in 1911 and by 1913 Karrier were building War Office subsidy-type B4 trucks. After 1920 a K-type for 3 to 6 tons was added, developed from the subsidy truck. Forward control was readopted in 1922 and lighter 1½ and 2-ton models were added to the range. From their early years Karrier were to be significant suppliers of municipal vehicles, including the low-loading CYR 2½-ton garbage truck. At the heavy end of the range Karrier introduced an 8-ton six-wheeler, the KW6 and KWF6, the latter being of forward-control layout. The lightest truck was the 1½-ton ZA model, built in 1929–30 and powered by a Dorman gasoline engine. The Karrier Cob 3-tonner, a rival to Scammell's Mechanical Horse, was introduced in 1931. There was also a 4-ton version called the Cob Major. This was also built with truck and municipal bodywork in rigid form. A most unusual vehicle of the early '30s was the Road Railer, which was designed with an extra set of special wheels so that it could run on the road or on rails. In 1932 a 12-ton six-wheeler, the Colossus, was introduced.

By 1934 Karrier were in difficulties and called in the receivers. A buyer was found in Humber Ltd of Coventry, which was part of the Rootes Group. Rootes had taken over Commer Cars of Luton in 1928 and they decided to transfer Karrier production to the Commer factory. Truck production at Huddersfield was discontinued in 1935. The company was now called Karrier Motor Successors Ltd. After the takeover Karrier was to become more and more specialized in light to medium municipal vehicles, their leading models being the 2-ton Bantam, the 3-ton CK3 and the 6-ton CK6. From 1950 the Bantam was relaunched with a stylish new cab based on the Commer QX. This also went on a new model, the 3 to 4-ton Gamecock which replaced the CK in 1952. A completely new cab design was introduced in 1962, fitted to both Karrier and Commer models. By 1967 Rootes was under the control of Chrysler, and Dodge production was moved to the Commer Karrier plant. A process of integration began, resulting in a new range, the Commando, launched in 1974. Chrysler UK sold out to PSA Peugeot Citroën in 1978. For a brief period the name Talbot Motor Company was adopted but then, in 1981–82, Peugeot resurrected the Karrier Motors Ltd title, but that was short-lived, disappearing when Renault Véhicules Industriels took control in 1981.

KUTAISI, GEORGIA

KAZ

■ RIGHT *A late 1970s KAZ 608V four-axled artic with tilt sleeper cab.*

Production of trucks to ZIS design began at Kutaisi, Georgia, in 1951 using machinery from Opel's former factory at Brandenburg. A dump truck, the KAZ 58, was later introduced. KAZ went on to build their own design of cabover tractor unit, the 606 Kolhida, with sleeper cab. This was followed by the modernised 606A, 608 and 608V with ZIL-130 V8 diesel. In the mid 1980s production at the Kutaisi factory was concentrated on agricultural dump trucks.

SEATTLE, WASHINGTON, USA

KENWORTH

In 1923 Harry W. Kent and Edgar K. Worthington adopted the new name Kenworth for the former Gerlinger Motor Car Co., which Edgar Worthington had acquired in 1917. Between 1917 and 1922 Gerlinger had produced the ruggedly built Gersix truck and the early Kenworths were developed from this. The success of this venture was helped by the closure of two competitive companies in Seattle – the HRL Motor Co. and Vulcan.

Kenworth's early models were solid-tyred bonneted types for payloads of 1½ to 4 tons, powered by Buda 4-cylinder gasoline engines. Eighty trucks were sold during 1924 and sales reached approximately two per week the following year. By 1925 there were five types on offer, the heaviest being a 5-tonner. A 78bhp 6-cylinder gasoline engine was introduced in 1927 and two years later Kenworth opened an assembly plant in Vancouver, B.C., to develop sales in Canada. Already Kenworth was adopting a customizing approach. Though a "standard" range was available, almost any vehicle could be built to the customer's special requirements.

In 1933 Kenworth became the first American truck manufacturer to install diesel engines (in this case Cummins) as standard equipment, and the same year began offering a sleeper cab option. Kenworth had stuck exclusively to bonneted types, but in 1936 launched their first forward-control truck prompted by legislation in the Motor Carrier Act. During World War II Kenworth was a significant producer of military trucks, especially their famous M-1 6×6 wrecker. In the mid 1940s increased use of aluminium in chassis frames, cabs and running units resulted in important weight savings.

In 1944 Kenworth became a wholly owned subsidiary of Pacific Car & Foundry (PACCAR) of Seattle. Kenworth was relocated at the former Fisher Body plant and a production plant was also built later at Kansas City. Sugar plantations in Hawaii became large customers for Kenworth in the immediate post-war period. Export sales were accounting for 40 per cent of Kenworth's turnover by 1950. In the early 1950s the company introduced the massive 853 for Middle East oilfield duties. In 1958 the 953 powered by a Cummins NTC350 was introduced. A half-cab CBE (cab beside engine) tractor unit was introduced in 1954. This was said to provide improved vision for drivers using mountain roads, but not all drivers

■ TOP *The W900 represents the timeless classic eighteen-wheeler conventional and offers a range of sleeper options.*

■ ABOVE LEFT *A 1980 K100 6×4 cabover engaged on heavy haulage in the UK.*

■ LEFT *A T800 dump with pusher axle and four-axled pony trailer.*

■ LEFT *A Canadian W900 with heavy-duty "low boy" trailer for transport of mechanical plant.*

liked it since it lacked interior space. In 1956 two icons of the company's history were launched, the W900 conventional and the K100 cabover. In the same year Kenworth produced an unusual underfloor-engined eight-wheel tractor unit for Pacific Intermountain Express. This formed part of a "dromedary" outfit. The Kansas City plant became operational in 1965 and the success of the new W900 and K100 saw record sales of heavy trucks, reaching 2037 in that year. In 1971 the PD series of cab-forward urban trucks, later marketed as the Hustler models, entered the market. At the other end of the weight scale Kenworth brought in their 6×4 Brute aimed at the construction industry.

A new plant at Chillicothe, Ohio was opened in 1974. Kenworths were also assembled in Australia where twin-steer four-axled rigids were developed. Kenworth also established a plant in Mexico building Kenmex trucks. Kenworth pioneered the high-roof long-haul tractor in 1976 with their top-of-the-range Aerodyne sleeper for both conventionals and cabovers. The archetypal American-style trucks underwent a new wave of styling changes in 1985 when the aerodynamic T600 claimed to reduce wind drag by 40 per cent. Cost conscious operators could benefit from fuel savings of up to 22 per cent from the sleeker lines of the new sloping bonnet (hood). Kenworth's new plant at Renton, Washington was opened on June 4th 1993, joining those in Seattle, Chillicothe, Vancouver, Mexicali and Bayswater, Australia. The same year Kenworth announced its Aerocab sleeper which could be described as a "home-from-home".

While European styling had been allowed to creep into the T600 and the lighter T300, the traditional United States style W900 with its slab-fronted radiator grille soldiers on, as does the long-established K range cabovers which have made only slight concessions to styling over the years.

Meanwhile the ultimate in aero-dynamics can be found in Kenworth's current T680 and T700, a progression of the T2000, which boast smooth flowing lines combined with exceptionally spacious integral sleeper compartments. Kenworth's parent company, Paccar, also owns Peterbilt, DAF and Leyland. Increasing international co-operation in the 1990s saw Americanized versions of Leyland DAF's 55 series, the K37, with the Kenworth name badge. Kenworth also market the Super Heavy-duty C500 for tough all-terrain applications.

■ LEFT *A T600 Chipliner powered by a Detroit Diesel 60 series at work in New Zealand.*

■ BELOW *A 1998 K100G cabover four-axled tractor engaged on heavy haulage in New Zealand.*

STOKE-ON-TRENT, ENGLAND

Kerr Stuart

■ LEFT *Britain's first production diesel truck was this short-lived Kerr Stuart 6-tonner.*

Kerr Stuart was a short-lived truck project but is worthy of its place in history as the first production British diesel truck, introduced in 1929. Kerr Stuart built locomotive boilers but designed a 6-ton chain-drive semi-forward-control diesel truck in 1928 using proprietary components. Initially a 6-cylinder Helios diesel engine was tried, but the first production vehicle had a 60bhp 4-cylinder McLaren-Benz. This had a governed speed of 800rpm and required a single-cylinder air-cooled JAP gasoline engine to start it. Within a year of their formation Kerr Stuart went bankrupt, and only five production models are believed to have been sold.

NICOSIA, CYPRUS

KMC

Truck assembly began at KMC Motors in 1973 using British-sourced designs from Dennis powered by Perkins diesels. When supplies of Dennis parts diminished, KMC based their trucks on Dodge and Commer, including Spanish Dodges. Trucks ranged from 16 to 30 tonnes gvw. During the 1980s KMC sourced their designs and components from a wider number of manufacturers, MAN becoming a major supplier of cabs and engines. Detroit Diesel engines are also available in some models.

■ ABOVE *The Cypriot-produced KMC 26/38DT 6×4 dump truck was based on the Spanish Dodge. It was powered by the Chrysler BS36 11.95 litre/728cu in 6-cylinder diesel engine.*

SPRINGFIELD, MASSACHUSETTS, USA

Knox/Knox Martin

Knox Martin is universally regarded as the world's pioneer of the articulated truck. As the Knox Automotive Co. it produced a variety of light and medium trucks from its formation in 1901 through to 1908. The earliest of them was a three-wheeler van version based on the Knox car. It was in 1909 that Charles Henry Martin, a former Knox employee, rejoined the company and patented his Martin Rocking Fifth Wheel. This was a device for coupling semi-trailers to tractor units. The weight of the semi-trailer front end was taken by the tractor rear axle as opposed to the tractor chassis. The first Knox Martin tractors were three-wheelers with a steerable single front wheel capable of an almost 90-degree lock angle. This made the outfit extremely manoeuvrable. Later a four-wheel truck was introduced. It is worth noting that it was the Knox Martin principle that formed the basis of the highly successful Scammell articulated six-wheeler in the UK in 1922. Knox Martin themselves ceased trading in 1924.

TOKYO, JAPAN

KOMATSU

■ BELOW *Komatsu are a major supplier of heavy dump trucks. This is their HD1200 of the late 1970s.*

Komatsu is a large Japanese manufacturer of dump trucks and other construction vehicles. Dump-truck production got underway from 1951 powered by licence-built Cummins diesel engines. Over the years Komatsu dump trucks have grown larger and more powerful. In the late 1970s the largest machine was the HD1200 with a 130-tonne payload, powered by a 37 litre/2220cu in, 1200bhp Cummins KTA-2300 V12 turbocharged, aftercooled diesel which drove an alternator providing current for the electric final-drive system. Each rear wheel had its own traction motor. Komatsu Mining Systems, formed in 1996 in a link-up with United States-based Modular Mining System Inc., is now Komatsu's global mining-equipment headquarters, and currently their range of dump trucks spans the 54 to 327 tonnes (59.5 to 360 US tons) payload range. The largest of these, machines employing diesel electric traction, is the 960E with a design gross vehicle weight of 580 tonnes (640 US tons) and a horse-power rating of 3,500.

KREMENCHUG, UKRAINE

KRAZ

■ BELOW *The 1999 KrAZ 5444 32-ton tractor is powered by 288bhp 14.86 litre/906cu in diesel.*

Production of YAZ trucks at the Yaroslavi works was transferred to a new factory at Kremenchug in 1959 and YAZ trucks were renamed KrAZ. The products were largely carried-over YAZ designs until 1966 when a new range of heavy trucks was launched. These were of 6×4 and 6×6 normal-control layout for use as dump trucks and as tractor units for articulated use. Their V8 diesels were built at the former YAZ plant which then became YAMZ. When marketed in Europe, KrAZ were badged as Belaz.

The current KrAZ range includes 37 bonneted 4×2, 6×4 and 6×6 heavy-duty tractors and truck chassis for gross weights from 17.3 to 75 tonnes, featuring a modern design of cab. The principal power unit is a 14.8 litre/903cu in V8 turbocharged diesel rated between 230 and 318bhp. The 4×2 tractor unit, type 5401, is for 32 tonnes gcw and has the 312hp engine. The largest tractors, the 6x6 '6446' with 330hp are marketed with a 48-ton Warz '9592' dump truck semi-trailer. Eurocargo trucks have also been built by KrAZ under a joint venture with Iveco formed in 1995.

AMSTERDAM, THE NETHERLANDS

KROMHOUT

Kromhout's history began in the mid 1920s when it built marine diesels, but in 1935 the company acquired a licence to build Gardner 4, 5 and 6-cylinder diesels which it used to power a range of Kromhout trucks. By the outbreak of World War II Kromhout Motoren Fabriek NV was offering a range of trucks and tractor units from 3 to 30 tonnes gcw. These were mainly of bonneted layout. Production was suspended during the war, but the range was reintroduced in 1945. In the late '40s Kromhout undertook assembly of Leyland vehicles for the Dutch market. Forward-control trucks for 10-tonne payloads appeared in 1953, and by 1955 normal and forward-control six-wheelers were added to the range. These featured Kirkstall overhead worm double-drive rear bogies. Kromhout developed higher powered diesels based on the 8.4 litre/512cu in Gardner up to 140bhp. Rolls Royce engines were also fitted as an option on the heavy six-wheelers.

Kromhout production ended in 1961 after the company merged with Verheul who, up until the merger, were mainly bus builders. Some Verheul trucks based on Kromhouts were fitted with the Kromhout-Gardner engine while others had Rolls Royce power units. Truck production at Verheul ended in 1965, by which time the company was AEC-owned.

■ ABOVE *A Kromhout 4VS-AN long-wheelbase dropside truck dating from 1956.*

ESSEN, GERMANY

KRUPP

Production of Krupp trucks began in 1919 with a chain-drive 5-tonner, although some early steam wagons had been built at the company's Kiel ship building works between 1905 and 1908. Fried Krupp Motoren- und Kraftwagen-fabriken went on to build a mixture of types in the early 1920s, including a 10-tonne payload bonneted tractor unit, and then, in contrast, a three-wheeled road sweeper. By 1925 the range was shaft-driven and consisted of 1½, 2, 5 and 10-tonners. Krupp's first forward-control trucks appeared in 1930 in both 4×2 and 6×4 form. From 1932 Krupp built Junkers opposed-piston two-stroke diesel engines. During the '30s a whole range of trucks continued to be built, but by the latter part of World War II the Krupp organization faced collapse. It was renamed Sudwerke GmbH and rehoused in a plant at Kulmbach where, between 1944 and 1951, trucks were also built under the name Sudwerke.

■ ABOVE *The 1963 Krupp 801 drawbar outfit for 34 tonnes gtw featured a 5.8 litre/355cu in 4-cylinder two-stroke diesel engine developing 192bhp.*

■ LEFT *A S960/12 articulated five-axled bulk cement truck powered by a Krupp-Cummins four-stroke V6 diesel engine.*

■ BELOW *A 1964 SF960/12 with sleeper cab powered by four-stroke Krupp-Cummins V6 developing 220bhp.*

■ BOTTOM *The 1960 Mustang 801 with 186bhp Krupp 4-cylinder two-stroke grossed 14 tonnes.*

Production transferred back to Essen in 1951 and a new range was launched, including the famous 8-tonne Titan and 5.5-tonne Buffel. A completely new range of normal and forward-control models, including the 701, 801, 901, 1001 and 1051, of very handsome appearance, was announced in 1956. These were powered by Krupp two-stroke diesels which were water-cooled, uniflow scavenged designs with 3, 4, 5 or 7-cylinders with power outputs ranging from 132 to 310bhp. From 1963 Krupp began offering the licence-built Krupp-Cummins V6-200 four-stroke diesel and most heavy-duty forward-control models became available with a tilt cab. All-wheel drive bonneted models such as the 760 4×4 and 360 6×6 were also available, as was a range of half-cab quarry dump trucks in 4×2 (MK) and 4×4 (AMK) form for payloads of 18, 23 and 30 tonnes. The heavy-duty on-highway trucks went up to 43 tonnes design gross train weight. In 1967 Krupp introduced a new 4×4 on-highway tractor unit with a 265bhp V8 engine, but the following year production of all trucks ceased owing to a fall-off in demand.

In 1968 Daimler-Benz took over the distribution of Krupp trucks, including their existing stocks and real estate. A small residue of forward-control tilt cabs was purchased by Atkinson Vehicles (Europe) SA to produce their Atkinson-Krupp models, of which very few were built. Krupp itself switched to the production of heavy-duty mobile cranes.

ALMA, MICHIGAN, USA

LaFrance

LaFrance is a name normally associated with American LaFrance fire appliances of Elmira, New York, but the company produced a 5-ton truck just before World War I. From 1914 onwards production was discontinued to concentrate on fire engines, but in 1923 a separate operation called the American LaFrance Truck Co. was formed in Bloomfield, New Jersey, offering a range of models from 2 to 7½ tons payload capacity. That enterprise was short-lived and in 1929 it was merged into the Republic Motor Truck Co. of Alma, Michigan, forming the LaFrance Republic Corp. Republic trucks went up to 6½ tons payload while heavier models of LaFrance design were added to expand up the weight range. The heaviest was a massive 20-ton gvw three-axled rigid called the Mogul, powered by an American LaFrance V12 gasoline engine of 240bhp. It attracted few sales and the whole business was taken over by the Sterling Motor Truck Co. in 1932, production being centred on Sterling's plant at West Allis, Wisconsin.

JURA, FRANCE

Labourier

■ LEFT ***Labourier's 3-tonner of 1960 had an unusual fibreglass cab with forward-sloping windscreen.***

While Labourier's main products were timber trucks and agricultural tractors, they produced a 5/7-tonne low-loading truck in 1947. Labourier's largest tractor was a 10-tonne 4x4 for oilfield work powered by a Deutz air-cooled diesel. In 1960 the company produced its only normal type of load carrier in the form of the TL3 forward-control 3-tonner. This had a modern fibreglass cab and a 1.8 litre/110cu in Peugeot diesel engine. Labourier continued to build specialized tractors, dump trucks and snowploughs through to their closure in the 1970s.

LETCHWORTH, ENGLAND

Lacre

■ RIGHT ***The 1913 Lacre O model had a 4-cylinder gasoline engine and chain drive. The payload was 2½ tons.***

The Lacre Motor Car Company's history began in January 1902 at Long Acre near Covent Garden in London, the name being an abbreviation of Long Acre. Until 1909 the products consisted of cars and light vans, the earliest being based on an Albion chassis. From 1909 a full range of trucks up to 9 tons payload capacity was available, one of the best-known models being the 2-ton O type with chain drive. Production moved to a new site at Letchworth Garden City in 1910. After World War I, during which they built military vehicles, Lacre switched to building road sweepers. For the first two years of the war all of Lacre's military production was sold to the Belgian Army, but trucks were also supplied to the British, Canadian and Indian forces. Road-sweeper production doubtless helped Lacre remain profitable during the post-war slump. Some ordinary load-carrying trucks were offered until the late 1920s, including the forward-control E type 2½-tonner noted for its easily removable engine which was mounted on a subframe. In 1928 Lacre was hit by financial problems and was wound up, the Letchworth factory being sold. A reconstituted company named Lacre Lorries Ltd was set up in Kings Cross, London, concentrating on road sweepers. In 1936 the company relocated again to Welwyn Garden City. During World War II the Ministry of Aircraft Production commandeered their factory so production of sweepers was suspended until 1947. From 1952 onwards Lacre only supplied sweeper bodywork on Bedford chassis.

TURIN, ITALY

LANCIA

■ LEFT ***The Lancia Esatau B of the early 1960s was powered by Lancia's own 6-cylinder diesel.***

Vincenzo Lancia and Claudio Fogolin formed Lancia in 1906. In 1912 the first trucks were built for the Italian army. The Iota and Diota of 1915 featured built-in electrics. The 2½-tonne Triota and Tetriota appeared in 1921. The Pentaiota of 1924 was Lancia's first true heavy truck, having a payload of 5.3 tonnes. In 1932 Lancia built their first diesel truck, the RO for 9.3 tonnes gvw powered by a vertical opposed-piston two-stroke engine built under licence from Junkers.

By 1938 Lancia had developed its own Type 102 5-cylinder diesel which was installed in the 3RO truck for 6½-tonne payload. More powerful 6-cylinder diesels were available in the Esatau of 1947, which was in production until 1963. Forward control appeared in 1955 with the 864A. These became the Esatau type B. During the 1960s Lancia's heavy trucks were the Esagamma and Esagamma E for 19 tonnes gvw, while heavier 6×2 and 6×4 versions were also available. Lancia joined Fiat in 1969.

SURESNES, FRANCE

LATIL

■ LEFT ***A Latil tractor purpose-built for shunting heavy trailers.***

Georges Latil was in vehicle building as early as 1898, having pioneered front-wheel drive in the Blum-Latil truck before establishing Cie des Automobiles Industriels Latil in 1914. The company specialized in all-wheel drive, all-wheel steer tractors. From the mid 1920s a range of trucks from 1½ to 10 tonnes was offered. In 1929 pneumatic-tyred trucks were introduced. Licensed production of Gardner engines began in the early 1930s. Latil tractors were licence built in the UK by Shelvoke & Drewry as Trauliers. After World War II Latil's comprehensive range was mainly diesel-powered. Until 1955 Latil remained independent, but it then became part of Saviem.

TOOWOOMBA, AUSTRALIA

LEADER

■ RIGHT ***The fibreglass-cabbed A6 three-axled rigid was part of Leader's Mid Ranger series.***

Leader trucks were the inspiration of a transport company that wanted a rugged truck tailored to Australian requirements. Cyril Anderson formed a transport firm in 1934. It grew into the nationally-based Western Transport. He also formed the Great Western Group. In 1972 it was decided to enter truck manufacture. The A series featured Caterpillar diesels, Fuller Transmissions and Rockwell axles. Detroit Diesel two-stroke V diesels were also available. Cabs were modelled on the Mack F series but built of fibreglass. There were two strains of Leaders – the Mid Ranger for short-haul work and the Overlander for long distance. These could be ordered with the Sundowner sleeper cab. A bonneted tractor, the Challenger, was also introduced. Leader were forced to pull out of truck manufacture in 1983.

LEYLAND, ENGLAND

LEYLAND

■ LEFT *A 1928 Leyland GH2 4-tonner powered by 4-cylinder gasoline engine. Pneumatic tyres were introduced in 1925.*

■ BELOW LEFT *The very first wagon to be built by the Lancashire Steam Motor Co. in 1896.*

■ ABOVE *Leyland's first gasoline-engined truck of 1904 was nicknamed the "Pig".*

■ BELOW *The Leyland Marathon introduced in 1973, developed by AEC.*

The origins of the UK's most famous truck maker lie in the Lancashire Steam Motor Co. set up in 1896 at Leyland in Lancashire. The young man at the centre of the enterprise was James Sumner, the son of Elias Sumner, who was village blacksmith at Leyland. Between 1884 and 1896 James had experimented with numerous steam-propelled vehicles. The passing of the 1896 Act, which lifted certain restrictive legislation, encouraged James to set up the Lancashire Steam Motor Co., for which he received financial backing from the Spurrier family. With the help of just 20 employees, Sumner completed his first vehicle, a 1½-ton steam van with oil-fired boiler, cart wheels and tiller steering. As orders for the steamers came in, new premises were found, being the "North Works" of Leyland's factory in later years. No less than 72 steamers were built over the first six years, and larger machines for payloads of up 3, 4 and 5 tons were developed. By 1904 the company was experimenting with gasoline-engined trucks, and following the first rudimentary machine, nicknamed the "Pig", an improved model appeared in 1905, production reaching 16 chassis. In 1907 the Preston-based engineering company, Coulthards, was taken over and the business was renamed Leyland Motors Ltd.

While steam-vehicle production continued until 1926, based at the company's Chorley works, Leyland's main focus was on the internal combustion engine. A bonneted 3-ton gasoline truck was approved under the War Office subsidy scheme in 1912. This became the famous RAF type. In its final form this had a 34hp 4-cylinder engine, cone clutch and 4-speed crash gearbox driving a double-reduction bevel rear axle. Over 5500 of these trucks were built, and they are regarded as one of Leyland's most famous machines. Notable classics of the 1920s were the Q-type 4-tonner, the SQ2 semi-forward-control 7-tonner of 1925 and the SWQ2 10-ton six-wheel derivative, which appeared in 1927. Leyland's early experiments with diesel power began in 1925 when a prototype engine of spark-ignition design was tried. By 1930 a direct-injection diesel was fitted into a six-wheeled Rhino for exhibition at the Olympia Show in London. By 1933 diesel engines were in full production.

From 1929–30 Leyland's famous Zoo range of trucks appeared with familiar names such as Beaver, Bison, Buffalo, Bull and Hippo, soon followed by the Rhino 6-tonner and the Cub 2-tonner in 1931. By now Leylands had taken on a more modern look, with fully enclosed cabs. UK legislation in 1933 led manufacturers to keep weight to a

■ RIGHT *Leyland's Hippo 12-tonner of 1937.*

■ RIGHT *Leyland's last important truck launch was that of the Roadtrain, which arrived on the scene in 1980.*

■ BELOW RIGHT *The mainstay of Leyland's early post-war range was this 22.O/1 rigid eight-wheeler powered by their O.600 diesel.*

minimum to avoid the excessive road tax that was based on unladen weight. Another phenomenon of the period was the rigid eight-wheeler. Though Leyland was not the first to exploit the 22-ton four-axled rigid, it had one available within a year of its rivals AEC, ERF and Foden. It took the appropriate name Octopus. A by-product of the twin-steer eight-wheeler was the Chinese Six. Leyland offered one from 1937 called the Twin Steer Beaver, but later renamed it just Steer.

Leyland became an important producer of battle tanks during World War II and also built thousands of trucks for military and essential civilian users between 1939 and 1945. In the late '40s Leyland rivalled AEC as Britain's largest heavy-truck builder. From that point on both companies embarked on ambitious expansion plans. Leyland took over Albion Motors in 1951 and Scammell Lorries in 1955. By this time AEC had become ACV Group and had taken over Maudslay and Crossley.

The post-war products of the two companies were also broadly similar. As part of the post-war export drive, Leyland introduced its bonneted Comet in 1947. A forward-control version came in 1953 and AEC matched it with their Mercury. Both companies built normal and forward-control heavies of similar weights and power outputs. AEC established numerous joint projects with European manufacturers, as did Leyland. Leyland's range, which consisted of the Comet and Super Comet four-wheelers and the heavier-duty Beaver four-wheeler, Hippo six-wheeler and Octopus eight-wheeler, received a new cab in 1960. This was the heavily styled LAD steel cab which, compared to its predecessor, lacked interior space.

■ RIGHT *Although badged Leyland, this Reiver was of Albion pedigree but was built at BLMC's Bathgate factory.*

In 1961 Leyland had bought out Standard Triumph and gained a facility to build a lighter truck, namely the Leyland 90. The same year ACV acquired Thornycroft. This was ACV's last expansion move as Leyland bought out the entire group in 1962. The resulting combine was called the Leyland Motor Corporation Ltd. It wasn't long before Leyland group products began to take on a family likeness. Their Ergomatic tilt cab of 1964 appeared on Leyland, AEC and Albion models. In the late '60s Leyland experimented with gas-turbine propulsion following the acquisition of the Rover Co. in 1966 which had extensive experience in this field. While a number of gas-turbine prototypes were built, the project was abandoned. Until the late '60s Leyland had remained reasonably successful and was easily the UK's largest producer and exporter of heavy trucks. Sadly, Leyland's fortunes were to take a down turn following an ill-planned merger with British Motor Holdings (BMH), which included BMC trucks and Guy Motors. BMC's range, built at Bathgate, was later marketed as Leyland Redline. The outcome of the merger, under which the company was now part of the British Leyland Motor Corporation (BLMC), was that BMH's ailing car operations starved the truck divisions of resources and investment.

The situation worsened until 1975 when the UK government was forced to nationalize the whole group and try to rescue what remained viable. Funds were put into a new range of trucks, desperately needed since Leyland had been unable to improve its range through lack of resources in the BLMC era. That new range was the T45, announced in 1980, which was highly successful. Unfortunately, by that time Leyland had lost most of its credibility and foreign competition had robbed most of its potential market, both at home and abroad. The BLMC years had all but ruined Leyland, which was once the jewel in the UK truck maker's crown. In spite of the excellent new T45 or Roadtrain range, Leyland suffered mounting losses and in 1987 the decision was reached by the UK government to sell off the company to DAF Trucks. Ironically, the relatively young Dutch company had originally built its reputation on Leyland technology during the 1950s. Henceforth Leylands were marketed as Leyland-DAF in the UK.

■ LEFT *During the 1990s Leyland Trucks Ltd. built the rugged Super Comet for export.*

THAME, ENGLAND

LEYLAND-DAF

■ RIGHT *Under Leyland-DAF the former Roadrunner was relaunched as the 45 series.*

The history of Leyland-DAF begins in 1987 with the sale of the UK's most prestigious truck manufacturer into foreign ownership, symbolizing the decline of Britain's once-thriving truck industry. Leyland's fortunes took a down turn after a series of expansion moves during the 1950s and '60s when it absorbed Albion (1951), Scammell (1955), ACV Group encompassing AEC, Maudslay and Thornycroft (1962), and finally the ailing car giant BMH, which included Austin and Morris trucks, as well as the Jaguar Group's Guy range, in 1968. It was the link-up with BMH to form the British Leyland Motor Corporation (BLMC) that eventually led to Leyland's problems. The car manufacturing divisions drained the group's resources until it faced collapse in the mid 1970s.

The British government stepped in and rescued the company in 1975 and British Leyland's truck and bus divisions were given greater autonomy, but the damage was done. All the truck plants except Leyland were either closed or sold off, including Southall, Wolverhampton, Scotstoun, Watford and Bathgate, and Leyland made a final bid to re-establish itself with the launch of the T45 series in 1980. In spite of the slimming measures and the launch of a first-class product, the company continued to suffer heavy losses. It changed its name to BL to disguise the British identity that was thought to convey a poor image. It was then relegated to being a member of the Rover Group. By 1986 the taxpayers could no longer be expected to prop up the state-owned truck maker and a buyer was sought. Bids were turned down from General Motors and Paccar, but in 1987 it was agreed that DAF would take a 60 per cent controlling share in Leyland and Freight Rover. Leyland was to be responsible for light and medium trucks while DAF concentrated on heavy trucks, and a new UK-based sales company would market the products as Leyland-DAF in the UK. In other markets the trucks were to be badged as DAF. Initially the new organization appeared to flourish, but then DAF ran into financial problems following heavy investment in a new range, the 65, 75 and 85 series. In February 1993 the company collapsed and was rescued by the Dutch and Belgian governments. However, the UK manufacturing plant at Leyland was not part of the deal and was the subject of a management buy-out, returning it to 100 per cent British ownership. The new company, Leyland Truck Manufacturing, formed an agreement to supply Leyland trucks to DAF to be marketed in the UK through Leyland-DAF Ltd, which is still owned by DAF. Leyland Trucks also builds certain DAF models and, for a period, undertook assembly of Isuzu trucks.

In 1996 Paccar, the American owners of Kenworth, Peterbilt and Foden, took over DAF. Two years later in June 1998 Paccar acquired Leyland Truck Manufacturing too. In September 1999 Paccar transferred Foden production from Sandbach to the Leyland plant where it continued until Foden's demise in 2006. The 'Leyland' was dropped from Leyland-DAF in 2000 and the factory at Leyland in Lancashire was put over to producing DAF trucks mainly for the UK market.

■ ABOVE LEFT *A heavy-duty 95 series 8×4 tractor engaged on UK heavy haulage.*

■ LEFT *The 85 series Leyland-DAF eight-wheeler is of DAF pedigree throughout.*

JABLONEC NAD NISOU, CZECH REPUBLIC

LiAZ

■ LEFT *The latest LiAZ 300 series long-haul tractor is this 19/41 TBV with 300bhp diesel.*

Liberecké Automobilové Zavody took over production of Skoda 706 trucks in 1951 at the former Avia plant in Prague which had built Skodas since 1946. The Skoda 706RT and 706RTS forward-control models appeared in 1957 with the direct injection 11.78 litre/719cu in diesel. The LiAZ name was adopted from 1974 when the long-running 706 models were joined by the modernized 100.05 trucks and 100.45 38-tonne tractor units powered by a turbocharged version of the 11.94 litre/729cu in diesel which had powered the 706 models in 1968. In turbocharged form for the 100 series it was rated at 270 or 340bhp.

From 1999 LiAZ trucks were produced by the Truck International AS Division of Skoda and the range included 4x2 models up to 19 tonnes gvw and 6x2s for 24.5 tonnes, all models grossing 40 tonnes with drawbar trailer. Also available were dump trucks in 4x2, 4x4, 6x4 and 8x4 form. The company ran into financial difficulties in the new millennium and production ceased in 2001. The last tractor units shared a new design of sleeper cab with Skoda.

USA

LIBERTY

■ RIGHT *Liberty trucks were built by a number of manufacturers and some were later converted for civilian use.*

Though Liberty was not officially a truck make in its own right, it was the name adopted for a standardized design of truck for the United States Army. In 1917 the United States Army drew up a specification for a standard Class B 3 to 5-ton heavy truck, to overcome the problems of having scores of different types needing huge stocks of non-interchangeable spare parts. Such was the demand for trucks in World War I that over 8000 Libertys were shipped to France during the latter part of the war. The Model B was built mainly by Selden of Rochester, New York, and Gramm Bernstein of Lima, Ohio, but they were also built by Garford, Pierce Arrow, Republic, Bethlehem, Diamond T, Brockway and Sterling. After the war a Belgian company based in Brussels began reconditioning the surplus United States Army Liberty trucks. Soc. Franco-Belgique de Camions Liberty went on to build modernized versions through to the start of World War II, the later ones having diesel engines. Liberty trucks were also rebuilt by Willème during that period before the company in Seine, France, went on to launch its own designs.

BRIDGEPORT, CONNECTICUT, USA

LOCOMOBILE

Locomobile existed for a very short period, its name being changed to Riker after just five years. The first Locomobile of 1912 was a cabover 5-tonner with chain drive. Other models for 3, 4 and 6 tons were added during 1915. Production ended in 1920.

■ RIGHT *A World War I Locomobile 3-ton truck with a 4-cylinder engine.*

ROUEN, FRANCE

LOHÉAC

The Lohéac story is an example of a transport contractor developing his own breed of truck to suit his specific needs. Beginning in the early 1950s Antoine Lohéac based his first tractor units on ex-United States Army H-542 Internationals introducing other makes of engine, mainly Berliet diesels. Over the years Lohéac introduced an increasing number of his own components, building the distinctive semi-forward cabs from fibreglass "in house". During the 1970s and '80s Lohéac used DAF and Scania engines and introduced a full forward-control tractor with Aramid fibre-reinforced cab. The Lohéac fleet is made up mainly of bulk liquid tankers. The company has also built its own semi-trailers.

■ ABOVE ***Lohéac built heavy trucks solely for their own use.***

■ LEFT ***Early Lohéac trucks were developed from the ex-army International H-542.***

COLNBROOK, ENGLAND

LOMOUNT

Lomount was a new name applied to Rotinoff heavy-duty tractors from 1960 to 1962. (See "Rotinoff".)

■ RIGHT ***One of two Rotinoff Viscount road-train tractors supplied for Australian livestock transport.***

LORRAINE, FRANCE

LORRAINE-DIETRICH

Formerly known as De Dietrich, whose history dated from 1896, Lorraine-Dietrich trucks first appeared in 1905. De Dietrich's earliest truck, a 3-tonner, took part in the 1897 Versailles Heavy Vehicle Trials achieving a top speed of 15kph/9mph. The early vehicles had complex transmissions combining belt drive and gearing, but a 2-tonne truck available in 1902 had chain drive. In 1907 the design rights were acquired from Turcat-Méry for a highly unusual three-axled truck with a central chain-driven axle and a lightweight steered axle fore and aft. By 1909 the truck range included bonneted models from ¾ tonne to 5 tonnes, the heaviest having a 5½ litre/335cu in gasoline engine. A cab-over-engine layout was adopted for a 3-tonner in 1911. Some shaft-drive 1-tonne trucks were built during the early part of World War I, but after that production ceased. A small number of trucks badged Lorraine were built under licence from Tatra in the 1930s, plus a few road-rail terminal tractors in the 1940s.

ALLENTOWN, PENNSYLVANIA, USA

MACK

■ LEFT ***The 1999 Mack Vision tractor has a 460bhp E-Tech turbo diesel with V-MAC electronic vehicle management and control.***

■ BELOW LEFT ***An early example of Mack's legendary AC Bulldog dating from 1917. Around 40,000 ACs were built between 1915 and 1938.***

The Mack Brothers Company was incorporated in New York in 1901 with John M. (Jack), Augustus F. (Gus) and William C. (Willie) Mack as directors.

From 1904 the brothers adopted the Manhattan name for their vehicles and in 1905 formed Mack Brothers Motor Car Co. in Lehigh County, Pennsylvania, with production facilities at Allentown. From 1910 it was decided to drop the Manhattan name and call the trucks Mack. The first trucks of 1905 were a bonneted 1½ to 2-tonner and forward-control models for 3, 4 and 5 tons payload – all powered by Mack's own design of gasoline engine.

To raise further capital the International Motor Company was formed in 1911 as a holding company for the Mack Brothers Motor Car Co. and the Saurer Motor Co. The latter built Swiss Saurer trucks under licence. A significant development was the introduction of the medium-weight AB of 1914 followed in 1915 by the legendary AC. It was the AC's rugged performance during World War I that impressed the British soldiers, so much so that they dubbed it the "Bulldog". The name stuck and from 1922 the famous bulldog motif was adopted as Mack's corporate symbol.

■ ABOVE ***The A50T tractor was launched in 1950 in the lead-up to Mack's 50th anniversary.***

■ BELOW ***An F series engaged on long-distance European international haulage.***

Over the years more famous models appeared, such as the BJ and BB of 1927. Then came the streamlined medium-duty Mack E models of 1936 with payload ratings up to 4 tons. Heavier E models followed, including the 6-ton shaft-drive EM, 6-ton chain-drive ER and EQ tractors for 10 to 12 tons.

During World War II Mack was a major supplier of trucks, including prime movers, personnel carriers, wreckers and tank transporters.

The 1950s saw important new models, including the B, H and G series. The bonneted B series of 1953 was one of Mack's best-known trucks. A total of 127,786 were built through to 1966, when it was replaced by the R series. The Thermodyne diesel was also introduced in 1953. A series of cab-forward medium-duty trucks began with the D series in 1955, followed by the N series which shared a design of Budd tilt cab with Ford. Then, in 1962, came the MB with Mack's own tilt cab. This was later developed into the MC in 1978. The H cabovers, nicknamed "Cherry Pickers" on account of their tall cabs, were specially designed to operate with 10.6m/35ft trailers within the 13.7m/45ft legal length limits. The G series of 1959 featured an all-aluminium cab and a choice of Mack or Cummins engine and was aimed at the West Coast users. Another significant development in the 1950s was the acquisition of the Brockway

■ RIGHT *The Ultra-Liner range came on the scene in 1982 with power ratings up to 500bhp.*

■ BELOW *A late 1950s H60 series cabover-engine tractor. Early H60s were nicknamed "Cherry Pickers".*

Motor Co. of Cortland, New York. This was allowed to continue with its own product line although Mack F series cabs appeared on certain models. Brockway was finally closed in 1977.

The famous F series appeared in 1962 and was sold in vast numbers throughout the world. For heavy-duty construction duties Mack introduced their rugged DM models. During the mid '60s assembly plants were set up in various countries, including an Australian plant in Queensland where specialized twin-steer four and five-axled rigids were built for roadtrain use. In 1963 Mack took over Camions Bernard in Arcueil, France, renaming it Automobiles Bernard. The tie-up only lasted until 1966 when Bernard was closed down. Owing to a shortage of working capital, Mack merged with the Los Angeles-based Signal Oil & Gas Co. in 1967. The late '60s saw Mack introducing the Maxidyne constant-horsepower diesel, Maxitorque triple-countershaft transmission and, in 1971, Dynatard, Mack's own patented engine brake. A 66 per cent interest was acquired in Hayes Manufacturing, the Canadian heavy truck builder, in 1969.

The W series Cruise-Liner was announced in 1975 as Mack's premium long-haul cabover while the RW Super-Liner conventional followed in 1978. In 1979 Renault bought a 10 per cent share in Mack, increasing this to 20 per cent in 1982. That year also marked the launch of the new MH Ultra-Liner range with the Max-Glass composite cab made of fibreglass around a steel frame.

During the 1980s closer ties were formed with Renault, including an agreement to market the Midliner city truck as the Mack Midliner in the United States. Mack's CH bonneted range was launched in 1988. By 1990 Mack was a wholly owned subsidiary of Renault Véhicules Industriels. A premium long haul tractor, the Vision, appeared in 1999. Mack is now part of Volvo Global Trucks since RVI was taken over by Volvo in 2000.

BARKING, ENGLAND

MACK

■ BELOW *The British-built Mack of 1956 featured a Bedford TA cab shell and front wings.*

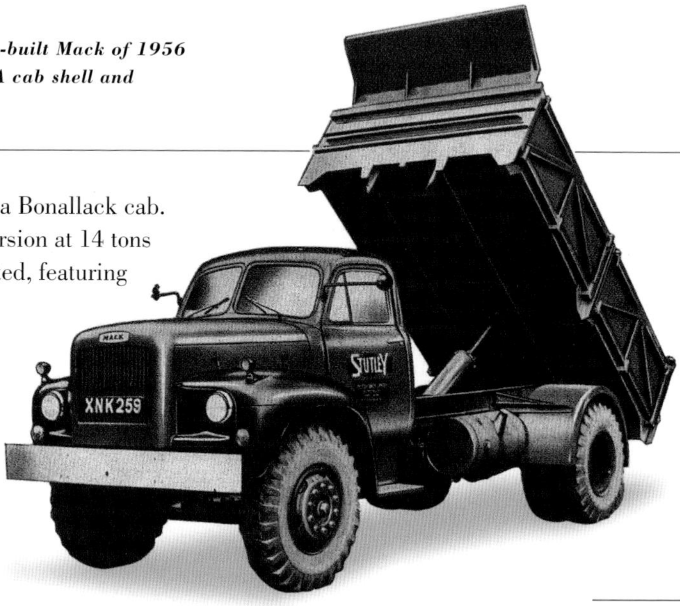

From 1954–64 a British-based company, Mack Trucks (Great Britain) Ltd, produced a small number of vehicles to its own design. Initially the company reconditioned World War II American Macks but, after an unsuccessful plan to import new Macks from America, the company marketed a Perkins-engined 7-tonner. Similar vehicles appeared, including a Leyland-engined forward-control 7-tonner with Albion gearbox and a Bonallack cab. A normal-control version at 14 tons gvw was also marketed, featuring an adaptation of the Bedford TA cab. In all, it is understood that the company only built around 20 trucks, closing its doors in 1964.

ULM, GERMANY

MAGIRUS-DEUTZ

■ LEFT *The 32-ton 200D16FS had a Deutz 12.6 litre/769cu in air-cooled V8 diesel engine.*

■ BELOW *Launched in 1951, the round-nosed Jupiter models had unique styling, as seen on this aircraft refueller.*

Prior to 1938, when Klockner Deutz Motoren absorbed Conrad Dietrich Magirus of Ulm, the latter was mainly concerned with the production of fire-fighting vehicles under the Magirus name. With its origins in 1903, Magirus first entered the truck market with a 3-tonner in 1916. This was followed by a 4-tonner in 1920. During the '20s many improvements were introduced, including pneumatic tyres and fully enclosed cabs, and the common power unit was a 4-cylinder 4.7 litre/287cu in gasoline engine. Six-cylinder engines appeared in the early '30s and in 1933 a range of military trucks featured a 7.5 litre/457cu in diesel. The 6.5-tonne M65 heavy-duty forward-control trucks of 1936 used a 150bhp horizontal 12-cylinder diesel with two opposing banks of 6-cylinders and a central crankshaft. The 10.63 litre/649cu in Z95D flat-twelve was mounted amidships behind the cab. This and the L265 bonneted 6½-tonner of 1939 were

■ ABOVE *In the mid 1930s the trucks were simply badged Magirus and prior to 1936 were all of bonneted layout.*

■ BELOW *A 1976 232D24K bonneted dump truck powered by FBL-413 V8 11.3 litre/689cu in air-cooled diesel.*

■ RIGHT *The 38-tonne gcw 340D22FS artic took its power from the Deutz air-cooled V12 340bhp diesel.*

■ BELOW RIGHT *This 209D14FS artic with day cab had a design weight of 35 tonnes gcw. The power unit is a 206bhp air-cooled V8 diesel.*

magnificent-looking machines and flagships of the Magirus range. The Magirus name badge, with its distinctive motif consisting of a letter "M" surmounted by the spire of Ulm cathedral, was still in use even though Klockner Deutz had acquired the company in 1938. Gradually the make was to become Magirus-Deutz, but the famous Magirus motif was retained. From as early as 1943 Deutz air-cooled diesels were beginning to oust the Magirus engines. The factory suffered extensive air-raid damage during World War II and was forced to close in 1945. Production resumed in a small way in 1946 with a mixture of products, including turntable ladders, tractors and a civilian half-track 2-tonner that was an important aid in post-war reconstruction.

A new 3-tonne payload truck was announced in 1946, outwardly resembling the pre-war designs that had the F4L 514 air-cooled diesel. They could actually handle 3.5 tonnes and were designated 53500 models. It was in April 1951 when Magirus-Deutz launched their sensational new Mercury and Jupiter ranges with their ultra-modern rounded bonnets (hoods) and ovoid grilles. The Mercury models for 5-tonne payloads had a 5.3 litre/323cu in, 85bhp 4-cylinder or 7.9 litre/482cu in, 125bhp 6-cylinder Deutz air-cooled engine. The heavier Jupiter for 8 tonnes payload had a 10.6 litre/647cu in producing 175bhp. In 1955 a number of heavy-duty 6×6 and 6×4 Uranus tractors were built mainly for military tank transporter duties. They were also used as a base for heavy armoured cars and as oilfield trucks. The planet names were dropped in favour of numeric designations from 1964. Forward-control trucks as well as bonneted versions became available from 1956 and an experimental tilt cab was tried in 1955. The fixed-cab 32-tonne 200D 16FS model was a particularly handsome machine. This carried the Deutz name badge plus the famous "M" and spire symbol. It was powered by the Deutz FBL714 12.6 litre/769cu in air-cooled V8 indirect-injection engine, but a 210bhp direct-injection version was also available.

During the 1960s a new design of forward-control cab in fixed or tilt form was introduced. This was of squarer appearance and had bumper-mounted oblong headlights but, in terms of styling, it was a retrograde step. That cab survived through to the late 1970s when it was replaced by the Fiat-Iveco cab and, in some dump-truck models, the cab was still fitted until the mid '80s. In 1971 Magirus-Deutz was one of four leading European manufacturers (the others were DAF, Volvo and Saviem) to form the Club of Four (officially called The Euro Truck Development Group) to develop a new range of medium trucks using a common steel tilt cab. In 1974 the company was reorganized as Magirus-Deutz AG and the following year was merged into the Fiat-led Iveco Group.

MUNICH, GERMANY

MAN

■ LEFT *The 10.212F has MAN's own cab. A Saviem cab appeared in the late 1960s.*

■ LEFT *A late 1950s 735L1 artic fuel tanker powered by 8.3 litre/506cu in 6-cylinder diesel.*

■ BELOW LEFT *A late 1970s 16.200 HAK bonneted four-wheel drive dump truck.*

Although Maschinenfabrik Augsburg-Nürnberg AG began truck building in 1920, its history dates back further to 1915 when it built Saurer trucks under licence in a former Saurer plant in Lindau. From 1916 the company was entitled Kraftwagenwerke MAN-Saurer GmbH and the licence-built Saurers were produced until 1918. In 1897 MAN made history by pioneering the first diesel engine in close co-operation with Dr Rudolf Diesel. In 1923 MAN built the first automotive diesel engine featuring direct injection. The 4-cylinder four-stroke engine developed 40bhp at 900rpm. A MAN truck powered by the engine was exhibited at the 1924 Berlin Show, but it was about three years before diesels were offered in production models.

In 1926 MAN launched a chain-drive six-wheeler with a 150bhp 6-cylinder gasoline engine. This became available with a new 6-cylinder diesel of 100bhp in 1927. During the early 1930s an impressive new range of trucks offered a choice of gasoline or diesel. The largest model was the imposing S1H6 of 1932, a long-wheelbase bonneted six-wheeler for drawbar use, powered by a 16.6 litre/1013cu in 140bhp diesel. During the '30s a comprehensive diesel truck range for payloads of 3, 3.5, 4, 5, 6 and 8 tonnes was available.

In 1936 MAN acquired ÖAF (Österreichische Automobilfabrik). For a period ÖAF manufactured axles for MAN but, during World War II, ÖAF assembled 4×4 4-tonne military trucks for the Wehrmacht. ÖAF operated as an autonomous division during the 1950s and '60s developing its own range of trucks, often using Leyland, Cummins and Mercedes engines as well as MAN, but the company came under closer MAN control in the early '70s when it also absorbed Gräf & Stift. MAN's wartime production was severely disrupted by bomb damage, but some production was resumed with the 5-tonne payload MK model from 1945. This had a 110bhp 6-cylinder diesel. There were two interesting engine developments in 1951 – the first turbocharged diesel and the first V8 diesel. In 1955 truck production was transferred to a new factory in Munich. By 1960 the MAN range included 4×2 trucks and tractor units for load capacities of 5 to 20 tonnes, and in 1961 six-wheelers for payloads of 16 to 20 tonnes. A program of technical co-operation with Saviem of France began in 1968, under which Saviem began using MAN engines while MAN benefited from Saviem's new tilt cab

■ LEFT *A 1992 F90 cabbed 35-332 8×8 dump truck with Meiller body, loading in Magdeburg.*

which replaced its own long-running all-steel forward-control cab. The latter had also been available as a tilt cab in the '60s.

At the same time MAN had acquired a financial interest in Büssing Automobilwerke AG and took over the company completely in 1971. This resulted in the demise of the famous Büssing range, which included a high proportion of underfloor-engined trucks. Such was the following for these among Büssing's former customers that MAN reintroduced them rebadged as MAN-Büssing. Demand was so great that the range survived through to the mid 1980s, the latter-day models featuring the Saviem-MAN pattern cab. During the early '70s MAN developed a rigid eight-wheeler aimed at the UK market and many European countries adopted the type. The Hungarian RÁBA company of Györ built MAN-based trucks under licence from 1970, renewing an association that had begun in the 1930s. From 1984 RÁBA began using DAF cabs but continued to use RÁBA-MAN engines. A similar agreement was formed with Autocamioane Brasov of Romania to build MAN trucks under the Roman name from 1971. These were also marketed as DAC.

During the 1980s MAN marketed their comprehensive F8 range from 16-tonne two-axled trucks up to 44-tonne tractor units, as well as special heavy-haulage tractors for gtw up to 105 tonnes. The F8 models were replaced in 1986 by the restyled F90, which featured a more modern MAN-designed cab. Further improvements came in 1994 with the launch of the 2000 range. When MAN needed a lighter range of trucks during the 1970s it entered a joint development program with Volkswagen. The result was the MT range using VW's LT cab. The MT continued in production for almost 10 years, after which it was relaunched as the MAN G90. Later still, after MAN took over Steyr Nutzfahrzeuge AG in 1991, the range was replaced by the L2000 models featuring a Steyr cab.

MAN Truck & Bus AG also build trucks in Turkey, India and South Africa. In 2000 MAN bought ERF in the UK from Western Star, eventually transferring ERF production to Europe from 2002 to 2007. The F2000 "Evolution" range was launched in 1999, and its successor, the TGA, a year later. Currently, MAN's flagship TGX features a restyled cab and produces 640bhp from its D38 Common Rail Euro 6 diesel engine.

■ ABOVE *MAN's original diesel-powered truck of 1924.*

■ RIGHT *MAN's impressive new TGX 2676 has re-styled cab and powerful D26 Common Rail diesel with 420bhp.*

STOCKPORT, ENGLAND

MANCHESTER

■ LEFT *The 1929 Manchester 1½-ton dump truck originates from the American Willys Overland.*

The Manchester was really an Anglo-American hybrid built between 1928 and 1933 by Willys Overland Crossley of Stockport near Manchester. The division of Crossley was set up in 1920 to assemble Willys Overland vehicles for the UK market and began using the Manchester name on the Willys Overland 25cwt truck in 1926.

The first British-designed Manchester was a 35cwt which was sometimes sold with a third-axle conversion. In 1930 a bonneted 2½-ton truck appeared and a forward-control version was planned, but the company folded in 1933.

INDIANAPOLIS, INDIANA, USA

MARMON-HERRINGTON

Marmon-Herrington's origins date back to 1851, but trucks were not produced until 1931 when the Marmon Car Co. was joined by Col. Arthur W. S. Herrington, an engineer with experience in all-wheel drive. The company went on to build specialized all-wheel drive vehicles and, later, some massive trucks for the Iraq Pipeline Co. It also carried out all-wheel drive conversions on Ford light trucks. A variety of military trucks were built during World War II.

In 1963 Col. Herrington's share was acquired by a private conglomerate. Designs for a new truck were sold to its south-west distributor, who put it into production under the name of Marmon. In 1985 Marmon-Herrington became part of Fontaine Inc. at Louisville, where it makes driveline components.

■ ABOVE *Marmon-Herrington had this 6×4 cabover on the stocks when it pulled out of trucks in 1963.*

DENTON & DALLAS, TEXAS, USA

MARMON

■ LEFT *The Marmon 6×4 cabover is part of a range of hand-built premium trucks made in Denton, Texas.*

In 1963, after Marmon-Herrington ceased truck production, a new company, Marmon Motor Co. of Denton, Texas, was formed by one of its distributors to build trucks that Marmon-Herrington had been planning. Marmon are premium trucks aimed at the owner operator. In 1973 the company was purchased by the Interstate Corporation of Chattanooga. In the 1980s Marmon's P 6×4 range became their main product. Marmon trucks later took on a more streamlined look in their D, L, R and S types, while the long-nosed P model retained the classic angular lines popular with long-haul owner operators. The premium, low-production nature of the trucks contributed to Marmon's demise in 1997.

COVENTRY & ALCESTER, ENGLAND

MAUDSLAY

The name that graced the front of Maudslay lorries from 1903–59 is older than almost any other name in the industry. Henry Maudslay was born in 1771 and founded his own engineering company in 1798 off London's Oxford Street. In 1831 it became Maudslay Sons & Field who built steam engines for the British naval fleet. It also pioneered one of the world's first commercial vehicles, Sir Charles Dance's steam carriage. Maudslay Sons & Field Ltd closed in 1900 and in 1901 Reginald, a great grandson of Henry Maudslay, founded the Maudslay Motor Co. A lightweight commercial vehicle was introduced in 1903. Advanced features included overhead camshaft engines and shaft drive. In 1912 Maudslay introduced new $1\frac{1}{2}$ and 3-tonners with 4-cylinder gasoline engines.

In 1923 a forward-control 7-tonner appeared. An even larger 8-tonner was announced in 1925. In 1929 it was joined by the L10 – a most impressive forward-control 10-ton six-wheeler.

During the 1930s truck sales all but dried up. The company was facing closure in 1935 when it was rescued by its major shareholder, Oliver Douglas Smith. A new truck range entered production at the end of 1939, consisting of the Maharajah six-wheeler, Mikado eight-wheeler and Mogul and Militant four-wheelers. Owing to the war, only a handful of six and eight-wheelers were built up until 1941, but four-wheelers were allowed to continue for essential civilian use. A wartime shortage of Gardner engines led to the use of AEC 7.7 litre/470cu in diesels in the Mogul while the Militant had the Gardner 4LW.

In 1946 a tractor unit named the Maharanee was introduced, and the following year a twin-steer six-wheeler, the Mustang. Production was transferred to a new plant at Great Alne, which was built as a shadow factory to escape Coventry's wartime blitz. Maudslay's last new models in 1948 were six and eight-wheelers. The six-wheeler was still called the Maharajah but the eight-wheeler became the Meritor. In May 1948 Maudslay was taken over by AEC, who discontinued the range and used the Maudslay plant to build AECs under the Maudslay badge. This continued through to late 1959 when the Maudslay name vanished. The Great Alne factory was sold in 1972 to the Rockwell Axle company.

■ LEFT *The 1927 forward-control Maudslay was heavily built and featured solid tyres.*

■ LEFT *A 1944 Maudslay Mogul II with AEC 7.7 litre/470cu in 6-cylinder diesel and 1500-gallon fuel oil tank.*

■ BELOW *Built in January 1951, this Meritor with AEC 9.6 litre/588cu in diesel was one of the last Maudslays ever made.*

MINSK, BELARUS

MAZ

■ LEFT *MAZ 504A articulated tanker seen at work in Budapest in 1992.*

■ BELOW *MAZ 64221 6×4 cabover with sleeper cab coupled to a tandem-axle tilt.*

The Minsk Automobil Zavod (or Minsk Motor Works) was formed in 1947 to build a range of trucks, dumpers and tractor units, a typical example being the MAZ-200 7-tonne payload cargo truck. This was of dated appearance and continued through to the mid 1960s when a forward-control range, the 500 series, entered production. This had an attractively styled steel cab of modern appearance and, in 4×2 form, had a payload rating of 8 tonnes. A 10-tonne payload six-wheeler was also available. Heavy dumpers and 8×8 tractors were added during the 1960s. In the early 1970s the 500 models underwent redevelopment and became the 9-tonne payload 500A. These had an 11.15 litre/680cu in 210bhp 6-cylinder diesel and grossed 15.8 tonnes while the 504A tractor grossed 28 tonnes.

The early '80s saw the launch of a heavy-duty range in tune with the advanced designs of Western Europe. Typical of new MAZ long-haul tractor units were the 5432 two-axled and 6422 three-axled cabovers powered by YaMZ V8 turbo diesels with power ratings of 280 to 320bhp. These were further developed into the 54321 and 64221 with increased output up to 360 and 425bhp. During the 1990s MAZ formed closer ties with MAN which gained a controlling interest in 1999, leading to further co-operation between the manufacturers. MAZ has recently begun assembly in Vietnam. Multi-wheeled dump trucks badged "Volat" are produced by associate MZKT or "Minsk Wheeled Tractor Plant", established in 1991. Prior to this it was known as the MAZ military vehicle plant.

HAYES & SLOUGH, ENGLAND

McCurd

The McCurd Lorry Mfg. Co. Ltd was a relatively short-lived maker. Between 1912 and 1914 some bonneted worm-drive trucks for 2, 3 and 5 tons were built at Hayes by engineer W. A. McCurd. After World War I, production of these was continued until 1921 but then suspended. In 1925 the company was relocated to Slough in Buckinghamshire as McCurd Motors and a few newly designed 2½-tonners were built up to 1927 when the company ceased trading.

■ LEFT *This 1913 McCurd 5-ton box van was powered by a 4-cylinder gasoline engine with an RAC rating of 32.4hp. The type was only built for two years.*

STUTTGART, GERMANY

MERCEDES-BENZ

■ LEFT *The Gaggenau cabover truck of 1910, built at the Süddeutsche Automobilfabrik (SAF), was the forerunner of the Mercedes-Benz.*

As the 21st century dawns, Daimler-Chrysler (formerly Daimler-Benz AG) is the world's leading truck manufacturer. The Mercedes-Benz marque has existed since 1926, but the company's origins go back to the late 19th century and the earliest recorded motor truck. Daimler-Benz was formed by the merger of Benz & Cie, Rheinische Gasmotorenfabrik of Mannheim and Daimler Motoren-Gesellschaft of Stuttgart-Unterturkheim. Daimler pioneered the truck industry with its 1896 rear-engined 1½-tonner, while Benz & Cie completed its first truck, of similar size to Daimler's, in 1899. In 1899, the year before Gottlieb Daimler died, his partners formed a separate truck-building company called Motorfahrzeug und Motorenfabrik Berlin AG at Marienfelde. This was subsequently absorbed by Daimler in 1914. Benz & Cie formed a syndicate involving Süddeutsche Automobilfabrik (SAF) of Gaggenau. Benz concentrated on cars while SAF became responsible for truck production. In 1908 Benz took over Süddeutsche to form Benz-Werke, Gaggenau. After developing along separate lines with broadly similar products over the next decade or so, Daimler Motoren-Gesellschaft and Benz & Cie were to merge in 1926. Gaggenau was to become the truck plant while Berlin Marienfelde became a repair centre.

From 1931 model designations had the prefix "L" (for "Lastwagen"). During the war years over 64,000 commercial vehicles were produced by Daimler-Benz, almost exclusively for military use. In 1938 the German government introduced restrictions on the industry and Daimler-Benz was only allowed to produce 3, 4½ and 6-tonne two-axled trucks, while all other production was suppressed. For a brief period towards the end of the war the company also built a batch of 3-tonne Opel Blitz trucks. The factories had been extensively damaged by Allied bombing, bringing production to a virtual halt.

When production resumed in 1949 the range was limited to the bonneted L3250 3¼-tonners and the L3600 and L4500 for 3.6 and 4.5 tonnes payload. Medium and heavy truck production was allowed to resume in 1951 and soon the bonneted L models were joined by the first cab-over-engine trucks, designated the LP. The "P" stood for "Pullman", implying Pullman car comfort. Heavy trucks were built at Gaggenau plant which also built the versatile new Unimog 4×4, while medium trucks were produced at Mannheim. The first LP model was the LP315 7-tonner of 1955. This was joined in 1958 by the LP333 twin-steer six-wheeler which operated at 16 tonnes gvw or 32 tonnes gtw, the 32-tonne limit having been approved in that year by the German government. An LPS333 tractor ("S" meaning "Sattelschlepper") was also available for 32 tonnes gcw. The second steering axle on this was mid-mounted 1.6m/5.25ft ahead of the drive axle. All these models

■ LEFT *An NK56 six-wheeler with Balloon tyres and a payload of 10 tons.*

■ BELOW *The LPS1620 tractor was powered by the OM346 6-cylinder diesel engine.*

had a bulbous full-width cab with split windscreen. A more compact version of the cab with single-piece screen was featured on the LP321, LP322 and LP337 for payloads of 6 to 7 tonnes.

By this time Daimler-Benz AG had several factories in Germany and had set up assembly plants in 24 countries. Gaggenau, near Baden-Baden, was still the main heavy truck plant and Mercedes-Benz accounted for nearly 75 per cent of Germany's medium to heavy truck exports. An ultra-modern production plant came into operation in 1963 at Wörth, located between Mannheim and Gaggenau. At first only cabs were built, but by 1965 full-scale truck assembly was underway. By 1967 the new Wörth factory had taken over totally from Mannheim and Gaggenau. A completely redesigned forward-control cab of squarer appearance was launched at the 1963 Frankfurt Motor Show. This was taller, and the engine was mounted very low to minimize engine cover intrusion. Coincidental with this Mercedes-Benz announced its first direct-injection diesel engine, the 10.8 litre/659cu in OM346. This effectively replaced the OM326 which, like all previous types, was of pre-combustion design.

Another important development of the mid 1960s was the new LPS2020 three-axled "rear-steer" tractor unit designed to take advantage of the legal weight increase from 32 to 38 tonnes. In anticipation of the higher power requirements Daimler-Benz developed a new family of V diesels in V6, V8, V10 and V12 form with power outputs ranging from 192bhp to 400bhp. The first to appear was the 16 litre/976cu in V10, designated OM403, with an output of 320bhp. This went in a range of new tilt-cab models in 1969 featuring a tilt version of the old "square" type cab. These were LP/LPS 1632, 2032 and 2232 models and were recognizable by their deeper front wheel arches, split near the cab rear face.

In 1970 Daimler-Benz took over Hanomag-Henschel Fahrzeugwerke GmbH, whose truck plant was at Kassel. The company's Bremen van plant was also an important acquisition, enabling Daimler-Benz to fill a gap in its weight range. In addition to its main truck plant at Wörth, Daimler-Benz now had 18 factories, including its car plant and headquarters at Unterturkheim. Truck plants had been established in Brazil, Argentina, South Africa and Spain while others in Turkey, Iran and Indonesia were mainly concerned with buses. Technical and financial collaboration with the Indian Tata Engineering & Locomotive Co. had begun in 1954 to build Mercedes-Benz designs under licence. In 1964 the company had formed Mercedes-Benz of North America. In 1968 it took over the distribution, including existing stocks and real estate, of Krupp Trucks when production ended at Essen. In 1972 it formed an agreement with FAP-Famos of Yugoslavia to supply cabs. A United States truck assembly plant was built in 1980 at Hampton/Newport News. The following year Daimler-Benz acquired the Freightliner Corporation of the United States. A further acquisition came in 1982 with the purchase of NAW, the joint company formed by Saurer and FBW at Arbon and Wetzikon, Switzerland. There were more takeovers to come.

■ TOP LEFT ***The stylish L6600 bonneted 6.6-tonne truck, produced from 1950–54, was powered by a 145bhp 6-cylinder diesel.***

■ TOP RIGHT ***An early 1960s LP333 twin-steer six-wheeler operated at 32 tonnes gtw with drawbar trailer.***

■ LEFT ***In the late 1960s this LPS1418 could operate at 32 tonnes gcw when coupled to a tri-axle trailer.***

■ RIGHT *This five-axled 38-tonne gcw dump truck features the attractive New Generation cab.*

■ RIGHT *Mercedes-Benz's medium range of the late '90s was the 'Atego', seen here in the form of a 1999 '1217' model with L cab.*

The most important truck launch of the 1970s was the New Generation range of 1973, so-called because of the "softer" styling of its new tilt cab. From that point on Mercedes-Benz trucks were predominantly forward-control, and bonneted types were gradually phased out after their production was moved to the old Henschel factory at Kassel. The first models to feature the New Generation cab were two and three-axled construction vehicles. By 1975 the cab had been introduced across the heavy truck range.

In 1988 the cab was facelifted with a new black grille, and relaunched as the SK. Detailed technical advances continued to be made during the 1970s and '80s. The EPS (Electro-Pneumatic Shift) gearbox appeared in 1985, followed in 1991 by an LEV (Low Emission Vehicle) range. IFA of Ludwigsfelde in the former German Democratic Republic was acquired in 1990.

Mercedes-Benz's first new range for over 20 years – the Actros – was launched in 1996, featuring a new cab and ground breaking 'Telligent' electronics controlling most functions including engine, transmission, suspension and braking. Medium weight trucks also received a new cab and were re-launched as the Atego. In 1997 Daimler-Benz and Freightliner absorbed Ford's American heavy truck operations, re-naming them Sterling. In 1998 Daimler-Benz merged with the Chrysler Corporation to form DaimlerChrysler, who owned Detroit Diesel.

DaimlerChrysler became simply Daimler AG in 2007. Additions to the truck range included the 'Axor' in 2002 which has proved popular in the UK. Daimler either owns or has joint ventures with Freightliner and Western Star in North America, Mitsubishi Fuso in Japan, CAMC and Foton in China, and Kamaz in Russia. In 2011 a new Actros range was unveiled featuring a completely new cab, a version of which went on a new construction range badged 'Arocs' announced in 2013. Having favoured V6 and V8 diesels for four decades Mercedes switched to in-line-six diesels for the new range, based on the Detroit Diesel 60 series.

■ BOTTOM *Launched in 2012 the new Mercedes Benz Actros boasts a stylish cab with superb comfort. This is a 2645 model in the UK.*

TOKYO, JAPAN

MITSUBISHI

Mitsubishi Shipbuilding & Engineering Co. Ltd built small numbers of light trucks of up to 2½ tonnes payload during the early 1920s, but large-scale commercial vehicle production did not begin until 1930. At first the company concentrated on buses, but trucks up to 3 tonnes payload also appeared in the mid 1930s when Mitsubishi developed its own diesel engines. Limited motor-vehicle production was centred at a factory in Kawasaki during World War II, but Mitsubishi were mainly preoccupied with military production. A range of heavy bonneted trucks was launched immediately after the war, these being diesel-powered 6 to 7-tonners bearing some resemblance to contemporary American designs.

In 1950, while under American occupation, the large Mitsubishi Group was dissolved and re-formed into separate companies. The two responsible for truck production became Mitsubishi Heavy Industries, Reorganized, Co. Ltd and Mitsubishi Nippon Heavy Industries Ltd. The former concentrated on the production of light vehicles, and later introduced the Jupiter 2 to 3-tonners.

Mitsubishi Nippon Heavy Industries was to build the heavier trucks under the Fuso name. A 7-tonner, the T3, developed from the 1946 design, appeared by 1956. This had the company's own DB31 8.55 litre/522cu in 6-cylinder diesel engine developing 155bhp. By 1961 this had been given a stylish new front-end treatment with a steeply sloping bonnet (hood) and full-width grille. It was now designated the T330 (long wheelbase) and T335 (medium wheelbase) and had the Mitsubishi DB31A 8.55 litre/522cu in diesel developing 165bhp. Options included power-assisted steering. Mitsubishi Fuso's other models for 1961 included T350 tractor units for 10-tonne payloads with a similar specification to the T330 but on a wheelbase of 3.45m/11.3ft. The W11D 6×6 dump truck and the W21 6×6 heavy-duty fifth-wheel tractor were based on World War II American designs. The W11D had the DB31W 8.55 litre/522cu in diesel with a 160bhp output, while the W21 had the 13.74 litre/838cu in DH21W producing 200bhp at 2000rpm. Both were fitted with air brakes. The W21, despite its heavy-duty specification was also designed for 24 tonnes gcw. The range also included a variety of forward-control two and three-axled mobile crane chassis with half-cabs such as the T380C, derived from the T330 truck, and the W13 and W25A 6×4s derived from the W11 and W22 trucks. A lighter half-cab 4×2 dump truck was also offered as the T52 for 6.5 to 7 tonnes. This had a downrated version of the 8.55 litre/522cu in DB31W producing 145bhp.

■ LEFT *A 1998 FV 6×4 tractor unit with side-lift container-handling equipment.*

■ BELOW LEFT *The 1934 TSS-28 2-tonner had a 4.8 litre/292cu in 6-cylinder gasoline engine.*

■ BOTTOM LEFT *Based on the FK model, this medium-weight artic is part of Allied Pickford's New Zealand fleet.*

■ LEFT *The Fuso badge was reinstated on Mitsubishi trucks as seen on this colourful drawbar combination photographed in Thailand.*

■ BOTTOM *An FV Shogun 6×4 tractor coupled to tri-axle fridge trailer.*

In the early 1960s a range of tilt-cab forward-control trucks was launched. This included the T380 8-tonne four-wheeler and the T390 11.5-tonne six-wheeler plus two tractor units, the T386 and T386S for 27 tonnes and 32.6 tonnes gcw respectively.

In 1964, just 14 years after the break-up of Mitsubishi, the two separate divisions, Mitsubishi Heavy Industries, Reorganized, and Mitsubishi Nippon Heavy Industries, rejoined forces, becoming Mitsubishi Heavy Industries Ltd, Motor Vehicle Division. The lighter Jupiter range carried on, joined by the Canter for payloads of up to 6 tonnes. The bonneted Jupiters consisted of the T10DAH (4.8 tonnes gvw), the T22DBH (6 tonnes gvw), the T30B and T33B (6.8 tonnes gvw). The T30B was diesel-powered while the T33B had the 3 litre/183cu in gasoline engine. A forward-control Jupiter T40B (diesel) and T41B (gasoline) was also introduced for 6.4 tonnes gvw.

The Canter was now called the Fuso Canter, Fuso being the name given to the heavy trucks. The Fuso Canter was, however, only rated at 3.7 tonnes gvw. A heavier version at 7.4 tonnes gvw using a similar cab design was introduced as the Fuso T620. All heavy trucks were now simply badged as Fuso.

In the early 1970s the Chrysler Corporation acquired a 15 per cent stake in Mitsubishi resulting in technical collaboration. Re-styled cabs appeared in 1972 and V6 and V8 turbocharged diesels of 190 and 310bhp were developed. The lightest trucks were the Fuso Canter (4.2 to 5.4 tonnes gvw) while the FK and FM series (9.15 to 14 tonnes) catered for the medium sector. The heaviest 4x2 was the FP at 15.4 tonnes, FU 6x2 and FV 6x4 three-axled models were rated at 21.4 and 25.4 tonnes gvw respectively. Heavy-duty bonneted trucks, the NP, NV and W series were also available. Articulated versions of the FP and FV series were for gcw's of between 34 and 51 tonnes. These took turbocharged V8 diesel engines. The range was marketed by Chrysler in Australia as the Dodge Fuso as was the lightweight Canter. The company was now called the Mitsubishi Motor Corporation. A black plastic grille gave the Fuso cab a new look in 1980 and trucks began wearing a Mitsubishi name badge instead of Fuso.

A brand new FP, FV and FS (8x4) range with new cab was unveiled in 1984. Power units included the 6D22-1A 11.15 litre/680 cu.in. 6-cylinder diesel with 225bhp, the LD 22-1AT3 turbo at 330bhp and the 16 litre/976 cu.in. V8 in two ratings – 320 bhp (naturally aspirated) and the 400bhp turbo. Eaton Fuller transmissions were featured in these models. The top-of-the-range FV 415 V8 truck was marketed as the Shogun. In 1998 another new generation of FP, FV and FS Shoguns with a stylish new cab was launched. These featured a new 19 litre/1158 cu.in. diesel, with an impressive 550bhp. In 2003 Mitsubishi Motors spun its truck division off which then became Mitsubishi Fuso Truck & Bus Corp and the Mitsubishi name badge reverted to Fuso. In March 2004 the company was absorbed into DaimlerChrysler AG which, in 2007, became Daimler AG after Daimler and Chrysler parted company.

BIRMINGHAM, ENGLAND

MORRIS

■ LEFT *A Morris FFK140 dump truck with 6-cylinder diesel engine.*

Following the merger of the Austin Motor Co. of Longbridge, Birmingham, and Morris Commercial Cars of Adderley Park, Birmingham, in 1951, a process of commonization began between the two companies' truck ranges, both of which consisted of mass-produced light and medium-weight vehicles in the 1½ to 5-ton bracket. A rationalized range of trucks that were virtually identical apart from the badges were announced in 1954. Although the Adderley Park company still traded as Morris Commercial Cars Ltd, the word "Commercial" was dropped from the badge in 1956. Thus, for the 12 years up to the formation of BLMC through the merger of British Motor Holdings (Morris Commercial's parent company) and British Leyland in 1968, the trucks were called Morris. After that they were all badged BMC. (See also "Austin" and "BMC".)

BIRMINGHAM, ENGLAND

MORRIS COMMERCIAL

William Morris, who later became Lord Nuffield, founded a cycle business back in 1893 and turned to motor-car production in 1912. In the early 1920s there were increasing numbers of low-cost American light trucks getting on to the UK market, and Morris saw an opportunity to compete in this sector with a mass-produced 1-tonner. A factory was purchased at Soho, Birmingham, in 1924 and the first Morris Commercial T type went into production using largely car-based running units. Commercial was added to the Morris name to distinguish the new trucks from the Cowley-built cars.

Very soon Morris Commercial began introducing heavier models like the D type six-wheeler for up to 2-ton payloads, introduced in 1927. This proved successful in both civilian and military roles. In 1930 Morris Commercial took over the old Wolseley Works at Adderley Park, Birmingham, and began to expand its truck range further. Following the appointment of a new chief engineer from AEC at

■ LEFT *This Morris Commercial T-Model has single rear wheels and semi-enclosed cab.*

■ BELOW LEFT *The semi-forward-control Equiload 5-tonner was first announced in 1938 and continued until 1948.*

■ RIGHT *A 1946 LCS 1¼-ton Post Office truck with 240cu ft/6.8cu m integral box body.*

■ BELOW *A 1947 LC 1½-ton truck still at work in New Zealand in 1998.*

■ RIGHT *The FV forward-control 5-tonner announced in 1948 was available with a 6-cylinder diesel engine based on a Saurer design.*

■ BELOW RIGHT *The CV11/40 was a bonneted 3-tonner with 3.5 litre/213cu in side-valve gasoline engine.*

Southall, Morris Commercial began to develop heavy-duty models like the 4/5-ton Courier, and there were plans to produce four and six-wheelers for payloads of 8 to 12 tons but some of these never left the drawing board.

A 2½-tonner called the Leader or P type appeared in 1933 followed by the C type in 1934, which was built in normal and semi-forward-control form. A heavier version of the Leader for up to 4 tons payload was also available. By 1938 the stylish CV range entered production. This was marketed as the Equiload and covered payload ratings up to 5 tons, the heaviest model being marketed as the semi-forward-control CVF 13/5 with a 4.9m/16.4ft body. The power unit was Morris Commercial's 3.48 litre/212cu in 6-cylinder gasoline engine developing 85bhp. The Equiload range, in reduced form, continued after World War II and in 1948 a full forward-control 5-tonner was announced. This was the FV with a simple but attractively styled cab featuring rear-hinged "suicide" doors. For the FV, Morris Commercial offered their own 4.25 litre/259cu in 6-cylinder diesel engine, a Saurer design built under licence. The diesel models were designated FVO. An 80bhp 4-cylinder gasoline engine was also available.

In 1953 a 6-cylinder gasoline engine developing 100bhp was offered. The diesel engine was not as successful as hoped, but was still offered up to 1953. In 1954 the forward-control trucks took on a completely new appearance with a new steel cab bought in from the Willenhall Motor Radiator Co. By this time Morris Commercial had entered the BMC empire, formed with the Austin-Morris merger of 1951. From then on Austin and Morris Commercial trucks began to develop along common lines, and the Morris Commercial name was discontinued from 1956 when the trucks were simply badged Morris. (See "BMC" and "Morris".)

OTHER MAKES

■ MANN

HUNSLET, LEEDS, ENGLAND

Mann & Charlesworth Ltd built their first steam wagon in 1897, an "overtype". The following year an undertype was tried. From 1900 the company became the Mann's Patent Steam Cart & Wagon Co. Ltd. Mann's 5-ton overtype of 1909 sought to provide extra load deck by having a side-fired boiler. Just after World War I a new 6-tonner replaced the 5-ton wagon. In 1924 Mann announced their shaft-drive Express undertype. The company went into liquidation in 1928.

■ LEFT *A mid 1950s Minerva 10-tonne artic with Perkins P6 diesel loaded with wool at Antwerp Docks.*

■ MINERVA

ANTWERP, BELGIUM

Minerva Motors SA built its first truck, a 2½-tonne payload cab-over-engine machine with overhead worm rear drive, in 1913. Power came from a 4-cylinder sleeve-valve gasoline engine. Production was suspended in World War I, but in 1923 a new model was introduced for 2 to 4-tonne payloads using the sleeve-valve engine. In 1925 Minerva absorbed SA Auto-Traction who were building Chenard-Walcker type tractors under licence. Production of these continued under the Minerva name. By 1927 a range of heavier trucks appeared with four-wheel braking and double-reduction rear axles. In 1932 they tried out sleeve-valve diesel engines, the largest being an 8.7 litre/531cu in 6-cylinder unit. In the last few years up to their closure in 1957 Minerva built very few trucks.

■ ABOVE *A Mol 8×8 500-tonne gtw tractor for Algeria's Electricity Company.*

■ BELOW *Once badged 'Mahindra Navistar' these Indian built trucks are now simply 'Mahindra' after Navistar pulled out. This 8x4 is seen in New Delhi.*

■ MOL

HOOGLEDE, BELGIUM

MOL Cy NV began building municipal chassis with low-line cabs and Deutz diesels in 1966, using GKN Kirkstall axles and Allison automatics. During the 1970s an increasing variety of models appeared including large 6x6 dump trucks, heavy haulage tractors, multi-axle mobile cranes, half-cab dock spotters as well as normal 38 tonne tractors. Typical of MOL's heaviest tractors were two 8x8 TG300 models for Algeria's Electricity Co. with 600bhp Cummins diesels and Clarke Power Shift transmissions for 500 tonnes train weight.

■ MAHINDRA

CHINCHWAD, PUNE, INDIA

In 2005 Mahindra & Mahindra formed a joint venture with Navistar International to build heavy trucks.

A wide range was offered as 'Mahindra-Navistar' and the trucks were designated 'MN' followed by the gross tonnage. (MN25, MN31, MN49, etc.). Power came from Navistar's SCR Maxxforce 7.2 litre/440 cu.in. diesel rated at 170/202/260bhp according to model. In 2013 Navistar sold their 49 per cent stake back to Mahindra and the 'Navistar' name was dropped.

The latest range unveiled in 2015 is called 'Blazo' and includes 6x4 rigids for 25 tons; 8x2 and 8x4 rigids at 31 tons and 10x4s at 37 tons plus tractors for gross ratings up to 49 tons.

OTHER MAKES

■ LEFT *A 1977 Mowag 32-tonne 8×4.*

■ BELOW LEFT *A 1920s Moreland truck.*

■ BOTTOM LEFT *An MTN 7-ton cabover.*

■ BOTTOM *A Multiwheeler Anaconda.*

■ MOWAG

KREUZLINGEN, SWITZERLAND

Formed in 1948 to take over the bodybuilding activities of Seitz und Ruf AG, Mowag (Mowag Motorenfabrik AG) began vehicle manufacture in 1951 with a 2-tonne 4×4 for military use. This was powered by a Chrysler 6-cylinder engine. Of more relevance to the truck world was the new range of forward-control heavy trucks launched in 1953. These were noted for their underfloor horizontal SLM (Swiss Locomotive & Machinery Works) diesel engines. Mowag built specialized trucks such as narrow-cabbed models for the carriage of long steel tubes. Other products included fire and armoured vehicles. One of Mowag's most interesting trucks was a forward-control 8×4, introduced in 1977, with an underfloor V8 two-stroke diesel. The 10.8 litre/659cu in Mowag M87K engine was turbocharged and intercooled, producing 500bhp at 2300rpm. An Allison 5-speed automatic transmission took the drive to Mowag double-reduction rear axles. The truck had a design gvw of 32 tonnes but was limited to 28 tonnes in Switzerland. Mowag continued to build specialized trucks and in 1999 it was announced that the company had been taken over by General Motors.

■ MTN

CROYDON, ENGLAND

MTN was the name used by Motor Traction Ltd of Croydon for most export territories. It is derived from the surname of Frank Manton, who founded the company. Rutland was used in the UK, while MTN was used for Spain, Portugal, South America and other export markets. The MTN model range was extensive, covering payload ratings from 2 to 3 tons up to 17 tons and the trucks were hand-built using bought-in propietary engines and drivelines. (See also "Rutland".)

■ MULTIWHEELER

SOUTH HARROW, ENGLAND

Between 1933 and 1941 a small number of Multiwheeler tractors, descendants of Beardmore-Multiwheeler, were built by Multiwheeler (Commercial Vehicles) Ltd. They used AEC and Gardner diesels, but with the outbreak of war the company turned to building trailers for military use. Multiwheeler Anaconda tractors feature the unique type of trailer coupling designed by Chenard-Walcker, giving them exceptional manoeuvrability.

CHICAGO, ILLINOIS, USA

NAVISTAR

The Navistar International Transport Co. was formed in 1986 after International Harvester were forced to abandon their worldwide expansion in the early 1980s. During the '70s the International Harvester Co. bought into numerous overseas companies, including DAF, ENASA, Seddon Atkinson and Pacific but, after being beset by financial problems, these interests were sold off and the company was reorganized under the Navistar International name. It still produces a full range of heavy trucks under the International name badge. (See "International Harvester".)

■ ABOVE *The Navistar International 9000 series conventional of the '90s had a wide choice of diesel power from Caterpillar, Cummins and Detroit Diesel.*

ZARAGOZA, SPAIN

NAZAR

■ LEFT *This mid 1960s Nazar forward-control 8-tonner has bold Spanish styling typical of its era.*

A range of forward-control trucks for 1½ to 9-tonne payload was offered by Factoria Napoles SA of Zaragoza from 1957. The lighter models used Perkins diesels, while heavier models featured Henschel diesels. They had heavily styled cabs, typical of Spanish designs in the 1960s, and production continued until 1967 when the factory was taken over by Barreiros.

CHAMPS-SUR-YONNE, FRANCE

NICOLAS

■ LEFT *A Nicolas Tractomas TR88G8C 400-ton 8×8 tractor.*

Nicolas specialized in heavy trucks for indivisible loads, and in 1979 the company turned to building heavy-haulage tractors too. The Tractomas range was developed during the 1980s. Their TRB6602 was a typical 6×6 for train weights up to 200 tonnes. It was powered by Mercedes-Benz's 20.9 litre/1275cu in OM404A V12 diesel engine producing 480bhp, while the ZF transmission incorporated a torque converter. The cab was a modified version of Berliet's Premier cab. An even more impressive machine is the 8×8 Tractomas TR88G8C powered by an 800bhp Detroit Diesel two-stroke 16V-92N. Gross train weight was 400 tonnes. An earlier 350-tonne version used a Cummins KTA-600 in-line-six engine and a Willème cab. Tractors of similar appearance were produced by Willème and Mol NV. Nicolas is currently one of the world leaders in heavy transport equipment, manufacturing Automas self-propelled transporters and modular trailers with steering multi-pendular axles capable of transporting payloads from 40 up to 8000 tonnes.

KAWAGUCHI, JAPAN

NISSAN/ MINSEI

■ LEFT *A Nissan UD TWA52T bonneted 6×4 tractor for 42 tonnes gcw powered by 14.3 litre/870cu in V8 diesel.*

■ FAR LEFT *A 1959 Minsei T80 7-tonner with 4.9 litre/300cu in two-stroke diesel engine.*

What has, for the past 40 years or so, been marketed as the Nissan Diesel UD had its roots in the Nippon Diesel Engineering Co. Ltd founded in 1935. This became Minsei Diesel Industries in 1950. During the late 1930s Nippon were granted a licence to build Krupp-Junkers two-stroke opposed-piston diesel engines, which were used to power a 7-tonne truck that continued in production until after World War II. From 1950 trucks were built under the Minsei name and, after several years of research, Minsei introduced its own two-stroke diesel, the UD, which stands for Uniflow-scavenged Diesel. The engine was used to power the new T80 7-tonne truck which was similar in appearance to the Krupp.

Forward-control Nissan/Minsei trucks appeared in 1960, forming the basis for later CK tilt-cab 8-tonners. A heavy-duty 6×4 for 15 tonnes was also launched, powered by a turbocharged 7.4 litre/451cu in two-stroke diesel developing 230bhp. In 1962 Nissan/Minsei developed new four-stroke diesels. Two-stroke engines were still offered until about 1970. At that time Nissan/Minsei had a comprehensive line-up from medium trucks to 32-tonne cab-over tractor units. There were also 6x2s and 6x4s for 15-tonne payloads. The largest model was a 40-tonne bonneted 6x6 heavy haulage tractor.

During the 1970s Nissan built up healthy exports to Australia and New Zealand where the trucks were marketed as Nissan-UD. Lighter trucks were also introduced, like the CMA at 9 tonnes gvw. The 1980s range included the CWA45 6x4 and 8x4, then in 1993 Nissan launched its Mikado range powered by a 350bhp engine. In 2007 Volvo, which has owned Renault Trucks since 2001, bought out Nissan Diesel, and made it a subsidiary. Nissan also has a close relationship with the Chinese truck manufacturer Dongfeng. In 2010 Nissan Diesel changed its name to UD Trucks, with the UD standing for "Ultimate Dependability".

■ ABOVE *A Nissan Mikado CG380 eight-wheeler and trailer.*

DARLEY DALE, ENGLAND

NORDE

■ LEFT *The 1964 Norde six-wheeler with Cummins V6 diesel and Bedford TK cab grossed 20 tons.*

With the advent of motorways in the UK in 1960, there was a demand for more powerful trucks. One haulage company set up its own manufacturing operation in 1961. Toft Brothers & Tomlinson formed Norde (short for North Derbyshire Engineering Co. Ltd) to build trucks of its own design. The first was a 24-ton outfit capable of 110kph/70mph over long distances. Power was from a 262bhp turbocharged Cummins, the drive being taken to an AEC axle through an SCG RV.30 semi-automatic transmission. Hendrickson-Norde suspension was used. Other models were introduced, including six-wheel rigids with Perkins 6.354 or Cummins V6.200 diesels and a Bedford TK cab. Sales were very limited and the company survived for one year, after which it concentrated on truck suspension systems.

VIENNA, AUSTRIA

ÖAF

■ LEFT *A mid 1960s Tornado FS9-200L 32-tonne artic powered by Leyland 0.680 diesel of 200bhp.*

ÖAF's origins go back to 1907 when Austro Fiat AG was set up to assemble Fiats. The association ended in 1925 and the company became Österreichische Automobilfabrik AG. The name AFN was used for a period. ÖAF began licence-building MAN diesels in 1934 and, in 1936, became a subsidiary of MAN. Production was suspended following the war and it wasn't until the early 1960s that ÖAF re-entered the heavy truck market. Their most important model was the Tornado. Engine choice included Leyland, Cummins, MAN or ÖAF's own diesel. The cab on forward-control versions was shared with Gräf & Stift, with whom ÖAF merged in 1970.

The last ÖAF announced before switching to MAN-based designs in the early 1970s was the 13-tonne gross Hurricane. ÖAF began to lose their individuality after 1970 and became almost identical to MAN. Since the late '70s ÖAF have specialized in the production of heavy-duty multi-axle trucks.

BRESCIA, ITALY

OM

■ LEFT *An early 1960s OM Tigrotto 4-tonne truck powered by a 75bhp 4-cylinder diesel engine.*

S.A. Officine Meccaniche was formed at the turn of the 19th century. In 1928 it became OM Fabbrica Bresciana Automobili. It acquired a licence to build Saurer trucks, which were marketed with OM badges. In 1933 the OM Brescia factory came under the control of the Fiat Group. One of the first new trucks was the 1CRD 3-tonner with a 60bhp diesel, still built under Saurer licence. In 1936 came the new BUD bonneted 7½-tonner. OM's Titano model – the Titano 137 six-wheeler – first appeared in 1937. Wartime production was disrupted through bomb damage but production was to resume, after reconstruction, in 1946. Now the first forward-control trucks began to appear, such as the Taurus 3-tonner and Supertaurus 5-tonner. In 1950 an important new range, including the Leoncino 2½-tonner, updated versions of the Taurus and Supertaurus, plus the Orione and Super Orione 9-tonner powered by the 10.6 litre/647cu in V8 diesel engine, was introduced.

The 1950s and '60s saw new models added, like the Tigre 6.3-tonner (12 tonnes with trailer) and the re-emergence of the Titano model, this time as a completely new maximum-weight range that made its debut in 1961. It boasted a 260bhp, 10.3 litre/629cu in in-line-six DG-L diesel and was claimed to be the most powerful truck in Europe at that time. It was offered in 4×2, 6×4 and 8×4 rigid form plus 4×2 and 6×4 tractor units. The 8×4 was rated for 22 tonnes gvw or 44 tonnes gtw and was OM's heaviest and most powerful truck.

In 1968 OM was fully incorporated into Gruppo Veicoli Industriali Fiat, which also included Unic of France. From that point on OM ceased to exist as an independent company, but the OM badge appeared on Fiat-based trucks through to the formation of the Iveco Group in 1975.

■ LEFT *Grossing 14 tonnes, this 1970 OM 150/L carries a 9-tonne payload. It has a 176bhp 6-cylinder diesel engine.*

TORTONA, ITALY

OMT

■ LEFT *The 1963 OMT MF4 with AEC AV690 diesel was one of Italy's first rigid eight-wheelers.*

Officine Meccaniche Tortonisi specialized in trailer manufacture but in 1963 introduced a heavy truck. To benefit from the maximum possible gross weight under Italy's legislation, it developed a twin-steer 8×2 truck using a Fiat cab and some Fiat running units. For its power it used an AEC AV690 6-cylinder diesel, but some were also built with Fiat diesels. The truck could gross 22 tonnes and carry a net payload of 13 tonnes but, when coupled to a four-axled drawbar trailer, it could legally run at 44 tonnes gtw. Some twin-steer tractor units were also built during the four years that OMT survived in production. The company then went back to trailer building. The OMT MF4 helped pioneer a breed of truck that soon dominated the Italian transport scene, but most were twin-steer models with proprietary fourth-axle conversions.

RUSSELSHEIM, GERMANY

OPEL

Adam Opel's history can be traced back to 1862. A 1-tonner was introduced in 1910. Opel was taken over in 1929 by General Motors. From 1931 the 2½-tonne Blitz appeared. A plant at Brandenburg was set up to build trucks. During World War II GM relinquished control as the plant was decommissioned and transferred to Russia. From 1948 GM re-established at Russelsheim, and production of light trucks continued to the mid 1970s.

OSHKOSH, WISCONSIN, USA

OSHKOSH

■ LEFT *A five-axled bonneted F series delivering to a construction site.*

■ BELOW *An E series 6×4 with drawbar trailer in New Zealand.*

The Oshkosh Motor Truck Manufacturing Co. was formed in 1917 and was originally called the Wisconsin Duplex Auto Company. The company built trucks using the front-wheel drive system invented by William Besserdich, who had earlier helped to develop the FWD. The first truck to enter full production was a 2-tonner. This was joined by a 3½-tonner in 1920 and a 5-tonner in 1924. Oshkosh went on to build heavier models during the 1930s with engines up to 200bhp. During World War II the company continued production of heavy all-wheel drive machines for the United States government.

After the war 6×6 models were introduced for oilfield and mining. Some 4×4s were characterized by their set-back front axles and long bonnets (hoods), designated the 50–50 series, launched in 1955. During the 1970s on-highway tractors were added, such as the cabover E series with its square cab and full-width grille. Oshkosh is synonymous with rugged trucks for construction, mining and military use. In the 1970s a South African plant was established at Paarl. Currently the range includes a variety of 8×8 military designs, some of which, such as the MK48, steer by pivoting in the middle.

RENTON, WASHINGTON, USA

PACIFIC

■ LEFT *A re-cabbed ex-army Pacific used on heavy haulage in the UK.*

The Pacific Car & Foundry Co., originally formed in 1905, were commanded by the United States government in 1942 to build 6×6 tank transporter tractive units. The Fruehauf Trailer Company built the 40-ton capacity transporter's low-loading trailer. The tractors were designated TR-1 and were powered by Hall-Scott 240bhp 6-cylinder gasoline engines. In the post-war years many of the Pacific tractors survived as heavy-haulage tractors but were largely re-engined with Cummins diesels and fitted with non-armoured civilian cabs.

VANCOUVER, CANADA

PACIFIC

■ ABOVE *A dual-steer Pacific PLW-500PSA Constructor 14cu yd/10.7cu m cement mixer powered by Cummins L10-300 diesel.*

In 1947 three former executives of the Hayes Mfg. Co. set up Pacific Truck & Trailer Ltd to build heavy-duty logging trucks suited to the tough Canadian lumber industry. Similar trucks were also built for construction and oilfield duties. In 1972 it became a part of International Harvester of Canada but was sold off in 1986. Pacific became a member of the Inchcape Group. During the 1980s it continued to build a wide range of heavy trucks and construction vehicles, such as the P500 and P.12.W series, using a variety of Cummins, Detroit Diesel and Caterpillar engines. Production was phased out in the early 1990s.

DETROIT, MICHIGAN, USA

PACKARD

■ LEFT *A standard Model E Packard truck of c.1918 for a payload of 4 to 5 tons.*

One of the oldest American motor manufacturers, Packard was building cars from the turn of the century and in 1905 began offering a 1½-ton truck with a horizontal twin-cylinder gasoline engine located beneath the driver. This was replaced by a new 3-ton bonneted truck in 1908 with a 4-cylinder vertical gasoline engine. Chain drive was used on the early trucks but in 1914 a worm drive was introduced on the lighter models. A 5-tonner that was announced in 1912 continued to feature chain drive, as did a 6-ton version but, from 1920, Packard switched to shaft drive. A new 2-tonner, the X, was the first to have pneumatic tyres in 1920. The range consisted of 2, 3, 5 and 7½-ton models during the three years up to when they finished production in 1923.

WIGAN, ENGLAND

PAGEFIELD

■ LEFT *A 1933 Pagefield Plantaganet rigid six-wheeler for 12-ton payload, powered by a Gardner 6LW oil engine.*

Pagefield Commercial Vehicles was set up in 1907. In 1911 a 2-ton truck appeared with 2-cylinder gasoline engine and chain drive. Four-ton and 5-ton trucks were added in the pre-World War I period, including a 5-ton dump truck with patent gearbox-driven screw-type rams. Subsidy type trucks were built during 1914–18 and in the early '20s a demountable body system for transporting horse-drawn dustcarts was introduced. This was the forerunner of today's swap-body container trucks.

In the 1930s the company developed chassis for garbage collection as well as a range of heavy trucks. The model types included the Pompian, Paladin, Pathfinder, Pegasix and Plantagenet, the latter two being six-wheelers. Gardner diesels and Kirkstall axles were fitted. Pagefield ceased trading in 1947. In 1948 Walkers & County Cars was formed to continue building municipal vehicles, and a Walker 5-ton truck was offered in the same period. Walkers & County Cars was disbanded in 1966.

PARIS, FRANCE

PANHARD

■ LEFT *A 1928 Panhard-Levassor 3-tonne payload truck with drawbar trailer.*

S.A. Etablissments Panhard & Levassor's history dates back to 1893. Light trucks were built during 1895 and by 1900 a 1½-tonne truck was entered in Military Trials. Heavier chain-drive trucks were added, as well as a military 4×4. By 1930 there were models up to 8 tonnes capacity. Trucks between 4 and 8 tonnes were Panhard's main products in the 1930s, and by 1939 there were forward-control models.

In 1954 Panhard joined Citroën and truck production was progressively cut back, ceasing altogether by 1959.

LYONS, OREGON, USA

PAYMASTER

■ RIGHT *The unique Paymaster P36 tractor later became the Ryder.*

Trucks do not come more unconventional than the Paymaster P36. It was the aim of designer Dean Hobgenseifken to shun all that had gone before and provide the owner, driver and mechanic with the ideal vehicle. It claimed to be quieter, safer and more comfortable, while minimizing costs and simplifying overhauls by having a removable engine, gearbox, axle and exhaust system in one "power module". It was the result of 10 years of design work. The engine was a Detroit Diesel 6V-92TTA two-stroke. Other engines were optional. The first trucks were completed in 1973 but the same year Ryder Systems of Miami, Florida, bought the design rights and the make was changed to Ryder. About 10 production vehicles were built by the Hendrickson Manufacturing Co. for Ryder's truck rental fleet.

MADRID, SPAIN

PEGASO

■ LEFT
The distinctively styled 1066 30-tonne gvw 8×2.

■ LEFT
The Pegaso II resembled its Hispano-Suiza forerunner.

■ BELOW LEFT
By the early 1980s eight-wheelers grossed 36.25 tonnes.

Spain's state-owned Empresa Nacional de Autocamiones SA (ENASA) acquired the Hispano-Suiza truck-building operations in Barcelona in 1946 and relaunched the Hispano-Suiza 66G as the Pegaso I 7-tonner. An improved model, the Pegaso II, for 8 tonnes payload, was developed from 1947, still virtually identical to the old Hispano-Suiza. There was a choice of gasoline or diesel power. The gasoline-engined Z-203 had a 5.65 litre/345cu in 6-cylinder unit developing 110bhp, while the Z-202 had a 9.3 litre/567cu in 6-cylinder diesel rated at 125bhp, soon uprated to 140bhp. The trucks had a gtw rating of 26.5 tonnes. An articulated version, the Z-701, had a design gcw of 22.7 tonnes. The Hispano-Suiza-based models continued to be built up to 1958.

Meanwhile, development work on a completely new design of truck, the streamlined Barajas, was underway. A prototype of this was exhibited at the Salon del Automovil in Barcelona in 1955. It took its name from a new factory opened at Barajas, Madrid, in the same year. The Barajas truck featured very individualistic styling with its curved lines and heavily ribbed panels. The Z-207, as it was designated, was a 6-tonner powered by a V6 diesel of 120bhp.

A heavier model, the Z-206 developed from the old 66G/66D, was powered by a big 9.3 litre/567cu in 4-cylinder diesel with a 140bhp output. A 165bhp horizontal diesel was used in a revolutionary new model in 1955 – the Z-210 twin-steer six-wheeler for 20 tonnes gvw and a 12-tonne payload. From the mid 1950s Pegaso collaborated closely with Leyland Motors of England in the development of new models. A double-drive six-wheeler, the Z-211 for 22.9 tonnes gvw appeared, followed by an even larger prototype model on four axles, the Z-212, which was built in the late 1950s and inspired by the Leyland Octopus. This was an 8×4 while the majority of rigid eight-wheelers, which became popular in Spain in the 1970s, were 8×2s – basically twin-steer six-wheelers with a self-steering fourth axle.

In 1960 Leyland Motors became a major shareholder in ENASA. This soon led to increasing use of Leyland running units and the development of the Pegaso Comet (a Leyland type name) for 8-tonne payloads powered by the Leyland 6.4 litre/390cu in 6-cylinder diesel and using an Albion gearbox and rear axle. In 1965 a lightweight 7-tonner, the 1100 Comet was added to the range.

■ LEFT *The 19-tonne gvw 1065 had a similar cab to the Comet 1090 but developed 170bhp as opposed to 125bhp. An Albion rear axle was fitted.*

This was powered by a 90bhp, 4.4 litre/268cu in 4-cylinder version of the 0.400.

Important new models were introduced in 1964, powered by Pegaso's own 10.5 litre/641cu in 200bhp diesel. These included twin-steer production vehicles, the 1063A 6×2 and 1066 8×2. The 1066 had a design weight of 34 tonnes and a payload capacity of 24 tonnes. In 1966 ENASA acquired a controlling interest in Sòciedad Anónima Véhiculos Automóviles (SAVA) which was mainly involved in the light to medium sector, although it assembled Berliet heavy vehicles as Berliet-SAVA. In 1968 ENASA took over SAVA and continued producing the BMC J4 vans which SAVA built under licence from the British Motor Corporation.

A completely new range of heavy trucks appeared in 1972. These featured a new, squarer design of full forward-control cab and new 10 and 12 litre/610 and 732cu in 6-cylinder diesel engines covering a horsepower range from 170 up to 310bhp and up to 352bhp in turbocharged form. The old Leyland-designed engine continued to be available on some lighter models and was turbo-charged to produce 155bhp. In 1975 a tilt version of the new cab was introduced.

During the late 1970s, in a declining market, Pegaso began making a loss. In 1981 the American International Harvester Company purchased a 35 per cent shareholding and took charge of the management. This arrangement was not to last long and International were forced to pull out of their European activities in 1983–84. International also had a large share in DAF and had bought Seddon Atkinson in the UK. In 1983 Pegaso acquired Seddon Atkinson for the token sum of one pound sterling from International.

Pegaso maintained its links with DAF, and the two companies formed Cabtec in 1984 to develop a new heavy truck cab. This went into production in 1987 on the new Troner model. It was also fitted to the DAF 95 series and the Seddon Atkinson Strato. The new Troner was launched at the 1987 Salon de Barcelona. The impressive new range was designed for gross weights up to 44 tonnes and featured a new 12 litre/732cu in, 24-valve 360bhp diesel. The Troner proved to be the last true Pegaso as ENASA was absorbed into the Italian Iveco Group in September 1990. By 1992 the Barajas factory was geared up to building the Iveco EuroTech and EuroStar.

■ LEFT *The 1972 1086/52 8×2 featured a new-style cab, 260bhp diesel and grossed 35.5 tonnes.*

■ BELOW *Pegaso's last new model was the 1987 Troner with Cabtec cab and 360bhp turbo-intercooled 12 litre/732cu in diesel.*

CLEVELAND, OHIO, USA, & SLOUGH, ENGLAND

PEERLESS

■ RIGHT *A 1931 Peerless LA-type Gardner-engined, forward-control 7-ton dump truck.*

From 1911–18 the Peerless Motor Car Co. built a range of heavy trucks of conventional design. Up to 1915 they were mainly bonneted 3 to 6-ton payload models with Peerless' own 4-cylinder gasoline engine and chain drive. From 1916 these were joined by a shaft-drive 2-tonner. All were of rugged, workmanlike build and large numbers of the early 4 and 5-ton models were shipped to the UK following World War I.

Large numbers of reconditioned war-surplus Peerless trucks were sold in the UK following World War I through Slough Lorries and Components Ltd. From 1925 the Peerless Trading Company took over to build trucks from spare parts and British-made components. As supplies of war-surplus parts diminished the British content increased until the British Peerless was a vehicle in its own right. By 1930 an 8-tonner with strengthened chassis was available with optional pneumatic tyres and a Gardner 4-cylinder diesel. A fully fledged 8-tonner, the chain-drive Trader, also became available with a Meadows 6-cylinder engine. The following year an updated range, the 90 series, featured a protruding bonnet (hood) and set-back front axle, and an impressive 12-ton six-wheeler with trailing axle and shaft drive followed. There were plans to build a lighter 4 to 5-ton range with Gardner engine, Meadows gearbox and Kirkstall axle, but in 1933 truck production was discontinued, Peerless Motors being re-formed to distribute Studebaker trucks.

OAKLAND & NEWARK, CALIFORNIA, USA

PETERBILT

■ LEFT *Peterbilt's 378 and 379 conventionals are the timeless classics of the United States highways.*

In 1932 the Fageol Motors Company of Oakland, California, was one of the casualties of the great depression, and was forced into bankruptcy after producing high-quality trucks for 17 years. The receivers, with support from the Waukesha Motor Company and the Central Bank of Oakland, kept the business going until 1939 when a buyer was found in the person of logger and plywood maker Theodore Alfred Peterman from Tacoma. Peterman had rebuilt army-surplus trucks and modified old logging trucks in the course of his own lumber business. As a man who did things his own way he bought the Fageol assets in order to build his own custom chain-drive logging trucks. From the outset Peterman put the emphasis on quality, not quantity. Finding a name for the new truck was easy. The Fageols had gained the nickname "Bill-built" after the company's president W. H. Bill, so the natural choice was Peterbilt. Over the years the name became synonymous with top quality and Peterbilts are often referred to as the Rolls Royce of trucks.

Soon after the start of production the company had to put all its resources into fulfilling government contracts for heavy trucks. The experience gained from this was invaluable in post-war development.

Following Peterman's death in 1945 the company passed into the hands of a group of employees, and in June 1958 it became a wholly owned subsidiary of Pacific Car & Foundry (Paccar). Early Peterbilts were all bonneted conventionals, but in 1950 the Model 350 cabover was introduced featuring a Kenworth cab. In 1959 the 90-degree tilt hood was introduced for easier servicing. From August 1960 production was moved to a new plant at Newark, California. Over 800 trucks were built in the first year at Newark and demand was such that a second plant at Madison, Tennessee, was opened. By 1973 an expansion

■ LEFT *This 1991 Cat-engined 357 transfer dump outfit operates around Vancouver and grosses 52 tons.*

■ RIGHT *Since Paccar took over Leyland-DAF, a new range of Peterbilt trucks uses Leyland's T45 cab.*

program doubled Madison's capacity. Another Peterbilt plant opened at Denton, Texas, in 1980. Meanwhile, in 1975 Peterbilt of Canada was set up to market the trucks throughout Canada. During the 1970s Peterbilt branched out into building more specialized trucks for municipal vehicles such as the CB300 garbage truck that developed into the 310 and, in 1987, the 320 built at the Denton plant. In 1984 the 349 construction range appeared with innovations such as an engine rear power take-off and self-steering lift axle. In 1986 came the aerodynamic 377A/E marking a move towards improved efficiency by reduced air resistance. The Unibuilt sleeper appeared in 1993 but the classic 379 remained a flagship model for 20 years until replaced in 2007 by the 389 – the ultimate long-haul truck for today's trucker. In 2017 Peterbilt joined the race to produce the autonomous truck of the future.

SOCHAUX, FRANCE

PEUGEOT

While Peugeot is normally associated more with light vans than trucks, the old established company did once build heavy trucks around the time of World War I. Established in 1897, Peugeot, from its earliest days, offered lightweight, tiller-steered chain-drive vans. By 1913 it had introduced a range of seven truck models, the heaviest of which was a 5-tonner with a 4-cylinder side-valve gasoline engine and chain drive. Production continued during the war, but by 1917 only 3 and 4-tonne models were being built, these now having worm-drive axles. Only light commercial vehicles up to 1½ tonnes were built from then on, but Peugeot became involved in truck production once more as recently as 1978 when it acquired Chrysler's European operations which included the Dodge and Karrier marques. Shortly after, Peugeot's Dodge operations were acquired by Renault Véhicules Industriels.

BUFFALO, NEW YORK, USA

PIERCE ARROW

■ RIGHT *A 1915 Pierce Arrow 4-ton truck. It featured worm drive when most contemporaries were chain-driven.*

In 1910 Pierce Arrow Motor Car Co. entered the truck market with a 5-tonner. It had chain drive and a cab-over-engine layout, but it was not pursued. Instead a normal-control, worm-drive truck (the R model) was put into production. Worm drive was unusual and its choice was influenced by Pierce Arrow's design engineer, John Younger, who was formerly with Dennis Bros. in the UK. A model X 2-tonner appeared in 1914. During World War I the company supplied large numbers of military versions of their trucks as well as building Class B Liberty trucks. In 1928 the company was merged with Studebaker of Indiana and some trucks were badged as Studebaker Pierce Arrow.

PRAGUE, CZECH REPUBLIC

PRAGA

■ LEFT ***The Praga S5T had a long production run from 1957–73 and was a rugged 5-tonner with air-cooled T912 6-cylinder diesel.***

The old established Praga factory dated back to 1907, established by an agreement between the First Czech-Moravian Machine Factory and the Frantisek Ringhoffer Co., the first Praga trucks under Dykomen licence appearing in 1910. They were shaft-drive models for payloads of 1½ to 5 tonnes. The 4 to 5-tonne V type announced in 1911 became a war subsidy truck. During the 1930s models included the MW 2-tonner and RN 2½-tonner. Diesel-engined versions appeared from 1930 using Deutz engines. The heavy-duty Type T was developed into the TN and TND by the late 1930s. The RN of 1938, which resembled the International K series, was also built in Yugoslavia and called the TAM.

In 1945 the factory was destroyed by bombing. In October that year it was nationalized, becoming Letecke Zavody Narodni Podnik in 1946 and Auto-Praga Narodni Podnik in 1948. RN production resumed after the war and in the 1950s Praga developed the V3S 6x6 powered by a Tatra air-cooled diesel. This and a 4x2 version, the S5P, continued being produced into the early 1970s. From 1974 to 1984 Praga built truck gearboxes but prototypes of a new multi-purpose truck, the UV80, were built in 1985. In 1992, as Praga Caslav AS, it began producing the UV80 and NTS265, a Deutz-engined 14 tonne 4x4. Since 2004 the company has undertaken some development of army vehicles.

BOMBAY, INDIA

PREMIER

■ LEFT ***The Premier PST-118 7-tonner was basically an Indian-built Kew Dodge with Perkins 6.354 diesel.***

During the 1970s and '80s Indian-built Dodge and Fargo trucks were sold as Premier. Outwardly the normal-control models were almost identical to the British-built Kew Dodge of the 1950s, while forward-control models often had locally built cabs of square appearance typical of Indian trucks. Power units included locally built Chrysler gasoline engines or Perkins diesels.

NORWICH, ENGLAND

PROCTOR

Proctors were developed by an operator seeking to improve on performance and economy. Proctor Springwood Ltd of Mousehold, Norwich, were hauliers founded in the 1930s, and after World War II they built a prototype 6-ton truck with a Perkins P6. It featured a Moss gearbox and rear axle. A short-wheelbase dump truck and tractor unit were added to the range. Proctor's distributor, Praill's Motors, took over production in 1949 but by 1952 the marque was withdrawn.

■ LEFT ***Proctor's lightweight 5/6-ton truck was built in small numbers from 1947–52.***

TELFORD, ENGLAND

QUEST

■ LEFT ***The highly unconventional Quest F1646 had a choice of Mercedes OM.352 or Perkins T6.354 diesel.***

Quest 80 was formed at Telford, Shropshire in 1979 as a design consultancy to develop trucks and buses for the South African Sigma Corporation. Technically the Quest F1646 truck was very innovative, having self-levelling air suspension and a very unusual design of cab with the instrument panel above the windscreen. Long and short-wheelbase versions were available. Of the few that were built, some had Perkins T6.354 and some Mercedes OM.352 diesels. ZF S6-36 gearboxes and Rockwell rear axles were used. In spite of having aluminium cabs, the trucks were very heavy, restricting payloads to 8 tons – 2 tons below average. This and the highly unconventional design features probably led to their demise. In 1984 the company was bought by the United Engineering Industries Group and only 18 months later production ceased. Currently the Quest Motor Corporation of Zimbabwe, owned by Leyland Overseas Holdings, assembles Leyland trucks.

GYÖR, HUNGARY

RÁBA

■ LEFT ***The Rába has a DAF cab, MAN diesel engine and Rába's own axles.***

Rába Magyar Vagon és Gépgyár of Györ has a long history. The company built its first truck in 1904. In 1912 a licence was acquired to build Praga 5-tonne trucks. Another agreement was formed with Fried Krupp of Essen in 1920 to build Krupp trucks under licence. By 1928 Rába had introduced its own 3-tonner. In the late 1930s Rába negotiated with MAN to licence-build its diesel engines. During the wartime occupation, the factory was dismantled. It wasn't until the late 1960s that truck production resumed.

From 1968 Raba built MAN diesel engines under licence and from 1970 complete trucks based on MANs featuring the MAN/Saviem cab. When MAN introduced a new cab design, the F90, Raba switched to using a DAF cab. Raba continued to offer a range of heavy trucks until early 2003. From that date the company has confined its production to buses and axles for heavy trucks.

JOHANNESBURG, SOUTH AFRICA

RALPH

■ LEFT ***Ralph, South Africa's only truck builder, survived in business for just four years. This 6×4 tractor had a Detroit Diesel 6V-71.***

Ralph were the only heavy trucks to be designed and built entirely in South Africa. The enterprise began in 1968 when Ralph Lewis and a small team of engineers built the first prototype. The company was registered as Rolway Enterprises (Pty) Ltd at Ophirton, Johannesburg, and the range included heavy-duty tractor units and rigids using proprietary units from Cummins, Detroit Diesel, Allison, Spicer, Fuller, Rockwell and Hendrickson. Ralph cabover 6×4 tractors bore a close resemblance to contemporary Kenworths.

Ralph built a 105-tonne tank transporter for the South African Government, and a couple of 50-tonne ore dump trucks powered by 700bhp V12 Cummins diesels. Limited production led Ralph to seek outside investment in 1970, and the company was taken over by the International Development Corporation who acquired a 51 per cent shareholding. The company underwent expansion but ran into further financial problems, closing down in 1971.

BILLANCOURT, FRANCE

RENAULT

■ LEFT ***This 1929 SG 5/6-tonner was among the last type of Renault to have the dash mounted radiator.***

■ BELOW LEFT ***This Renault G290 artic has the Club of Four pattern cab in high roof sleeper form.***

■ BOTTOM LEFT ***The Renault Magnum has one of the tallest cabs on the market.***

France's leading truck manufacturer built its first truck in 1903, a 1-tonner. The company was founded as Renault Frères to build cars in 1898. By 1909 it began building heavy-duty trucks, including a bonneted, 4-cylinder gasoline-engined 3-tonner, soon followed by a 5-tonner with a 6.1 litre/372cu in 4-cylinder gasoline engine with 4-speed gearbox and chain drive. A forward-control 3-tonne truck was introduced in 1910 and, just before World War I, an artillery tractor with four-wheel drive and four-wheel steering was developed. For the next few years production was concentrated on military vehicles, but in the early 1920s a full range of trucks for payloads up to 7 tonnes entered production. They were instantly recognizable by their dash radiators and "coal scuttle" bonnets (hoods).

In the late 1920s the characteristic "coal scuttle" front ends gave way to conventional front-mounted radiators, and as early as 1930 Renault were introducing heavy-duty diesel engines. These included a 7.25 litre/442cu in 4-cylinder and a 10.5 litre/641cu in 6-cylinder, both direct-injection. The 10.5 litre/641cu in became available in 1931. Another innovation of the early '30s was a 5-speed gearbox for the heavier models. By 1935 Renault's heavy trucks boasted a forward-control cab of very modern and handsome appearance, while mechanical improvements, including power-assisted braking and power steering, were becoming available. Just before the advent of World War II Renault was offering a comprehensive truck range, their largest models being for 15 tonnes payload and powered by 6-cylinder diesels of 12.5 litre/763cu in capacity.

After France was liberated from German occupation in 1945 Renault was nationalized, becoming Régie National des Usines Renault, and an impressive array of forward-control trucks was put on the market in the early 1950s. These were the full forward-control underfloor-engined models for payloads of 5 and 7 tonnes (as rigid 4×2s) and 12 tonnes in articulated form. These had the 105bhp, 6.23 litre/380cu in AAA6 horizontal diesel engine and 5-speed overdrive gearbox with steering-column gearshift. Heavier models of similar specification followed over the next couple of years, like the R4153/54/58 for 8.25 tonnes payload powered by an uprated engine, the 512, developing 120bhp.

A major landmark in Renault's history took place in 1955 with the formation of Saviem (Société Anonyme de Véhicules Industriels et Équipements Mécaniques) by the merger of Renault, Latil, Somua and Floirat. Very soon, the group vehicles were appearing with Saviem and Saviem-Renault badges. Some were also badged Saviem-LRS. The unmistakable underfloor-engined Renaults survived up to the mid 1960s, becoming the Saviem Tancarville TP-10 in 1962, by which time the engine was included in the new Fulgur family and had been bored out to a 6.84 litre/418cu in capacity and developed 150bhp. The TP-10s had floor-mounted gearshifts.

■ RIGHT *In 2013 Renault VI unveiled a completely new range including this 'Range T' for long distance haulage up to 44 tonnes.*

From 1965 the Renault name disappeared from heavy trucks although it was still used on lighter commercials. However, Renault was to re-emerge as a major truck marque in 1980 after some organizational changes. In 1975 Saviem acquired the Berliet truck business from Citroën, which had owned the company since 1967. Peugeot merged with Citroën in 1974 and disposed of Berliet to Saviem. This meant that Saviem had a new range of heavy trucks in the form of Berliet's TR first introduced in 1972. After Renault Véhicules Industriels (RVI) was established in 1977, the Berliet range was relaunched as the Renault R-series, becoming an important seller in the heavy-duty market. Renault was re-establishing itself on the truck scene and expanding its empire with the acquisition of Chrysler's former truck business in the UK in 1981. This had been owned by Peugeot since 1978. At the same time, RVI acquired Chrysler Espana, builders of Spanish Dodge trucks at the former Barreiros plant. Meanwhile it was acquiring an increasing share in Mack of America.

Trucks built after 1980 (at which time the Saviem name was dropped and Renault reinstated) inherited their cabs from two different sources. One was the Berliet Premier or KB, the other an updated version of the Club cab. The Berliet TR, originally launched in 1972 while the company was under Citroën ownership, became the R-series. Later still, in 1990, it was marketed as the Renault Major. The other cab, which was fitted both to medium and heavy trucks, was a legacy from the Club of Four project. The same basic design was fitted to Volvo's F6 and F7. In Renault's range it appeared on the Midliner medium trucks and on the G-series heavy tractor units. The latter were relaunched in 1991 as the Manager. The following year 6×4 and 8×4 rigids with the cab were named Maxter.

There was an important launch in 1990, namely the Magnum with its high-datum flat-floor cab. It boasted sufficient headroom for the driver to stand up and move around. Power came from Renault's 12 litre/732 cu.in. in-line-six diesel with 390 to 470bhp or an optional Mack V8 16.4 litre/1000 cu.in. with 560bhp. In Australia the Magnum wore a Mack badge and had the 565bhp Cummins Signature 15 litre/914 cu.in.

In 1996 came the stylish new Premium suited to both distribution and long-haul operations. Completing the range were the Kerax 3- and 4-axle rigids powered by Renault's 9.8 litre/598 cu.in. 6-cylinder turbo diesel with 260-400bhp. The 'Midlum' replaced the Midliner in 2000 – the year that RVI was absorbed into Volvo Global Trucks.

In 2006 Renault came up with the new Premium Lander aimed at the construction industry. At the end of 2013 came a completely new range, namely the Range T long-haul trucks and Range C construction vehicles plus the Range D for distribution. The Range T won International Truck of the Year in 2015. The Magnum ceased production in 2013 and was replaced by the Range T 'High' which was only built with LH steering until 2018 when it became available in the UK. It has three levels of cab specification – 'International' features a rotating passenger seat, flat floor and standard bunks. Power ratings are 440 or 480bhp. The 'Driver' spec has the added luxury of leather seats and an extra power option at 520bhp. Then comes the 'Driver Lux' which has an even more luxurious package. Engines include the DTi11 (11litre/671 cu.in.) and DTi13 (13 litre/793 cu.in.) with outputs from 380 to 520bhp.

■ LEFT *Renault's new 2013 range catered for all types of operations. The 8x4 'Range C' is aimed at the construction industry.*

LANCING, MICHIGAN, USA

REO

■ ABOVE ***A late 1930s Reo Speedwagon 3-ton dump truck powered by the 6-cylinder Gold Crown gasoline engine.***

The man who formed Reo, Ransome Eli Olds, was one of the pioneers of the American motor industry. Born in 1867, Olds built a steam car in 1886 and introduced a gasoline-engined car in 1897. Owing to a disagreement with the board, he left Olds in 1904 and founded the Reo Motor Car Co. The original company, Olds Motor Works, also survived and was absorbed into General Motors in November 1908. Olds Motor Works went on to build a variety of trucks under the Oldsmobile name up to 1939. The Reo company entered the truck market in 1913 with a 2-ton payload bonneted Model J which featured electric starting and lighting. The volume seller was Reo's legendary Speedwagon range, first introduced in 1915. It remained in production for about 10 years and was then modernized, continuing to be offered through to the late 1930s. From 1925 a 6-cylinder engine was available, and this was to become the main type of power unit. In 1928 heavier models for 3 and 4-ton payloads were available. Reo also built up a healthy export business and a UK assembly plant was set up in 1929.

A 4-tonner, introduced in 1932, had an 8-cylinder gasoline engine and in 1934 Reo offered their 6-cylinder Gold Crown gasoline engine across the range, which now included a heavier 6-ton model. After World War II their Model 30 and 31 bonneted trucks appeared, the heaviest being for 10-ton payloads and powered by Continental gasoline engines up to 200bhp. The first diesel-powered Reos were introduced in 1956 using turbocharged Cummins engines. In 1957 the company was acquired by the White Motor Co. The following year White also acquired Diamond T, and production of both Reo and Diamond T was concentrated in Reo's Lancing plant from 1960. By that time a new series of heavy-duty tilt-cab forward-control models, the DC range, was in production. In the final years of production a wide variety of heavy-duty trucks was offered, including 4×2, 6×4, 6×6 and 8×6 with, in some cases, diesel engines up to 335bhp. In 1967 Reo ceased to exist as an independent marque, the products becoming Diamond Reos.

CHESTER HILL, AUSTRALIA

RFW

■ LEFT ***RFW trucks were custom-built. This is an 8×4 site vehicle on test.***

Robert Frederick Whitehead founded his engineering company in the mid 1940s after serving as a fitter in the RAAF. A self-taught engineer, he turned to truck making in 1969, when he produced a Scania-engined twin-steer eight-wheeler fitted with a Bedford KM cab. RFW went on to offer a range of custom-built trucks in which quality and durability were more important than price. An almost endless choice of diesel engines was available, including Detroit Diesel, Cummins, Caterpillar, Scania, AEC, Rolls Royce and Nissan UD. Power ratings ranged from 190 to 550bhp. Model types included 4x2, 4x4, 6x4, 8x4 and 8x8.

During the late '80s on-highway trucks gave way entirely to custom-built specials including fire trucks and road-rail vehicles. In 2000 RFW was bought by Birrus International of Dandenong who introduced trucks based on Tatra technology but very few were built.

BRIDGEPORT, CONNECTICUT, USA

RIKER

The Riker name was adopted for Locomobile trucks from 1917 after the name of Locomobile's founder Andrew Riker. All were built on a 3.8m/12.5ft wheelbase and powered by a Locomobile 4-cylinder gasoline engine. Production of the 3 and 4-ton bonneted trucks continued until 1921, passing to Hares Motors in 1920.

BRASOV, ROMANIA

ROMAN

The Roman name was applied to a range of MAN-based trucks introduced by Autocamioane Brasov in 1971. The range was also marketed as DAC. Interprenderea de Autocamioane Brasov was originally the ROMLOC company, which built locomotives and rail wagons back in the early 1920s. It then became SR (Steagul Rosu, which means "Red Flag") and began truck building, under the SR, Bucegi and Carpati names, from 1954. The new Roman range was based on MAN/Saviem technology and, in some cases, was sold through MAN dealers. The Saviem-designed MAN cabs were built under licence as were Rába-MAN diesel engines. A wide range from 16-tonne 4x2s up to heavy tractors and 8x4s was offered. In 1990 the company was re-named Roman SA and the trucks were badged as DAC. In 2000 a new cab, called the "Millennium", was introduced. These particular models were badged as Roman.

■ ABOVE RIGHT ***Roman trucks of the 1970s were basically MAN designs built under licence. This six-wheeler is UK-registered.***

■ RIGHT ***The MAN origins are clearly evident in this 38-tonne artic with the MAN/Saviem pattern sleeper cab.***

COLNBROOK, ENGLAND

ROTINOFF

■ LEFT *Very few Rotinoffs entered civilian operations. This one worked in the UK.*

Rotinoff Motors Ltd was formed at Colnbrook, near Slough in Buckinghamshire, in 1952 by George Rotinoff, a White Russian immigrant, to build heavy tractors suitable for military tank transport. After suitability trials, the 6×4 Rotinoff Atlantic GR.7 was approved by the Swiss Army. The first example appeared in 1955. It had a maximum gross train weight rating of 140 tons, was powered by a 12.17 litre/743cu in Rolls Royce C6.SFL Series 109 direct-injection supercharged diesel developing 250bhp, and had a David Brown 12-speed (four main, three auxiliary) transmission. Kirkstall axles were fitted. Later models had the 275bhp C6.TFL Rolls Royce turbocharged diesel and 15-speed transmission. A heavier Super Atlantic GR.7 took the C8.TFL 16.2 litre/988cu in "straight eight" Rolls Royce turbo diesel giving 335bhp. These were fitted with 15 or 18-speed transmissions and were capable of gross train weights up to 300 tons. As well as the Atlantic and Super Atlantic, Rotinoff built a 7.3m/24ft wheelbase Viscount GR.37/AU load-carrying drawbar tractor suitable for Australian roadtrain operations. This had the additional option of a Rolls Royce B.81.8P 8-cylinder gasoline engine rated at 220bhp, designated the Viscount 64.GKS. Also listed was a forward-control Viscount 84.BJS rigid eight drawbar tractor. An estimated 35 Rotinoffs were built. From 1960 onwards the company changed its name from Rotinoff Motors to Lomount Vehicle & Engineering Ltd. Later still, when Lomount ended production in 1962, the design rights were acquired by Atkinson Vehicles Ltd of Walton-le-Dale, Preston, who briefly marketed the trucks under the Atkinson name badge.

LISKEARD, ENGLAND

ROWE-HILLMASTER

■ BELOW *The 1960 Rowe-Hillmaster tractor unit had a wide engine choice. This one was powered by an AEC AV470.*

Rowe's Garage Ltd of Dobwalls, Liskeard in Cornwall, were coach operators who turned to building a coach of their own design in 1953. A Meadows 4DC diesel engine was used. Only five coaches were built, but proprietor Maurice G. Rowe turned to truck building in 1954. The aim was to build a powerful, rugged truck which could master the steep hills in Rowe's native Cornwall. The appropriate name Rowe-Hillmaster was adopted, and the first model was a 6 to 7-ton payload forward-control four-wheeler powered by a 90bhp Meadows 4DC-330 diesel engine. An 8-ton version of this also became available but with an Eaton 2-speed axle as standard. In 1955 an underfloor-engined 7-tonner was available powered by a Meadows 4HDC-330 mounted amidships behind the front axle, a layout already tried in an earlier coach chassis. By this time Maurice Rowe had sold the garage and coaching business and set up a truck-manufacturing operation under the name M. G. Rowe (Motors) Doublebois Ltd. The company went on to offer an extensive range of trucks with payload ratings from 6 to 14 tons, plus an artic tractor for a 15-ton payload. A 10-ton four-wheeler, the M/10 at 14 tons gvw, announced in 1956, had a Meadows 5.4 litre/330cu in 4DC-330 but it was also available as a 9 to 10-tonner with a wide choice of power units. The L/9-10 had the Leyland

■ RIGHT *Most Rowe-Hillmasters were sold in their home territory. This livestock truck was based at Liskeard, Cornwall, where it was built.*

Comet 0.350, the A/9-10 had the AEC AV470 and the G/9-10 had the Gardner 5LW. Others, for 6/7-ton payloads, were available with the Gardner 4LK or 4LW, according to model. No less than 14 basic models were listed by 1959, including a 14-ton six-wheeler with Hendrickson bogie and a choice of Meadows 6DC-500, AEC AV470, Gardner 5LW or 6LW.

For an extra charge – according to model – almost any Rowe-Hillmaster could be supplied with underfloor engines from Meadows, Gardner, AEC or Leyland. The trucks were fitted with coachbuilt cabs supplied by Jennings of Sandbach. Despite Rowe's high engineering standards and custom-build approach, sales were mainly limited to south-west England, and the company ceased trading in 1962 after nine years in business.

CROYDON, ENGLAND

RUTLAND

■ LEFT *Though a small company, Motor Traction offered a very wide range. This is a typical Rutland 6-tonner dating from 1957.*

Motor Traction Ltd was established in 1951 at New Addington, Surrey, to build Rutland trucks. These were sold as MTN in certain export markets. The origins of the company date back to 1946 when Frank Manton left the Royal Navy and set up Manton Motors at Tee Van Road, Addiscombe, Croydon, with a Commer distributorship. He began building his own design of truck called the Manton, powered by a Perkins P6 diesel and grossing 8 tons gvw. These sold well in Spain, and Frank Manton established an agency at the Mack Distributors, Sumassa, in Madrid. As there were restrictions on the number of vehicles one agent could sell, the name MTN was introduced to double the quotas. Those sold in the UK were usually badged Rutland.

To avoid clashing with Commer, Manton transferred his truck-manufacturing business to new premises, under the name of Motor Traction Ltd. In the five years the company survived, an amazingly diverse range of trucks was built. To keep costs down, items such as spring hanger brackets were fabricated rather than forged or cast. The range covered almost every conceivable type, from the 2 to 3-ton payload M4 up to a projected TH 10716 rigid eight-wheeler at 24 tons gvw. Both bonneted and forward-control models were built. Many had type names like the Toucan 5 to 6-tonner, the Albatross 6 to 7-tonner, and the Stuka and Eagle 7-tonners. Motor Traction could fit almost any engine and drive-line the customer wanted, and cabs were custom-built by almost any coachbuilder. There were well over 50 different types on offer, including 4×4s and special mobile-crane chassis. However, production figures were low, some even being one-offs. The firm folded in 1957. The name Rutland was derived from the county of Rutland where Frank's father, Arthur C. Manton, was born.

OTHER MAKES

■ RAMIREZ

MONTERREY, MEXICO

Grupo Industrial Ramirez built heavy-duty trailers at their subsidiary, Trailers de Monterrey SA, and in the late 1950s began building 4×2 and 6×4 bonneted highway tractors, typical of which is the R-22, powered by a Cummins NTC-350 diesel. Most components are licence-built in Mexico to American design, including Spicer transmissions and Rockwell axles. Gross train weight capabilities extend up to 54.5 tonnes.

■ LEFT ***The 1966 Ramirez 4×2 bonneted tractor features all-American drive components but these are locally produced under licence.***

■ RAPID

DETROIT & PONTIAC, MICHIGAN, USA

One of the United States' pioneer truck builders, the Rapid Motor Vehicle Co. was established in 1904 after brothers Max and Morris Grabowski had built their first truck back in 1900. That was a very basic single-cylinder affair capable of about 16kph/10mph. In 1905 production moved to Pontiac. By 1907 Rapid was building 1-ton and $1\frac{1}{2}$-ton forward-control models with a driver-over-engine layout. In 1907 Max Grabowski pulled out of Rapid and set up the Grabowski Power Wagon Co., which survived until 1912. Meanwhile the newly formed General Motors Truck Co. showed an interest in Rapid, absorbing the company in 1911.

■ ABOVE LEFT ***Relay's massive Duo-Drive 300A 6×4 of 1931 had twin 8-cylinder gasoline engines producing 275bhp.***

■ LEFT ***The 1930 Relay 3/4-tonner featured a unique final drive referred to as the "Surmounting Principle".***

■ RELAY

LIMA, OHIO, USA

The Relay Motor Corporation was set up in 1927 with substantial financial backing. It was formed as a consortium of three existing manufacturers, namely the Commerce Motor Truck Co. of Ypsilanti, Michigan, the Service Motor Truck Co. of Wabash, Indiana, and the Garford Truck Co. of Lima, Ohio. Eventually all production was centred at the Lima plant. The three individual makes were retained and a separate Relay range was introduced. This included eight bonneted models for payloads in the 1 to 4 tons range. While the Commerce, Service and Garford trucks featured worm drive, Relay adopted a unique final-drive arrangement in which drive pinions engaged with toothed rings in the rear wheels, enabling it to "climb" over obstacles – Relay referred to it as their "Relay Surmounting Principle". In 1931 a 7-ton payload 6-cylinder truck was introduced.

Relay's last grand gesture before folding up in 1933 was their high-powered Duo Drive – a 6×4 monster powered by two Lycoming Type AEC straight-eight gasoline engines mounted side by side with combined output of 275bhp. Each engine drove one rear axle through its own air-shift Fuller 5-speed gearbox. Other features included power steering, hydraulic clutches and full air brakes. Cleco-Gruss air springs were mounted at the front, and the cab incorporated a sleeping bunk. Relay advertised it as the world's most powerful truck, but it attracted few sales.

■ REPUBLIC

ALMA, MICHIGAN, USA

Beginning in 1913 as the Alma Motor Truck Co., Republic built light to medium trucks from 1914 with payload capacities of around 1 ton. By 1917 heavier models for up to $3\frac{1}{4}$ tons were available, powered by Lycoming, Continental or Waukesha gasoline engines. These were marketed in the UK as Whiting by Whiting (1915) Ltd of North London. Early trucks had Torbensen drive, but this was soon abandoned in favour of Timken and Eaton worm drive. During the 1920s heavier models still were added, the biggest being a 5-ton payload machine. However, Republic were suffering financial difficulties. In 1928 they acquired the Linn Manufacturing Co. of Morris, New York, which built half-track tractors. The following year Republic merged with the American LaFrance Truck Co., forming the LaFrance Republic Corporation. This survived until 1932 when it was taken over by the Sterling Motor Truck Co. of West Allis, Wisconsin, production carrying on until 1942, but the latter-day LaFrance Republics were basically Sterlings under a different name.

ARBON, SWITZERLAND

SAURER

■ LEFT *The Saurer C type truck was a great classic with its origins in the 1930s. This is an early '60s 7-tonner.*

■ BELOW LEFT *Saurer's first truck was this 1903 shaft and pinion drive 5-tonner.*

Adolph Saurer was experimenting with gasoline-engine design back in 1888, and by 1896 had produced his first motor car. This pioneer of the European motor industry entered the truck market as early as 1903 with a 5-tonner powered by a 25 to 30hp T-head gasoline engine. In 1905 lighter trucks for $1\frac{1}{2}$, $2\frac{1}{2}$ and 3 tonnes appeared, and the following year an improved 5-tonner on solid rubber tyres. Saurer vehicles scored many successes in international trials in Europe. In 1909 the Zurich-based Safir Co. took out a licence to build Saurers and it was there that Saurer's first high-speed diesel engine was built.

As early as 1910 truck factories were set up in Germany and France to assemble Saurers for these markets. Also, the International Motor Co. of Plainfield, New Jersey, began licensed assembly (see "Mack").

In 1918 Saurer introduced its A types for civilian customers, and by the early 1930s was building 2, 3, 4 and 5-tonners. The B type appeared in 1926. The first diesel appeared in the B types which, by 1930, included trucks for payloads of 2 to 6 tonnes.

In 1929 Saurer acquired its Swiss rival, Motorwagenfabrik Berna AG of Olten, but the Berna name was allowed to continue. During the late 1920s a British operation was established, and from 1931 Saurers were built in

Newcastle-upon-Tyne under the Armstrong Saurer name. Diesel-engine development continued throughout the 1930s, the first direct-injection Saurer diesel appearing in 1934. Later that year the company introduced its famous C type which was of very modern appearance.

During World War II Saurer developed a highly innovative 8x8 military truck plus 4x4 and 6x6 versions. After the war the C type resumed production and a forward-control C type was also introduced, the heaviest being a 7-tonner. Heavier models, including the 10-tonne payload 6C, appeared in 1956 and the C range continued to 1963. By the late 1950s D type trucks were under development, consisting of two basic chassis, the 2D and 5D. These were offered in a variety of wheelbases, powered by diesel engines of 120 to 240bhp. All-wheel drive versions were also offered. From 1971 the 2D became the 4D while the 5D continued. The largest and most impressive 5D model, the 5DF 8×4 rigid eight-wheeler, was launched in 1974.

From 1976 the main models were the D180/D230 4×2 and the D290/D330 which were built in various configurations as 4×2, 6×2, 6×4 and 8×4s. Declining sales in the early 1980s saw the two leading Swiss truck makers, Saurer and FBW, forming a joint organization called NAW (Nutzfahrzeuggesellschaft Arbon & Wetzikon). In 1982 Daimler-Benz acquired a major shareholding in NAW and soon took full control.

■ RIGHT *The D model designation covered the entire range from the 1970s onwards. This is the heavy-duty D290.*

■ LEFT *Successor to the C type was the D type, which bore a strong family likeness to its predecessor but had a facelifted cab with flush mounted headlights.*

SEINE, FRANCE

SAVIEM

Saviem, an acronym of Société Anonyme de Véhicules Industriels et Équipements Mécaniques, came into being in 1955 when Latil, Renault, Somua and Floirat merged. It was primarily a marketing organization, and for two years or so the various companies' trucks were marketed as Saviem Latil, Saviem Renault, Saviem Somua, Saviem LRS and Saviem Floirat. The widely differing model types led to a complex range. Renault's distinctive underfloor-engined models had little or nothing in common with Latil and Somua's vertical-engined types. Latil were still producing their unusual four-wheel steer timber tractors and Somua offered a choice of heavy-duty dump-truck chassis. Clearly there was room for rationalization in such a conglomeration of models, and by 1960 some simplification was taking place, notably in the range of diesel engines. Saviem Fulgur 4 and 6-cylinder diesel engines of 4.6 and 6.8 litre/281 and 415cu in capacity were introduced in 1961 and some of the older designs were phased out. A diesel engine plant was set up in the former French Government's Limoges armaments factory, which had been producing engines for military use. Also in 1961 Saviem entered a brief association with the German company Henschel, under which Henschels were to be marketed in France as Saviem Henschel. The arrangement was ended after only two years.

■ ABOVE ***After the formation of Saviem, Renault's old underfloor-engined models were given a new lease of life as the Tancarville.***

■ BELOW ***The JM240 artic featured a stylish new cab and a 235bhp MAN diesel.***

New models, badged Saviem, appeared in the early 1960s, including a medium-range, the S5, S7 and S8 for 5.5, 7.5 and 8.5-tonne payloads respectively. There was also an

■ **RIGHT** ***Saviem's SM range had a lot in common with MAN, resulting from technical co-operation in the late 1960s and '70s.***

■ **RIGHT** ***Later versions of the Saviem cab had this full-width black grille, giving them their own identity.***

■ **BELOW RIGHT** ***The mid 1970s J range of medium trucks had the Club of Four cab.***

articulated model for up to 16.5 tonnes payload. Engine choice included the 3.0 litre/183cu in Renault 591 4-cylinder diesel and the 5.8 litre/355cu in Perkins 6.354 diesel. These models had a column-mounted gearshift, carrying on a Renault tradition. The 1962 heavy-duty range, featuring a stylish new cab with four headlights, consisted of the JL with payload ratings from 6.8 tonnes up to 12.75 tonnes. There were also seven heavy-duty tractor units ranging from the JL21 at 18 tonnes gcw up to the JL32 at 32 tonnes gcw, plus the JL20 and JL20/200 for 35 tonnes gcw. The latter featured a Henschel 520D6T 6-cylinder 204bhp direct-injection diesel and a 10-speed gearbox. Latil's 4×4 timber tractor continued to be available, marketed as the Saviem TL23. Certain models from the underfloor-engined Renault range were still marketed as the Saviem Tancarville TPIO, powered by the 150bhp F646 horizontal diesel and featuring a floor-mounted gearshift.

In 1971 Saviem became a member of the Euro Truck Development Group, otherwise known as the Club of Four. Along with DAF, Magirus-Deutz and Volvo, they developed a tilt-cab medium truck range, appearing in 1975 as the Saviem J models. These were powered by an MAN 5.5 litre/335cu in diesel licence-built by Saviem at their Limoges factory. Technical co-operation between Saviem and MAN of Germany, which had begun in the late 1960s, resulted in a new range of heavy-duty trucks, the SM models, with a new tilt cab of Saviem design. This became standard fitment on MANs as well as Saviems, while MAN engines were fitted in the Saviem versions. Many of these models also featured a steering-column gearshift.

A major development in 1974 was the acquisition of Berliet from the Citroën Group. This resulted in an even more complex range, with certain Berliet designs being marketed with Renault and Saviem badges. By 1978 the organization had undergone rationalization and became known as Renault Véhicules Industriels. The Berliet and Saviem names were replaced by Renault and by 1980 Saviem no longer existed as a make.

WATFORD, ENGLAND

SCAMMELL

Scammell's Articulated Six-wheeler of 1922 set the scene for the company's highly individual approach to truck design throughout its 66-year history. Scammell Lorries Ltd, which set up at Tolpits Lane, Watford, in 1922, was an offshoot of the coachbuilding and steam wagon repair company, G. Scammell & Nephew Ltd of Spitalfields, whose history dates back to 1837. In 1919 the company began experimenting with a matched three-axled articulated truck using a design closely based on the American Knox Martin. The weight of the trailer, or "carrier" as Scammell preferred to call it, was taken on semi-elliptic leaf springs attached to the tractor rear axle.

Shortly after setting up their Watford factory, Scammell took on a young engineer called Oliver D. North, who was responsible for a number of important designs at Scammell. However, his first project was less than successful. He tried a 3-cylinder radial engine in a light delivery Scammell called the Autovan. Only four were ever built, and the project was abandoned. The same year a decision was made to develop the legendary 6×4 and 6×6 Pioneer which was an unqualified success.

■ TOP *From 1924, Scammell's articulated truck could have "four-wheels-in-line" twin rear axles enabling a payload of up to 12 tons.*

■ ABOVE *Heavy tractors were Scammell's forte, like this Cummins-powered 240-ton Contractor of 1967.*

■ BELOW *In the 1960s Scammell modernized its Rigid 8 concept by launching the Routeman. This is a Routeman III.*

North's next project was equally sensational. In 1929 plans were drawn up for what was claimed to be the world's largest truck – the Scammell "100-tonner". The heavily built chain-drive machine was matched to a massive "carrier" (trailer) with a steerable rear bogie. Only two were built. Initially they were fitted with Scammell's standard 4-cylinder 7 litre/427cu in gasoline engine, geared to a maximum road speed of 10kph/6mph. During their working lives they were both re-engined with Gardner diesels.

Scammell also began offering 6-ton four-wheelers, which were basically longer versions of their motive units. The first appeared in 1929. Then came a six-wheeled rigid in 1933. This, like all Scammells up to 1934, was fitted with the 4-cylinder gasoline and chain drive although, by then, pneumatic tyres were standard. Within a year, Scammell's technology had taken a leap forward with the introduction of a Gardner 6-cylinder diesel and shaft drive. Until 1933 the company had devoted all its

■ RIGHT *Scammell's Rigid 8 continued in production until 1958.*

attention to heavy-duty trucks, but then it launched its famous Mechanical Horse articulated lightweight truck for town deliveries.

Scammell's next significant design was their first rigid four-axled truck which they named the Rigid 8, presumably to distinguish it from their earlier Artic 8. It was powered by a Gardner 6LW and had a 6-speed overdrive gearbox. The first went into service in 1937.

Just after World War II Scammell designed and built a series of special heavy four-wheeled fairground generator trucks called Showtracs. Also, a modern-day equivalent to the Pioneer was built in the shape of the 6×6 Explorer. Other heavy tractors, often aimed at the overseas market, included the Mountaineer and Constructor.

In 1955 Scammell was absorbed into the Leyland Group, but because of the specialist nature of its products it was allowed to carry on as their Special Vehicles division.

■ RIGHT *The Scammell Highwayman kept alive Scammell's long tradition of bonneted artics.*

■ RIGHT *This 1973 Crusader represents Scammell's modernized range. The engine was a Rolls Royce 220 or 280 diesel.*

In 1958 the old Rigid 8 was due for updating, and Scammell launched the Routeman which had similar running units. A fibreglass cab was fitted. Shortly after, in 1962, the completely new Routeman II was launched with a striking fibreglass cab styled by Giovani Michelloti. During the 1950s the Artic 8 became the Highwayman tractor unit using a conventional fifth wheel in place of Scammell's patented Spherub semi-permanent coupling.

By 1968 new designs were appearing in the form of a heavy-duty Crusader 6×4 tractor and later a 4×2 version. The standard power unit for this was a Rolls Royce Eagle 6-cylinder diesel, but 6×4s were powered by 8V-71 Detroit Diesel two-stroke engines. A solitary eight-wheeled version called the Samson was built for Pickfords, the heavy-haulage contractors. Super heavy-haulage tractors, like the Contractor of 1966, were designed for gtws of 75 to 240 tons.

The Highwayman was phased out in the late 1960s, and the Routeman was replaced in 1980 by the new Leyland Constructor rigid eight which, though developed by Scammell, was badged Leyland. During the 1980s Scammell continued building heavy vehicles in the form of the S24 and the Commander tank transporter but, following the acquisition of Leyland by DAF Trucks in 1987, the plant closed in 1988.

SÖDERTÄLJE, SWEDEN

SCANIA

The Scania name appeared on trucks from 1903–11 and was not to reappear until 1969. Between 1911 and 1969 the trucks were marketed as Scania-Vabis. The first Scania truck, named the Tor, was built in 1903. The company's origins can be traced to 1891 when a Swedish agency was set up at Malmo by Danish-born Fredrik Petersen to assemble English-designed Humber bicycles. Svenska Aktiebolaget Humber & Co. manufactured the bicycles under licence. Bicycle production was discontinued from 1900 and a new company, under Petersen's directorship, was formed under the name Maskinfabriksaktiebolaget Scania.

Vagnfabriks Aktiebolaget i Södertälje (VABIS) was established even earlier, in 1892, building railway rolling stock and horse-drawn wagons. From 1897 Vabis began design work on internal combustion engines led by engineer Gustaf Erikson. From 1907 the company began to concentrate on automotive engines and passenger cars which were marketed under the Vabis name. After suffering financial difficulties during 1909–10, Vabis merged with Scania to form A.B. Scania-Vabis in 1917.

Prior to the merger, each company had begun developing its own designs of trucks. While Scania had produced the Tor in 1903, Vabis had already built its first truck, a 1½-tonner, in 1902. By 1908 there were Vabis trucks for 2 and 3 tonnes payload, powered by their own designs of gasoline engines. These included the E2V V-twin 12hp (later increased to 15 and 18hp) and the E4 four-in-line 5.4 litre/330cu in, producing up to 36hp. Shaft drive was used. Some 20 Vabis trucks were built prior to the merger. Scania's pre-merger truck production included a forward-control 1½-tonne chain-drive truck designed in 1902.

The first Scania-Vabis trucks were based on Scania chain-drive designs, but by 1913 a new range from 1½ to 6 tonnes payload capacity was launched. These were of bonneted layout with chain drive and gasoline engines with power ratings from 30 to 70hp. By the end of World War I Scania-Vabis had developed a four-wheel drive army truck which also found customers in the civilian market. This was unusual in having four independent drive shafts, one to each wheel, from a centrally mounted transfer box. A double-drive six-wheeler was launched in 1923. Other important developments of the era were a double-reduction drive axle and a patented design of progressive road spring.

Experiments with diesel power began in 1927, resulting in the Hesselman-Scania oil engine. This used gasoline for starting before being switched to diesel oil. It was some years before Scania's high-speed diesel engines actually entered production, the first appearing in 1936.

■ LEFT *Vabis' first truck of 1903 carried 1½ tonnes and had a top speed of 12kph/7.5mph.*

■ BELOW LEFT *A forward-control, chain-drive 1½-tonner with 12hp twin-cylinder gasoline engine.*

■ BOTTOM LEFT *A 112M 32-ton artic with low datum P sleeper cab. The "M" signifies "medium duty".*

All pre-World War II Scanias were built with right-hand drive as Swedish traffic, like that of the UK, drove on the left and did not change over to the right until September 1967. Most Scania trucks were of bonneted layout, but as early as 1933 forward-control conversions were being built, inspired to some extent by the Bulldog buses that appeared in 1932. They were called Bulldogs because of their "flat-faced" design, which enabled the driver to sit beside the engine. The Bulldog principle was introduced on trucks in 1934, with the very functional-looking 34511 4½-tonner featuring a cab-ahead-of-axle layout with long doors and a low-entry step.

Major expansion plans were underway at the end of the 1930s and truck production was stepped up. During the war, fuel-oil shortages led to the wide use of producer gas, and civilian demand for trucks diminished as road fleets were laid up. Lack of civilian orders was compensated by demand for military trucks, and by 1943 Scania-Vabis production was entirely geared to the war effort. From the end of 1944 civilian production resumed. New bonneted heavy-duty trucks, the F10 and L10, were unveiled in 1944. The F10 was a four-wheel drive of 8.5 tonnes gvw while the L10, at the same design weight, was a 4×2. These were the first production Scania-Vabis to have left-hand drive. Large numbers of these trucks were fitted with third-axle conversions. A heavier version for 10/11 tonnes gvw, the L20 (4×2), soon followed and a factory-built 6×2 version, the LS20 for 15 tonnes gvw, was also introduced for 1946.

During the 1950s Scania-Vabis was seeking to increase its export sales to remain profitable. Many new models, mainly bonneted heavy-duty trucks, were launched and direct-injection diesels, based on Leyland technology, were introduced. To power the heaviest trucks, like the experimental LS85 6×2, the D815 8-cylinder in-line engine of 11.3 litres/689cu in was tried. This was turbocharged to boost the output from 180 up to 205bhp and was claimed to be the first-ever production turbo diesel. Bonneted 6×2 trucks up to 22 tonnes gvw and 4×2s of 13 to 15.5 tonnes gvw were Scania-Vabis' most common models of the 1950s and '60s, but in 1963 the forward-control LB76 ("B" standing for "Bulldog") entered the scene.

The company established a very important production plant in Brazil in

■ ABOVE LEFT *The LB76, introduced in 1963, led to an expansion in sales, especially in the UK.*

■ ABOVE RIGHT *Scanias, like this late 1970s 141, had reserves of strength and power to cope with their domestic weight limit of 52 tonnes.*

■ RIGHT *T-cabbed Scanias were great favourites among image-conscious operators from 1995 to 2005.*

■ LEFT *A completely new design of cab gives the 'Next Generation' Scanias of 2017 an up-to-the-minute image.*

1962. To gain an improved share of the European market another plant was opened at Zwolle in The Netherlands in 1965. The LB76 played an important part in establishing Scania-Vabis as a major force in Europe and the UK. The replacements for the LB76, the LB80 and LB110 of 1968 consolidated the company's position as one of the market leaders. In 1968 Scania-Vabis, which was owned by the Swedish Wallenburg empire, merged with SAAB. As SAAB-Scania the company dropped the Vabis name and the trucks were just badged Scania from 1969. The LB80/81, 110/111 and 140/141 were replaced in 1980 by the 2 series (82, 112, 142). The outwardly similar 93, 113 and 143 range followed in 1988. The 9, 11 and 14 signified the engine capacity in litres. Next came the 4 series consisting of the 94, 114, 124 and 144. These were dubbed the New Program models and were pre-fixed G, P, R or T. G and P were low cabs, R high cab and T bonneted cab. In 1995 Scania and SAAB separated, SAAB passing to GM. Scania launched the R series in 2004 powered by new engines, the biggest being the 16 litre/976 cu.in. V8 with 580bhp, later uprated to 680. The T cab range was phased out in 2005 through lack of demand.

In August 2016 Scania unveiled a completely new range, the 'Next Generation' featuring a new style cab and a striking new flagship model in the form of the 'S'. The S730 represents the top of the range with its Highline flat floor cab and 730bhp V8.

LETCHWORTH, ENGLAND

SD

■ LEFT *T series municipals sometimes fulfilled other roles, like this tanker.*

■ BELOW LEFT *SD's most famous municipal model was the W type.*

Harry Shelvoke and James Drewry developed a unique concept in municipal chassis while employed at Lacre Lorries. In 1922 they left to start their own company, Shelvoke & Drewry, or SD. Their unusual transverse-engined low-loading truck, the Freighter, was a great success. The company also built the Latil tractor under licence, using the Traulier name. One of SD's most famous trucks was the W type. This had SD's own 3.9 litre/238cu in gasoline engine but, from 1954, a Perkins P4 diesel was offered. As the 1950s and '60s progressed, SD developed larger trucks, aimed at the municipal market. The TW of 1960 had a choice of SD gasoline or Perkins P6 diesel and grossed 11 tons, while the new fibreglass-cabbed TY of 1963 grossed 14 tons and featured a Leyland O.350 diesel engine.

In 1975 the company launched its SPV (Special Purpose Vehicle) division and branched out into heavier-duty 4×4 and 6×4 crash tenders and fire trucks. In 1984 SD was taken over by the American-based Dempster Co. and then traded as Shelvoke-Dempster. The SPV range was discontinued and SD's share of the market declined until it was sold to a private investor in 1988. It was then to trade as Shelvoke, but the venture failed and the company had vanished from the scene by 1990.

OLDHAM, ENGLAND

SEDDON

Seddon was a relative latecomer to the truck industry compared with most of its rivals in the north-west of England. The company was formed as Foster & Seddon in 1938 at Salford, near Manchester in Lancashire. Foster & Seddon were hauliers and truck agents who realized the potential for a low-weight diesel truck that could weigh under 2½ tons unladen and was, therefore, exempt from the 32kph/20mph restrictions then in force. The object was to move a 6-ton payload over long distances at minimum cost. The higher 48kph/30mph legal speed meant faster turnaround and diesel power was more economical, giving more km/miles per gallon, on fuel that was half the cost. The formula was a sound one and the first Perkins P6-powered Seddon fulfilled all its promises. At first production was limited, owing to the cramped premises at Salford, but increasing demand justified a move to bigger premises at Oldham, where their Woodstock factory began full production in 1948.

There the Mk.5 forward-control four-wheelers were built in increasing numbers, and Seddon built up export business as well as healthy sales in the home market. In the 1950s Seddon, which was renamed Seddon Diesel Vehicles Ltd in 1951, began to widen the range with lighter and heavier models. The first was the Mk.7 3-tonner powered by a Perkins P4 diesel. An even lighter model, the bonneted Twenty Five 1¼-ton delivery vehicle, took the P3. By then Seddon was making extensive use of fibreglass in its cab and bodywork and was a pioneer of this technique. Cabs were built by a subsidiary called Pennine Coachcraft.

Seddon continued to generate increasing export business, selling into the Far East, Central and South America, Spain, Portugal and Europe. In the mid 1950s it began to move up the weight range, the UK weight limit having been increased to 14 tons and the 32kph/20mph limit having been abolished. A stylish new cab with curved screen appeared in 1956.

■ TOP *Seddon built its reputation on its Perkins-engined Mk.5.*

■ ABOVE *The Sirdar heavy-duty 30-ton 6×4 was aimed at the export market.*

■ BELOW *The Cummins-engined 34:Four of the early 1970s era was Seddon's last tractor unit as an independent maker.*

■ LEFT *Seddon entered the maximum-weight sector in 1958 with their SD8 and DD8 rigid eight-wheelers.*

■ LEFT *A 1968 six-wheeled beer tanker grossed 22 tons and was available with an AEC AV470 diesel.*

■ BELOW LEFT *The 16:Four dump truck was powered by a Perkins V8-510 and features a Motor Panels cab.*

There was also a 14-ton gvw model, the Mk.14 with Gardner 6LW engine, and a Seven-tonner which was also available in artic and six-wheel form for up to 15 tons gvw. In 1958 the 14-ton gvw Mk.15/10 appeared with a choice of Perkins, Leyland and Gardner diesels.

In 1958 Seddon announced a completely new heavy-duty range, including a 24-ton gvw rigid eight-wheeler, the DD8 (8×4) and SD8 (8×2). This had a design weight of 28 tons in anticipation of increased weight limits. The new eight-wheeler had a choice of Gardner 6LW, 6LX or Cummins HF6, one of the first Cummins installations in a UK heavy truck. Another vehicle of interest in 1958 was the Sirdar 30-ton six-wheeled heavy tractor in bonneted or forward-control form, for up to 45 tons gtw. This was powered by a 198bhp Cummins NH.B.6.

Seddon benefited from being an assembler rather than manufacturer of its own components, and was able to offer a broad range of optional power units. In 1962 the range underwent some simplification and the rigid eight received a number of changes, becoming the 24DD8 or 24SD8. One was a very advanced design of tapered-leaf high-articulation rear bogie called the Maxartic. In 1964 the range was updated with a new model, the 13:Four, which featured a completely new steel cab bought in from Motor Panels. The 13:Four was powered by the Perkins 6.354 6-cylinder diesel. The following year a heavier model, the 16:Four (the first two digits indicated the gvw) with a 170bhp Perkins V8, was introduced. With an increase in demand for tractor units on the UK market, the eight-wheel range was dropped in 1964 and, by 1966–67, heavy-duty tractor units for 28 to 34 tons gcw were available, the heaviest being the 32:Four powered by Gardner 6LXB 180 or Rolls Royce 220bhp diesels.

There were few new models in the early 1970s, these being mostly heavy tractors, plus a 16-ton drawbar model for 32 tons gtw. A 34-ton tractor unit, the 34:Four with a choice of Rolls Royce Eagle 220, Cummins NH 220 or Gardner 8LXB 240bhp diesel became available. In 1970 Seddon acquired Atkinson Vehicles of Preston and by 1974 Seddon's and Atkinson's individual models were phased out, to be replaced by the new Seddon Atkinson range. (See "Seddon Atkinson".)

OLDHAM, ENGLAND

SEDDON ATKINSON

■ LEFT *The 400 tilt-cab range appeared in 1975, with a choice of Gardner, Cummins and Rolls Royce diesel engines.*

■ LEFT *From 1992 Stratos began appearing with the Iveco Group cab, as seen on this 44-ton drawbar outfit in New Zealand.*

Atkinson Vehicles of Preston was taken over by Seddon Diesel Vehicles Ltd of Oldham in 1970 but, for five years or so, each company retained its identity. A new joint product, the Seddon Atkinson 400, was under development when International Harvester purchased the company in 1974. The first Seddon Atkinson 400 came on the market in 1975. The next models to appear were the 200 and 300 series, which featured International diesels. Seddon Atkinsons were fitted with a Motor Panels steel tilt cab. From 1982 the range was updated with the 201, 301 and 401 series, recognizable by their black plastic grilles. At the same time Atkinson's famous circle "A" badge was reinstated at customers' request. Also, International engines were supplemented by Perkins and Cummins alternatives on certain models.

By 1986 the range was again updated, becoming the 2-11, 3-11 and 4-11, and International engines were deleted. By this time International had sold Seddon Atkinson to the Spanish ENASA Group. The Motor Panels cab was phased out after the introduction of a new long-haul truck, the Strato, which shared Cabtec design used by DAF and Pegaso. In 1992 ENASA was taken over by Iveco, and very soon Seddon Atkinsons began to be fitted with similar cabs to Iveco-Ford.

The Oldham factory closed in 2002, with production being transferred to Madrid. For a period Iveco continued to offer 8x4 models, a 6x4 tractor and municipal chassis but, with dwindling demand, Iveco announced that the Seddon Atkinson brand would be axed in October 2006.

■ ABOVE *The 200 series four-wheeler with International D-358 diesel engine was available from 1976–82.*

■ RIGHT *Between 1988 and 1992 the top-of-the-range Strato featured a version of the Cabtec cab developed by DAF and ENASA.*

SHREWSBURY, ENGLAND

SENTINEL

■ LEFT *Sentinel's legendary Super undertype steam lorry first appeared in 1923.*

■ BELOW LEFT *The S type steamer of 1934 was an advanced design but, even so, could not compete with diesel trucks.*

While Sentinel is synonymous with Shrewsbury, the company was originally established in 1906 as Alley & MacLellan Ltd based at Polmadie, Glasgow. Their Standard 5-ton steam wagon featured a vertical water-tube boiler incorporating a super-heater coil, an undertype 2-cylinder engine and single chain drive. So successful was that early wagon that it remained in production with relatively few changes through to the launch of Sentinel's famous Super of 1923. Alley & MacLellan had changed its name to the Sentinel Waggon Works Ltd when a new factory was opened at Shrewsbury, Shropshire, in 1915. In 1920, after being beset by financial problems, the company was reorganized as Sentinel Waggon Works (1920) Ltd. The highly successful Super wagon incorporated many advanced features, including a crankshaft differential and twin chain drive.

The DG series was a direct development of the Super, appearing in 1926. The DG4 had a payload rating of 6 to 7 tons, and had the benefit of 2-speed gearing for a better performance span between hill climbing and flat roads. The same year a six-wheeled version, the DG6, appeared for payloads of 12 tons. An even larger DG8 four-axled version was introduced in 1929. This has the distinction of being the first British rigid eight-wheeler but only a small number were built and, in practice, legal weight limits meant they could not carry any more than the DG6.

Sentinel and Foden dominated the steam market, but the 1930s were to see the demise of both ranges as new legislation forced the development of lighter trucks. Sentinel survived the longest. In 1934 they defied all odds and launched a new and very advanced steamer – the S type with a single-acting 4-cylinder underfloor engine with longitudinal crankshaft suited to cardan-shaft drive to an overhead worm-drive axle. It was lighter and featured a modernized driver's cab with a set-back boiler. It came in four, six and eight-wheel form, designated S4, S6 and S8. In spite of its sophisticated design, it could not compete with diesel trucks for all-round convenience and payload capacity, and it was phased out in the late 1930s. However, that was not the end of Sentinel's involvement with steam, since the company built about 100 wagons for export to Argentina as late as 1950.

By that time the company had become Sentinel (Shrewsbury) Ltd, and had developed a new range of diesel trucks. The first, the DV44, went into production in 1948 and was powered by Sentinel's own 4-cylinder horizontal indirect-injection engine, mounted in much the same location as that of the S4 steamer. David Brown gearboxes and Kirkstall overhead worm rear axles were standard. The all-steel 3-seater cab was of very handsome appearance and featured sliding doors. Prototypes of an underfloor gasoline-engined truck had been under development during the war, but the gasoline engine option was

■ RIGHT *From 1948 Sentinel Diesels entered full production. This is a 1955 Sentinel DV46T coal dump truck.*

soon abandoned. In late 1950 the DV46 light six-wheeler, basically a DV44 with trailing axle, became available, followed in 1952 by the DV66 heavy six-wheeler with a direct-injection 6-cylinder engine. The 4-cylinder was also revised to direct-injection design. Despite Sentinel's superbly engineered trucks, sales were diminishing during the 1950s, and by 1956 the company was forced to pull out of truck production. The factory was bought by Rolls Royce for diesel engine production, while the remaining stock of parts and vehicles was taken over by Sentinel's main dealer, North Cheshire Motors Ltd of Warrington, who formed a new company, Transport Vehicles (Warrington) Ltd in 1957 to build Sentinel-based designs under the TVW name.

SHEFFIELD, ENGLAND

SHEFFLEX

■ LEFT *This six-wheeler was one of Shefflex's largest trucks in the early 1930s.*

During World War I, when Commer Cars were working at full capacity to meet demands for their RC military trucks, the Sheffield Simplex Car Co., builders of luxury passenger cars, sub-contracted manufacture of lightweight 1½ to 2-ton Commers. When Commer returned to normal peacetime production, the contract with Sheffield Simplex was ended. Commers built at Sheffield were then marketed as Shefflex, but surplus stock was sold to R. A. Johnstone, an operator and motor dealer. Johnstone set up a production plant to build more, and production continued through to 1935. In 1930 heavier models were introduced, including a 5-ton payload 6×2 and a 6-ton articulated truck. Forward-control models were also offered. Engines used included Dorman, Meadows and Petter.

NANTERE, FRANCE

SIMCA

■ BELOW *During Simca's brief presence in the truck market it offered this Cargo 5-tonner.*

The history of Simca (Société Industrielle de Mécanique et Carroserie Automobile) is more concerned with cars than trucks, but in 1954 it acquired the French S.A. Ford operation at Poissy, which provided it with an established truck factory. A 5-tonne payload forward-control truck was marketed as the Cargo. A bonneted 5-tonner powered by a Ford V8 gasoline engine, the Caboteur, was also built briefly from 1957, but the following year truck production was transferred to Simca's associate company, UNIC.

HELSINKI, FINLAND

SISU

Sisu, built by OY Suomen Autoteollisuus AB, is Finland's leading truck make. Sisu began production in 1931 with a bonneted 3-tonner, the SH, powered by a 6-cylinder side-valve gasoline engine. In 1943, under a Finnish government nationalization plan, Sisu was merged with the newly formed Vanaja company, Vanajan Autotehdas OY, and production was concentrated on military vehicles that went under the Yhteissisu name. In 1948 Yhteissisu was de-merged, and Sisu and Vanaja became independent companies. Most Sisus built in the late 1940s ran on wood gas, wood being a plentiful commodity in Finland. Sisu's first diesel engines were available by the mid '50s. The 8.7 litre/531cu in 140bhp engines powered new bonneted trucks up to 13 tonnes gvw. By the late '50s Sisu had standardized on Leyland diesel engines, but continued to build its own axles. Its range now included 6×2s up to 20 tonnes gvw, with electro-hydraulic lifting devices on the trailing axle to transfer weight on to the drive axle. This system also became a universal feature of Scandinavian six-wheelers and was widely adopted in many other countries. In the mid 1960s, tilt-cab forward-control trucks appeared and in 1966 normal-control models were restyled using fibreglass bonnets (hoods). The K normal-control models covered 16-tonne 4×2 and 4×4 up to 24-tonne 6×2 and 6×4, while there were two KB cabover models – a 4×2 tractor and a 6×2, both for gcws of 38 to 45 tonnes. A lighter-bonneted range, the U models, covered the 15 to 22 tonnes gross bracket.

In 1967 Sisu took over Vanaja, reuniting the two manufacturers that had split up 20 years earlier. By the early '70s a complete range of 14 heavy trucks, in normal and forward control, was available, plus "half-cab" terminal tractors for yard shunting. The largest truck built by Sisu was a 180-tonne gcw bonneted 6×6. During the 1970s Leyland and Rolls Royce engines were the main fitment. The M-series of 1971 had a new design of forward-control tilt cab. At that time Leyland and Saab-Scania both had a 10 per cent stake in Sisu, but by 1974 it had returned to Finnish state ownership. Leyland and Rolls Royce engines were phased out in favour of Cummins. The SR bonneted and SM forward control models were restyled in the mid-1980s, and by then Sisu offered a wide range, including 8×4s and 10×4s up to 60 tonnes.

In 1997 Sisu signed a co-operative agreement with Renault Vehicules Industriels to market Renaults in Finland and some Sisus were built with Mack engines and Renault cabs. In 2010 the company launched its current Polar range based on the Mercedes Benz Actros with power outputs up to 600bhp.

■ TOP *Hauling a 125-tonne trailer in the early 1970s is this Sisu K42 bonneted 6×6 tractor.*

■ ABOVE *The M series of the 1970s had a new design of tilt cab that Sisu also supplied to Dennison.*

■ LEFT *Sisu trucks like this 'Polar' 4-axle tridem dumper feature an adaptation of the Mercedes Actros cab.*

MNICHOVO HRADISTE, CZECH REPUBLIC

SKODA

Emil Skoda's engineering business originated in 1859 and grew to be one of the largest engineering companies in Europe. During World War I it was the largest arms manufacturer in the Austro-Hungarian Empire but, after the war when military production ended, new products had to be introduced. Skoda built locomotives, ships, aircraft, power stations and many other projects. In the mid 1920s it entered truck production, first building Sentinel DG steam wagons under licence from 1924 and, the following year, absorbing the old established truck builder Laurin & Clement AS of Mlada Boleslav to the north-east of Prague. Laurin & Clement had built trucks since 1907, a range from 2 to 6-tonne payload capacity being produced around the World War I period. Skoda-Sentinel steam wagons were phased out around 1932. Meanwhile, existing Laurin & Clement trucks were built under the Skoda name. New and improved trucks appeared in the late 1920s and early '30s. Skoda's first diesel truck appeared in 1932 as the 605D model for 5 tonnes. An 8-tonne payload six-wheeler, the 706N was introduced in the same year. By the mid '30s Skoda's largest trucks were bonneted 6×4s for up to 10-tonne payloads.

During World War II, while under German occupation, most Skoda companies were incorporated into the German war-related industries. The works was nationalized in 1945 and truck production was centred at Liberecké Automobilové Závody (LiAZ) in Jablonec nad Nisou. This was officially established as a Czechoslovakian state enterprise in 1951. One of Skoda-LiAZ's best-known trucks, the forward-control 706RT was launched in 1956 and carried the Skoda badge. The Mlada Boleslav plant concentrated on cars. Although the trucks were sold as LiAZ, they also carried the "winged arrow" trademark of Skoda. In 1974, when the 706RT was phased out, the modernized 100 series made its debut. Production of the 706RT continued in Bulgaria under the Madara name badge.

From 1999 LiAZ truck production came under the Truck International AS division of Skoda. In 1992 LiAZ AS had become a privatized stock company and in 1995 a majority share was acquired by Skoda Plzen. It then traded as Skoda Mnichovo Hradiste or Skoda-LiAZ AS, the Skoda name being reinstated on a new long-haul tractor called the "Xena". This 42-tonne gcw tractor featured a stylish tilt cab, Detroit Diesel 60 series engine and Eaton RTSO 16-speed gearbox. The Skoda-LiAZ operations ran into financial difficulties in the new millennium and truck production was phased out in 2001.

■ ABOVE *The **706RT** was one of Skoda's most memorable trucks.*

■ BELOW *Skoda's last range of the late 1990s included this Xena with Detroit Diesel power.*

ST OUEN, FRANCE

SOMUA

LEFT ***Mid 1950s Somua four-wheelers grossed up to 19 tons. This stylish example is Dutch-registered.***

The Société d'Outillege Mécanique et d'Usinage Artillerie was formed in 1914, combining three existing engineering companies, including the vehicle-building activities of Societé Schnieder of Le Havre. Somua chassis were built mainly for municipal use until the early 1930s, when a range of heavy-duty semi-forward-control diesel trucks for payloads of 10 to 13 tonnes, including six-wheelers, was introduced. A lighter range for 5 to 8 tonnes payload had gasoline engines. In the late '30s full forward-control trucks of two and three-axle type became available with a choice of gasoline or diesel. During World War II a large proportion of Somuas were converted to run on producer gas and production was suspended altogether between 1943 and 1946. Production of diesel-engined trucks resumed in 1946 with a new model, the JL15 11-tonner, being added. In 1955 Somua introduced the JL19 four and six-wheelers powered by a 9.3 litre/567cu in diesel of 150bhp output. A tractor-unit version was also available. In 1956 Saviem (Société Anonyme de Véhicules Industriels et Équipements Mécaniques) was formed, encompassing Latil, Renault, Somua and Floirat.

HAMBURG, PENNSYLVANIA, USA

SPANGLER

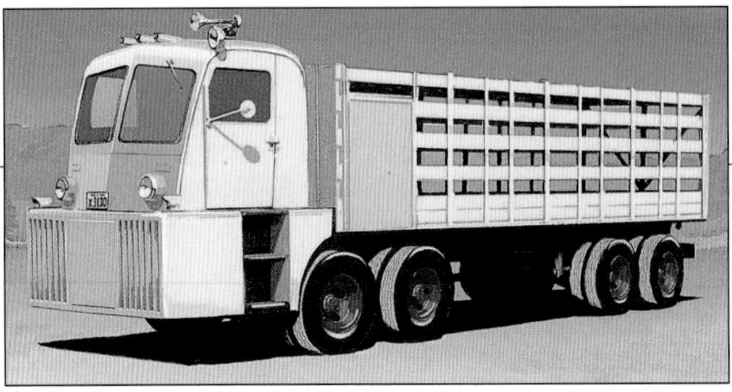

LEFT ***The unique Spangler Dual had twin Ford V8 engines and dual wheels on all four axles.***

The Spangler dual-engined 8×4 truck announced in 1947 was unusual in having front and rear bogies of equal capacity. They featured a walking-beam arrangement suspended on coil springs, and the front axles had dual-ratio steering, 25:1 for on-road use and 50:1 for low-speed manoeuvring, selected by a lever on the steering column. Running units were of Ford manufacture and servicing was through Ford agents. Power came from two 100bhp Ford V8 gasoline engines mounted side by side under the cab. Each drove one rear axle independently. Vacuum hydraulic braking operated on all wheels and each driveline had an emergency transmission brake. Three wheelbases were offered for bodywork of 4.9 to 8.2m/16 to 27ft.

Only a small number of the trucks were built up to 1949. They were built by Hahn Motors at Hamburg, Pennsylvania, and took their name from D. H. Spangler, Hahn's president. After 1949 Spangler carried out twin-steer conversions on various makes.

WOLVERHAMPTON, ENGLAND

STAR

The Star Engineering Co. built light vans from 1904 until 1907 when a heavier chain-drive truck for 4 tons was announced. By 1909 the range had been extended, and the heaviest 4-tonner had a 6.2 litre/378cu in 4-cylinder gasoline engine. After World War I a 2½-tonner and a 1½-tonner featured worm-drive rear axles, and pneumatic tyres became standard on the lighter model. Star had a reputation for quality engineering. From the mid 1920s front-wheel braking became standard. A new bus chassis that appeared in 1920 evolved into the 1927 Star Flyer, the company's best-remembered model. The VB-4 Flyer for truck or bus use was introduced in 1928. As a truck it was one of the fastest available, being capable of well over 80kph/50mph. After the Star Flyer there were no further truck models introduced, and the business was sold to Guy Motors in 1928 who kept production going on a small scale until 1931.

STARACHOWICE, POLAND

STAR

■ RIGHT *The 1980 Star TRL38 5-tonne truck featured a forward-control cab by Chausson.*

Just after World War II Poland established its own truck industry. Fabryka Samochodów Ciezarowych began with the Star Model 20 3½-tonner powered by an 85bhp gasoline engine. Articulated and dump-truck versions followed. A 6×6 was introduced in 1958 and in 1961 diesel engines became available. The Series 28/29 launched in the late 1960s had a modern steel cab from the French company, Chausson. In the 1970s and '80s Star's principal models were the TRL38 5-tonne forward-control, the 200 series 6-tonner and the 266 6×6 powered by the 359-62 6.8 litre/415cu in 6-cylinder diesel of 150bhp. Current Star models are the 3-tonne payload 742 with Andoria power unit, the 12-155 7 to 8-tonner with MAN diesel and the 1142 available as a 12-tonne gross four-wheeler or lightweight 12-tonne gcw artic, both powered by Star's own 150bhp diesel engine. Since 1998 the Star plant has been owned by the MAN Group.

MILWAUKEE, WISCONSIN, USA

STERLING

■ LEFT *The Sterling chain-drive with end-dump bodywork dates from 1928.*

The Sterling Motor Truck Co. was formerly known as the Sternberg Motor Truck Co. The latter produced early designs of cabover trucks from 1 to 5 tons capacity between 1907 and 1915. In 1914 it had introduced a normal-control truck for up to 7 tons using chain drive. Concerned about anti-German feeling aroused by World War I, founder William Sternberg chose to rename the company Sterling in 1916. Wartime production included Class B Liberty trucks. In the 1920s chain-driven 5 and 7-tonners powered by Sterling's own 4-cylinder gasoline engines continued to be built, a distinctive feature being wooden inserts in the chassis frame. The mid '20s saw a 6-cylinder engine added to the range and heavier models appeared, including tractors for up to 12 and even 20 tons. The classic bonneted F series was launched in 1931 and, to expand production, the LaFrance Republic Corporation was taken over in 1932. Another development of the early 1930s was the introduction of Cummins diesels, Sterling being one of the first manufacturers to offer them as an alternative to their gasoline engines.

In the mid 1930s demand for cabover trucks was on the increase and Sterling designed an unusual tilt cab, part of which tilted backwards, leaving the front section, windscreen and wings undisturbed. By 1937 this had been abandoned and an orthodox forward-tilt cab had appeared as the G series, setting a trend that was eventually adopted throughout the industry. The Oakland-based Fageol Truck Co., established in 1916, ceased trading at the end of 1938 and Sterling stepped in and purchased its assets. Retaining ownership of the sales network, Sterling sold the manufacturing rights to T. A. Peterman, who formed Peterbilt Motors at the former Fageol plant. Sterling was a significant producer of heavy-duty military trucks during World War II. After the war Sterling specialized in extra-heavy-duty trucks but a downturn in the market led to the company being taken over by White Motor Co. of Cleveland, Ohio, in 1951. For a couple of years production continued as Sterling-White.

WILLOUGHBY, OHIO, USA

STERLING

■ RIGHT *The 1999 Sterling 7500 L-Line 6×4 had a choice of Cummins or Caterpillar diesels.*

In 1997 the Ford heavy truck operations in the United States were absorbed into the Freightliner Corporation, which is owned by DaimlerChrysler, and the products have since been marketed as Sterling. The model line-up can be divided into five basic groups. The Cargo series consists of medium-duty cabovers for city deliveries and features the former UK Ford Cargo tilt cab first introduced on the European market in 1981. The 7500 series is a conventional range for short-haul and urban duties. Then comes the heavy-duty conventional 8500, available with a choice of mid-range diesels as an all-round general-purpose range. The 9500 series is the long-haul range of conventionals, with performance and driver comfort for heavy-duty operation combined with powerful on/off-road models for construction work. The top-of-the-range tractor, for line-haul work, was the Sterling Silver Star, offering a combination of luxury, durability and performance.

BUFFALO, NEW YORK, USA

STEWART

The founders of the Lippard-Stewart Motor Co. of Buffalo, Thomas R. Lippard and R. G. Stewart, parted with the company in 1912, within one year of its formation, and set up the Stewart Motor Corporation also at Buffalo. Lippard-Stewarts were lightweights up to 2 tons and featured a "coal scuttle" bonnet (hood). They ceased production in 1919. Early Stewarts resembled their Lippard-Stewart counterparts, but in 1916 they launched the K model 1-tonner with a driver-over-engine layout. Heavier models, up to 3½ tons, appeared powered by engines from Buda, Continental and Milwaukee. By the early 1930s there was a range of six models up to 7 tons payload, Waukesha gasoline engines being the most common fitment. In 1938 Stewart offered their first cabover for payloads of 1½ to 3 tons. Stewart's president, Thomas R. Lippard, left to join Federal in 1939. Three years later Stewart ceased production.

VIENNA, AUSTRIA

STEYR

■ LEFT *This early 1990s 19S31 drawbar outfit was available with Steyr WD815 V8 turbo intercooled diesel of 355bhp.*

Steyr trucks began production in 1922 at the former weapons factory of Osterreichische Waffenfabriks-Gesselschaft AG situated at Steyr near Vienna. The company had been in arms production since 1864 and, following World War I, it turned to vehicle building to supplement its dwindling weapons activities. The first Typ III 2½-tonne truck was a shaft-drive machine on solid tyres, powered by a 34hp 6-cylinder gasoline engine. In 1926 the company was officially renamed Steyr-Werke AG and continued to offer a range of trucks, mainly in the light to medium-weight bracket.

■ RIGHT *This Steyr Typ III features street-sprinkling equipment.*

■ RIGHT *The 1965 Type S862 bonneted tanker had a Steyr 6-cylinder diesel.*

■ BELOW RIGHT *The Steyr Plus 1291 38-tonne artic had a choice of in-line-six or V8 diesel engine.*

In 1935 it joined forces with two other Austrian vehicle builders, Austro-Daimler of Vienna and bicycle manufacturer Puch Werke. Austro-Daimler was formed in 1900 as a subsidiary of the German Daimler company and had built trucks from 1900 through to 1920. The merged businesses became known as Steyr-Daimler-Puch AG. Until the post-World War II period Steyr-Daimler-Puch produced light and medium trucks, including military vehicles, but a new range of trucks, mainly of normal-control layout, appeared for payloads of 4 to 8 tonnes. These were designated the 380 (4-tonner), 480 (5-tonner), 480z (6-tonner), 586z (7-tonner) and the 780 (8-tonner).

From 1968 a new truck range, the forward-control Plus models, entered production. These featured a modernized cab design and spanned a wider payload range from 5 up to 16 tonnes. The heaviest were powered by Steyr's own 320bhp 6-cylinder diesel engine. A wide choice of drive configurations was offered, including 4×4 and 6×6 models. From 1975 the already comprehensive range was joined by rigid eight-wheel models that were becoming popular in Switzerland, following a change in weight legislation. An assembly plant for Steyr trucks was set up at Thessaloniki in Greece in 1974 and later another in Bauchi, Nigeria. During the 1980s Steyr-Daimler-Puch's truck divisions were in a loss-making situation despite bold export-marketing plans.

In 1990 the truck building activities were taken over by MAN of Germany. Steyr's last range before the takeover included the 17S18 and 17S21 4×2 17-tonne gvw models featuring a modern steel tilt cab (which Steyr also supplied to ERF in the UK for their ES models), and their 195 4×2 tractor powered by a choice of Steyr's WD615.63 6-cylinder 9.7 litre/592cu in diesel engine or their 12 litre/732cu in V8 providing up to 386bhp. Both were turbocharged and intercooled. The high-powered tractors were marketed as the Gottardo, named after the famous mountain pass. Similarly, their heavy V8-powered 8×4, aimed mainly at the Swiss market, was called the Simplon. The Steyr plant was eventually turned over to MAN production and some MAN models were marketed as Steyrs in certain territories.

BRISTOL & TWICKENHAM, ENGLAND

STRAKER-SQUIRE

■ BELOW *A Straker-Squire 5-ton chain-drive brewer's dray powered by a 4-cylinder gasoline engine.*

A steam-wagon builder from 1906, Sidney Straker & Squire Ltd of Bristol had a manufacturing agreement with Büssing of Germany to sell Büssing vehicles as Straker-Squire in the UK. The earliest models were 3-tonners with 4-cylinder gasoline engines. The arrangement with Büssing lasted until 1909, from which point Straker-Squire began building its own designs. A heavy 5-ton Colonial truck was produced in 1910 and a 3 to 4-ton truck was introduced in 1913 and was built in large numbers for military use during World War I. After the war the company suffered along with others from a slump in the market. A semi-forward-control 5-ton truck with 4-cylinder engine and worm-drive axle, the A type, was introduced in 1919. The Bristol factory closed in 1918, production moving to Twickenham and, later, Edmonton. Production ceased in 1926.

BRENTFORD, ENGLAND

STRAUSSLER

Hungarian-born Nikolas Straussler was a consulting engineer who specialized in designing military trucks during the 1930s. He set up Straussler Mechanization Ltd at Brentford, Middlesex, in 1935 to build specialist civilian trucks, the first of which was a highly unconventional one-off 8×4 chassis for the Anglo Iranian Oil Company. The short-wheelbase chassis marked a completely new approach to truck design, the drive going to the front two axles. A Straussler 7.2 litre/439cu in twin overhead camshaft V8 gasoline engine provided 150bhp and had two separate radiators side by side cooled by a fan on each bank. All eight wheels were independently sprung. The truck was built in Hungary by Nikolas Straussler's former employer, Manfred Weiss of Csepel, and originally carried the MW badge. It was shipped to England where it was fitted with a 16,820 litre/3700 gallon spirit tank body by Thompson Bros. of Bilston. Other Straussler products included a 7-ton payload 4×4 with a rear-mounted Ford V8 engine. Smaller military vehicles were also built, but the company ceased production in 1940.

■ ABOVE *The unusual Straussler front-wheel drive 8×4 with V8 gasoline engine developing 150bhp.*

SOUTH BEND, INDIANA, USA

STUDEBAKER

■ LEFT *The 1962 Transtar had a 170bhp V8 gasoline engine.*

■ BELOW *The Studebaker 2R16A of 1950 with 3.7m/12ft stake-side body had a 102bhp L-head 6-cylinder Power Plus gasoline engine.*

The history of one of America's oldest truck manufacturers, Studebaker, dates from 1852 when the Studebaker family built horse-drawn wagons. In 1902 they began building electric vehicles. Their first gasoline-engined truck appeared in 1913. Heavier trucks did not enter the scene until 1927, with 3-tonners powered by a 5.9 litre/360cu in 6-cylinder gasoline engine. The following year Studebaker joined forces with Pierce Arrow, leading to the trucks being called Studebaker Pierce Arrow. During 1932 there was a brief tie-up with the White Motor Co. By the mid '30s Studebaker was independent again, with normal and forward-control models being listed for 1936. The heaviest of these was for 3 tons payload. Military 6×4 and 6×6 trucks were built during World War II, powered by Hercules engines. The post-war period saw updated light trucks for 1½ to 2 tons. It wasn't until 1962 that Studebaker really ventured into the heavy-duty market when the E45 19-ton gcw tractor unit, featuring the same cab as the lightweight 2-tonners, appeared. This had a 3.5 litre/213cu in 4-53 Detroit Diesel two-stroke engine delivering 130bhp. Gasoline-engined versions of these "heavies" were marketed as Studebaker Transtar, having the Power Star 4.2 litre/256cu in V8 delivering 170bhp at 4200rpm. The heavy-duty trucks were short-lived, the company ceasing truck production in 1964.

OTHER MAKES

■ SCOT

DEBERT, CANADA

The Atlantic Truck Manufacturing Company of Debert, Nova Scotia, entered the market in 1972 with the Scot conventional 6×4 tractor unit. It had a Cummins NTC335 engine and a Ford Louisville cab. By 1977 the company had developed its own cabs, including forward-control versions. Scot went on to diversify into specialist vehicles such as logging trucks, fire engines and aircraft refuellers. Some have gross train weights up to 180 tons, and power units include Detroit Diesel, Cummins and Caterpillar up to 600bhp.

■ SR

BRASOV, ROMANIA

Autocamioane Brasov began truck production in 1954 with the SR101 ("SR" is taken from Steagul Rosu or "Red Flag" works at Brasov). Based on the Russian ZIS-150, the 101 was a ruggedly built 4-tonner powered by a 90bhp gasoline engine. The 101 was replaced by a more modern design in 1962 under the Bucegi and Carpati name. The emblem on the bonnets (hoods) of the new trucks was changed to AB (for "Autocamioane Brasov"). Since 1990 the company has been renamed Roman S.A. and currently manufactures DAC trucks. (See also "Bucegi", "DAC", and "Roman".)

■ BELOW *A 1950 SR 101 truck.*

MARIBOR, YUGOSLAVIA

TAM

■ LEFT *The Yugoslavian TAM 6½-ton dump truck is based on Magirus-Deutz technology.*

TAM (Tovarna Automobilov Maribor) trucks first appeared in 1947, being Czechoslovakian Pragas built under licence. Production of these carried on until the early 1960s but in the meantime, in 1957, an agreement was formed with Klockner Humboldt Deutz to manufacture Magirus-Deutz designs, including Deutz air-cooled diesels, under licence. Pragas were soon phased out. Models included 4×2, 4×4 and 6×6, the 4×4 and 6×6 being for both civilian and military use. In 1996 TAM became MPP Vozila d.o.o. after bankruptcy and a new group of 14 smaller companies owned by the Slovakian Government carries on the production of TAM trucks. The main selling truck is the TAM 90T-50 in both 4×2 and 4×4 form.

JAMSHEDPUR, INDIA

TATA

■ LEFT *The 1978 forward-control Tata LPT1210E grossed 12 tons and was powered by 4.8 litre/ 292cu in 6-cylinder diesel.*

■ BELOW *This hard-worked semi-forward-control 1210SK has similar mechanical specification to the LPT1210E above.*

The Tata Engineering & Locomotive Co. Ltd was established in 1945 to manufacture steam locomotives, but in 1954 the company entered into a collaborative agreement with Daimler-Benz of Germany to manufacture heavy commercial vehicles. By 1969 Telco had been fully established as a truck manufacturer in its own right, with an almost 100 per cent local content. Telco is the largest truck producer in India, building a complete range from 5 tonnes gvw up to 35 tonnes gcw. The company has plants at Pune, Lucknow and Dharwad, as well as its main plant at Jamshedpur. While Tata trucks are based largely on Mercedes designs, Telco has undertaken its own developments and also builds Cummins diesels under licence.

Tata trucks have used model designations similar to those of Mercedes-Benz. The LPS1516/32, for instance, was a forward-control tractor unit introduced in 1980. This had a tractor gvw of 15 tonnes and a 6-cylinder turbocharged diesel, designated the 697, developing 160bhp. Other popular models were the 1210SK which featured an adaptation of Mercedes-Benz's semi-forward-control cab. Some models have cabs of local design, while others have adaptations of Mercedes cabs.

The range remained broadly unchanged for some years, until the addition of the new "Novus" models based on Daewoo designs. South Korean Daewoo was absorbed into Tata in 2004 and renamed Tata Daewoo, who jointly developed the 2009 Tata World Truck range. The latest "Prima" models, with stylish new cabs, include tractor units up to 49 tonnes and a choice of rigids up to 10×4s at 37 tonnes.

KOPRIVNICE, CZECH REPUBLIC

TATRA

■ LEFT *The all-wheel drive Tatra TerrNo1 grosses 41 tonnes and has a choice of diesels up to 320bhp.*

■ BELOW *An 815 Jamal 6×6 36-tonne gvw dump truck with 360bhp V8 diesel for export to Russia.*

Tatra's origins lie in the Nesseldorfer Wagenbau-Fabriks-Gesellschaft formed in 1898 at Nesseldorf in Austria. The first Nesseldorfer or NW truck was built in 1899, a tiller-steered forward-control design with a rear-mounted Benz gasoline engine. NW's next truck, in 1915, was a 2-tonner featuring shaft drive. This was followed by a 4-tonner the following year. While both were to continue until the mid 1920s, those built after World War I were called Tatra. As a result of the war, Czechoslovakia had been formed, taking in the region of Austria where Nesseldorf stood. The town changed its name to Koprivnice.

A completely new concept in truck design came in 1925 with the introduction of Tatra's unique tubular "backbone" chassis with independently sprung, fully floating half axles. From 1935 these principles were applied to a heavy truck, the Type 24 six-wheeler for 10-tonne payloads.

In 1942 Tatra's air-cooled V4, V6, V8 and V12 diesels were developed and the legendary 'T111' 6x6 was introduced. The T111 grossed 20 tonnes and had the 14.8 litre/900 cu.in. V12 with 180bhp. It continued in production for 20 years. In 1957 came the 'T138' for 12 tonnes payload, powered by the T-928K V8 with power outputs of 180-220bhp.

The new '813' 8x8 Kolos appeared in 1961, later developing into the T815 in 1983. Tatra celebrated its centenary in 1999 and, in that year, launched the new T815-2 'TerrNo1' range of 4x4, 6x6 and 8x8 models plus the T163 'Jamal' 6x6 dump truck. As well as civilian trucks Tatra produce their 'Armax' and 'Forte' military trucks up to 12x12 models.

In 2001 Tatra became part of SDC International of America and the following year Terex Corporation bought into the company, following which some models began to be marketed as ATC (American Truck Corporation) and built at Fort Wayne, Indiana.

In 2006 Terex sold their share in Tatra which returned to Czech ownership. Their current 'Phoenix' range features a DAF cab and engine since DAF took a 19 per cent share in Tatra in 2011.

BENSCHOP, THE NETHERLANDS

TERBERG

■ LEFT *The Terberg FM2000 8x8 has a design gvw of 55 tonnes but is limited to 46 tonnes for road use in its native Netherlands.*

Automobielbedrijf en Machinenfabriek W.G. Terberg & Zn began by rebuilding ex-United States Army trucks, and from 1965 turned to building its own designs. As war-surplus parts diminished, Terberg began manufacturing some of its own units, such as axles, and then complete trucks. The first was a 6×6 dubbed the N800, and used a DAF diesel engine. This was followed by the 6×4 semi-forward-control SF1200 model featuring a Mercedes-Benz cab and diesel engine. The heavier SF1400 6×4 for 14-tonne payloads had a cab to Terberg's own design, but later models began to feature the Volvo N series cab. Since the 1980s Terberg has continued to market a wide range of specialized heavy trucks including 6x4, 8x4, 8x8, 10x4 and 10x8 with Volvo cabs. It trades as Terberg Benschop BV.

BASINGSTOKE, ENGLAND

THORNYCROFT

■ RIGHT *An 1899 Thornycroft 3-ton undertype steam wagon with vertical water tube boiler and a horizontal compound engine beneath the driver.*

■ RIGHT *A 1935 Bulldog CE/GD4 4-ton truck powered by a 3.6 litre/219cu in 4-cylinder gasoline engine.*

One of the pioneers of the motor industry, John Isaac Thornycroft built his first steam van in 1896 at his Chiswick boatyard on the banks of the River Thames. It was powered by a lightweight marine engine with chain drive to the front wheels. Tiller-operated steering acted on the rear wheels. A new works was set up nearby to build road vehicles while Thornycroft's main business of boat-building continued. The Thornycroft Steam Wagon Co. of Chiswick soon outgrew itself, and a new factory was built at Basingstoke in 1898. In the meantime, improved designs of wagons for 3 and 4 tons had been developed and in 1898 Thornycroft built one of the world's first articulated goods vehicles.

Their first gasoline-engined truck, a 4-tonner, appeared in 1902. By 1907 the company was pulling out of steam but a subsidiary, Stewart & Co. of Glasgow, continued to build some steamers up to 1910. World War I saw a significant increase in truck production when the firm's J type 3-ton War Office Subsidy models appeared. Some 5000 were built, powered by 40hp 4-cylinder gasoline engines. The X type 3-tonner of the 1920s was a derivative of the J type. A lighter model, the A type for 1½ to 2 tons, was introduced in 1923. This had pneumatic tyres and electric lighting.

From 1931 model identification was simplified by the use of names rather than letters. Among the truck models were the 2-ton Bulldog, the 2½-ton Speedy and the impressive 6½-ton Jupiter and Taurus with their long "snouted" bonnets (hoods) and set-back front axles. By 1933 diesel engines were becoming available on the heavier models.

One of Thornycroft's largest trucks of the mid 1930s was the 12-ton Stag six-wheeler. Officially designated the XE type, the Stag was a high-speed, long-distance 6×2 machine powered by a 100bhp 6-cylinder gasoline engine with 8-speed gearbox.

In 1934 the Trusty 7½ to 8-ton full forward-control four-wheeler was introduced, with a choice of a 4 or 6-cylinder Thornycroft diesel. Another significant model of the 1930s was the long-bonneted 6×4 Amazon used mainly as the basis for mobile cranes.

During World War II some 13,000 trucks were built for military service, as

■ BELOW *This Trusty PF/NR6 eight-wheeler dates from 1953 and is powered by a 6-cylinder diesel engine.*

■ LEFT *A 1960 Trident RG/CR6/1 for 12 tons gvw, powered by a 90bhp 6-cylinder diesel engine.*

■ BELOW *Dating from 1949, this Sturdy ZE/TR6 4-tonner has a 6-cylinder diesel engine.*

well as 2000 civilian models for essential users. Civilian production got going again from 1945, the main models being the Nippy 3-tonner, Sturdy 5/6-tonner and Trusty VF four, RF six and PF eight-wheelers for payloads of 8, 12 and 14 tons. The Sturdy, which had taken on a new look in the late 1930s, became available with a new indirect-injection 6-cylinder diesel. The Trusty also appeared in a new guise including an eight-wheeled version originally planned just before the war. This was powered by the NR6MV 7.88 litre/481cu in diesel engine developing 100bhp, but an alternative gasoline-injection power unit was also tried. This did not enter full production.

In 1948 the automotive side of John I. Thornycroft was renamed Transport Equipment (Thornycroft) Ltd to distinguish it from the boat-building division. An uprated Sturdy, the Sturdy Star, was announced in 1948, and over the next couple of years important new models included the Mighty Antar heavy tractor for up to 100 tons gtw. This was originally powered by an 18 litre/1098cu in Rover Meteorite Mk.101 V8 diesel developing 250bhp. It was fitted with twin radiators. Other models aimed at the export market were the bonneted Trident and Trusty.

Medium-weight vehicles like the Sturdy and Sturdy Star received a new-style Motor Panels Mk.1 cab in 1952. Along with their road-going trucks, Thornycroft offered a variety of heavy-duty specialized trucks mainly for the overseas market, such as the Nubian and Big Ben. The lightweight 4-ton Nippy Star of 1952 and the slightly heavier Sturdy Star were phased out in 1957 when the new Swift and Swiftsure were introduced.

Thornycroft vehicles were built almost entirely from in-house components, which meant that developing new models was costly. However, a new version of the Trusty eight-wheeler, the PK model with the higher powered 130bhp 9.8 litre/598cu in QR6MV diesel, was announced in 1956, entering production in 1957. Its cab resembled that of another new model, the Mastiff, which appeared shortly after in four and six-wheel form, plus a tractor unit. By 1960 Thornycroft were beginning to concentrate more on heavy-duty specialized trucks for military and export use, the main sellers in the UK being the Trusty eight-wheeler and Mastiff range.

In a declining market, Thornycroft were struggling to keep their large works productive, and in 1961 the company was taken over by the ACV Group which was the parent company of AEC. Very soon those models that competed with AECs were phased out and production turned to specialized trucks like the Nubian, Big Ben and Antar. ACV itself was taken over by Leyland. Leyland already owned Scammell, which they regarded as their special vehicles division, so it was almost inevitable that the Thornycroft and Scammell ranges would be rationalized. The last Thornycrofts were built not at the Basingstoke factory but at the Watford plant of Scammell, the Basingstoke plant having been sold off in 1969.

MAIDSTONE, ENGLAND

TILLING STEVENS

The old established Tilling Stevens company is probably remembered more for its buses than for its trucks. Beginning in 1897 as W. A. Stevens Electrical Engineers, they developed a gasoline-electric vehicle in 1906. In 1907 Stevens began an agreement with Hallford (J. & E. Hall of Dartford) to convert their gasoline trucks to gasoline electric. An important customer, Thomas Tilling, took over the Stevens company, ended the agreement with Hallford and renamed Stevens "Tilling Stevens Ltd". As well as buses, Tilling Stevens produced trucks for 2 and 4-ton payloads in both gasoline electric and conventional gasoline-engine form. These were based on the TS3 and TS4 chassis. Many TS3 models entered war service during World War I. Truck and bus production resumed after 1918, and during the 1920s a full range was on offer, payloads going up to 4 tons. The company sought new investment in 1930 and was refloated as T. S. Motors Ltd. In 1933 TSM acquired the Vulcan Motor & Engineering Co. of Southport, Lancashire, which was in receivership. This led to the production of Vulcan trucks at Maidstone from the late 1930s, using Vulcan's own gasoline engines or Perkins diesels. Although some Tilling Stevens trucks were built during World War II, the bulk of the company's production was concentrated on buses through to its takeover by the Rootes Group in 1949. Production of all models, including Vulcan, ceased in 1952.

■ LEFT *A Tilling Stevens equipped with hand-operated tower wagon for overhead servicing.*

MILWAUKEE, WISCONSIN, USA

TITAN

Between 1917 and about 1931 the Titan Truck & Trailer Co. built a variety of heavy trucks, the first being a 5-ton payload, solid-tyred model with a 4-cylinder gasoline engine. Lighter models appeared later for payloads of 1, 2 and 3 tons, powered by Buda engines. Production continued until the early 1930s.

BACKNANG, GERMANY

TITAN

Beginning in 1970 at Appenweier, Titan Spezialfahrzeug GmbH built heavy multi-axle crane chassis and special vehicles for logging, earthmoving and oilfield duties. In 1977 a range of 6x6 and 8x8 heavy tractors was launched at the instigation of German heavy haulage concern, Schutz. The tractors, with train weights up to 200 tons, were Mercedes-based. The company relocated to Backnang in 2011 and continues to build Mercedes-based heavy haulage tractors like the Z64-600F 8x8 shown with a pull capability of up to 1000 tonnes. Such models have the Mercedes OM 502 LA in-line-six diesel with 609bhp and reinforced chassis with Kessler axles. The range includes 6x6, 8x6 and 8x8 models featuring Mercedes cabs.

■ LEFT *Titan heavy-haulage tractors like this Z64-600F 8x8 are based on Mercedes-Benz engineering.*

■ BELOW *The 1964 DA90 with gvw of 10.5 tonnes had a Toyota 2D 6-cylinder diesel developing 130bhp.*

■ BOTTOM *The DA115 7-tonne truck grossed 11.5 tonnes and was powered by a 140bhp 6.5 litre/397cu in 6-cylinder diesel.*

TOKYO, JAPAN

TOYOTA

While Toyota ranks among the world's largest motor manufacturers, its commercial vehicle range has, in recent years, been limited to light trucks. Production of medium to heavy trucks is left to its associate company, Hino. What was originally the Toyota Automatic Loom Works Ltd, based at Kariya City, began building light trucks in 1935. The first vehicle was a bonneted 1½-tonner. The company was re-formed into the Toyota Motor Co. Ltd in 1937, and production of lightweight trucks continued through to 1951 when their first medium-duty truck, the BX 4-tonner, appeared.

By the early 1960s larger normal and forward-control trucks for 5 to 6-tonne payloads were in production. These were available with a choice of gasoline or diesel power. The DA80 ("D" indicated "diesel") had a gvw of 9.5 tonnes, while the DA90 and DA95 grossed 10.5 tonnes. The power unit was Toyota's own 6.5 litre/397cu in 6-cylinder indirect-injection diesel with an output of 130bhp. The lighter DA80 had a 5.9 litre/360cu in version producing 110bhp. A 4.23 litre/258cu in 6-cylinder gasoline engine was available as an option on all models, and gasoline variants were the FA80, FA90 and FA95. A 4-tonner, the FC80, was only available with gasoline engine. A 6×6 truck, the ZDW15L, closely resembling a World War II United States Army design, was also available for a payload of 4.5 tonnes (on-highway) or 2.3 tonnes (off-highway).

From 1965 a new range with a completely restyled cab was available as the FA100 and FA115 (gasoline) and DA110, DA115 and DA116 (diesel). The DA range of diesel trucks had an increased gvw of 11.5 tonnes and a payload rating of 6.5 tonnes. The power output of the 6.5 litre/397cu in diesel was increased to 140bhp. A 5-speed synchromesh gearbox was standard and a 2-speed rear axle was optional.

Production of the DA and FA continued into the mid-1980s but since then Toyota has concentrated on light vans and pick-ups. Heavy truck production is undertaken by Hino, which has been a subsidiary of Toyota since 2001.

ST LOUIS, MISSOURI, USA

TRAFFIC

■ LEFT *This 1918 Traffic 2-ton forward-control truck used a Continental 4-cylinder gasoline engine and 3-speed gearbox.*

Formed in 1918, the Traffic Motor Corp. built a $1\frac{3}{4}$-ton four-wheel truck with a Continental 4-cylinder gasoline engine. Up to 1925 the appearance of the Traffic was quite distinctive, thanks to its rounded front and rear chassis crossmembers that served as bumpers. Solid tyres were standard, but pneumatics could be supplied to special order. In 1927 Traffic launched 2 and 3-ton models with more powerful 4.15 litre/253cu in Continental engines. By then the front and rear crossmembers were of conventional design. Production ended in 1929, and during that year a 4-tonner with 6-cylinder engine appeared briefly.

WARRINGTON, ENGLAND

TVW

■ LEFT *TVW trucks were developed from Sentinel designs.*

■ BELOW LEFT *This early TVW is a converted Sentinel fitted with a Gardner engine.*

Transport Vehicles (Warrington) Ltd was established in late 1957 to build a range of heavy-duty trucks largely based on Sentinel designs. Sentinel of Shrewsbury folded in 1957 and their main UK dealer, North Cheshire Motors Ltd, purchased the remaining vehicle and parts stocks to set up its own truck-building operation

under the TVW name. The range consisted of tractor units and six and eight-wheeled rigids in the 19 to 24 tons gvw bracket. Sentinel's practice of using horizontal diesel engines was abandoned and TVW offered a choice of Gardner, Meadows, Perkins, Leyland and Rootes diesels, the latter being the unusual 3-cylinder opposed-piston two-stroke used in Commer trucks. The trucks were fitted with proprietary cabs from Boalloy and a local coachbuilder, Williams of Grappenhall, Warrington. The best-selling TVWs were their rigid eight-wheeler and their 24-ton gcw tractor, but most sales were to associate companies that had helped raise finance for the venture. An estimated 100 trucks were built up to 1961 when the company closed.

PUTEAUX & TRAPPES, FRANCE

UNIC

The history of one of France's most famous truck manufacturers, Unic, began in 1905 when SA Etablissements Georges Richard was formed, but only light vehicles and taxi cabs were built through to the 1920s. It was then that a 3-tonne truck, the M5C, was introduced. By 1931 a range of heavier trucks for 6 to 11 tonnes payload was available. The largest model, the CD3, was a bonneted rigid six-wheeler powered by a licence-built Mercedes-Benz 6-cylinder 8.6 litre/525cu in diesel engine. "CD" stood for "Codra Diesel". CODRA was the Compagnie des Diesel Rapides, which held the licence for Mercedes diesels in France. In 1937 Unic introduced its own diesel engine – the first to be entirely designed and built in France. It was a 10.3 litre/629cu in indirect-injection 6-cylinder unit.

During World War II the company formed an association with Bernard, Delahaye, Laffly and Simca under a government-led plan called Groupement Français de l'Automobile (GFA). It was disbanded in 1951. From 1945 Unic offered their ZU range, which featured a stylish new semi-forward-control cab.

From 1952, faced with the need for new investment for modernization, Unic joined forces with Simca, which was formed in 1934. By 1958 Unic had become the Industrial Vehicle Division of Simca. Simca had also purchased the Ford France truck business. The Ford Cargo medium trucks were built alongside Unic heavy-duty trucks. In 1956 Unic, still under Simca ownership, was merged with Saurer France.

Four years later another administrative change took place when Simca de-merged their Automobile Division (which was assigned to Chrysler) and their Industrial Vehicle Division. From that point Unic only had their heavy-duty range as Cargo production ceased. To fill the light to medium gap they marketed imported OM models from 4 to 7 tonnes gvw. The mid 1950s Unic range of heavies included their superbly designed "long-nosed" ZU94 Verdon and ZU122 Izoard of which there were many almost identical variants under other names like Auvergne and Tournalet. The long-nosed cab was called the Longchamp while a new forward-control cab, introduced in 1960, was the Vincennes.

In 1966 Simca Industries was absorbed by Fiat France and there was increasing product exchange with the Italian parent. It was in 1960 that Unic introduced their M625 V8 diesel using Saurer fuel injection. In 1969 a higher-rated version, the 14.9 litre/909cu in V855 developing 340bhp, was announced. Between 1971 and 1973 production of Unic trucks was transferred from Puteaux to Trappes, and in 1975 it became part of the newly formed Iveco Group. The Unic name was phased out in the early 1980s.

■ **TOP** ***An Izoard T270 38-tonne artic with 270bhp V8 diesel engine.***

■ **ABOVE LEFT** ***The Unic Vercors dump truck grossed 17.8 to 18.2 tonnes with 5-cylinder or 6-cylinder diesel engine.***

■ **LEFT** ***Latter-day Unics had the Iveco Group cab. This refrigerated van is virtually identical to a Fiat 110C.***

GAGGENAU, GERMANY

UNIMOG

■ LEFT *The 1998 Unimog 2540 artic is powered by a 240bhp Mercedes OM366-LA turbo diesel.*

Unimog's light 4×4 might be of marginal relevance in truck terms owing to its highly specialized nature, but it is worthy of mention in view of its legendary history. It has its origins in an all-terrain military design that was under development in the early part of World War II but finally emerged in 1948. In its more familiar guise it was developed by Gebr. Bohringer GmbH of Goppingen and was aimed at the agricultural industry. Unimog stands for Universal Motor Unit or UNIversat MOtor Gerat. It was powered by a Mercedes-Benz 1.7 litre/103cu in 4-cylinder diesel. In 1951 manufacturing rights passed to Daimler-Benz.

In 1954 a new model appeared as the Unimog S powered by a Mercedes 2.2 litre/134cu in 6-cylinder gasoline engine. The versatility of the Unimog was explored to the full during the 1970s and '80s with heavier models up to 9 tonnes gvw, powered by diesels up to 200bhp, capable of gross train weights of 50 tonnes plus. There were countless variants, such as road/rail shunters, long-wheelbase self-loaders and 6×6 fire appliances. Currently there is a heavy-duty Unimog 2540 articulated version for a gcw of 31 tonnes. This is powered by a 5.9 litre/360cu in OM366-LA turbocharged diesel developing 240bhp.

LONDON, ENGLAND

UNION

■ LEFT *Union ballast tractors were built and operated exclusively by the Union Cartage Company.*

In the late 1930s the Union Cartage Company of London required a rugged ballast tractor to haul meat-container trailers and, unable to find an off-the-shelf model, it decided to build its own. Some 42 tractors were built in total, all powered by Gardner 5LW diesel engines. Many Union tractors survived in operation well into the 1960s.

PERIVALE & WATFORD, ENGLAND

UNIPOWER

■ RIGHT *A 1972 Unipower 4×4 tractor unit with Motor Panels cab and Perkins V8 diesel engine.*

Universal Power Drives was formed in 1934 with its head office at Aldwych, London, and a factory in Perivale, Middlesex. It specialized in Unipower third-axle conversions. In 1937 Unipower introduced a 4×4 timber tractor which was produced in large numbers during World War II when the UK government stepped up timber production. The Forester tractor was built along similar lines to the French Latil. It had a 4-cylinder Gardner 4LW oil engine. In the late 1940s a 5LW-powered Hannibal was introduced. Production continued until 1968 and, in the meantime, a short-lived Centipede four-wheel steer version was introduced in 1956.

In 1972 Unipower switched to building a forward-control 4×4 called the Invader, powered by a choice of

■ LEFT *An Alvis-Unipower HET 8×8 heavy tank transporter powered by a Cummins SQK 19 litre/1158cu in 750bhp diesel.*

Perkins V8 or Cummins V8 diesel. This was aimed at on/off-road, fire-fighting, municipal and construction use. A heavier model with Motor Panels cab and a choice of Rolls Royce gasoline or Cummins NTF365 diesel was also offered. The company was taken over by AC Cars in 1977, and production moved to Thames Ditton in Surrey. With the closure of Scammell Lorries in May 1988, Unipower set up a new factory at Watford to carry on production of certain Scammells. It introduced the C-series heavy tractor and a range of military trucks. In 1994 Unipower was bought by Alvis PLC but production ended when Alvis sold it off some six years later.

■ BELOW *A 1952 Unipower Hannibal 4×4 timber tractor powered by an 85bhp Gardner 5LW diesel.*

MIASS, RUSSIA

URAL

■ BELOW RIGHT *Ural 6×6 trucks can be supplied for both civilian and military duties.*

In 1942 part of the ZIS (Zavod Imieni Stalina) operations was relocated to a shadow factory at Miass in the Chelyabinsk Region of the Ural mountains to ensure continuity of production if the Moscow plant suffered war damage. The trucks were called Ural-ZIS, the Ural-ZIS 5 being a 3-tonner. Production carried on after the war. The trucks were now simply called Ural.

In 1961 the first of Ural's own designs appeared as the 375D 5-tonne 6×6. A ZIL 7 litre/427cu in V8 gasoline engine was fitted. In 1964 a heavier-duty 6×4 7-tonne 377 appeared with a V8 diesel. These trucks continued in production with little change, but recently Ural developed its own air-cooled diesels as well as using Kamaz engines. In recent years the truck range has expanded to include heavy duty 8x8s in both civilian and military specifications, using an adaptation of a Fiat cab from the 1970s.

PORTSMOUTH, ENGLAND

USG-PITT

■ LEFT *The rear end of the USG-Pitt front-wheel drive truck could be lowered to facilitate loading.*

The USG-Pitt R35 front-wheel drive low-loading truck was designed and built between 1964 and 1967. It was based on the Bedford RLC1 and had a gvw of 9.5 tons and a wheelbase of 5m/16.5ft. It had a 5.4 litre/330cu in, 107bhp 6-cylinder Bedford diesel and a 4-speed gearbox coupled to a transfer box that took the drive forward to a Bedford steer-drive axle. Only a small number were built, and the truck was aimed at operators such as electricity-generating companies. The rear end of the load platform could be lowered to form a ramp on to which cable drums or similar loads could easily be winched. It was a joint development of United Services Garages, a Bedford truck main dealer, and Pitt Trailers Ltd.

GOTHENBURG, SWEDEN

VOLVO

The two men behind the formation of Volvo, economist Assar Gabrielsson and engineer Gustaf Larsen, both spent part of their careers at Svenska Kulgerfabriken, better known as SKF, the famous Swedish ball-bearing manufacturer. "Volvo" is Latin for "I roll", and a company of that name had been formed as a subsidiary of SKF in 1915. Assar Gabrielsson secured the rights to the dormant company in 1926.

Volvo avoided the high overheads of in-house component manufacture by sub-contracting their work to established firms like Pentaverken (the Penta Engineering Works) of Skövde. Penta produced Volvo's car and truck engines from the outset, and in 1931 Volvo took the company over, renaming it AB Volvo-Pentaverken in 1935. Likewise, gearbox and rear-axle gearing were farmed out to Köpings Mekaniska Verkstad at Köpings. When pressed-steel cabs became standard, Volvo turned to Olofströms Stålpressings AB (the Olostrom Pressed Steel Co).

■ ABOVE *With Sweden's generous length limits, bonneted tractors like this N88 were popular in their home country.*

■ LEFT *Until the 1960s nearly all Volvos were bonneted, such as this early 1950s L220 4-tonner.*

■ BELOW *In the medium-weight class the L465 with a 4.7 litre/287cu in 6-cylinder diesel was an important seller in the 1960s.*

In the late '20s Volvo introduced a 1.5 tonne bonneted truck, the LV40 followed in 1929 by the LV60 2-tonner with 6-cylinder 3.0 litre/183 cu.in. gasoline engine. A larger 6x2 model followed, the LV66/67, with 4.1 litre/250 cu.in. 6-cylinder engine. A short-lived forward control truck, the L75 'Bulldog' appeared in 1932 but only about 250 were built before it was with-drawn in 1935.

New models appeared in 1935, namely the LV81, 83 and 93, the heaviest being a 4-tonner. These had a more streamlined appearance and set back front axle. Around the same time Volvo offered a Hesselman 'diesel' – a gasoline engine using fuel injection and spark ignition. During WW2 Volvo developed trucks running on producer gas, some having the equipment on a trolley ahead of the front bumper to save it taking up load space behind the cab.

In the post war era Volvo stepped up their exports and by the 1950s had a presence in South America, Cuba, Middle East, Spain, Turkey and most of Europe.

Heavier trucks, still bonneted, appeared in 1951 as the L295 14-tonne gross Titan with improved styling. Power came from the D96AS 9.6 litre/588 cu.in. 6-cylinder diesel with up to 150bhp. A 6x2 version grossed 19 tonnes. A turbocharged diesel, the DT96, appeared in 1954 with 185bhp.

The L385 Viking appeared in 1953 with a gvw of 12.5 tonnes and the D67 6.7 litre/408 cu.in diesel with 115bhp. A 6x2 version grossed 16 tonnes.

Up until 1962 Volvo had concentrated on bonneted trucks but realised forward-control 'cabovers' were in demand for export. It launched its 'Tip Top' tilt cab models in 1962. These were mechanically similar to the Viking and Titan and designated L475, L485 and L495.

One year later Volvo unveiled its famous 'System 8' range. The concept was based on the eight components that underwent major renewal, namely engine, gearbox, rear axle, frame, steering, brakes, suspension and cab.

The new range put Volvo on the world map. In 1964 Volvo acquired Gosta Nystrom's Karosserifabrik at Umea which became its cab plant. In 1969 the Volvo Trucks Division was formed as an autonomous operation.

In the UK the F86 and F88 were enthusiastically received when former Scottish haulage contractor Jim McKelvie set up his Ailsa Trucks dealership. Within three years Volvo had gained a commanding position in the UK market. A Scottish assembly plant was established in 1972 and was responsible for developing the first F86 eight-wheelers although similar models appeared in Australia around the same time.

Alsemberg Plant in Belgium had been building Volvos since 1951 while Ghent had opened in 1965 followed by a Peru factory in 1966. Volvo went on to open an assembly plant in Brazil in 1980 followed later by a plant in Morocco.

The Volvo-White Truck Corporation was formed in 1981 when Volvo bought the ailing White business. In 1986 it took over GM's heavy truck division. In 1971 Volvo joined the 'Club of Four' (aka Euro Truck Development Group) to develop a new cab for the F4 and F6 models of 1975. The F7 followed in 1978, using the same cab.

In 1977 the F88 and F89 were replaced by the F10 and F12, the latter having the TD120 diesel with ratings from 330-385bhp. The low cab FL7/FL10 appeared in 1985.

Volvo continued to set the pace with the new FH of 1993 and the lower cabbed FM in 1998. A bonneted version, the NH, is built in Brazil while the VN conventional is marketed in the

■ ABOVE LEFT *Rigid eight-wheelers such as this 1978 F731 were developed and built at Irvine in Scotland.*

■ ABOVE RIGHT *Tilt-cab forward-control System 8 trucks enabled Volvo to expand its European sales.*

■ RIGHT *This 1973 F88 artic with TIR tilt trailer was used on international services from the UK.*

United States, where assembly takes place in Dublin, Virginia. VN Engine options include Volvo, Cummins, Caterpillar and Detroit Diesel.

Volvo took over Renault VI and its Mack subsidiary in 2000 to form Volvo Global Trucks. In 2006 came Volvo's most powerful truck at that time – the 660bhp FH16 with its SCR D16E engine.

Volvo have since introduced a Euro 6 750bhp, D16K powered FH16, featuring a new cab and many innovations including the availability of independent front suspension and dynamic steering on left hand drive models. Volvo also offer LNG-powered trucks with the D13X engine and is showing interest in electric power for urban distribution trucks.

RESENDE, BRAZIL

VW

VW Caminhoes e Onibus is a subsidiary of MAN SE (Societas Europaea) and part of MAN Latin America. In 1979 Volkswagenwerk AG bought a 67 per cent stake in Chrysler Motors do Brazil, taking full control the following year to form VW Caminhoes Ltda. Truck production began in March 1981, the main models being 4x2 medium trucks for gross weights of 11-13 tonnes. Power came from Chrysler-designed MWM diesel engines with outputs of 130bhp. The cab was from the LT van and light truck range.

Following a brief tie-up with Ford Motor Co as part of Autolatina between 1990 and 1995, VW became independent and was re-named VW Caminhoes e Onibus with a factory at Resende, near Rio de Janeiro.

The range expanded to cover heavy-duty trucks which took the names 'Worker' and 'Titan' and were produced in both rigid and articulated form. At that time the small LT cab was still being used on the heaviest models.

By 2001 VW had become truck market leader in Brazil. In 2005 it launched its most important range, the 'Constellation' for gross weights of 13-57 tonnes, featuring a stylish new cab befitting a heavy truck. Power units consist of a choice of Cummins or MAN diesels according to model.

An associate company named 'BMB' was established in 2006 to carry out special conversions on certain models such as converting 6x2 rigids to 8x2 and 8x4 configurations.

MAN Latin America market VW heavy trucks alongside MAN trucks, the latter focusing the heaviest weight category which, in Brazil, extends up to 74 tonnes gross. However, in 2017 a heavier VW 6x4 tractor unit, the '33.440', was introduced, raising the VW maximum from 57 to 74 tonnes, and powered by an MAN 440bhp diesel.

■ ABOVE LEFT ***In the United States Volvo's latest VNL has sleek aerodynamic styling.***

■ ABOVE RIGHT ***For decades Volvo have led in the power stakes with trucks like this 750hp FH16.***

■ ABOVE ***The Brazilian scene is dominated by locally built trucks like this VW 'Constellation' grossing 57 tonnes.***

OTHER MAKES

■ VANAJA

HELSINKI, FINLAND

Vanajan Autotehdas Oy of Helsinki was once a body-building company and began building trucks around 1943 when it was merged into Sisu (Oy Suomen Autoteollisuus) to manufacture military trucks under the Yhteissisu name. After the war the two companies were de-merged and Vanaja became a make in its own right. Initially it produced medium-weight trucks with a 6-cylinder 5.0 litre/305cu in gasoline engine. During 1954 it began offering a diesel which then became standard.

As the range expanded, Vanaja formed an agreement with the British AEC company which supplied it with engines. Trucks included 4×2, 4×4 and 6×4 tractor units that offered extra traction to cope with Finland's severe road conditions. The 6×4s were driven on the front and the first rear axle – in effect a 4×4 with a trailing third axle. After AEC was absorbed into Leyland in 1962 some forward-control Vanaja trucks were fitted with the Leyland Ergomatic cab. One such model was the TTB 8×4 crane chassis. In 1967 Vanaja was taken over by its former partner Sisu.

■ VERHEUL

WADINXVEEN, THE NETHERLANDS

Verheul was originally a coachbuilder and in 1961 it acquired Kromhout of Amsterdam who were truck manufacturers. Verheul continued production of some Kromhout models, but introduced a new range of normal and forward-control cabs. These carried a large "V" motif on the grille. Both were taken over by the British ACV Group in 1960, and greater emphasis was placed on bus models. Truck sales were limited and the range was withdrawn in 1965.

■ VOMAG

PLAUEN, GERMANY

Vogtlandische Maschinenfabrik AG once specialized in printing and textile machinery, but in 1915 it began building chain-drive 3 and 4-tonne trucks. Some were also built with shaft drive. After the war a 1.5-tonne truck was the main production model until the mid 1920s when a comprehensive truck range for payloads of 3, 4, 5, 6 and 7 tonnes was offered. Four-cylinder gasoline engines were the standard, but from 1930 Vomag built diesel engines. Some impressive bonneted trucks appeared up to the outbreak of war, including a 9-tonne six-wheeler with 140bhp diesel. Production ceased in 1939.

■ VULCAN

MAIDSTONE, ENGLAND

Vulcan's history began at Southport, Lancashire in 1907, as the Vulcan Motor & Engineering Co. Ltd. It turned to building light trucks in 1914. In the early 1920s a variety of models ranging from 1½ to 4 tons payload was available. A light-weight articulated model appeared in 1922.

Financial difficulties, resulting from a couple of unsuccessful joint ventures, contributed to the company's collapse in 1931. In receivership, it continued to offer a small range in the 1½-ton to 4-ton payload bracket, while a 5/6-ton forward-control model was added in 1934. The option of a Dorman or Gardner diesel engine was also offered. Owing to persisting financial problems, the company was taken over in 1938 by Tilling Stevens Ltd. It was relocated to Maidstone in Kent and renamed Vulcan Motors Ltd.

From then on a new forward-control range appeared, but full production was interrupted by the war. Vulcan was allowed to build limited numbers of 6-tonners for essential civilian users. After the war it resumed full production, the range including the 6VF (gasoline) and 6PF (Perkins P6 diesel) 6-tonners in short and long-wheelbase form, plus a tractor unit. Tilling Stevens was taken over by the Rootes Group in 1950. The same year a new range for 7-ton payloads was launched, the 7GF with Gardner 4LW engine. These had a new cab design. However, under Rootes' ownership Vulcan was phased out in 1952.

■ TOP ***Finnish Vanaja trucks were generally powered by AEC diesel engines.***

■ ABOVE ***1927 Vulcan VSD 2-tonner powered by Vulcan's own design of 4-cylinder gasoline engine.***

■ ABOVE ***This Perkins P6-engined Vulcan 6PF dropside truck dates from 1948.***

VOORHEESVILLE, NEW YORK, USA

WALTER

■ BELOW *Cummins-engined Walter type ACU 4×4 Snow Fighter had unique drive system with automatic differential locks.*

Walter specialized from the outset in 4×4 trucks. Its founder was William Walter, a Swiss engineer who emigrated to New York in 1883. He began by making confectionery machinery, but in 1898 turned his talents to motor cars. The first Walter truck was made in 1909, and this formed the basis for his first 4×4 of 1911. The early trucks had a dashboard radiator and "coal scuttle" bonnet (hood) reminiscent of the old Renault and Latil designs. Some conventional rear-wheel drive versions were also built. Until 1920 Walter built its own gasoline engines, but later used Waukesha units. The heaviest truck went up to 7 tons payload. By the mid 1920s the trucks began to take on their distinctive snout with the front axle set back under the cab – a Walter trademark for much of its history. In 1929 the first Snow Fighter snow-clearance truck was launched, and during the '30s the company diversified into specialized fire appliances, concrete trucks, articulated dump trucks and logging outfits. Some 4×4 medium artillery tractors were supplied to the army during World War II. Over the past five decades Walter has remained a major force in the specialized all-wheel drive market, building a wide range of snowploughs, crash tenders and similar machines, some with power ratings up to 540bhp.

ELMIRA, NEW YORK, USA

WARD LAFRANCE

Although Ward LaFrance became a prominent manufacturer of fire appliances, it has no direct business connection with American LaFrance except that it was formed by a member of the same family in Elmira, New York. Ward LaFrance was set up in 1918, some 13 years after American LaFrance, and built trucks from 2½ to 7 tons payload capacity powered by 4-cylinder Waukesha gasoline engines. A 6-cylinder model was added in 1926. During the 1930s much heavier trucks entered the scene, many being custom-built bonneted heavy tractors. Ward LaFrance was among the earliest American companies to offer diesel power using Cummins engines.

During World War II the company specialized in building 6×6 heavy wreckers, as well as 6×4 and 6×6 Cargo trucks. A new range of on-highway trucks appeared in 1945, the handsome bonneted D series for up to 30 tons gcw. By the mid 1950s more emphasis was being put on fire appliances, which had first been available in the pre-war period. Trucks were discontinued from about 1956, production being given over entirely to fire vehicles and airport crash tenders. In the late 1970s heavy-duty 8×8 trucks were supplied to the United States Army, powered by 600bhp diesels. During the '80s the company continued building fire appliances but, after financial losses, it closed in 1993.

KELOWNA, CANADA

WESTERN STAR

Since 1981 Western Star has been a make in its own right, but it began as an offshoot of White Trucks in 1968 when that company launched a new model aimed at the West Coast market. White Western Star 4900 conventionals soon earned a reputation for ruggedness and reliability in the United States and in Canada where White had set up the production plant at Kelowna, British Columbia. When White collapsed in 1980 and was taken over by Volvo Trucks in 1981, the deal did not include Western Star and the division was re-formed into Western Star Trucks Inc, owned by two Calgary-based companies. As well as the familiar conventionals, some cabover Western Stars were built featuring the White Road Commander cab.

By 1990 the company was experiencing another downturn and it was bought by Australian, Terrence Peabody. Under new ownership, sweeping improvements were introduced plus new models for on/off-highway duties. More engine options were added, including the Detroit Diesel 60 Series. Fom 1983 to 1993 Western Stars were assembled at a plant in Queensland, Australia, where new models were developed especially for the Australian and New Zealand markets. The company reached an agreement with DAF of The Netherlands to market Western Stars through DAF dealers, and some technical collaboration led to the production of a small number of Western Star 1000 Series rigid eight-wheelers with DAF 95 cabs when Western Star couldn't offer its own cabovers.

During the 1990s the company saw a remarkable turnaround, and in 1996 it acquired the British ERF concern as well as Orion Bus Industries of New York and Ontario. In the same year it launched its new Class 8 Constellation. Manufacturing was located at Kelowna except for the Commander range which was built at ERF in the United Kingdom. In March 2000 Western Star sold ERF to MAN of Germany. Four months later Western Star itself was absorbed into Freightliner, part of Daimler Trucks North America. In 2002 production was moved to Portland, Oregon in the United States.

■ ABOVE ***Constellation 4964FX B-train for bulk cement transport in Canada.***

■ LEFT ***The Commander 8×4 features an ERF EC cab.***

■ BELOW ***5964 dump truck features aerodynamic cab styling.***

CLEVELAND, OHIO, USA

WHITE

■ LEFT *This 6×4 tractor is a good example of White's stylish WA and WB conventional models of the 1940s era.*

■ BELOW *Between 1932 and 1955 Labatt's Streamliners became legendary. This one is based on a 1948 WA122 with Mustang 6-cylinder gasoline engine.*

Under the curious title of the White Sewing Machine Co., this company built its first commercial in 1901, a light car-based van nicknamed the "Pie Wagon". Prototype steam trucks for 3 and 5 tons payload were built around 1906 but went no further than White's own transport fleet where they spent some years in service. The company's origins can be traced back to 1859 when Thomas Howard White formed his sewing machine company. His son, Rollin H. White, travelled to Europe to observe the developing car industry. He was particularly impressed by Leon Serpollet's flash tube boiler, and on his return home began work on a modified version which he installed in the first White steam car of 1898.

Production got underway in 1900, and by 1906 the White Co. was formed as a separate entity to build cars and trucks. In 1910 White turned from steam to gasoline power and built its first real heavy truck, the bonneted GTA 3-tonner with 30hp engine and chain drive. Lighter models for 1½ tons also appeared. In 1912 the TC 5-tonner was introduced. Both the GTA and TC continued in production until 1918.

During World War I the United States Army ordered 18,000 military trucks for the Allied Forces in Europe. Some organizational changes took place in this period and the name was changed to the White Motor Co.

The first 6-cylinder gasoline truck appeared in 1928 as the Model 59, and was for a 3 to 4-ton payload. Three-axle variants of the heaviest model were introduced in 1930 for a payload of 10 tons. In 1932 White purchased the Indiana Truck Corp. of Marion, Indiana, from the Brockway Motor Truck Co., and production was transferred to Cleveland. The same year White became involved with Studebaker Pierce Arrow, assembling Pierce Arrows at Cleveland until 1934.

The most striking model of the period was White's first cabover, the heavy-duty 730 of 1935, which was powered by a 7.6 litre/464cu in version of an 8.3 litre/506cu in opposed-piston horizontal 12-cylinder gasoline engine first tried in buses in 1932. The fully rated 8.3 litre/506cu in was offered later. Despite its impressive specification, the 730 series did not attract many sales due to poor economy and reliability. Subsequent forward-control vehicles, like the 800 series, used in-line-six engines. The 800s appeared in 1937 and were White's first truly competitive cabovers, some of which featured tilt cabs.

During World War II much of White's production was given over to military vehicles, including 6×4 and 6×6 trucks. A replacement for the 700 and 800 series appeared in 1940 as the WA in both normal and forward control. Normal-control WA models were succeeded by the WB just after the war, although these were of very similar specification. In 1949 a further development of the WA and WB appeared as the WC, and this bonneted range was to become one of White's best-sellers during the 1950s. White's next new model was the memorable 3000 with its futuristic styling. The bulbous set-forward cab was equipped with a motorized tilting system. These were built mainly as gasoline-engined trucks as those fitted with diesels suffered cooling problems owing to the design, which featured a flat cab floor and a set-back engine. The 3000s aerodynamic appearance was timeless, but it was an expensive cab to produce and repair. It was eventually replaced by the 1500 series which went to the other extreme, having a box-like appearance similar to that of the Mack MB.

In 1951 White formed an agreement with the Freightliner Corporation to sell and service its trucks as White Freightliner. This arrangement continued until 1977. White was very profitable in the 1950s and was able to take over a

number of other makes, the first of which was Sterling, in 1951. Some trucks were sold as Sterling-Whites up until 1953. The same year, White took over Autocar. Autocar survived as a make in its own right within the White organization.

Reo Motors was the next acquisition, in 1957. The following year Diamond T was acquired and was soon merged with Reo leading to the Diamond-Reo marque. New designs of White's own trucks continued to appear, like the fibreglass-cabbed forward-control 5000 series of 1959. This signified the continuing trend towards cabovers, to maximize trailer lengths under the prevailing United States limits. Diesel engines became standard on the 5000. With a 124cm/50in BBC, it could haul 12.2m/40ft semis.

Meanwhile, longer bonneted trucks were announced in 1966 as part of the 4000 series, and in 1968 White formed Western Star to serve the West Coast market. White Western Star conventionals were built in a new plant at Kelowna in British Columbia, Canada. In the early 1970s White started converting Cummins diesels to run on gasoline, calling them White Giesels, but they proved unsuccessful. Instead White bought in diesels from Detroit, Cummins and Caterpillar.

During the remainder of the 1970s White over-committed itself with big investments in new factories. Production was transferred to New River Valley, Virginia, in 1975 and only a year earlier a new plant at Ogden, Utah had been commissioned to build the Autocar. There was also heavy investment in a planned new model range. This level of commitment, combined with a downturn in the market, led the company into financial difficulties in 1980. White went into liquidation and in August 1981 became part of Volvo as the Volvo White Truck Corporation.

Volvo White continued to market White trucks and even introduced new models. In 1983 the successor to the Road Boss appeared as the White Conventional with a longer bonnet (hood). The Road Commander 2 was also revamped, becoming the White High Cabover. These now carried the Volvo diagonal stripe on their grilles. In 1987 came the droop-snoot Aero plus an extended sleeper for the long-nosed conventional. As Volvo's influence increased, its engines and drivelines were introduced, as they also were on Autocar. Eventually the White name disappeared, and from 1995 all the trucks were badged Volvo.

■ TOP *By the early 1990s White had become WhiteGMC, most models having an all-Volvo driveline.*

■ ABOVE *The tilt-cab 3000 series became a market leader in the 1950s.*

■ LEFT *Following a marketing agreement, Freightliner trucks were sold as White Freightliner from 1951–77.*

NANTERE, FRANCE

WILLÈME

■ BELOW *During the 1970s Willème concentrated more on the production of heavy-haulage tractors like this 8×4. Engines included Detroit Diesel, Mercedes and Cummins.*

Etablissement Willème of Neuilly, Seine, was set up in 1919 to recondition ex-United States Army Class B Liberty trucks in the aftermath of World War I. There were large numbers of the 5-ton workhorses left over from the hostilities, and they were refurbished and sold to civilian customers as Liberty-Willème. Various improvements were later introduced, including pneumatic tyres and the fitment of more powerful engines. By 1930 there were Liberty-Willème 4×2 dump trucks for 7½-tonne payloads and 6×2 conversions for payloads up to 12 tonnes. Later, some models were fitted with CLM-built Junkers opposed-piston diesels.

From about 1930 Willème began manufacturing its own designs under the Willème name badge, the first being a 1-tonner. By 1935 heavier trucks appeared for payloads of 8 to 15 tonnes in both normal and forward control. After World War II Willème built some massive heavy-haulage tractors, including 8×4s for up to 150 tonnes gtw.

In 1962 Willème formed a joint agreement with AEC, under which AEC supplied it with diesel engines. Some models also featured a high degree of AEC technology in their chassis and running units. After AEC was absorbed into Leyland in 1962, Leyland curtailed AEC's technical collaboration with other manufacturers and, instead, Willème began producing BMC trucks under licence. These were badged Willème-BMC. In 1965 financial problems led to the closure of Willème but a manufacturing licence was granted to Pinez et Raimond, who developed a range of massive heavy-haulage tractors for gross train weights as high as 1000 tonnes. These were renamed PRP from 1978.

■ LEFT *The early 1960s Willème 38-tonne gcw artic was powered by an AEC AV690. It featured a ZF gearbox and Willème's Horizon cab.*

OTHER MAKES

■ WABCO

PEORIA, ILLINOIS, USA

Though Wabco has not built on-highway trucks in the normally accepted sense, the company is worthy of mention as the builder of some of the world's largest dump trucks. Wabco was formed in 1956 by the Combustion Equipment Division of the Westinghouse Air Brake Company. In 1953 Westinghouse took over the Le Tourneau Co. which was an old established manufacturer of earth-moving equipment, forming the Le Tourneau-Westinghouse Co., which began building dump trucks under the Haulpak name. This became Wabco from 1958.

The colossal off-highway dump trucks, like the 320B, for the mining industry can carry up to 235 tons and are powered by GM EMD 127 litre/7620cu in V12 two-stroke diesels developing 2475bhp. The drive is transmitted to the ground by hub-mounted electric traction motors. The main engine has a compressed-air starter motor and the vehicle, which has an all-up weight of 393 tons, is carried on hydro-pneumatic suspension. Access to the cab is up a nine-rung ladder. Wabco has since become part of the Komatsu D Corp.

■ WICHITA

WICHITA FALLS, TEXAS, USA

Between 1911 and 1932 the Wichita Motor Co., later renamed the Wichita Falls Motor Co., built a range of trucks of between 1½ and 5 tons payload capacity powered by Waukesha gasoline engines and using their own axles as well as Timken's.

■ WOLSELEY

BIRMINGHAM, ENGLAND

Wolseley's early designs, from its formation in 1901 as the Wolseley Tool & Motor Car Co., were the work of Herbert Austin, who left in 1905 to set up the Austin Motor Co. A varied range appeared in the early years, the largest being a 4-ton army truck with a 4-cylinder horizontal engine. J. D. Siddeley took over in 1908 and a vertical-engined Wolseley-Siddeley was introduced. An X-type chain-drive 3½-tonner also went into production, but by 1908 Wolseley-Siddeley abandoned trucks. In 1912 J. D. Siddeley moved on and Wolseley resumed production. By the start of World War I, it was offering 1½ and 4-ton subsidy types for the War Office. Wolseley were no longer in the market from 1919.

■ **ABOVE RIGHT**
A Wolseley 1½-ton truck from around 1912, with shaft drive and 4-cylinder gasoline engine.

■ **RIGHT**
Among the largest trucks in the world is this Wabco 3200B, with a 235-ton payload capacity powered by a GM EMD V12 of 2475bhp.

YAROSLAVI, RUSSIA

YAZ

YAZ were the forerunners of KrAZ, their history dating back to 1925, when production began of their 3-tonne YA-3 powered by an AMO gasoline engine. In 1928 the YA-3 was replaced by the YA-4, powered by a Mercedes-Benz 6-cylinder gasoline engine. An even heavier truck, the YA-5 for 4.5 tonnes appeared in 1929. Between 1925 and 1945 YAZ were known simply as YA. After World War II they became YAZ or sometimes YAAZ. The range was extended to include trucks for payloads of 7 to 12 tonnes. The trucks were of simple but rugged construction and included all-wheel drive 6×6 variants. Engines were licence-built GM 6-cylinder two-stroke diesels. From 1959 truck production was transferred to a new factory at Kremenchug and the trucks were renamed KrAZ (from Kremenchug Auto Zavod). The YAZ plant concentrated on diesel engine production for KrAZ and was renamed YAMZ (Yaroslaviski Motornoi Zavod).

LEEDS, ENGLAND

YORKSHIRE

As its name clearly implies, the Yorkshire Patent Steam Wagon Co. Ltd, formed in 1903, was concerned only with the building of steam wagons. Its speciality was the patented double-ended transverse locomotive boiler, which had a central fire-box. This unusual arrangement, which overcame the limited loadspace problem associated with locomotive boilers, was to be used by the company through to the end of steam-wagon production in 1937. Aware that steam was losing out, Yorkshire began considering a gasoline-engined truck as early as 1912.

In 1933 it built a forward-control 6-ton payload four-wheeler powered by a Dorman Ricardo 4-cylinder diesel. This was the first WK model, and Yorkshire offered it with a standard crash gearbox or a Wilson pre-selector. One of the problems that faced steamer drivers transferring to diesel trucks was their lack of gear-changing skills and the Wilson gearbox made a diesel easier in this respect. In 1935 a Gardner 6LW-engined six-wheeler for a 12-ton payload appeared, and the following year came an even larger 15-ton payload rigid eight-wheeler, the WK6. This had a Gardner 6LW, David Brown gearbox and Kirkstall rear axles. However, sales of Yorkshire diesels were limited and production ended in 1938. The company continued to trade after World War II, supplying municipal bodywork on various makes of chassis.

NANJING, CHINA

YUEJIN

■ RIGHT ***A late 1970s Yuejin NJ23A 4×4 truck for 4.8-tonne gvw powered by a 6-cylinder gasoline engine.***

The Yuejin 2.6-tonner was a long-running make of Chinese truck built in 4×2 form for civilian duties and as a 4×4, restricted to 1.6 tonnes payload, for military and civilian use. Production of the 4×2 NJ130 began as long ago as 1958, the truck being a copy of the old Russian GAZ-51. The NJ230 entered production in 1965. An NJ230 with winch was also built as the NJ230-A.

TULSA, OKLAHOMA, USA

ZELIGSON

■ LEFT *A Zeligson 6×6 forms the basis for this recovery vehicle powered by a Cummins diesel.*

This company was formed in 1946 by ex-serviceman Samuel Zeligson and two colleagues to refurbish war-surplus trucks for civilian use. All-wheel drive conversions were also carried out on 4×2 and 6×2 trucks for off-road use. Zeligson's founder also formed CCC, the Crane Carrier Corporation, which built specialized construction and concrete mixers. In the 1960s and '70s Zeligson built special trucks for the oil and mining industries using a variety of military and proprietary components, including Detroit Diesel two-stroke engines. In 1980 the company was sold to a new owner, who carried on a similar business on a small scale until finally closing down in 1989.

MOSCOW, RUSSIA

ZIL

■ LEFT *A 1985 ZIL 4331 artic for a 14-tonne payload, powered by a 185bhp diesel engine.*

ZIL trucks were in fact ZIS trucks under a new name. As a development of the old AMO (Automobilnoe Moskowvoskoe Obshchestvo) company, which built Fiat trucks under licence from 1924, the ZIS plant was formed in 1933 in honour of the Russian leader Joseph Stalin. ZIS stood for Zavod Imieni Stalina, and the first ZIS trucks of 1934 were virtually identical to AMOs. Heavier 6×4 4-tonne versions were added in 1935. During World War II a shadow factory was built in the Ural mountains and trucks built there were known as URAL-ZIS. In the post-war era ZIS introduced its 150 4-tonner based loosely on the American International Harvester K series.

In 1957, during the de-Stalinization of the USSR, the ZIS name was changed to ZIL, the "L" being in homage to the company's manager, Mr Likhacheva. During the 1960s ZIL developed its own models like the ZIL-130 bonneted 5-tonner which was produced in vast numbers. A 5-tonne gvw 6x6, the ZIL-131 with a 150bhp V8 gasoline engine, was built for the army. Heavier 133VJA 6x4s took a Kamaz V8 diesel with 210bhp.

In 1999 there were plans for Volvo and later Renault to build heavy trucks in collaboration with ZIL but these joint ventures did not come to fruition. ZIL continued to build a range of trucks, including bonneted and cabover models up to 24 tonnes gross but production ceased in 2013.

SLOUGH, ENGLAND

ZWICKY

■ LEFT *Typical of Zwicky's products is this purpose-built airport runway sweeper powered by a Ford engine.*

Zwicky specialized in fire appliances, aircraft refuellers, runway sweepers and similar machines for airfield use. They were in production from 1910 until about 1970. Ford engines were used.

GLOSSARY

Aftercooling: Where air, in turbocharging, is cooled before entering the combustion chamber.
Artic: Combination of tractor and semi-trailer which articulates on a "fifth wheel".
BBC: Measurement from bumper to back of cab.
Bhp: Brake horse power – the power developed by an engine as tested on a dynamometer.
Bogie: A pair of axles linked by a compensating suspension system.
Bonneted: See "Conventional".
Bore: The diameter of an engine's cylinders.
Cab-over-engine: North American term where the cab is placed directly over the engine. In Britain and Europe it is known as "forward control".
Constant mesh: Relates to a gearbox where the gear wheels on the main shaft are permanently meshed with those on the layshaft and can spin freely until gear selection locks the relevant gear wheel to the shaft.
Conventional: North American term where the cab is behind the engine. Known as "normal control" or "bonneted" in Britain and Europe.
Differential: Every driving axle has its own "diff" unit that transmits the drive to the road wheels. It also enables one wheel to travel further and faster than the opposite wheel when the vehicle is cornering.
Dolly: An axle supporting a fifth-wheel coupling and drawbar used to convert a semi-trailer into a full trailer.
Double: An artic coupled to a drawbar trailer (A-train) or an artic with a second semi-trailer coupled to the rear of the first semi-trailer by a fifth wheel (B-train). Also called "double bottom".
Double drive: When two rear axles on a vehicle are both driven.
Double reduction: A drive axle with a secondary set of reduction gearing. (See also "Hub reduction").
Drawbar trailer: A full trailer drawn by a rigid or artic.
Eighteen-wheeler: A North American term for an artic consisting of a three-axled tractor and a two-axled semi-trailer.
Eight-legger: British slang for a four-axled rigid truck usually with four steerable front wheels.
Fifth wheel: The coupling device on a tractor unit, consisting of a heavy steel plate with a hole into which the kingpin of the semi-trailer is connected.
Forward control: See "Cab-over-engine".
Fully-floating axle: An axle where the wheel bearings are located on the outside of the axle tube that bears all the vehicle's weight, and torque is transmitted by the drive shafts.
Gasoline: petrol.
GRP: Glass-reinforced plastic – sometimes used for cab manufacture.
Gcw: Gross combination weight. The gross vehicle weight as applicable to articulated combinations. Also called "gcm" or "gross combination mass".
Gtw: Gross train weight. The maximum permitted weight of a towing vehicle and its trailer when loaded. Also called "gtm" or "gross train mass".
Gvw: Gross vehicle weight. The maximum permitted weight of a vehicle when loaded. Also called "gvm" or "gross vehicle mass".
HGV: A British abbreviation for "heavy goods vehicle" (now superseded by "LGV").
Hub reduction: A drive axle with epicyclic reduction gearing in the hubs, reducing torque loads on the drive-shafts.
Intercooling: See "Aftercooling".
Jack-knife: Where an artic skids and the tractor and semi-trailer slide around towards each other.
Kerb weight: The weight of an unladen vehicle in full operating condition, including all equipment but excluding the driver.
kW: Kilowatt – a European alternative to brake horse power (1kW = 1.34bhp).
LGV: Large goods vehicle (alternative to "HGV").
Naturally aspirated: Where air is drawn into the engine's inlet manifold at atmospheric pressure, as opposed to being turbocharged.
Normal control: See "Conventional".
Overtype: A steamer with the engine mounted over the boiler.
Payload: The load that can be carried by a vehicle within the maximum gross weight limit.
Plate: The specification plate on British heavy trucks that displays the vehicle's maximum gross weight and individual axle weights.
P.T.O: Power take-off. Where auxiliary equipment is driven off the vehicle's gearbox or engine.
Range change: A gearbox with two sets of ratios possible from the same gears by the use of an auxiliary reduction set.
Reefer: Slang for a temperature-controlled box van.
Rigid: A non-articulated truck.
Semi-trailer: A trailer with no front axle, coupled to a tractor.
Skeletal: A semi-trailer or truck with no body designed to carry a lift-off container.
Sleeper: A cab with sleeping accommodation.
Spiral-bevel axle: An arrangement of the crown wheel and pinion within the axle where the centre lines of the gears are in the same plane.
Splitter gearbox: Alternative to a range-change gearbox. This type uses a wide ratio main box and the additional gear-set "splits" each of the main ratios.
Stroke: Distance travelled by a piston in a cylinder.
Susies: The pipes on an artic that connect the air-braking system from the tractor unit to the semi-trailer.
Tachograph: An instrument to record a truck's speed, mileage, distance and driver's working hours.
Tag axle: An add-on axle fitted to the back of a truck to increase permissible payload. Widely used in the United States to achieve compliance with the Bridge Formula.
Tandem: Two axles closely linked together often with a common suspension system.
Tare weight: See "Unladen weight".
TIR: Transports Internationale Routiers. European carnet system to facilitate international movement of goods.
Torque: The turning force of an engine at its crankshaft output flange. Usually measured in Newton metres (Nm) or pounds-feet (lb ft).
Tri-axle: A semi-trailer with three close-coupled axles.
Turbocharging: A process where air is forced into the induction system of an engine at higher than atmospheric pressure by a turbo-blower driven by waste exhaust gases.
Twin-steer: A 6×2 vehicle with two steered axles at the front and one driven rear axle. Popularly known in Britain as a "Chinese six".
Undertype: A steamer with the engine mounted below.
Unladen weight: Includes the kerb weight, driver and any additional equipment.
Wheelbase: The distance between the centre lines of the front and rear axles. For vehicles with twin rear axles, the centre line is usually taken as being midway between the two rear axles, and the distance from this point to the front axle is known as the "mean wheelbase".
Worm axle: An axle where the crown wheel is driven by a worm gear mounted either above or below.

INDEX

GLOBETROTTER